Colonising Plants
in Bihar (1760-1950)

In memory of life that was

Colonising Plants in Bihar (1760-1950)

Tobacco Betwixt Indigo and Sugarcane

Kathinka Sinha Kerkhoff

PARTRIDGE

A Penguin Random House Company

To order additional copies of this book, contact
Partridge India
000 800 10062 62
orders.india@partridgepublishing.com

www.partridgepublishing.com/india

FOREWORD

This book illustrates the fact that the history of tobacco in colonial Bihar cannot be understood in isolation. Unless we include the history of other plants, our tale remains incomplete. Though not totally unimportant, the history of the poppy plant proved less vital than that of sugar cane. Even more, it was the history of indigo that coloured tobacco in Bihar. It was experience in the contemporary tobacco fields of Bihar that gave me an inkling of this verity. In this foreword, I would like to share this understanding.

Research on tobacco in colonial Bihar had started in September 2007, yet an eight-month search for information in Indian libraries, archives, and record rooms had ended quite fruitless – or so I thought – and had driven me out. Instead, I tried my luck in Bihar's tobacco fields.

Figure 1. Darbhanga Raj record room. Photograph by author.

Kathinka Sinha Kerkhoff

Shahpur Baghauni Village in Tajpur Block of Samastipur District, Bihar
7 May 2008

Along with research assistant Masoom Reza, I walk towards the Madarsa Chowk in Shahpur Baghauni and inquire about tobacco-growing families who reside in the village. 'You meet Mr Hasan,' we are told. 'He is one of the leading tobacco growers in this village.' Land in this village was expensive and sold at the rate of Rs. 25,000 in 2008, whereas agricultural land in other districts of Bihar such as in Purnea or Araria could be bought for Rs. 2,000 per *katha*. This particular village mostly housed Muslims, almost all involved in tobacco cultivation.

Figure 2. Helal Ahmed, age sixty-seven, Satanpur (Samastipur). Interviewed on 15 March 2009, with his sun-cured chewing tobacco. Photograph by Masoom Reza.

Mr Hasan must have been around sixty years old and explained that here villagers (men, women, and children) had been involved in tobacco growing 'from time immemorial'. We also come to know that in other parts of

Samastipur, Hindus (upper castes as well as lower castes) are also involved in tobacco cultivation and transport.

Figure 3. Loading sun-cured tobacco on a truck.
Photograph by author.

More information was provided by Hasan, who explained that every part of the tobacco plant was sold. The most important part was the leaf, and it was of various varieties but mainly divided into good-quality and bad-quality leaf, depending on usage. The bigger leaves were named *morhan* by the villagers and used for the production of chewing tobacco. The smaller leaves were used for *zarda*, mainly manufactured in Lucknow, situated in Bihar's neighbouring state Uttar Pradesh. The roots were used to manufacture *gul*, a cheap powdered tobacco product produced in Jharkhand, the state adjacent to Bihar's southern part. Such smaller tobacco leaves were sold to traders arriving from Bihar's capital Patna or from Kolkata, the capital of the state of West Bengal, another of Bihar's neighbours. These leaves suited as fillers of *biris*, hand-rolled 'Indian cigarettes'. 'Our leaf cannot be used for *bideshi* (foreign) cigarettes,' some men added to the information we had already received from Hasan while continuing their work of sorting and bundling dried tobacco leaves seated on the ground.

Figure 4. Sorting and bundling tobacco leaf. Photograph by Masoom Reza.

Almost a tobacco specialist, but with still minute knowledge of tobacco's colonial history in the region, a last bit of information follows:

In this particular village, apart from tobacco, farmers also grow potato and rice. One plot is always used for tobacco and another plot for other crops, yet highland is used for tobacco only. Besides, when the tobacco plants are already in the field and the leaf has become larger, farmers sow maize seed in between them. After cutting the tobacco plant in March–April, maize remains in the field till it is ready for harvesting. Thereafter, till August–September, when tobacco seeds are sown, the land remains barren. After the tobacco plant is harvested, it is left to dry in the field for about thirty to forty days after which it is taken to a shed, daily turned over, and sprinkled with water. Jute bags are used to cover the leaf. After around a fortnight, this curing process is ended, and the tobacco leaves have obtained accurate colour and texture to be sold in bundles.

Figure 5. Bundles of dried tobacco leaf. Right: Innamul Haque (Annu), age sixty-six, with another tobacco cultivator in Rampur (Samastipur). Photograph by Masoom Reza.

'Tobacco seed', Mr Hasan added to this, 'is purchased from the Pusa Farm'. Inquiry regarding this 'Pusa Farm' bore fruit. 'Pusa is very old,' I was told. Still eager to know more about the historical roots of all what we see, hear, and smell, we decided to have a look over there, direction Pusa.

Tobacco betwixt Indigo and Sugar Cane in Bihar

From Samastipur railway station, we thus proceeded to Pusa and encountered villages Dharampur, Datpur, Garwara, Bela Pachrukhi, Morsand, Birauli, Garhia, Bishanpur, and Harpur, all situated at the bank of or near the river Gandak.

Figure 6. Little Gandak. Photograph by author.

Famous as the tobacco-growing region of Bihar and (still) interested in its history, we decided to take this route. Yet we witnessed the legacy of another but vanished commodity in the region: indigo. We encountered ruins of old indigo vats/tanks, some ramshackle and vacated 'indigo planters' bungalows', their graveyards, and remains of beautiful gardens of yesteryears and also more *kotis* well-maintained by new Bihari inhabitants.

Figure 7. Old but well-maintained British indigo planter's house in Samastipur. Photograph by author.

Figure 8. Old indigo vat at Pusa (Samastipur) used for indigo improvement experimentation. Photograph by author.

Mr Choudhary born in a village close to Biroli in 1929 was more than willing to tell us all about those 'indigo days'. 'My father worked for the (British) planter here,' he started off. 'This planter had two married brothers residing in neighbouring villages while he himself had remained unmarried. He used to interact a lot with the local people as he had needed the services of the washerman, barber, and carpenter. Choudhary also knew that this particular planter had owned nine horses and had taken out a different one every day to oversee his factory and fields. The two brothers had children, but Choudhary – also a child at the time – had neither played with them nor had ever entered their houses. Around 100–125 landless labourers had worked for this planter and', Choudhary added, 'on very low wages.' Apart from indigo, sugar cane, wheat, paddy, and vegetables had been cultivated in the fields of this planter. Planters had replaced indigo plants in particular by sugar cane during the first decades of the twentieth century, and when we arrived at Pusa, we came to know that a sugar cane research institute had been established under the Government of India (GoI) in 1932 there.

Figure 9. Sugar Cane Research Institute established in 1932 at Pusa. Photograph by author.

Traces of tobacco's history in the region remained elusive however. After our inquiry, Choudhary replied, 'Tobacco? No, no, no tobacco!' Choudhary clarified, 'Tobacco was the crop of the people not of the "British" planters.'

A perceived lack of relevant sources is often related to scholars' faulty searches than in fact, Amin demonstrated in his book on sugar cane in colonial India.[1] After my return to Ranchi (Jharkhand), where I reside, the simple sentence uttered by Choudhary as well as the legacy of indigo plants and sugar cane in the contemporary tobacco region of Bihar made me review the sources already collected from the archives. My first field visit – reinforced by three other visits later on – indeed taught me that I had carried out a wrong data search till then. After this visit, I realised that in order to unearth the roots of tobacco in Bihar, I had to delve into the history of indigo and sugar cane in the region. What is more, I now began reading already collected sources in a different way. 'Tobacco had been "a crop of the people",' Choudhary had said. 'Indigo and sugar cane had been possessed by the British "foreigners".'

A simple description of Bihar's landscape by James Routledge in 1875, which I had read without much interest before, after a second reading now revealed many things as my visit to the tobacco fields had provided the clue for

---

[1]   Amin, S. *Sugarcane and Sugar in Gorakhpur: An Inquiry into Peasant Production for Capitalist Enterprise in Colonial India*, Delhi: Oxford University Press, 1984.

further analysis of sources. Following the trade far up the Gandak, Routledge had observed:

> We found at that time from fifty to sixty native vessels at the mouth of the Gunduck river [. . .] Some were laden with rice, some with fodder, some with salt, linseed, wheat, gunny-bags, cotton, oat-straw, oil-seeds, tobacco, hardware, sugar, and so on. [. . .] On the banks of the river, or rivulets, you see *tobacco plantations, mostly native*; *indigo plantations, mostly European* [italics mine]; a landscape at places beautiful and green as an English park, at others bearing marks of the devastation of floods, or the caprice of the stream, which often in a day removes the landmarks of centuries. Everywhere you see that you are not among an idle but an industrious and wealth-producing people. How little we know of all this.[2]

The second time I read this passage, I looked at the landscape in the way James Routledge, a colonial administrator in the 1870s, had done. I looked at the 'wealth' of nature around me and saw plants like wheat, cotton, sugar cane, indigo, and tobacco. These plants constituted a splendour that ugly floods could destroy, taken away from me. I saw wealth that I already owned, indeed had colonised, that is indigo plants. I also saw wealth that 'the natives' (still) possessed (i.e. tobacco and sugar cane). I could acquire, rather colonise, the latter two if I could save these crops from floods and droughts, once I knew more about them. This rereading exercise taught me a lot about how to go about tobacco's history. I had to study the colonisation of other plants, in particular indigo and sugar cane and even poppy to some extent, in order to understand tobacco's history in Bihar. At that point, tobacco seemed indigo's (and sugar cane's) counterpoint. Indigo-producing plants were 'owned' by the Europeans in the 1870s, whereas tobacco (still) belonged to the 'natives'. These plants had to be studied together in order to understand them separately. They were each other's reverse but flew in one colonising history. The present book is the result of this insight.

---

[2] Routledge, J. 'Indian Notes: No. III. Commerce and Manufactures', *Macmillan's Magazine*, Vol. 32, May/October 1875, p. 459.

ACKNOWLEDGEMENTS

'Tobacco smoke isn't pouring out of your ears yet?' My Dutch friends used to ask me during the last couple of years (i.e. *Heb je er nog steeds geen tabak van?*). Thanks to them, this book's project ended. I embarked on this 'tobacco project' when I joined Willem van Schendel, Marcel van der Linden, Anil Persaud, Ulbe Bosma, and Ratna Saptari in 2008 to work on a multiyear research project 'Plants, People and Work: The Social History of Cash Crops in Asia, Eighteenth to Twentieth Centuries'. During those years, I was affiliated to the International Institute of Social History in Amsterdam (IISH) while still working till 2010 as director of research at the Asian Development Research Institute (ADRI) at Ranchi (India). The project brought me to international conferences in Yogyakarta, Daejeon, Amsterdam, Berlin, and Wageningen, where I presented papers, some of which will be published in due course of time. I was also connected to colleagues assembled in similar projects such as the 'Anti-Commodity' working group, the 'Global Collaboratory on the History of Labour', the 'Indigo Academic Network', and the 'Commodities of Empire Project'. These visits, meetings, the research as well as the papers, and this book, which resulted from those, could never have materialised without the funds provided by the Netherlands Organization for Scientific Research (NWO).

My special thanks are to Ratna Saptari and Jean Stubbs for introducing me to the trajectory of tobacco in Indonesia and Cuba, respectively, to Ulbe Bosma and Anil Persaud for updating me on the history of sugar cane in Indonesia and India, to Willem van Schendel, Prakash Kumar, and Ghulam Ahmad Nadri for sharing their extensive 'indigo knowledge', to Rana Behal and Marcel van der Linden who introduced me to global labour history, and to Jonathan Curry-Machado whose vast knowledge on imperial commodities benefitted me tremendously. I am also extremely thankful to Anand Yang who not only commented on several of my 'tobacco papers' but whose in-depth knowledge of Bihar's history continues to inspire me. I also like to thank Bhaswati Bhattacharya, Touraj Atabaki, Paul Streumer, and Karin Hofmeester for their enthusiastic engagement in their own works on the history of coffee cultivation and consumption, the 'Social History of Labour in the Iranian Oil Industry 1908–2008', the history of the Hos in Jharkhand, and Karin's work on global commodity chains, especially diamonds, respectively. They encouraged me in my own endeavour. I am very grateful indeed to Sandip Hazareesingh, Harro Maat, Ulbe Bosma, and Willem van Schendel who painstakingly went through earlier versions of the manuscript or chapters and versions thereof.

The greatest practical help, like always, I received from Md. Masoom Reza be it during our research trips in the tobacco fields of Bihar or in national and state archives and libraries in Patna, Delhi, and Calcutta. Masoom's continuous support during all these years and his valuable assistance in data collection, transcription of interviews, data entry, scanning, photographing, and ordering processes, and what not are extremely appreciated. Noor Alam, too, helped me with interviews and photographs in the Hajipur and Samastipur regions of Bihar. I like to thank staff of the National Royal Library in the Hague (KB), who provided archival documents online, and also the Forum Library in Wageningen, the National Library and Asiatic Society in Kolkata, the Nehru Memorial Museum and Library in New Delhi, the staff at the library of the Centre of South Asian Studies, University of Cambridge (courtesy C. A. Bayly), and the Heritage Archives of Bangladesh in Rajshahi (courtesy its Chairman Md. Mahbubar Rahman). Furthermore, I received help from A. K. Singh and Mr Para at the Maharajadhiraja Kamleshwar Singh Kalyani Foundation and from Hetukar Jha in Darbhanga. At Pusa (Samastipur) in Bihar, the staffs of the Rajendra Agricultural University were helpful. My warm thanks also to all tobacco cultivators in Samastipur and Darbhanga, who were interviewed by us. During writing stages I received most support from my husband, Vinod Kumar Sinha, who made it possible for me to remain isolated during many long days and nights, and to Pongo, who kept me company. My apologies are for many including my in-laws and my daughter, Trishla, who, as a result of my absentmindedness, suffered somewhat at times.

Much of the material, some of which is mentioned in the selected bibliography at the end of this book, was found through Internet searches. In this regard, I am very happy with sites such as that of the ProQuest Information and Learning Company, books.google, onlinelibrary, wiley.com, Springerlink. com, JSTOR, Project MUSE, the EBSCOhost, a programme situated in the British Library called the Nineteenth Century Programme, the Digital South Asia Library, and foremost with the immensely valuable archives I procured through Internet Archive (www.archive.org) and Project Gutenberg. I like to thank Eve Watson Head of Archives Royal Society of Arts who helped me in a special way. The initiative of some publishers and educational institutions in India and elsewhere to reprint original work published before 1923 is also highly appreciated, and my special thanks are for the Asian Educational Services, Rupa, Elibron Classics, The Cornell University Library Digital Collections, Printsasia.com, General Books, Concept Publishing, and the Logos Press, some of which granted me copyrights of images that are included in this book with due acknowledgement. The Wi-Fi connection of the Central Institute of Psychiatry (CIP) at Kanke in Ranchi (Jharkhand), where I reside, made actual access of these online resources an absolute delight. Brother Nimalya Chakraborty of the computer section of CIP deserves special mention as he greatly assisted me with scanning of many of the photographs included in this book.

A few more people and then you can start reading the book. Sincere thanks to Bob Janes, who allowed me to use the unpublished autobiography of an indigo planter named William Sharpley. Hope this autobiography will be published one day. I am deeply indebted to Charles Allen, who allowed me to use photographs included in his mother's autobiography describing Joan Allen's life as a planter's daughter in British India. He also sent me even more scanned photographs (*vide* the photograph of the Bihar Light Horse members on the cover of this book) (courtesy Rosie Llewellyn Jones, honourable secretary of BACSA). The British Association for Cemeteries in South Asia (BASCA) kindly granted me permission to use a photograph similarly displayed in this book (*vide* sugar cane in Chapter Eight), which was derived from yet another biography by Betsy MacDonald. Finally, the book is published, thanks to Partridge Publishers, which also did its editing. Many of my friends might not go beyond these pages. Yet my dear friend and colleague Jos Mooij would have. Not long before her sad demise last year, she inquired about the progress of my 'tobacco book'. I miss her critical but benign judgement.

CONTENTS

INTRODUCTION

This book concerns the radical reorganisation of agriculture as planned and executed by British administrators during the nineteenth and part of the twentieth centuries in Bihar, British India. In his book *Seeing Like a State*, James C. Scott analysed agricultural schemes that intended such reorganisation. Defining agriculture as the 'radical reorganisation and simplification of flora to suit man's goals', Scott analysed why certain agricultural schemes, though aiming at 'improvement', had nevertheless failed. A somewhat similar analysis is completed in this book. In the chapters that follow, a particular 'scheme' that aimed at 'tobacco improvement' in colonial Bihar is focussed upon. As shown, this 'scheme' was long-drawn, covering about one-and-a-half century, and diverse. In fact, it consisted of various smaller schemes implemented in different phases over time. Besides, 'radical reorganisation' of agriculture was intended to suit the aspirations formulated by men during Britain's imperial century who aimed at commercial prosperity and the preservation of Britain's industrial and commercial predominance in the world. These schemes also had a prehistory starting around the time that Britain had promoted itself as the new rulers in Hindustan. I therefore reserved the term 'colonisation' to describe these reorganisation efforts planned and executed by colonial agents and their collaborators in colonial Bihar.

From the end of the 1780s, in Britain, men in government had periodically talked of ambitious projects that could put on hold the prosperity of the Spanish empire on both its Atlantic and Pacific coasts. After the victory of the American revolutionaries in the 1780s, attention was focused more on India and 'how to develop techniques of regenerating non-European societies, which, in comparison with industrial Britain, appeared to be stagnating'.[1] Yet it was only five decades later, by the 1830s, that a great number of large-scale projects and possible blueprints were under consideration which cumulatively

1

amounted to 'a grand design for remoulding much of the world, a full-scale "cosmoplastic" (world-shaping) plan'. A key thematic word in the various projects that were formulated around the time in early Victorian Britain was 'development'.[2] The reorganisation of the vegetable kingdom in British India belonged to one of these projects of empire designed to 'improve' plants by making them more useful to men.[3]

Yet neither was the empire unified by one coherent philosophy nor by any coercive policy. I agree, therefore, with Ronald Hyam who argued that local administrators defined the strength of imperial rule, adding that the authority of the imperial government seldom existed at the local level. We thus have to look at the local level in order to understand how this global agricultural 'improvement project' of the British empire – carried out in many other British possessions simultaneously – actually took shape and functioned, succeeded or failed in British India.[4] We then will understand how the global influenced the local but also vice versa.

This book concentrates on tobacco improvement schemes in colonial Bihar (till 1912 part of Bengal), which were part of an immense agricultural project in India, here defined as plant colonisation.[5] This kind of colonisation encompassed commerce and industry as well as that it included knowledge systems, science, and technology.[6] Naturally, colonisation of plants required 'colonisers' and the colonisation of not only plants but also people. Moreover, there were 'dynamic relationships among plants, peoples, states, and economies'.[7]

Had initially tobacco colonisation referred to commerce, as shown in Chapter One, from around 1800 onwards it related to tobacco cultivation as well. From that time on, not only did colonial botanists study, name, cultivate, and market tobacco, schemes for its 'improvement' were also in place. Yet this tobacco colonisation could not be studied in isolation and was part of a wider agricultural context in which several schemes functioned or failed. Tobacco improvement schemes in Bihar were not even always the ones that earned most colonial attention.[8] Besides, these various schemes for plant colonisation did not operate independently from each other. In colonial Bihar, only to some extent, the ups and downs in poppy cultivation influenced tobacco schemes, yet as born out in this book, it was, in particular, developments in the indigo fields that coloured tobacco. Besides, an analysis of developments in sugar cane cultivation in Bihar and their mutual interaction with the cultivation of indigo-producing plants proved essential for our understanding of tobacco schemes.

In fact, tobacco in colonial Bihar was betwixt and between sugar cane and indigo. In this introduction, I place these three plants in their wider context, viewing them as part of a great plant colonisation project of the British Empire, the reigning international regime during the nineteenth century.

Towards Plant Imperialism in Bengal

One of the first in-depth treatises on the agriculture ('husbandry') and commerce of Bengal was written by Henry Thomas Colebrooke (1765–837), whose father had been chairman of the Court of Directors of the East India Company (EIC), explaining the Indian career for the son. In 1782, Henry Colebrooke became a writer in the Bengal and spent thirty-two years in the service of various EIC's civil departments. In 1786, Colebrooke was appointed as assistant collector at Tirhut, the region in Bihar that forms the central place of action in this book. His revenue duties in Tirhut forced him to evaluate the agricultural scenario there, and he thus became engaged in a minute examination into the state of husbandry in Bengal. The results of his inquiries were privately printed in 1795. This book was an agricultural survey of not only Tirhut but all the regions governed by the presidency of Fort William at that time, including the *subas* of Bengal and 'Behar' and even some parts of the *subas* of Allahabad, Berar, and Orissa. This book also was a searching criticism of the policy pursued by England as well as the company in these regions and a comprehensive view of what, according to Colebrooke, that government policy ought to be. In his book, Colebrooke opposed the renewal of the EIC's monopoly and advocated free trade. As his study gave no little offence to the EIC directors, it was not considered advisable to get the book published in England.

The second part of the original treatise was, in fact, mainly composed by one called Lambert, a non-EIC merchant of Calcutta, and related to the manufactures and external commerce of Bengal, while the first part mostly contained the observations of Colebrooke and were confined to the 'internal traffic' of Bengal. It was the second part of the original treatise which was published in 1806 and reviewed in the *Edinburgh Review or Critical Journal* of 1807.[9] Though the reviewer in 1807 did not question Colebrooke's sincerity, it was nevertheless doubted whether his policy recommendations would benefit England or even Calcutta-based non-official British merchants like Lambert.

Most of all, however, the reviewer from England doubted whether Colebrooke's recommendations in the field of agriculture would benefit the people of Bengal (referred to as 'natives' during the nineteenth century and even during the first half of the twentieth century), that is, 'the hardy and intelligent inhabitants, quietly submitting to a sway exercised by a handful of strangers, cordially espousing their interests, and sacrificing their lives on the field of battle for the support of their authority'. The reviewer also warned that Colebrooke's ideas were not liked by the English in England 'who think that the state of society in other countries, either is, or ought to be, precisely what they see it at home'.[10]

The reviewer's ideas of 'justice' and 'policy' did, therefore, differ from those of Colebrooke. Colebrooke had written, for instance, that an 'ignorant husbandry' exhausted the land and neglected 'the obvious means of restoring its fertility and of reaping immediate profit from the operations which might restore it'. These native 'husbandmen' also used 'rude implements, inadequate to the purpose for which they are formed and requiring much superfluous labour'. This labour also was, according to Colebrooke, 'ill-divided and of course employed disadvantageous', and all this 'loudly called for amendment'.

Colebrooke, therefore, recommended a change in Bengal which implied an adaptation of radical different agricultural techniques and implements, namely those that were used in English agriculture back home. Agricultural improvement in his view meant 'mighty innovations' and a total removal of the existing local institutions in Bengal to which he attributed all 'the evils' that existed in rural Bengal. However, the reviewer in the *Edinburgh Review* in 1807 totally disagreed and was even offended by the way Colebrooke depicted the Bengal peasantry 'in a querulous tone, as the result of their own mismanagement and the consequences of their unenlightened industry' and as 'being blind to obvious improvements'.[11] Instead, the reviewer proposed:

> It will frequently be found, that customs which appear to strangers the result of negligence and want of refinement, have their origin in local peculiarities, and may, on further information, be traced to a series of profound and continued practical observations. We are disposed to think that the author's strictures on the plough, and on the rotation of crops used in Bengal, may be found in this predicament. [. . .] To enable his readers to judge how far the Hindus are scientific

and intelligent cultivators of the soil, we lament that Mr Colebrooke has not given the names adopted by them for the different species of lands, discriminated by their respective level above the line of inundation, and the peculiar mode of culture appropriated to each [. . .] What we have said will suffice to prove that the Bengal peasantry do not proceed without fixed principles for their guidance, and those probably derived from a remote antiquity, and possibly the best adapted to their soil and climate.[12]

The *Edinburgh Review* concluded by refuting 'the hints suggested by the enlightened benevolence of Mr Colebrooke, for the amelioration of our Indian dominions'. These consisted of two propositions. The first proposition was the capital employed in agriculture is too small and injudiciously applied. Colebrooke had suggested:

If Bengal had a capital in the hands of enterprising and intelligent proprietors, who employed it in agriculture, manufactures and internal commerce, these arts would be improved; and with more and better productions from the same labour, the situation of the labourers would be less precarious, and more affluent.

The *Edinburgh Review* wanted to know, however, 'who are the intelligent and enterprising proprietors, to whose assistance he would have recourse?' And the reviewer asked whether Colebrooke wanted to 'recommend the rescission of the act of Parliament which precludes Englishmen from purchasing or farming lands (in Bengal)? [. . .] An act of justice and enlightened policy, without which, we will venture to affirm, one half of the lands of Bengal would, ere this, have become the property of Englishmen, and the natives would have been strangers on their own soil.'[13] The *Edinburgh Review* certainly argued against the abolishment of this act and hoped it may be 'the wealthy natives' and 'their habits of industry, their enterprise, and their capital, under the encouragement held forth by a permanent assessment (of revenues)' that would 'be advantageously employed in rural concerns'.

The second proposition of Colebrooke had been that Bengal's agriculture could be encouraged by the facilitation of exportation of its agricultural wealth to England. This in Colebrooke's view would be possible through the lowering of the rates of freight and the duties of Bengal's produce such as sugar in England. Here, again the *Edinburgh Review* had its misgivings and pointed to the 'jarring interests' such a policy would induce.[14]

I defined the 'great change' that took place in the agricultural field during the more than 150 years here under review as a 'radical reorganisation and simplification of flora to suit man's goals' brought about by a colonisation of plants through English/European capital, new (English) knowledge systems ('skill'/'science') and manpower under the (English) flag of 'improvement'.[15] Yet like most social changes, this reorganisation – though radical – were neither sudden nor complete. Besides, many such agricultural schemes aimed at 'improvement' failed. Importantly, this colonisation was not absolute or uncontested, and schemes were various and multidimensional.

Though proposed by people like Colebrooke, during the first decade of the nineteenth century, this 'great change' still was very much contested in England as well as by many a British man in Bengal itself.[16] Such new policy recommendations were part of the emergence of what Sunil Agnani described as 'colonial modernity' and the evolution of nineteenth-century 'liberal imperialism' and were formulated in 'a complex context of contradictory pronouncements and positions on empire'.[17] By the end of the nineteenth century, however, 'colonial modernity' was more or less fully accepted and guided all government agricultural policies. Indeed, if we compare 1800 with the situation in Bengal hundred years later, plant colonisation, as defined above, had become an accepted part of imperial policy by 1900, and contestation was marginal and seen as a novelty. It will be evident from the proceedings in the book before you that it was Colebrooke-like's views and recommendations that dictated government policies in the long run. This implied more and more British/European capital, skill (science), and manpower in the agricultural field of colonial Bihar. In other words, by 1900, the ideology of plant colonisation had reached its climax, and the idea of plant improvement through English (government and non-official), science, and manpower ('experts') was firmly upheld by the state. It had taken a century to mature however, and during the first half of the nineteenth century, all the three aspects of this colonisation process were still very much matters of dispute.

A British Imperial Plant Colonisation Project in Bengal

This book concerns more than 150 years of agrarian history of colonial South Asia during which there were multiple projects in various regions. Retrospectively, I have been able to club such projects in Bihar together in one broad category of plant colonisation. Yet such a colonisation project during the years that the English EIC ruled in Bihar was qualitatively different from that of post-1857 Bihar when the British Crown had taken charge. While all the different schemes during these 150 years of British rule in India were part of the same 'radical reorganisation and simplification of flora to suit man's goals' – and here clubbed together as plant colonisation – those that were designed before 1857 by state agents to improve nature and make it more useful to men were qualitatively different from those designed afterwards. The essential difference pertained to the identification of the target population for whose benefit agrarian improvement schemes were designed. Before 1857, the 'ideology of improvement', as David Arnold substantiated, attended to 'the company's material needs'.[18] After 1857, 'imperial needs' had to be satisfied.

Plant colonisation by the EIC in Bengal[19] can be said to have started even before 1800, though then it had less to do with agriculture and more to do with trade, that is, the 'seizing of commodities' in Irfan Habib's (Marxist) terminology.[20] As detailed in Chapter One of this book, colonisation of tobacco between 1757 and 1800 mostly meant efforts by EIC servants to dominate in the internal trade of this commodity.[21] This period fell into a wider period of 'mercantilism' during which 'state-making' activities – both political as well as economic – among European nations were pursued. Rila Mukherjee defined the period as 'a time when powerful national economies were built on the basis of extensive colonial possessions'. She also argued that as Britain's geography limited the extent of the market and thereby restricted its trade profits, it ventured into the seas with the 'aim to establish trade in regions which they could dominate and thereby acquire windfalls gains'.[22] The creation of the EIC had been, in fact, effected in accordance with these intentions.

When the English became masters in Bengal (and southern India) during the decade and half following the middle of the eighteenth century, the EIC acquired the power to levy and collect land revenue and other taxes. In 1783, the EIC constituted Europe's third largest territorial power and had become a political as well as an economic force in the world. Yet the power of the

EIC was somewhat reduced because of its servants' dependence on powerful merchant-capitalists in London. Financed mainly by the export of part of the collected revenues and taxes begotten, these merchants along with EIC servants conducted a trade in – among others – indigo. These so-called investments in commodities such as indigo were huge, and indigo was sold in markets throughout the world with great profits. The EIC servants were therefore hunting for indigo and other profitable plants which had the 'whole world as their market'.[23]

These 'plant hunters'[24] in Bengal were continuously critiqued, however, even by insiders. In fact, this criticism only grew during the period after 1800 till the 1830s when the colonial objective changed from 'seizing Indian commodities to seizing the Indian market'. This changed objective, as Irfan Habib described, 'not only made the East India Company's monopoly over Indian internal commerce and overseas trade obsolete, but positively required free trade'. This was largely accomplished through the 'Charter Acts of 1813 and 1833'.[25] Now several plant colonisation schemes were initiated by official and non-official Europeans (not in service of the EIC) in particular in Bengal. This region included Bihar and Orissa in north-eastern India that measured 161,978 square English miles and was considered by many in England as the company's jewel.

The transformation towards 'free trade' had been accompanied, however, by a change in British colonial ideology which had been prompted by the fear among some in England as well as in Bengal itself that the 'wealth' of Bengal was squandered by EIC servants before it could be harnessed for the nation. In Britain, some even argued against the company which not only worked, or so some felt, against British interests but also caused suffering and unrest among the inhabitants of the Bengal Presidency, referred to as 'the natives', as well as acted against the interest of the 'native government', therewith antagonising it.[26]

The EIC had made no attempt to cultivate 'the hearts and souls of the natives', noted one of its critics William Bolts, merchant, adventurer, and alderman of the Mayor's Court at Calcutta, held against this trading company that had also assumed administrative powers in Bengal. Edmund Burke, another critic, added in 1783 standing before the House of Commons that 'the prosperity of the natives must be previously secured before any profit from them whatsoever is attempted', as without such reform, 'the transmission of great wealth to this country would be in jeopardy'. In other words, during this period, as elaborated upon in Chapter One, the colonisation efforts of EIC servants not only met with resistance from 'native' quarters but also faced criticism from non-EIC (private) English traders as well as from men at home.[27] The latter in turn formulated other plant colonisation schemes that befitted 'the imperial plan' for plants to grow under the British flag.[28]

Stephen Vella illustrated that during this period (from the end of the eighteenth century to the early nineteenth century), there was a shift from trading empires to state-managed empires. Vella argued that,

> Narrowly focused, short-term profiteering was no longer consistent with a powerful state's project of extending British sway [. . .] The language of formal Empire – made explicit in opposing the power of private trading companies – found its formulation in the late-eighteenth century and laid the basis for the 'official' and self-righteous imperialist ideologies of the nineteenth.[29]

Indeed, during the greater part of the nineteenth and part of the twentieth centuries, British officials constituting the colonial state and living and working in what now is known as India imagined the landscape surrounding them to be a part of a British empire. The people, behaviours, buildings, artefacts, flora, and fauna in this landscape was commented upon by them and categorised. Initially, it had been EIC servants themselves who had acted as 'foot soldiers' in 'the botanical wars', as Patrice Bret remarked, hunting for tropical resources.[30] Yet with a 'shift from military fiscal adventurism' to a more 'bureaucratic system' of EIC rule,[31] increasingly 'botanists' were brought in, who accommodated 'exotic' or 'tropical'[32] plants in the 'vegetable kingdom'[33] and further typified them as part of the wealth of Bengal. Consequently, while some plants were degraded as 'mere weeds' that did not deserve much colonial attention, others won status as 'agricultural/cultivated plants' or even better were categorised as 'useful', 'economic', 'industrial', or 'commercial' and 'most promising' plants.[34] The latter category of plants became part of colonial agricultural schemes; that is, they were selected for colonisation.

Of course, this labelling was in a flux, and the status of plants kept on changing. For example, trees were at times seen as 'jungle', part of 'wastelands' and obstacles to the growth of 'more useful' agricultural plants in particular the 'economic plants' among them, whereas in other periods they were cultivated as 'most valuable timber', cash crops themselves, or sought to be preserved for their 'intrinsic value'.[35] They could be all this at the same time too or were differently validated in diverse geographical circumstances. Colonial rulers in British India, first the company's servants and later on those serving 'Her Majesty' directly, perceived parts of nature around them as beautiful and exotic but also as ugly, useless, and increasingly as (potentially) useful. Besides, as dominant conquerors, they believed that they rightfully owned the plants in their 'possessions'. Furthermore, as they owned these, they could do whatever they wanted with them. They could trade, preserve, or destroy them, learn from them, and thus distil new (botanical) knowledge or even better 'improve' these plants using their own understanding of plant cultivation.[36]

Chapter Two of this book starts at a point when everything was still quite open; the British could opt for colonising tobacco trade within Bihar, in and out of the region, or concentrate on overseas trading too, to England for instance. They could decide to just claim the harvest or go for interference in plants cultivation. As I will show in the rest of this book, however, in the case of tobacco grown in Bihar, the British decided the cultivation of this plant should not remain without assistance of 'European capital, skill, and manpower'. If 'improved' in this way, tobacco might even attain 'export quality' and fetch a much higher price in the London market. This would benefit all; it was argued that it would benefit tobacco cultivators categorised as raiyats, traders, capitalists, as well as consumers within Bengal and in the homeland (England) and therefore add to the general welfare of the (imagined) British empire.

To understand this changed political economy in Bengal – from trade colonisation only to colonisation of cultivation as well – and in which commodities such as tobacco, indigo, sugar cane, and poppy were grown and traded, I consider Christopher V. Hill's work useful. With him I argue that from around 1800 onwards – and independently of its outcomes – a new colonial value system impinged on increasingly more plants categorised by British (amateur) botanists in the 'Vegetable Kingdoms of the Tropics'.[37] Christopher V. Hill explained that this changed condition was the outcome of a long process:

> [B]eginning in the late 15th century, European merchants would arrive in large numbers, bring with them an environmental ethic that saw nature merely as a commodity

and an accompanying desire for a vast array of products from South Asia. These included spices, jewels, timber, cotton, tobacco, indigo, and opium, all of which had to be culled from nature. When the demand for goods culminated with the British colonization of India in the last half of the 18th century, *commodification* [italics mine] became the established policy in the subcontinent.[38]

Hill defined commodification as a 'change in attitude and values in which nature is seen only for its value as commodity'.[39] I would like to add 'possible' before Hill's 'value as commodity' as not all plants (and nature's other components) were stirred by Hill's 'commodification'. I also like to emphasise that such a 'commodification' can only take place in a colonial context – or under similar conditions – in which the attitudes and values of 'the other(s)' (the colonised, subaltern, marginalised, 'natives', etc.) regarding plant breeding or crop choices, for instance, are either ignored, degraded, or incorporated in established policy if colonisers find them 'useful'.[40]

Utsa Patnaik described a similar change in attitudes and values towards nature among colonial rulers but called it 'commoditisation' which she considered 'under colonial conditions' to have been 'quite distinct from commercialisation of agriculture in capitalistically developing countries'. The key to the difference was, Patnaik added, 'the universal transfer of resources and profits away from India to Britain'. Peter Robb also contributed to this debate and concluded that, therefore, 'there is a distinctive context in India which has significantly shaped the nature of its agriculture'.[41] What thus mattered most in the colonial setting under consideration was who had the power to decide, which plants were 'useful' and for whom, and who had the power to decide which ones had to be 'improved' to make them more useful.

Without using the word 'commodification', in this book, my argument throughout is that the 'distinctive context' in rural colonial Bihar was that its political economy was shaped by this new ideology disseminated by those in power. This ideology – supporting a colonisation of nature[42] – guided state's agricultural and later on industrial engineering in rural Bihar till 1950 at least, if not beyond. As shown in this book, it fundamentally impacted agricultural developments in colonial Bihar where cultivators' choices and production of botanical knowledge were now regulated by colonial policies that sought the preservation and advancement of the imagined British Empire.

British Empire's Demand for Tobacco, Poppy, Indigo, and Sugar Cane from Bihar

The establishment of new transoceanic routes permitted the widespread adoption by Europeans for several commodities from the Americas and 'the Orient', which had been either unknown or were not yet widely consumed. In the seventeenth century, two commodities with particular great demand in Europe were tobacco and sugar, but other commodities followed suit. All the European powers that established colonies in the Americas experimented with the cultivation of both the tobacco plant as well as the sugar cane. This 'agricultural colonisation' in the so-called New World was made profitable by the use of slave labour, and from the 1660s onwards, as John Darwin described, among the plants, 'sugar was king, with tobacco a distant second and cocoa and chocolate trailing behind'. Darwin viewed these plant colonies as 'the bizarre offspring of European expansion', and he described how everything that was needed to make them profitable – except the soil itself – had been brought from outside: capital, management (the European planters and overseers), labour (African slaves), and in some cases even the plants themselves. The planters in British colonies lived as if they were in England, and according to Darwin, it is wiser to see the Atlantic trading world, at least until 1750, 'as the vital prop of a commercial *ancien regime* rather than as a dynamic element in the industrial transformation of even the most advanced European economies'.[43]

The Portuguese and Spaniards initially reigned, supplying markets in Lisbon and Seville, but it was the maritime states of Northern Europe that finally proved best placed to enhance their prosperity, and a notable feature of the period was the rise of large port cities such as Amsterdam, Hamburgh, and of course London. The English merchant fleet doubled in size between 1660 and 1690, and among these European 'core' states, a struggle was waged for outright hegemony in commerce and empire. Yet these maritime economies of north-west Europe never enjoyed a clear predominance over inland economies in this pre-industrial age.[44] However, this had changed by the end of the eighteenth century when the British marched into the subcontinental interior of India with relative ease. Starting with Bengal, considered the most prosperous region at the time, the British could draw on the income of a long-established system of land taxation – the 'land revenue'.[45] By 1800, Darwin described, 'India provided its European invader with the resources that could be turned to the task of conquest'. 'India was a project, not an abuse,' and London became quite tolerant of the EIC's imperialism. By the 1840s, India was looked upon as a major asset for a trading empire, and Darwin concluded that here, 'British rule was fiercely defended as the only path to social progress'.[46]

During the sixteenth century, tobacco had become a great source of wealth for European merchants and had become an economic resource of interest to governments too, since it was made subject to taxes and began to produce substantial returns for European states. Despite the taxes, the consumption of tobacco increased tremendously and was in particular appreciated by consumers in Europe in powdered form (snuff). This demand for tobacco in Europe determined a rise in production in the colonies of the Americas during the early seventeenth century.

In 1614, James inscribed, 'I had established taxes on "foreign" tobacco in order to favour tobacco from its own colonies', and in 1625, Charles inscribed, 'I of England had imposed a tax on the first shipments of this plant from North America.' Tobacco taxing had thus become a preferential source of income of the royal treasury of this nation.[47] Yet by the 1650s, other European powers than the Spanish and Portuguese had begun to promote the cultivation of tobacco in their colonies in the hope of meeting the increasing demand and obtaining commercial benefits. England was among these powers and altered its taxing system for tobacco from their American colonies. Remarkably, at the close of the seventeenth century, it was England that had not only one of the highest levels of tobacco consumption but also a most developed tobacco market. Throughout the eighteenth century, the growth of British tobacco imports remained constant, and the majority came from Virginia, and whereas the Spanish concentrated on 'high-quality' tobaccos appropriate for smoking and snuff, the British North American colonies cultivated 'chewing tobaccos'. In fact, tobacco became a key commodity of the (old) British Empire.

Pius Malekandathil argued that it was a Jesuit priest who introduced tobacco in India, and though there were various other versions regarding the first arrival of the commodity in India, the Portuguese were involved in tobacco trade in Bengal during the mid-seventeenth century. In 1675, Bahian tobacco from Brazil was introduced in India in the form of snuff made in

Lisbon, and eventually, tobacco was used in India for chewing, smoking, and sniffing. Indo-Portuguese traders used to take tobacco to Bengal, and by 1750, the Portuguese had drafted a plan to launch a trading company in Bengal to obtain saltpeter and textiles from Bengal with proceeds from tobacco. Though Portuguese officials did not show much interest in it, some Indian merchants joined together to form the Bengal Trading Company for the same purpose.[48]

During the period between 1675 and 1775, the use of tobacco became widespread in many places of India including Bengal, which in turn necessitated networking of ports of Bengal with Goa, Bahia, and Lisbon. At the same time, the cultivation of tobacco had spread to Bengal, including Bihar. The story of its colonisation by the British is highlighted in this book but cannot be understood without the knowledge of colonisation of other plants in Bihar in particular that of indigo, poppy, and sugar cane. Apart from tobacco, these three other plants had also had prominent functions in the building up and sustenance of the British Empire.

Though indigo had come into prominence in the seventeenth century, the cultivation of indigo-producing plants had been concentrated in districts elsewhere in India such as around Ahmadabad, Aligarh, and Agra. Yet during the reign of Aurangzeb, indigo had been exported from Bengal. The so-called Bayana indigo was also used within Bengal as it formed the basic material for washing and bleaching ordinary cotton cloths to a pure white colour. Yet trade in indigo declined after Aurangzeb 'on account of accidents of season and uncertain political conditions'.[49] The blue dye was in high demand among Europeans by the end of the eighteenth century, and having lost its supply from other sources, English administrators now put all hopes on indigo from Bengal, which included present-day Bihar at the time.

After the above-mentioned Charter Act of 1813 that supported 'free trade', European agency houses in Bengal brought in private English merchants who flourished in particular because of this indigo trade. But for a time, West Indian competition destroyed their hopes of continuous expansion of indigo exports, and this brought about a crash of the agency houses in 1832–33. By the early 1830s, therefore, a solution was sought as the realisation of tribute from Bengal had taken the form of indigo exports mainly. Export of other commodities such as raw cotton and silk was thus considered. But finally, the solution to this 'realisation problem'[50] was found in opium, and by 1858, opium exported to China in exchange for tea and silk had advanced to the position of the premier article of export of Bengal, dwarfing other exports of commodities such as sugar cane and indigo.

During the time that Bengal had been part of the vast Mughal Empire, poppy had also been an important crop that was in particular highly taxed during the reign of Akbar. Apart from Benares and a wide expanse of western India, where it came to be known by the generic name Malwa, it was cultivated in eastern India and was despatched from there in large quantities by water.[51] When the EIC established a monopoly over opium trade in Bihar, the drug was shipped from Patna to Calcutta and smuggled from there into China by private traders because of the official interdiction of the trade by the Chinese authorities. From that time onwards, poppy, from which this opium was extracted, was grown under strict company's supervision in Bihar and thus became the first plant to be totally colonised by the British in Bihar.[52] Tirthankar Roy even concluded that opium 'cemented and stabilised the British Empire'.[53]

Regretting that the company's opium monopoly should restrict the free expansion of its cultivation and thus sacrifice 'a great national advantage', 'free traders', therefore, again focussed on the possibilities of indigo but at the same time that these 'European entrepreneurs' became (again) interested in indigo-producing plants cultivated in Bengal and sugar cane grown in this province also received their attention. Bengal had occupied a most important place in sugar production from sugar cane during the reign of Akbar already. Its cultivation had extended to several places in Bihar during the seventeenth century and from there exported to Arabia, Mesopotamia, and Persia. Though the Portuguese had also been involved in this trade, by the last quarter of the eighteenth century, England became in particular interested in Bengal sugar and for the same reasons that the country had looked towards Bengal for its supply of indigo and tobacco.

It had been the War of American Independence (1776–83) as well as the Haitian Revolution of 1791 that not only changed English sugar trade and cultivation policies but also those concerning indigo and tobacco. As a result of the above-mentioned political developments, the production of these commodities in Britain's North American colonies diminished considerably. The English now considered whether Bengal, being just acquired, could become an alternative supplier of these 'lost' plants (i.e. sugar cane, indigo plants, and tobacco). It is at this point that our 'colonisation' story really begins from Chapter Three onwards. Chapter Four illustrates that these 'state interests' as well as the interest of 'free traders', that is indigo and sugar cane entrepreneurs or so-called planters, finally converged by the 1860s.

Colonisation of Plants through Agricultural Science

During the first decades of the nineteenth century, colonisation of plants in Bengal was executed by a botanical enterprise of the (changing) colonial state with roots in various European countries, where earlier botanical gardens had been established which had experimented with plants from their overseas dominions. In England, the first botanical garden of public nature was the Royal Garden at Hampton Court and efforts cumulated in the establishment of the Kew Royal Gardens. W. T. Thiselton-Dyer, assistant director of these Royal Gardens, wrote in a paper read at the Colonial Institute in 1880: 'The closing years of the eighteenth century inseparably attach Kew to Colonial history, for it was by the voyages of Captain Cook and Sir Joseph Banks [. . .] that the vegetable productions of the southern hemisphere were first introduced into English gardens.'[54] Peter Collinson, a leading plant introducer of the day, described Kew as 'the Paradise of our world, where all plants are found, that money or interest can produce'.[55] During the period that followed, several botanical gardens were established in the English colonies themselves, and India became 'the first and foremost' location where these 'principal seats of the botanical work of the Empire' were established, which according to Thiselton-Dyer 'from the beginning' considered botany as a 'thoroughly practical science'.[56]

Lucile H. Brockway in her historical–anthropological study on science, colonial expansion and the role of the British Royal Botanic Gardens concluded that the nineteenth-century British botanist felt no conflict between pure science and its application 'to enrich the Empire through satellite gardens in the hinterland and at the expense of captive colonial labour forces there'.[57] Richard Grove also specified that 'the foundation of the new botanic gardens' in south-west India – which he traced to the Portuguese and Dutch activities in the field and reflected their 'Constructions of Tropical Nature' – clearly was 'connected with the early expansion of the European economic system'.[58]

However, plant colonisation was a slow process, and while the project continued throughout the nineteenth century and beginning of the next, individual schemes often failed. Grove also demonstrated that not all such schemes were 'used to root colonial claims to possession'. Vinita Damodaran added that until the mid-nineteenth century, botanists and other Europeans responsible for the establishment of botanical gardens in India, among others, often roped in indigenous knowledge, exemplified in names attributed to plants for instance. Damodaran emphasised that 'while this appreciation of indigenous ideas diminished by the latter half of the nineteenth century, it was still a force to reckon with in the earlier period'.[59]

The Calcutta Botanic Garden established in 1786 was meant to function as 'the headquarters of botany in India'.[60] Its inspiration had come from an army officer, Lt. Col. Robert Kyd, who was an ardent horticulturist. In June 1786, he forwarded a scheme for the foundation of a botanic garden to Gov. Gen. Sir John Macpherson. The latter passed it on to the Court of Directors of the EIC. Kyd's proposal had firmly rested on economic lines, and the cultivation of 'rare plants as things of mere curiosity' had repelled him. He instead envisaged the growing of plants 'that might benefit the peoples of both India and Great Britain'. The Calcutta Botanic Garden was largely staffed by men trained at Kew, such as Christopher Smith, who was appointed as botanist at Calcutta in 1794. After Kyd's death in 1793, William Roxburgh succeeded him after having been the company's botanist at Madras. Roxburgh started the cataloguing of plants which remained the central work at Calcutta. Along with banks in Kew, he also continued the work on 'economic plants', and Roxburgh became known as the 'Father of Indian Botany'.[61]

These 'amateur' scientists[62] were thus involved in a physical and cognitive reorganisation of tropical nature based on contemporary 'scientific' principles and in close relation with the Royal Botanic Gardens in Kew.[63] From the beginning, such 'practitioners of natural history' or 'natural philosophy' ('naturalists',[64] 'plant taxonomists', 'plantsmen', and 'botanists') were encouraged to provide inventories of the botanical 'potential' of the territory in possession of the EIC. The EIC was greatly interested in such a scheme as it offered them, as colonial administrators, the opportunity 'to try and cultivate plants which had hitherto been confined to lands owned by foreign powers'.[65] Consequently, a plant science, botany, developed that identified plants that were thought to have potential to become export commodities (to England). Botanists at Kew, around 1790, concentrated their activities on such commercial crops, and this was reflected in the work carried out in Calcutta.[66] Though not founded with the same goals in mind, both the gardens in Kew and in Calcutta were thus chiefly involved in the study and distribution of so-called economic plants. In this regard, the development of 'economic botany', as a formal science, was most significant. Originally, it was defined as 'all activities which pertain to the past, present, and future uses of plants by man'.[67] Increasingly, it became part of a general 'imperial agricultural science' that encompassed more components, as shown in Chapter Six.

By 1840, colonial officials were convinced of 'the capability of India for all kinds of culture, and the probability of the almost indefinite extension of these, with increased improvement in most of the principal staples of Indian Commerce'.[68] Yet such 'improvement' would not materialise without the application of 'science', officials thought.[69] After 1860, when the EIC had been dethroned, there was a constant invocation of (colonial) 'agriculture science' by the new administrators in British India.[70] MacLeod commented:

> [. . .] the potential usefulness of new knowledge in the economic development of a predominantly agricultural country could not be ignored. The active spirit of capitalist enterprise among Englishmen in India as in her other colonies, had, from the early eighteenth century, directed itself to the development of plantation industries. The cultivation of the natural history sciences, notably botany and geology, typically followed.[71]

Natural resources had, in the first instance, to be tapped to sustain British (economic) hegemony, yet there was a qualitative difference in the 'improvement ideology' of the new players, that is Indian Civil Servants who had taken over charge from the EIC servants. Recurrent shortages of food-supplies resultant in famines and 'law and order' threats prompted such administrators to apply science to agriculture to stimulate its 'improvement'.[72] What is more, the very definition of improvement changed. Improvement had meant making plants useful to England and those who served it (i.e. the company's servants). After 1860, it was increasingly argued that plant improvement would have to serve the whole British Empire, which of course included India and the Indians too. A general disappointment with the outcomes of agricultural experimentations during the first half of the nineteenth century urged officials to 'come for a careful reconsideration of our management of the land of the country.' Late secretary to the GoI, A. O. Hume, had questioned, for instance, in 1879:

> The land revenue in all historical periods has been the main
> financial resource of every successive Government, Hindoo
> or Mahomedan. We have done much for the country, have
> enormously increased the value of its produce, yet province for
> province we are not receiving much more than many of our
> predecessors, Akbar for instance, did. Are we really making
> the most out of the land?

Certainly not, Hume had felt, and he admitted that stupendous errors had
been made, and the Permanent Settlement of Bengal that related to the land
revenues had been one of these. The latter had only created 'a multitude of
absentee landlords and rent-charge holders' and had left 'the masses [. . .] worse
off and more miserable than those of any other part of the empire'. Yet as the
Permanent Settlement was there to stay, Hume and many of his contemporaries
urged the establishment of a Department of Agriculture through which the GoI
could enact 'systematic improvement in its agriculture', which 'might prove a
remedy for many of India's present troubles'.[73] The application of 'science' in
this effort was a sine qua non. 'Scientific agriculture', as an adviser to the GoI,
James MacKenna explained, had slowly progressed even in England. However,
all these decades (1840–80) had gone by with lots of talk but no action. Yet
when by 1880 British agriculture faced a period of depression, an 'awakening
of a *real* [italics mine] interest in scientific agriculture' could be witnessed in
England, and MacKenna wrote:

> Scarcely had this development in England begun before
> we brought this gift to India – a gift the meaning of which
> was not, perhaps, fully realised and the immediate necessity
> of which was not accepted by many, including not a few
> of the older type of Government official, whose opinions
> were conservative and who thought it a vain task to teach
> the cultivator his own business. But what a scope Indian
> agriculture offers for scientific investigation!

As administrators now 'really' believed in using scientific agriculture for
agricultural engineering, an increasing number of scientists was invited from
England to start work in one of the newly established agricultural institutions

in India. Administrators now believed such scientists could do wonders in the agricultural fields.[74] MacKenna wrote:

> The appeal is irresistible, and, just as England had its early enthusiasts, so these young exiles, influencing the Government under which they worked, stirred up from the beginning an agricultural policy and directed the attention of Government to the improvement of agriculture (in India).[75]

Though the application of 'science' to agriculture itself was not new, the fact that colonial administrators hoped 'agricultural science' would provide practical solutions to economic and political problems faced within British India was a novelty. Special experimental stations were founded or funded by them, calling for scientists to man them and carry out the great imperial agricultural project, that is the colonisation of plants. In Chapters Six, Seven, and Eight, by following in particular tobacco but also indigo and sugar cane, I evaluate the institutionalisation of agricultural science at Pusa in Bihar and argue that three groups of 'white colonisers'[76] – in colonial Bihar at least – that is, 'colonial administrators', 'European planters', and other 'non-official British'[77] along with British scientists, for quite some time, shared a broad technocratic ideology of agricultural development. It was technocratic in assuming that the major obstacles to sustain agricultural growth in Bihar were ultimately technical rather than social or political.[78]

Thus had the first half of the nineteenth century been the golden age of botany, after 1860, botanists not only studied plants but also started transforming 'tropical agriculture' as (economic) botany became part of an 'agricultural science'.[79] Daniel R. Headrick described the gradual changes. During the first half of the nineteenth century, botanists

> had before them the example of numerous valuable plants transferred and commercialized in earlier centuries, such as cotton, tobacco, maize, manioc, and sugar cane. These early plant transfers had resulted from amateur initiatives. From the late eighteenth century on, however, plant transfers became official policy.[80]

By the end of the nineteenth century, Headrick continued, the emphasis in economic botany had turned from collecting and transferring plants to improving their potential through scientific research. For this purpose, 'experiment stations' or 'model farms' had been established that, unlike botanical gardens, concentrated on a small number of crops such as tobacco and sugar cane and, Headrick explained, 'studied them from the point of view of soil chemistry, mycology, entomology, genetics, and agronomy'.[81] Such model farms were followed by agricultural research stations such as the one established at Pusa in Bihar in 1903 and analysed in detail in Chapters Six and Seven. Through these research stations, a new science was generated, 'agricultural science' sponsored by British administrators in England as well as in India who, as David Ludden noted, saw the colonial state as the only good landlord, the only one capable of commanding the requisite knowledge for agricultural production, its problems, and improvement.[82] Accordingly, scientists entered government service, got involved in government's plant colonisation schemes, and were made to understand that the 'requisite knowledge' needed by the British administrators in India had to be 'useful'.[83] Addressing his audience, William Thiselton-Dyer, in his lecture on 'The Botanical Enterprise of the Empire' in 1880, echoed:

> I think that you will be interested in hearing these antiquities of the subject, because you will see that from the beginning botany has always been a thoroughly practical science. It is my object to-night to show to you that it is as true to its traditions to-day as it was three centuries ago. All that we ask as scientific men is free scope for using the organisation (Kew Royal Gardens) which is a necessity of any intelligent attempt to turn the resources of the vegetable kingdom to account, for purely scientific as well as for useful and commercial ends. Our aim is to make this organisation do a double duty; and I hope that I shall succeed in satisfying you, whether as administrators or as merely practical men, that in botanical pursuits such a combination of interests, while it adds enormously to the range of scientific activity, is also of the greatest service to the community from a merely material point of view.[84]

Clearly, scientists either in Kew or in British India had to take into account the (commercial) interests of the empire.[85] Useful knowledge had thus to be generated from 'nature', and plants were given 'a civil status'; that is, they had to be identified and named scientifically.[86] In other words, the science and scientists were 'in the service of imperialism', and in this way, the vegetable kingdom was 'scientifically recast'.[87] This process had started when the first natural science scholars had arrived in Bengal during the company's rule and continued under the crown. During the process, some plants lost their status and became 'kings' or kings in the waiting/making. *Watt's Dictionary* brought out between 1889 and 1893 is an excellent example of such 'scientific recasting' of plants. George Watt (1851–930) is best remembered as editor of the well-known six-volume *Dictionary of Economic Products of India* and for the later *Commercial Products of India* brought out in 1908 to update the *Dictionary*. Importantly, the *Dictionary* concerns itself mainly with plant resources, and Watt himself mentioned that 'the economic products belonging to Animal and Mineral kingdoms have been but very imperfectly touched upon'. He hoped, however, that they would receive adequate attention in a future edition.

The first volume by Joseph Hooker and entitled *Flora of British India* had appeared in 1875. If we analyse these volumes separately, we do not only get to know which plants were included (and by default of course also which not) but also get to know which had been given status as 'economic plants'. Besides, among the latter, some plants (in some regions) received more importance than others (judged by the number of pages devoted to them). Comparison of the various editions demonstrates which plants, over the years, had become 'outcastes', why, and when. Finally, an analysis of these volumes provides a good idea about (past) state policies and intentions. Importantly, the successor to the *Dictionary* was entitled *The Wealth of India*. Needless to add, that all Watt's efforts wonderfully illustrate that during his years, administrators strongly believed in the potential 'improvement' of India's agricultural wealth not only through (European and native capital) investments but also through the application of 'agricultural science'. What is more, such a colonisation of plants also needed (more) white colonisers.

Colonisation of Plants through New Settlement Policies

Plants could not effectively be 'colonised' by colonial science and capital alone, however. Colonial Bengal needed colonising people too, that is men who could control the power of vegetation and make commodities out of plants.[88] During the first part of the nineteenth century, colonial policy had sought the transformation of 'nature' into an 'agricultural state'. By the end of 1830s, most of the vast plain of 'Hindostan' was said to be 'in a state of cultivation':

> The original productions of nature have been effectually rooted out, and the plants and grains fitted for human use have been substituted, except in a few districts where political misrule has been paramount, or where the power of vegetation, from the combination of heat and moisture, has been found even greater than that of man to control it.[89]

During the nineteenth century, the principle staples chosen by British administrators for control by man were sugar cane, poppy, and indigo in Bihar, but other plants such as wheat, rice, and tobacco also received attention in particular after the 1870s. It was maintained, however, that most of these cultivated plants were in a 'degenerated' state and only useful for internal consumption. Nevertheless, it was judged that the introduction of British industry, machinery, capital, and skill 'would in a short time produce a supply adequate to the consumption of the whole empire'.[90] Therefore, there was an increased demand for not only 'a thorough freedom of commercial intercourse between the European and Indian dominions of the Crown' but also a thorough freedom of 'an unrestricted settlement of Englishmen in India'. The official attitude of the EIC had been, however, quite conservative regarding the former and in particular the latter. Though the EIC did consider European capital and skill the two 'grand and essential instruments for improving our Eastern Colonies and rendering them useful to the mother country', it had been wary of 'liberals' such as John Crawfurd who argued in 1829 in favour of an increasing number of Englishmen in Bengal:

> Everyone knows that it is the freedom which has existed in respect to these two essential and indispensable points which, even in spite of blundering legislation, neglect of the mother

country, inauspicious localities, and occasional imprudence on the part of the settlers, has assured the rapid prosperity of almost every colony which England ever possessed; it is unquestionably the interdiction of the same freedom which has made the Indian commerce always insignificant – often retrogressive – [. . .] a heavy burden to the mother country, and which has, for the most part, after sixty years rule, kept our Indian fellow-subjects in the same unaltered state of poverty and barbarism in which we found them.[91]

During the 1830s and 1840s, an increasing tension could indeed be witnessed between the EIC – a trading company administrating government – and non-official settlers in Bengal. Free trade and settlement was advocated by the latter, who in particular argued against monopolies, namely, those of silk, salt, tobacco, opium, or tea.[92] In Bengal, it was the relation between the Court of Directors of the EIC and so-called indigo planters that in particular deteriorated during the 1830s. The latter, involved in the colonisation of sugar cane and indigo in Bengal, held that from their 'uninterrupted residence in the Mofussil', they had contributed to the 'advancement of the "greatest happiness" of the Empire'. These white planters, therefore, demanded that 'the privilege of holding lands being freely granted to British-born subjects'. One of the supporters of a much more lenient government policy towards British settlers in the interiors of Bengal remarked:

> A journey ('*tempo permitiendo*') to the district of Tirhoot, the 'Arcady' of India – or if time and opportunity do not permit – then an excursion into the neighbouring districts of Nuddeah, Jessore, Fureedpore, and Dacca – all bordering more or less upon each other, and affording the most incontestable proofs of the benefits which have already resulted from the uninterrupted residence in the Mofussil, of that useful and respectable body of men, the Indigo Planters, whose boast it may justly be 'To scatter plenty over a smiling land.' And read their history in a nation's eyes.[93]

During the century of consolidation of colonial rule (1757–857), the expatriate capitalists living in the villages of Bengal (proper) and Bihar (the so-called *mofussil*) pointed to the success of 'colonisation', which in their opinion should be 'the ardent wish of every friend to improvement in India'. One of them defended his opinion by stating that only if Europeans would be allowed to become landholders or at least renters, agriculture, commerce, and manufacturing would advance by rapid strides. Besides, 'the establishing of this intimate connection between British capital and energy, and the soil of India' was indispensable as 'no other circumstance will so speedily and certainly arrange the existing mischievous confusion and uncertainty of rights and tenures connected with land, into the known relations of landlord, tenant, and labourer'.[94] In this way, the amount of revenue collected would very much increase as the interests of a British population in India would be identical with those of the (colonial) government. Yet after having experienced the developments in the American colonies during the last few decennia of the eighteenth century, British government officials were not convinced of the latter truth. British settlers ardently argued, however, around 1832 that such a (non-official) British population would add security to the empire and this, 'without power of being dangerous to the government, will have the means of being useful in its support':

> Because the colonies of America revolted, it is therefore supposed, *that the exclusion of British subjects from India will give stability to our Asiatic Empire, without any advertence to the difference of the cases;* without any thought of the danger, which the exclusion of British Subjects must induce.[95]

Though there had been some change in attitude towards free settlement of British-born subjects in India, during the 1830s and 1840s, many servants of the company were still not convinced that enlarged facilities should be given for the successful application of non-official British skill and capital in developing the great natural resources of India and especially that the privilege of holding lands should be more freely granted to British-born subjects. To the contrary, in the opinion of some of these executives of the company's government prevailing unrest in Bengal at the time was caused by conflicts between 'natives' (*zamindars* or *raiyats*) and European (indigo) planters. Therefore, till the rising of Indians against 'whites' in 1857 known as the Mutiny, the attitudes of the state machinery towards European (English) planters remained ambivalent, and therefore, official colonisation of plants during the first half of the nineteenth century was carried out through European and native capital and official British skill and manpower involving only a handful of (British) non-official 'colonisers'. The latter being involved in their own plant colonisation schemes that often worried the EIC government servants and administrators at home alike.

Though there had been violent and varied resistance against the colonial regime even before 1857, between 1857 and 1859, there were more gigantic and widespread challenges to British authority in Bengal and elsewhere.[96] Immediately after these disturbances, there were some officials who questioned 'the value of India as a part of the British Empire'.[97] Yet the so-called Civil War of 1861–65 in the southern states of America had wrecked, at least temporarily, some of its export crops, and this induced Britain to again put its hopes on agricultural producers in Bengal. Indeed, by 1862, the ship of the state had been righted, and the powers formerly delegated to the EIC were now in the hands of the ministers of the Crown. Colonisation, that is settlement of British/European men in Bengal, now became openly backed, and it was considered 'no small advantage to England that her educated middle classes, whose numbers are rapidly increasing, find in India scope for honourable ambition and personal enterprise, with remunerative employment for skill and industry'.[98] As a result, and as Eric Hobsbawm described, after the end of the company's rule, a new community rose of expatriate British, accompanied by their wives, which increasingly emphasised its separatism and racial superiority and which increased social friction with the new indigenous strata.[99]

By 1833, the commercial activities of the EIC had already become incompatible with its administrative responsibilities, and the Parliament in London had prohibited the company's servants to engage themselves in trade or industry. As a result, the company's investments in the indigo business went in private hands (only). In some cases, private indigo entrepreneurs were able to even purchase estates, but in general, they dealt with the tenants of Indian landlords in the vicinity of their (indigo) factories (concerns), binding them to their interests by becoming their creditors. In this way, a large number of European planters had settled in Bengal proper, but in Bihar, too, such indigo planters multiplied. Significantly around 1860, after widespread agitation against them in Bengal proper, officials in Bihar were quite unguarded in showing their liking for these English planters who were now defined as 'an intelligent, enterprising, and human class, who have conferred great benefit on the districts in which they reside'. It was also maintained that during the so-called rebellion or Mutiny of 1857–58, these indigo planters, without exceptions, had held their ground and had carried on their industrial pursuits, unprotected by European troops and 'in the midst of thousands of ryots whom they were said to oppress and maltreat'.

The official opinion now was that doubtless, there had been instances of individual injustice, but in general, these planters were supposed to be or could become very useful.[100] Indeed, around the beginning of World War I, the interest of these planters and those of the official 'rulers' in Bihar did seem at par. Sir Joseph Bampfylde Fuller, administrator and author of *The Empire of India,* described this indigo entrepreneur of Bihar in 1913 as 'a dominating and picturesque figure in society, representing the sporting tastes, open-air life, and generous hospitality which Thackeray has associated with the planter squires of Virginia and the Carolinas'.[101] As shown in Chapter Six, along with administrators, scientists, British American capitalists, and some Indian collaborators, these English planters were thus entrusted to carry out the great imperial agricultural project of plant colonisation, which included schemes for the colonisation of tobacco plants in Bihar.

Indian Collaborators

Colonisation of the Indian economy, including agriculture, meant that raw materials would be supplied by India, and Indians and European skill, manpower, and/or capital would do the rest; that is, the latter would 'improve' this raw material, such as plants, in such a way that it would be of greater value in particular when transported abroad. After 1857, all trust was put in the development of the 'wealth of India' through 'science'. Apart from imperial railway projects,[102] commercial, industrial, and scientific cyclopaedia, handbooks, and dictionaries of the economic products of British India were published, and Indian produce was exhibited in one of the great exhibitions organised all over the world.[103] Post-Mutiny colonial schemes in the field of agriculture were ambitious, and expectations were especially high in this regard. The ultimate aim was 'plant improvement', which would stimulate overseas trade as well as ameliorate rural conditions. In order to realise this aim, officers employed in the newly established agricultural departments prepared lists of selected economic plants and provided them with new Latin-based names rather than preserving vernacular botanical nomenclature.

Western-educated Indians often acted as intermediaries between the two worlds of empire and colony, and one of them, T. N. Mukharji, commented on his position in 1883: 'We look upon our European brethren to teach us how to develop the resources of our country, and to share with us the profits arising from it. Neither should we think them as intruders, nor should they think us mere hackers of wood and drawers of water.' 'Western science', Mukharji believed, 'would help Indians to see through the eyes of the Europeans and discover that certain plants that Indians might think of as useless could become a source of national wealth.'[104]

Apart from these Indian scientists, other groups of 'natives' were accommodated in this great plant colonising project of the British Empire, as explained in Chapter Six. In order for the project to succeed, merchants were needed, and rather than from Britain, these came from Bengal (proper). Besides, quite a number of, in particular, Bengali traders transferred 'miscellaneous manufactures of Europe' from Calcutta to Patna city in Bihar. A survey among the old Bengali families in Tirhut in Bihar, where English 'skills, manpower, and capital' were concentrated, indicated that many of the first generation of Bengali migrants had come to north Bihar to assist the EIC servants in trade of various articles produced locally like saltpeter, indigo, opium, and grains.

Opium was manufactured as a government monopoly in Patna, where the final process of preparing the drug in balls for the Chinese market was conducted. Sub-deputy opium agents were Englishmen, but among the subordinate officials of each 'factory' were many a Bengali. Some other Bengalis had become general order suppliers to English indigo concerns (*nil-kuthis*) in Bihar.[105] Plant colonisation in Bihar did also not stand a chance without some help of Indian savings that were transformed into British-controlled capital. Besides, there was the entry of some of these moneylenders and bankers into the ranks of the *zamindars*. They and other landowners became the new collaborators in particular during, as Irfan Habib defined it, 'the new post-mutiny policy of befriending the *zamindars*'.[106]

In Bihar, the source of the EIC's profits had been lying not in commerce but in land revenue. Maximisation of land revenue had been necessary for the maximisation of profits, but this had led to tremendous pressure upon, among others, *zamindars*. Permanent Settlement proclaimed in 1793 had meant a compromise to these *zamindars,* though their position often worsened during the first decennia of the nineteenth century. In turn, these landlords had put even more pressure on the peasantries known as *raiyat, raaya, asami,* or *mazara,* who were the actual cultivators of the land, besides, of course, agricultural (landless) labourers. According to Marxist historian Habib, this had a 'polarising effect on the rural population'. After 1858 and under a new regime, these *zamindars* were now urged to 'collaborate' in the imperial agricultural project executed in Bihar. As reward, these *zamindars* could demand higher rents along with a relatively stationary revenue demand. This, according to Habib, was only possible because under the new regime, the emphasis had shifted 'from the levy of direct tribute through land revenue to the exploitation of India as market and as source of raw materials.' An alliance between 'the modern Indian landlord' and 'imperialism' was thus created that could be employed for further plant colonisation during the second half of the nineteenth and beginning of the twentieth centuries.[107]

Colonial Withdrawal without Decolonisation of Agriculture

The 'Great Imperial Agricultural Project' that unfolded during the first half of the nineteenth century was concurrent with the process that, according to Immanuel Wallerstein, took place during 1750 and 1850 and in which the Indian subcontinent became incorporated into a world economy as colonial states with Britain as the 'hegemonic core'.[108] In such a context of 'plant imperialism', it was not the Bihari peasantry, the overall agricultural livelihoods of peasant cultivators and/or locally defined ecological factors but British men (officials and non-officials) who decided on crop choices and crop shifts. It also was the English market, commercial laws, and interests that judged plant quality and the need for and direction of crop improvement in Bihar.[109] Such plant imperialism had its heyday during the first decade of the twentieth century. Yet by the beginning of the World War I, while some 'plant improvement schemes' designed during the nineteenth century were pronounced as successful (i.e. tea, mulberry groves, sericulture, etc.), many more had ended in a 'spectacular failure'.[110] In Chapter Seven, the faith of the tobacco improvement scheme in Bihar is described.

The political climate in Bengal had changed significantly by the beginning of the twentieth century. Political movements, sometimes drawing upon economic and industrial arguments, had been growing for years, and in particular, British economic imperialism[111] was attacked by Indians as well as by some British residents in Bengal itself. Roy M. MacLeod informed that now 'Local Government', devolution and demands of Indian democracy were the watchwords of the day. By 1914, British economic hegemony had started crumbling and along with it also a firm belief in Western science:

> This hegemony, in many respects, reached its zenith in the period 1900–1914, a period which also witnessed the first stages in several very slow movements – movements away from a complete domination by the perspectives of British and European science, as influenced by the interests of Imperial development – towards programmes and policies conditioned by increasing desire of India to develop indigenous industrial technologies. In many cases, and for many years, these programmes, of course, continued to be determined by British officials and scientists and not by Indians. By the turn of the century, however, the British administration included men whose years of experience on the subcontinent had led them to acquire views of science and its social functions far different from those of their contemporaries [. . .] Beginning about 1910, and gathering momentum during the First World War, there grew a determination that science in India should be cultivated without direction from London. At the same time, the war, as in Britain, placing immediate demands upon the country's industrial and technological capacity, began a slow shift in Government science from domination by the 'natural history' sciences towards public sponsorship of industrial technology.[112]

Other developments were also underway; one of which was Britain's slow but steady loss of interest in India and its focus on other colonies that could better supply its 'plants of desire'. Research outcomes generated through the Imperial Agricultural Research in Pusa (Bihar), established in 1905 as an 'epoch-making development' and which were 'invaluable lessons of our Indian administration and economic progress' and had been 'the results of much costly experience and research', should not be solely used within borders of states. Instead, these histories of 'successes and failures' should be made available to all bureaucrats, policy makers, and scientists resided in other British 'tropical dependencies' as well as in Great Britain itself.[113]

At the same time, recurrent food shortages had forced colonial administrators to look beyond mere 'economic plants' and concentrate on the improvement of staples such as rice and wheat. In some cases, it made administrators to de-emphasise research on the vegetable kingdom altogether. However, this did not mean that 'nature' was 'freed' from colonisation but only that it was its other components (rivers and forests for instance) that now had to be 'colonised'. Besides, instead of research on plants, these officials thought that for the development of agriculture, irrigation-, steamer-, railway-, canal-, drainage-, water power-, or other water-related research projects had to be promoted.[114] These projects continued to affect the development of plants, of course, though more indirectly.

Yet in colonial Bihar, even more than persistent food scarcity, famines, floods, and droughts, other factors were at work that forced authorities to change their agricultural policies. Economic tensions during the last decades of the nineteenth century had multiplied anti-imperialist arguments, and by the end of the 1880s, the Indian National Congress – the main vehicle of Indian nationalism – had come in existence, and its influence increased during the next century. In particular, after 1920, political developments in rural Bihar forced administrators, English/European[115] planters, scientists, and private businessmen to pay attention to something else than (technocratic) schemes for plant improvement. Policy makers, as pointed out earlier, had approached agricultural development problems as technocratic obstacles to sustained agricultural growth in Bihar. The autocratic agricultural science that had developed did not (allow) consider(ing) – even less an analysis of – social or political factors as causes for agricultural underdevelopment.

However, by 1920, a few British scientists as well as administrators in British India had become disillusioned with the results of scientific research. Not only did they become convinced that 'science in India should be cultivated without direction from London',[116] but also some of them believed that agricultural science should encompass research on and even with and for (colonised) peasants (*raiyats*) apart from being studies of plants/nature. As detailed in this book, the colonial context in which such scientists worked did not provide much space to men or women with such ideas, however.

Yet during the 1920s and 1930s, the colonial structure of the agrarian landscape was increasingly undermined by 'the colonised' themselves, who, as I illustrate in this book, ultimately compelled British administrators, private businessmen, scientists, and planters to 'decolonise' tobacco-, opium-, and indigo-providing plants in Bihar. The case of 'tobacco imperialism' is worked out in detail in this book, but it is shown how indigo colonisation coloured tobacco developments, and the concluding chapter (eight) shows what sugar cane had to do with all this. The colonial tobacco improvement schemes ended as failures in Bihar, after more than one and a half century of colonial experimentations as described in this book. Instead of a conclusion, in my afterword, I analyse this 'failure' in detail and chew over its advantages and disadvantages for tobacco cultivators and consumers in the present-day state of Bihar in India.

In the last chapter of this book (eight), I illustrate that plant colonisation in Bihar did not stop with the abandonment of indigo, poppy, and tobacco colonisation as sugar cane and other plant improvement schemes replaced such schemes. Moreover, after 1947, when India became an independent republic, no fundamental change took place in agricultural science that had developed during the colonial regime and was based on an – again invoking Scott's adept terminology – 'imperial or hegemonic planning mentality' with its 'authoritarian disregard for the values, desires, and objections of their subjects' and which – unfortunately – remained guiding the government even after India became an independent nation. This study, therefore, provides more insights than only those that stimulate a better understanding of the political, socio-economic, and cultural context of tobacco cultivation in colonial Bihar. A spin-off of this study on the travails of tobacco in colonial Bihar is knowledge generation regarding what Scott called the 'missing links'[117] that caused some plant improvement schemes to fail in British India.

CHAPTER ONE

British Interest in Tobacco Trade and Improvement in Bengal

Tobacco had played a fundamental role in the old British Empire. Yet after the so-called American Revolutionary War (1775–83), that 'empire' had crumbled. This forced England to analyse whether their 'possessions' in the East could function as alternative suppliers of tobacco and other 'lost' commodities such as indigo. A decade later, the colonial West Indies sugar industry collapsed due to the revolt of the slaves in 1791, after which British officials wondered whether England could obtain sugar from Bengal instead. During the last quarter of the eighteenth century, England's commercial gaze was thus increasingly on Bengal. Meanwhile, the British EIC had busied itself mainly with the internal tobacco trade within the region. This company changed from a trading only into a trading-cum-administrative body in Bengal after English military successes in Mughal India and defeat of other European competitors. Then the EIC also looked into tobacco's export potential. Yet as the trading company soon realised, Bengal was not the Chesapeake, and tobacco in Bengal was heavily protected by the local (puppet) rulers and other local 'native' stakeholders. Besides, the quality of Bengal's tobacco was different from the popular 'Virginia tobacco', so much prized at the London market just like the sugar India produced. The quality of Bengal's indigo as well as other commodities like opium were also judged excellent, and while during the first decades of the nineteenth century indigo was increasingly left to non-official European planters to colonise, the EIC fully colonised the latter through a government monopoly. These non-official European agrarian entrepreneurs became known as 'Indigo planters'. At the same time that export trade had been considered, it was in particular EIC servants who desired continuation of their participation in the internal tobacco trade, encompassing the whole Indian subcontinent, yet the EIC directors in London were neither eager to allow this privilege to non-EIC traders nor even to their own EIC servants who had been doing privately. By the 1830s, however, they finally 'freed' tobacco trade and now even hoped European 'indigo planters' would invest capital and apply skill and manpower to improve Bengal's tobacco in such a way that London would be interested in purchasing it. By this time, however, Bengal's tobacco had been placed betwixt indigo-producing plants and sugar cane. In this chapter, we follow these travails of tobacco in Bengal from around 1760 to 1857.

England's Tobacco Needs Supplied by Virginia

During the sixteenth and early seventeenth centuries, tobacco plants domesticated in the America spread all over the world helped by early European colonialism and trade. By 1630, the use of tobacco leaf for smoking, chewing, or sniffing had become popular in Europe, various regions on the African subcontinent, the South Asian subcontinent, China, Japan, and South-East Asia. Though tobacco, thus, easily transplanted to most climates, initially it was cultivated in the America only. The quality of those tobacco plants was very much liked in Europe and thus started competition among the European colonial powers in the America aimed at the procurement of this valuable commodity. Up to the middle of the seventeenth century, Portugal and Spain dominated the world trade, and these countries also began to cultivate tobacco plants in the West Indies and the Philippines. Spanish planters, for instance, transferred the seeds of the cultivated variety that grew in Yacatan (in Mexico) to Santo Domingo, and through various experiments, they eventually – around 1575 – developed a leaf with a fragrance very much liked in Europe. As a result, the Spaniards were in practical control of the rapidly growing European market.[118] England had also begun the cultivation and export of the plants not only in England itself[119] but also in its colonies.[120] Yet the tobacco exported from the Spanish and Portuguese colonies was *tabacum*, while the English colonies in America at first only had had the less-prized *rustica*. This stimulated a quest for this type of tobacco[121] among the English through experimentation with different soils, seed varieties, fertilisers, and various methods of cultivating and curing practices. These initial English efforts in colonial North America to produce improved tobacco for chewing or snuffing continued throughout the century but were later on carried out to produce 'brighter' and 'milder' tobacco – that could be used for smoking.[122]

Such experimentation began during the days of John Rolfe, who brought seeds, that were later on termed as *Nicotiana tabacum*, from Trinidad and Venezuela to the Jamestown Colony in Virginia. In 1612, these imported seeds were cultivated along the banks of the river James, and by 1613, a first experimental shipment went to England. This new produce became known as 'Virginia tobacco' and was very much liked in London, and this allowed the English colonies in America to grow and market these tobacco plants, which had become the king among the many tobacco species, at least according to European opinion at the time. Interestingly, 'Virginia tobacco', later also known as 'the Golden Leaf' because of the colour of its cured leaf, had become famous without being 'native' to the Virginian soils and thus constituted an 'engineered commodity'.[123] By 1700, tobacco had become an all-important commodity in England's colonial trade. It also firmly linked up England and the Chesapeake, mainly encompassing the colonies Maryland and Virginia, and it was tobacco in particular that made Britain big.[124]

Yet England had taken its time to reach this point. Tobacco had come to England in the 1560s and 1570s where poorer sections of society had been introduced to the foliage by sailors, and among the higher socio-economic classes, it had been popularised by Sir Walter Raleigh. Though King James I (1566–625)[125] had at first strongly condemned tobacco use in his famous essay *A Counterblast to Tobacco*, just a few years later this king of England, Ireland, and Scotland had changed his mind.[126] He may have realised that tobacco use was unstoppable, that a reasonable tax would bring money into royal treasury, and that the English settlers in the Virginia colony needed tobacco exports. Whatever the mixture of reasons, the strong royal objection to tobacco was abandoned, and in order to satisfy people's longing for nicotine all over Europe and to fill state pockets, in seventeenth century, England imported almost all its tobacco from its American colonies to (partly) re-export it subsequently.[127]

Throughout the seventeenth century – and according to the prevailing doctrine of mercantilism – tobacco in England remained subject to governmental control. As the seventeenth century was also characterised by various tobacco duties and monopolies of continental Europe that affected England's trade as well as that these inflicted heavy damages upon Virginia and Maryland planters,[128] policies were adopted to drive out competitors in its trade, such as the Dutch and Scotch, so that England alone would reap the full advantage of the 'Virginian tobacco' so popular in Europe. In particular, after the reign of yet another king (Charles I) who ruled from 1625 to 1649, English policies aimed at everything possible to encourage the colonial planter to cultivate this particular leaf. At times even, the economic interests of some Englishmen in England/Scotland/Ireland[129] were sacrificed, while a distinct advantage was bestowed upon the colonies. For instance, though vehemently opposed by English farmers, the planting of tobacco within England became prohibited.[130] Furthermore, pressure of groups within England concerned with the tobacco trade of Virginia resulted in adoption of certain policies that practically gave Virginia and Maryland a monopoly of the English market by the middle of the seventeenth century.[131] Nevertheless, transatlantic tobacco trade provided employment to thousands in England, who were engaged in it both for home consumption and for foreign trade (re-export). Undeniably, therefore, the tobacco plantations in the colonies had thus been of great use to many in England too.[132]

Tobacco thus played a fundamental role in 'the old British Empire'.[133] In 1853, John Crawfurd, as introduced in the introduction, described that during the eighteenth century, tobacco had become an all-important object of foreign commerce and a useful instrument for levying tax in England.[134] In a similar vein, George Arents,[135] whose great-great-uncle had been Maj. Lewis Ginter, the co-founder of the Allen & Ginter tobacco manufacturer in Richmond, Virginia, in 1875, concluded his address in 1939 in Williamsburg, Virginia, stating that 'thus, the extension of English boundaries in this part of North America was to a degree dictated by the general occupation of tobacco growing'.[136] During the eighteenth century, the staple trade of this commodity had thus firmly linked colonial Virginia with England, and tobacco had become an 'economic plant' that was strongly related to the political, that is the preservation or even development of a British Empire.

Yet after the so-called American Revolutionary War (1775–83), the old British Empire crumbled, which forced England to look for alternative 'possessions' elsewhere from which to procure its requirements. England then started looking more intensely towards its Asian possessions to assess whether commodities such as tobacco could be procured from there. Though England had – for some time to come – lost North America as its main tobacco provider, Price reminds us that this commercial dynamism between colonial Virginia and England had left behind 'something arguably more significant than specific markets for specifics products – namely, an infrastructure of great utility to the entire economy in the ensuing area of rapid industrialisation and attendant export (and import) growth'. By 'infrastructure' Price did not mean 'merely roads, canals, docks, waterworks, and other physical improvements' but also 'the myriad commercial and financial institutions' as well as 'commercial practices and law, commercial education, an improved postal system, to say nothing of the human capital'.[137] This infrastructure could in turn be used by England to import the lost 'exotics', not only tobacco but also sugar, indigo, tea, cotton, and coffee now from its Asian possessions. In other words, these were the tools that could be used to 'colonise' such plants in other regions too.

Tobacco in the Mughal Empire[138]

Tobacco was introduced into India from South America, Berthold Laufer, 'curator of anthropology', wrote in his book *Tobacco and Its Use in Asia*, published in 1924. Tobacco in India, therefore, was not 'native to its soil', Laufer argued, and he repeated an anecdotal account – later often quoted by others as well – that described the introduction of tobacco in the Indian subcontinent. This account had initially appeared in *Wikaya-i-Asad Beg* in 1605 when Asad Beg had been an officer at the court of the Mughal Emperor Akbar (1542–605). It went as follows:

> As I (Asad Beg) had brought a large supply of tobacco and pipes, I sent some to several of the nobles, while others sent to ask for some; indeed, all without exception, wanted some, and the practice was introduced. After that the merchants began to sell it, so the custom of smoking spread rapidly. His Majesty (Akbar), however, did not adopt it.[139]

Most scholars agree that tobacco had been brought along from Brazil (Bahia) by the Portuguese somewhere at the beginning of the seventeenth century[140] when they traded in the southern parts of India, and thence it was diffused to northern India.[141] Around 1615–20, tobacco was found in many places all over the subcontinent. Laufer mentioned, for instance, an Edward Terry from England who had spent some years in western India from 1616 to 1619 and subsequently wrote in his memoirs that he had seen tobacco in abundance in this part of the subcontinent. Terry had complained, however, that the 'natives' like those he had frequented in the West Indies did not know how to cure tobacco and make it strong. This Terry also described the so-called hubble-bubble or *hookah*.[142] During the whole of the seventeenth century, other European travellers-cum-merchants in India also mentioned in their accounts that the cultivation as well as sale of tobacco had been in abundance.[143]

Scholarly accounts on tobacco in seventeenth-century India[144] in particular mention its availability in Guntur, the port of Masulipatnam, the town of Rajahmundry, the Deccan Sultanate of Golcondo (Hyderabad), Bijapur, and more in the western part of the South India.[145] B. G. Gokhale, for instance, wrote a singularly interesting article on tobacco trade in seventeenth-century India.[146] Using contemporary travel accounts and documents related to the English factories in India as his primary sources, Gokhale concluded that tobacco was initially introduced into two separate areas of India, the present state of Gujarat (Surat-Broach area) and the state of Andhra Pradesh (Masulipatam and interior) before 1600 even. Gokhale observed that this was quite remarkable in view of the fact that tobacco as an English industry began around 1616 only in early Virginia, which had exported some 500,000 pounds by 1630.[147] The cultivation and use of tobacco must have spread rapidly throughout India thereafter, Gokhale concluded, and 'became a rich source of government revenue' during the seventeenth century. Irfan Habib described how during the reign of Jehangir, son of Akbar, who assumed the throne after his father's death in 1605, the cultivation of tobacco 'began to predominate over other crops' and soon was grown almost everywhere.[148]

Also Bengal saw the growth of tobacco cultivation throughout the seventeenth century, and travel accounts of that and the next century bore out that the consumption of tobacco, either through smoking it in the *hookah* or chewing it within the leaf of the betel vine (*pan*), had spread throughout Bengal and was popular among diverse classes, caste and age groups, religious communities, and among men as well as women. R. J. Barendse commented on the cultivation, consumption, trade, and quality of tobacco in Bengal:

By the late seventeenth century the tobacco trade involved both huge volumes and huge investments. Large areas in rural Bengal and in the Deccan were now reserved for the cultivation of tobacco. Indian tobacco was cheap but quite coarse and only used among the poorer classes; 'quality' tobacco was being imported from Persia, Turkey, Egypt, Europe, and even – in bulk – from distant Brazil.[149]

During the eighteenth century, there was an enormous volume of trade in agricultural produce throughout Bengal, and tobacco was one of the 'valuable crops' traded within Bengal, imported as well as exported from there. P. J. Marshall argued that tobacco had not only been widely grown in Mughal Bengal but also been part 'of a large trade, often over longer distances'.[150] Later on, certain districts came to specialise in supplying Calcutta, as others specialised in supplying older cities in Bengal such as Dacca, Murshidabad, and Patna. A substantial amount of Bengal's tobacco was exported to Burma, and huge quantities of tobacco were also traded between north Bengal, Bhutan, Duars, Tibet, Lhasa, Assam, Cooch Behar, and Rangpur (in present-day Bangladesh).[151] In Mughal Bengal, this tobacco trade was regulated by its government, and tobacco 'farms' existed in the areas where tobacco was produced.[152] Early in the eighteenth century, it was this internal tobacco trade that quickly became an object in itself for many an Englishmen. This trade, to obtain tobacco for export within the region over land and to dispose of imports, had been an inevitable adjunct to trading by sea, and in 1727, the governor of Bengal had assured the director of the EIC in London that every EIC servant in Bengal was free to improve his fortune in any way that he chose, 'either in inland or by sea'.[153]

Yet in Mughal Bengal, the extent of Englishmen's privileges was determined not by what the directors in London would accept but by what *nawabs* in Bengal could concede, and in 1731, these *nawabs* as well as their officials vehemently had denounced the English trade in this commodity. To Englishmen in Bengal at the time, it was obvious that these *nawabs* wanted, thus, to protect the exclusive grants and special duties related to commodities such as tobacco, which provided a considerable part of their revenue. Indeed, any attempt by Englishmen to apply the *dastak* to tobacco provoked confiscation and protests among these officials. In order, therefore, to keep peace with the *nawabs,* orders from the directors in London had been issued, stipulating that Englishmen in Bengal should not deal with tobacco trade and other such 'inland commodities'.[154]

The Call for 'Free' Tobacco Trade during East India Company Rule in Bengal

There had been commercial relationship between England and Bengal throughout the seventeenth century.[155] Yet though the EIC had traded with the East Indies, it had had difficulties in selling.[156] The company had shared this problem with other West European companies trading to the East Indies such as the Dutch EIC. They all had found the locals less eager to buy what they had to sell, making overseas exports a much greater problem than imports from Bengal to Europe. Therefore, these countries had found it necessary to export silver and some gold to balance their trades. Yet the English company was released from this pressing problem of silver scarcity when that organisation had started collecting local taxes in Bengal in the 1760s.[157] Thereafter, the Bengal *subah,* in particular, was looked upon by the English as the most important possible alternative in India that could replace the lost British colonies in America and supply all the required commodities.[158]

After 1760, trade activities greatly increased, and as contemporaries could witness during the later part of the eighteenth century, there had been a passing away of the old order and the birth of a new in which London and Calcutta became firmly commercially connected.[159] In the new order of things, the place of the 'natives' in EIC-ruled Bengal was definitely subordinate however.[160] In 1820, Walter Hamilton of the Bengal Civil Service wrote in his preface to his 'Description of Hindostan' that the result of the late operations in India had been the establishment of 'the supremacy of the British government, as to leave the native chiefs in a situation of very secondary importance':

> Hindostan, therefore, must not now be viewed as a mere assemblage of Nabobs, Sultans, and Rajas, but as a component portion of British empire, changed and modified in its territorial distribution by the effect of British domination, and in its internal economy by the promulgation of British laws and regulations.[161]

Though the old British Empire had thus vanished, by the end of the eighteenth century, the American colonies were replaced by England's newly acquired possessions in the East Indies, and its already created 'infrastructure', in particular the EIC, could now be utilised to acquire useful plants from Bengal. Indeed, within a century, Bengal fully transformed into an alternative supply region for England. However, the EIC was not interested in the trade of all cultivated plants, and at first, it was in particular cotton, mulberry, poppy, indigo, sugar cane, *and* tobacco that became identified as 'economic plants'. And their cultivation, manufacture, and trade had received the keen attention of the EIC traders and administrators.

When British power advanced in Bengal, *nawabs* had no longer been capable of maintaining any control over the activities of English traders, and the directors in London decided to control the trade themselves. In their concise history of modern India, Barbara and Thomas Metcalf concluded that 'Nawabi sovereignty' (Mir Kasim at the time) was thus visibly demeaned 'as the British took for themselves the trade in a range of valuable commodities, notably salt, betel nut, tobacco, and saltpeter'.[162] During the last half of the eighteenth century, the EIC recognised two 'branches' of trade in Bengal. The primary objective of the company was the external trade, 'the investment' as it was called. This concerned the export of cotton, muslins, raw silk, indigo, sugar, and so on, to Europe and opium to Eastern ports. Monckton Jones explained, in 1915, that 'it was the first duty of the company's servants to collect a sufficiency of these wares against the coming of the East Indiaman and to dispose of their English cargoes'.[163] The second branch was the so-called inland trade, the local commerce of goods from one part of the province to another and the supply of 'the ordinary commodities of life' to the inhabitants. The main commodities dealt with in this trade were salt, grain, betel nut, rosin, and English goods. Tobacco also belonged to the second branch of 'inland trade'.

Though the company was not supposed to intervene in this latter trade, its servants, who felt they were inadequately paid, as well as private Englishmen had found it a great (extra) source of income and had continued to take part in it despite the prohibitions by the *nawab's* administration and their own masters, the Court of Directors. In fact, when the English had replaced the Portuguese in matters of trade, participation in the inland tobacco trade had become a means of private gain at the cost of Indian merchants and the official English administration.[164] Thompson and Garratt explained:

> Every Company employee continued to assert a right of inland trading free of customs to which the country's natives were liable; and especially in such necessities and common commodities as salt, betel and tobacco. The youngest assistant lived like a king by selling his *dustuck* to Indians. Other Indians, without going to the expense or formality of purchase, merely put the English flag up.[165]

Though the Court of Directors inveighed most bitterly against such abuses, forbidding such trade year after year, 'the malpractice continued unabated'.[166] In 1764, the directors therefore decided that tobacco trade in future should be carried out solely through Indian *gumastas*. However, as this did not work out in favour of the EIC directors as they had hoped, Maj. Gen. Robert Clive, governor of the presidency of Fort William (Bengal), devised a new scheme for the inland trade that concerned, among others, tobacco trade. In 1768, he started the Society of Trade, which was an attempt to regulate the trade throughout Bengal in 'the most controversial' inland articles such as salt, betel nut, and tobacco. In fact, the scheme was a kind of monopoly under which all three commodities were supposed to go to the society which would market them wholesale to Indian merchants. This society was intended to provide the company's servants with a profit and the company with revenue and the local people with reasonable prices for the three commodities.

This new policy laid down devised by the EIC in 1773 for 'inland trade' fixed one rate of duty on all articles, yet tobacco (along with salt and betel nut) was 'freed' thereof. Instead, however, it became a government monopoly – albeit for a short time – rated more highly even and earmarked for the provision of certain EIC salaries. It was in particular non-official Englishmen in Bengal who protested against this scheme, and though eventually tobacco was left out of the scheme in 1773, these private Englishmen were still officially excluded from tobacco trade in Bengal as under new EIC rule, this trade was reserved for EIC employees only. The 'evidence' one non-EIC employed English named Harwood was quoted in the *House of Commons Report* in 1783. Being asked to mention the staple articles of Bengal, he quoted salt, betel nut, tobacco, opium, saltpeter, rosin, and grain of different kinds. Being subsequently asked whether he thought 'the natives' possessed capitals sufficient to carry it on without aid from the revenue of the company if trade was 'left free', he answered, 'Yes, if left free.'[167]

After 1813, this company's quasi-monopoly of the Indian tobacco trade came to an end, yet it was not until 1833 that the export trade from India on the company's account was finally discontinued. Henceforth, the company was solely concerned with the territorial GoI and had no longer part in trading affairs.[168] Yet even after the cessation of the EIC's trading activities, the EIC directors in London were not fully prepared to 'free' tobacco in Bengal, and tobacco, whether in leaf or in prepared state, remained subjected to importation or exportation custom duties.[169] In 1830, arrangements were made between the EIC and the growers to deliver the produce for exportation to the government.[170] The latter arrangement did not last long, however, as the tobacco provided by these growers was considered not suitable for export to England. Thereafter, it was only implemented in the Madras Presidency. Nevertheless, custom duties levied on tobacco cultivated in Bengal remain high during the first half of the century. Ross Donnelly Mangles in his book on the *Wrongs and Claims of Indian Commerce* published in 1841 had complained:

> We have not yet, however, exhausted the specification of those unjust distinctions, by which the agriculture and commerce of our noblest dependency have been so unfairly depressed. The case of tobacco is a flagrant instance. This article, if the produce of, and imported from any British possession in the West Indies, America, or the Mauritius, pays a duty of 2s. 9d. per lb.; if the produce of British India, it pays a duty of 3s., being the same that is levied upon all foreign tobacco, principally the produce of slave labour: – with this aggravation, that as, at present, the tobacco of India is very inferior to that of the United States, Cuba, and Manilla, the duty bears, of course, a much higher relation to its value, than it does to the produce of those and other foreign countries. The general result is, that of 22,000,000 lbs cleared for home consumption but 45,000 lbs are imported from British India.[171]

John Crawford (the same John Crawfurd mentioned earlier) in his treatise on the history and consumption of tobacco favoured a freedom from taxation for tobacco and believed that tobacco was never made an object of taxation 'in any country of the East subject to native rule' such as Turkey, Japan, and China, and in those countries, the only taxes imposed on it were 'those which it occasionally bears on importation or *in transit*'.[172] Not only did non-official Englishmen complain about such duties, which in their view prevented Indian tobacco being exported to England in huge quantities, but they also demanded a complete 'free trade', that is the participation of Englishmen in trade of all commodities in Bengal. In his *Notes on the Settlement or Colonization of British Subjects in India* published in 1833, John Crawfurd, for instance, had demanded:

> British subjects to be permitted to carry on any species of trade or manufacture, or any branch of industry whatsoever, which may be carried on by any Native of the country or other person, and the prohibition to carry on the internal trade in salt, tobacco, rice, &c. to be replaced.

Crawfurd added that 'surely nothing can be more mischievous, or ridiculous, than the prohibition, to British-born subjects to deal in the internal trade, in such staple articles as salt, tobacco, grain, and beetlenut'. Crawfurd contended that though indeed the official 'tobacco monopoly' was limited to a few districts under the Madras Presidency, the tobacco policy in Bengal was 'still more mischievous than the salt or opium monopolies (of the EIC)'.[173] Men like Crawfurd, however, pointed out that 'fixed duties' were still more preferable than monopolies like the one that existed in France and Spain at the time. They, therefore, had convinced the government of the ill-advisedness of 'monopolies' as existed at the time (1829) in Bengal for salt and opium for instance. Nobody less than the Right Hon. His Majesty's Principal Secretary of State for the Colonies, E. G. Stanley, showed for instance that under a scheme of fixed duties, the tobacco revenue was much more for England than the revenue of France, which operated under a system of monopoly.[174]

Demand for Tobacco Improvement in Bengal

Englishmen such as Mangles and Crawfurd supporting 'free trade' were disgusted with 'all the obstacles to the progress of the Indian trade'. The most injurious, according to John Crawfurd, was 'the exclusion of the industry, for example, and capital of Europe'. Crawfurd, therefore, not only supported free trade but also supported free settlement of Englishmen in Bengal as in his opinion it was in vain to expect that the agriculture of India could ever become of the vastness and importance of which it was susceptible 'until improved and extended by the unlimited and unshackled application of British capital and intelligence'. Crawfurd had exclaimed:

> The free settlement of Englishmen then is loudly called for, as a measure not only of expediency, but of real necessity, if India is ever to be rendered a valuable acquisition to this country. The whole productions of Indian industry that are abandoned to the exclusive management of the natives, through the restraints and penalties of the monopoly, are inferior to the similar productions of every other tropical country; they are not only inferior to the production of British colonial industry, but to those of the French, Dutch, and Spanish, even to those of the Portuguese industry; they are in every case also inferior to the corresponding productions of Chinese industry.[175]

In a similar vein, Mangles had complained:

> How grievously this noble field has been neglected or mismanaged, the great inferiority of the cotton of India to that of America, and of its silk to that of Italy, and even of China, – the comparatively petty quantity of sugar which it is able to export, and the high cost of production, and the wretched quality of its tobacco – will sufficiently demonstrate.[176]

According to Crawfurd, this inferiority of the agricultural products of Bengal was caused by 'the slovenliness and ignorance of a semi-barbarous people'. The quality of cotton and sugar was really deplorable, but 'Indian tobacco', according to Crawfurd, was an even better example of the 'slovenliness of Indian husbandry'. Notwithstanding tobacco's long culture and use, tobacco in India, due to the 'sheer ignorance and negligence of the native grower', was the 'very worst in the world and nearly unfit for any foreign market, altogether so, indeed, for the market of Europe'.[177] Such non-official Englishman thus concluded that 'improvement' of the quality of the agrarian produce of Bengal was a first priority. On this point, the EIC administrators and these non-officials eventually agreed, and this even brought forth scope for collaboration. Such Englishmen reasoned that as in the 'new order', it was the London market, or rather the Board of Customs in England, that decided on 'quality' (or 'standard goodness') of the produce of Bengal. In other words, instead of local tastes and customs, it now was England that had become the arbiter of quality and would decide on 'improvement' and it means.[178] Hence, it was ruled that apart from capital, expertise also had to be imported from England to improve the cultivated plants of Bengal.

Already in 1758, the EIC had shown interest in the 'productions of the soil', and in that year, the council in Calcutta had written to the Court of Directors (in England) that they desired to encourage the planting of cocoanuts, betel, and tobacco in Bengal. Actually, this interest of EIC officials in the cultivation of these plants had been inspired by their hope to be able to export such 'economic plants' to England. But in the case of tobacco, they had been disappointed as London had rejected the 'bad-quality tobacco' of Bengal. Subsequently – and increasingly – EIC servants started interfering in Bengal's cultivation matters.[179] In 1789, as Chandra Prakash N. Sinha mentioned in his analysis of the decline and destruction of agriculture in Bihar during early British rule, the Court of Directors desired the 'commercial residents' in Calcutta to obtain precise information regarding tobacco and cotton produced throughout their domains in India. They wanted to know about the quantity and the usual price of tobacco produced in the districts as well as the growth of this article.[180] British experimentation with tobacco cultivation in Bengal dates back to as early as this year.[181]

Yet more systematic and official efforts had come only after 1800 when it was felt that besides the Indigo branch, 'European capital and enterprise' should concentrate on other valuable crops such as tobacco, sugar cane, cotton, mulberry, and the poppy, which were considered the most important productions of Bengal. In 1803, Rev. William Tennant, one of His Majesty's chaplains in India, wanted special attention to be given to the 'culture of opium and tobacco'. Accordingly, Tennant had described tobacco 'in the northern and western provinces' which required 'as rich a soil as opium and an equal share of manure'. 'Tobacco, therefore', Tennant further explained, 'is most frequently raised on the rich plots interspersed among the dwellings of the peasantry.' Though requiring a laborious cultivation, tobacco, according to Tennant, could become very profitable in particular in the southern districts of Bengal, where the soil was excellent for this crop: 'In these provinces a sufficient number of hands and perhaps a sufficient quantity of land could be afforded for the supply of the whole market of Europe'. Yet for the time being, the species cultivated were considered 'too weak to fit the market'. Tennant concluded, however, that the known enterprise of Europeans and the 'effect of large capitals invested in the trade' would certainly help to make Bengal tobacco a profitable enterprise.[182]

In 1819, the Agricultural and Horticultural Society had been established in Calcutta, and this society increasingly spent time in observing the 'native methods' of rearing plants with a view to 'improve' them, and in 1829, the GoI had expressed its wish to cooperate with this society 'to promote the production of articles of raw produce of an improved description for importation'. In 1836, this society explained that

> it was thought at this epoch by many, that the attention of the Society had been hitherto too much confined to the introduction of what, with reference to the climate of Lower Bengal, and the residence of the majority of the Subscribers, might be termed exotics: they conceived, that the efforts and the funds of an Indian Agricultural Society might be far better applied, and more in consonance with the original draft of proposals for its formation [. . .] in a word, that Sugar, Cotton, Coffee, Silk, and other great staples of commerce, were far more legitimate objects of its special encouragement, deriving, as it did, and hoped still more to do, its chief support from the Commercial and Agricultural community, than the introduction, at a heavy expense, of European fruit trees, with other pursuits of the same nature, which, however laudable in themselves, few have the leisure to attend to, or feel the want of, whilst all are interested in seeing our commercial resources augmented, by improvements in our Agriculture.[183]

Therefore, the real take-off of a 'colonial tobacco improvement scheme' (later to be transformed into an imperial tobacco improvement scheme) in Bengal has to be located in the 1830s when the EIC government began to finance tobacco experiments conducted under the aegis of the Agricultural and Horticultural Society particularly in their newly established experimental farm at Akra near Calcutta but also elsewhere in Bengal.[184] In 1851, 'East Indian tobacco' had even been included in the 'Exhibition of the Works of Industry of All Nations'.[185] Yet notwithstanding all experimentation, even by this time though it was now widely known that tobacco was grown 'to considerable extent in various parts of India', EIC officials still argued that generally tobacco in India was 'of very inferior quality'.[186]

Tobacco betwixt and between Sugar and Indigo in Bengal

To recapitulate and as Raymond K. Renford described in detail, the curtailing of trade prospects in the West caused by the American War of Independence had induced more 'free merchants' to turn to Bengal. Moreover, in Bengal, the ban upon private trade by the company's servants, other than those in the commercial branch, had left much of the 'internal and county trade' to such private merchants.[187] These merchants traded in several commodities however, and tobacco was just one of them. Besides, it was only in 1830 that the EIC decided for once and for all that tobacco should really be 'freed' in the sense that it should not be part of any kind of government monopoly and that European capital, skill, and manpower should 'freely' be applied to improve its quality. Contradictory, this announced the real beginning of what I call 'tobacco colonisation'.

The case of poppy was different however, and the cultivation of this plant and its manufacture into opium was retained as a monopoly by the EIC and had become an important source of revenue. Holt Mackenzie, one of the principal witnesses, interviewed by the Commons' Committee in 1832 believed that

> from that source (opium) also they (EIC servants) derive a very large revenue, the excess of the sale prices beyond the first cost constituting such a tax as I would think it hopeless to get by any other device; and though, commercially speaking, there are strong objections to the system, yet we must set against that the necessity of the revenue; and my belief is, that the same amount of revenue cannot be otherwise got.[188]

Non-official Englishmen had thus been deprived of partaking in this trade or in the cultivation of the poppy plant in Bengal, and as the EIC had for long also made it difficult to participate in tobacco trade and the trade/cultivation of other commodities that had been categorised as 'important economic plants', British merchants, therefore, concentrated on two other types of 'useful' plants, that is those which produced indigo and sugar.

By 1790, there had been some fifteen Agency Houses in Calcutta, a majority of them British and mostly run by former company servants.[189] These Agency Houses actually served to channel into trade the private funds of company officers and officials barred from trading in their own names. As such, these houses were able to support a further penetration of the internal trade of Calcutta's hinterland (including Bihar). Yet it was indigo and sugar cane and not tobacco that in this way were getting 'colonised' by foreign capital, skill, and manpower. As this book bears out, during the following hundred years, tobacco in Bihar remained 'betwixt and between' these two commodities.

During the first decades of the nineteenth century and like British tobacco traders in Bengal before them, 'indigo planters', as these new private forces were also called, entered into skirmishes with the EIC however. Using the arguments of Adam Smith against restrictions on trade, they attacked all monopolistic restrictions of the company and were backed by the agency houses. They aimed at the removal of the 'annoying restraints' upon their acquiring a legal title to land in the interior of Bengal. In 1833, the outcome of this struggle meant a significant victory for the 'planters' embodied in a new Charter that allowed 'natural-born subjects of His Majesty' to legally proceed to, reside in, or pass through most of British territory in India without a licence. Moreover, such persons were now legally empowered to acquire and hold lands or any right, interest, or profit therein for any terms of years in the Indian territories in which they were authorised to reside. However, and as illustrated in this book, for long these planters still had to contend with an often unsympathetic EIC administration.[190]

Nonetheless, planters who settled in the 'interiors' of Bengal even before 1833 had taken up indigo and sugar production and had often been very successful too.[191] As for sugar, around 1790, a number of events had occurred which greatly influenced the sugar trade between Bengal and England afterwards. Between 1698 and 1789, England had got its sugar almost entirely from the West Indies supplemented from about 1740 onwards by some sugar from France. Yet the West Indies sugar industry had been crippled by the revolt of the slaves in 1791, and a resolution in 1792 by the general court of the proprietors of the EIC had urged the Bengal government to 'speedily and permanently supply a considerable quantity of sugar for the relief of Great Britain'. However, 'these English had found the quality of Bengal sugar as 'so poor' and so to high the price of the sugar available, it had been decided to send this *khandsari* to Britain for further refining into the 'better' crystal sugar, which was so much in demand in Europe. Nevertheless, sugar from Bengal was preferred above that of the West Indies 'because it was made by freemen' and not by slaves, antislave movement supporters in England argued. Thus, there was enough incentive for British 'planters' to try their luck with sugar trade and cultivation in Bengal.[192]

Sugar cultivation and manufacture in Bengal had long predated European intervention, and refined sugar had long formed an item of long-distance internal and overseas trade; unrefined sugar (*gur*) had been a peasant produce and had circulated locally and over middle distances even more actively. Yet in the nineteenth century, refined sugar went through several cycles as an item of trade in European hands and as an item of European manufacture, as explained by Amiya Kumar Bagchi. The manufacture of crystalline sugar was the finishing stage of a long process, and it was only at this stage that many of the European enterprises were involved. Thus, only the crushing of sugar cane in a centralised sugar factory and the refining of the juice by the centrifugal process were carried out in factories under European control.[193]

European/British planters in Bengal considered indigo even more promising than sugar. In fact, after the collapse of handicraft exports from Bengal, indigo became one of the major export crops and a principal means of remitting 'the tribute' and earnings of individual European officials and traders to England. Though some Indians also owned a considerable number of indigo concerns and cultivated and manufactured sugar, in evidence before the Lord's Committee of 1830, it was however stated that their indigo and sugar were 'not as good' as that manufactured by Europeans. Sugar and indigo thus provided the GoI seated in Bengal with ample proof that with the aid of European capital and skill many more plants in Bengal could become profitable export commodities.[194]

During the 1820s, tobacco was situated betwixt and between these two commodities, that is sugar and indigo, and tobacco was still largely considered a product of the 'natives', whereas sugar cane and, to an even larger extent, indigo was being colonised already. It was now proposed to start 'colonising' tobacco as well.

Colonisation of Tobacco in Bengal by English Planters

Some territories in India were said to possess the most esteemed and superior 'country tobacco', and others possessed soils eminently suited for tobacco cultivation that produced 'a fine variety of tobacco' that could be used for cigar manufacture and even be sold at higher prices than 'any American' cigars.[195] Yet nonetheless, European capital and skills were needed to prepare this tobacco for the London markets. Thus, around 1830, the Court of Directors had appointed a Select Committee of the House of Commons to look into 'the possibility of improving the culture, in the East Indies, of some articles which are now chiefly supplied by the United States of America, particularly of Cotton and Tobacco'. About 'Indian tobacco', it said the following:

> Tobacco is another article of commerce, the consumption of which is very great, and although it is believed not to be an indigenous production of India, it is nevertheless in general cultivation there. Occasional small consignments of tobacco have been made to Europe by the Company and by individuals, but without success, arising from the cheapness of American tobacco, and the higher cost and inferior quality of the Indian. In the year 1824, our Bombay Government sent to London a sample of Kaira tobacco, which we entrusted to the management of persons eminent in that business, but the result was unfavourable. Part of this tobacco, manufactured in various ways, was sent back to Bombay, with specimens of approved kinds of American and Turkey tobacco; and in 1827, our Bombay Government sent us a further parcel of Kaira tobacco, prepared with greater care than the former parcel, but still objectionable and unfit for the British market [. . .] The difference between the freight of ships from India and from

America will perhaps be a permanent obstacle to the general importation of Indian tobacco into Europe, unless it can be overcome by superiority of quality; but even if a market cannot be opened in Europe for the Indian tobacco, an improvement in the article for the internal consumption of India is a very desirable object [. . .] Under this view we have taken measures for procuring supplies to tobacco seed from Virginia and Maryland, a portion of which will be sent to you.[196]

In this report, Thomas Lack, a 'most obedient humble servant' of the EIC, furthermore explained:

It has been represented to their Lordships that the cotton of India is inferior to that of Carolina, not through any inferiority in the soil in which it is grown, but through a defective mode of cultivation; and it is thought that this deficiency might be supplied by a judicious application of skill and capital. The same representation is made as to Tobacco [. . .] The peculiar system of administration which the legislature has sanctioned for British India, forbidding Europeans to settle in the country, prevents the operation of the encouragement ordinarily afforded by an extensive market and favourable tariff [. . .] Their Lordships apprehend that the important article of indigo has flourished under encouragement of this nature.[197]

The *Select Committee Report* of 1832 added that the cultivation of tobacco in Bengal could be carried to any extent 'with due encouragement on the part of government'. Presently, however, Indian tobacco was not worth one-third of what American tobacco was, and this was ascribed to the want of skill on the part of the grower and the preparer. Tobacco in China and Burma[198] was considered much better than Indian tobacco as – it was argued – more care was taken by the cultivators and curers/manufacturers there. In Bengal, much more attention had to be paid to selecting the seed, to choosing the soil, to weeding, to reaping the crop and its after preparation, and to packing. It was envisaged that Bengal, or in fact the whole of India, could never compete with American tobacco, but Indian tobacco could become extensively consumed in

England for particular purposes if only European skill and capital were applied to it.[199] In fact, this message was again and again repeated during the 1840s and 1850s albeit in different forms, forwarded by different media and meant for various readerships.

In 1841, for instance, Mr Melvill quoted the opinion of 'parties conversant with the trade' who argued that if the duty on tobacco were reduced to 2s. 9d., 'a very considerable consumption of East Indian tobacco would ensure'. Melvill's informants had continued that although shipments to England of 'East Indian tobacco' had hitherto been very limited,

> we have obtained sufficient knowledge of the quality that might be produced; and we have no hesitation in stating, that if more care were taken in the cultivation, and the sorts of tobacco cultivated, a very superior description might be grown and to an extent quite sufficient, even in the finer descriptions calculated for cigars, to supersede the use of Colombian tobacco and second-rate qualities of Havannahs [. . .] and there is little doubt that, as in the case of coffee, the reduction of duty would result in such an increase of consumption as would effectually protect the revenue from loss, if not improve it.[200]

In Bengal, the price cultivators received for tobacco seemed to have been more than they received for poppy, which was prevented to be sold in the 'free' market. Around 1820, in Bihar, it was the *kories* who had been induced by government to cultivate the poppy and it was the *koerie* who also took care of tobacco and vegetables. At this point in time, tobacco differed from poppy, however, in that the former was considered a 'native' cash crop, whereas the latter was associated with the colonial government. The *koerie* cultivated both and was said to 'go anywhere where a good garden land is to be found'.[201] The low-caste *koerie* had been selected by the government for poppy cultivation as he was known for his 'industrious habits', and he differed from another poppy-growing caste, the *kurmi*, who had a 'special hereditary cultivation – sugar cane', whereas the *koerie* as a caste of gardeners had chosen tobacco apart from poppy. Benoy Chowdhury, in his ground-breaking study on the *Growth of Commercial Agriculture in Bengal (1757–900)*, mused over the association of this caste with poppy cultivation and observed:

What exactly confined the cultivation of poppy largely to the *koerie* caste cannot be clearly ascertained. The *koerie* was the caste of gardeners and it is likely that when poppy came to be extensively grown, he transferred his skill from one crop to another. It is, moreover, not altogether unreasonable to hold that in the first phase of poppy cultivation, marked by a certain amount of compulsion [. . .], cultivation of a low caste could be more easily compelled by the village headmen to take to poppy cultivation; low social and economic status was more compatible with the success of coercive methods. Besides, trouble and care indispensable to a successful growth of poppy prevented the common run of peasants from changing over to the poppy crop. On the other hand, used to agricultural operations of a certain type for over a long period, the *koerie* found it convenient to stick to it. Moreover, within a settled village with a given pattern of distribution of crops, the *koerie* really found it difficult to jostle his way into an already crowded field.[202]

During the 1830s, government decided that the quality of tobacco in Bihar should be improved; it was this *koerie* who was seen as a potential cultivator who could be induced by Englishmen to change his ways. In the decades following the new Charter of 1833, in particular, non-official Englishmen had come out in greater numbers. They mainly swelled the numbers in the three presidency towns, including Calcutta, but few ventured upcountry into the *mofussil* and took to indigo and sugar planting.[203] The Charter had thus thrown open the trade between Bengal and England, and 'the unfettered application of British skill, capital, and industry to the commercial and agricultural resources of India' could be started by these non-official Englishmen with support of the colonial government.[204]

In 1838, it had occurred to the Right Honourable the governor general of India to address the home authorities 'on the subject of the advantage likely to accrue to the British Indian Empire by undertaking, at the expense of the state, experiments on an extensive scale for naturalising in India useful and desirable plants indigenous to other countries'.[205] On the occasion, Professor Lindley had deliberated:

From the great extent of the British possessions in India, and the infinite modifications and combinations of soil and climate to be found within them, there can be no doubt whatever, that almost every production of every climate except the Arctic, may be so completely naturalized, that when they are of any importance as objects of cultivation, they may be brought to all the perfection of which they are susceptible in other countries; provided skill and care are shown in the selection of their situations.[206]

By the 1850s, tobacco in Bengal was also enlisted as one such plant that should be 'colonised' by European capital, skill, and industry, and the authorities looked upon the European/British (indigo/sugar) planters in the *mofussil* with great expectations in this regard.

CHAPTER TWO

Away from Bengal Proper: Colonial Gaze Drawn to Bihar

Sugar cane cultivation as well as manufacture in Bengal had attracted British planters from the West Indies when the industry had petered out in the latter colonies around 1780. In particular, the Tirhut region in Bihar (that time part of Bengal) had seemed promising in this regard. Though in the same region the EIC had commanded a government monopoly for opium, EIC directors in England had encouraged the establishment of cane cultivation and refineries in Bengal without stipulation of such a monopoly but having been prompted by despair over of the 'loss' of cheap supplies of white sugar from other colonies. Though for some time sugar in its raw state was successfully exported from Bengal and further refined in the United Kingdom, experiments had also started in order to improve the quality of sugar cane as well as techniques of refinery within Bengal. Around 1850, these developments were put on hold, however, and would remain so for some decades that followed. All expectations of the EIC government as well as planters were on indigo instead. Till 1860, indigo in Bengal proper, though facing ups and downs and therefore considered a risky business, nevertheless remained the most important plant towards which colonisation efforts were directed. However, by 1860, public opinion in Bengal proper was definitely against indigo. Its cultivation had become too unpopular among Bengali peasants to foster its continuation in that part of Bengal, and planters looked upon Tirhut in Bihar as a possible alternative region where indigo colonisation could proceed. Subsequently and after the so-called Mutiny of 1857, the newly established GoI that had replaced the company's rule indeed acknowledged these indigo planters as partners in their 'Agricultural Improvement Project' in Bihar but not without taking in Bihari *zamindars* (landowners) too, however. This chapter follows this process during which the colonial gaze as regards indigo colonisation was drawn away from Bengal proper and increasingly focussed on Tirhut in Bihar part of 'Upper Bengal'.

The Fate of Sugar in Bengal (1780–860)

By the time the EIC took charge in Bengal as an administrative body, sugar had been exported from the Indian subcontinent for centuries and also to Europe.[207] During the seventeenth century, both *khand* ('refined' raw sugar) and *gur* ('unrefined' sugar which contains molasses in addition to sucrose) were exported from Calcutta, and for instance, Dutch traders shipped Bengal sugar from Masulipatam.[208] Moreover, around 1789, developments in the sugar trade elsewhere in British colonies, in particular in the West Indies, made England decide to try whether the *khand* and *gur* from Bengal could be utilised for further refining into crystal sugar (white sugar or 'industrial sugar') so much in demand in Europe.[209] As this was found possible, sugar in this form was shipped from Bengal to England by private Englishmen as well as EIC traders. Yet this sugar known as East Indian sugar had to compete with sugar from the West Indies.[210] A prohibitive duty on Indian sugar – till removed in 1836 – had made many Europeans involved in this export trade, take up indigo rather than sugar as the former was considered more lucrative.

Nevertheless, a few Europeans had tried their luck in cane cultivation and even in the manufacture of so-called muscovado from cane on 'West Indian lines' and refinery from *gur* within their own factories in Bengal and elsewhere in the subcontinent.[211] For instance, a slump in the sugar export in the second half of the eighteenth century due to a rise in the price of Bengal sugar had caused some Europeans to undertake sugar manufacture in Bengal on 'West Indian lines' in the hope this would make sugar cheaper. Moreover, reacting to the huge demand of the profitable European market for white sugar, the EIC had encouraged *gur* refining in the last decades of the eighteenth century as well as cultivation of sugar cane in Bengal.[212] Yet in 1811, the demand for Bengal sugar from London was minimal, and the EIC decided to discontinue trade as part of their regular investments. Thereafter, sugar factories in Bengal incurred losses and were either wound up or converted into indigo *kuthis*.[213]

However, in 1813, when the EIC's trading monopoly was abolished, there once more had been a temporary increase of sugar exports from Bengal, though this East Indian sugar remained in competition with West Indian sugar. In 1837, after an equalisation measure between duties of sugar from East and West Indies, sugar export from Bengal was again taken up by Europeans with new hopes. New sugar factories were also established by them. Yet hopes were soon converted into despair as it now was the invasion of beet sugar stimulated by Prussian and French government since the 1830s which had captured a great part of European markets.[214] As a result, the production of cane sugar was increasingly put under pressure in Bengal.[215]

During the second half of the 1830s, it was argued that 'improvement' of the quality of sugar cane would be the solution to increased competition. In the *Quarterly Journal of Agriculture* of 1837–38, it was, for instance, proposed that the Hindustani cultivators could not help that they used 'degenerated species' of cane as they had not been supplied with better. The result was that the sugar cane produced in the east of Hindustan was 'considerably inferior in strength to that of the West Indies'. Though this cultivation of the cane 'was practiced in the East from the most remote antiquity' and even exported to Syria at the time, 'the application of capital and skill' was now recommended 'to the improvements of an article whose inferiority is alone consequent on the want of these'. The government was urged to do something in this respect as:

> In the event of any sudden emergency, how could England expect India to meet in quality or quantity the requisite demand? In times of profound peace it may be well enough; but should political convulsions ever have the misfortune to recur, by which our Western Colonies may fall into the hands of a foreign power, the value of East India sugars would then, if they do not before, claim the serious and most liberal consideration on the part of the legislature, to give due encouragement to the present limited extent of sugar exports from this country (India), which has the natural effect of attracting attention to increased cultivation in other parts of the globe.[216]

Experiments in the nursery garden of the Agricultural and Horticultural Society of Calcutta had indeed been carried out in a desperate effort to be able to compete globally through the 'improvement' of Bengal sugar and cane.[217] Treatises for European planters were also compiled, teaching them how to cultivate sugar according to 'modern knowledge'. Robinson had been one such compiler who even believed that such experiments and treatises had resulted in sugar in Bengal to go through 'the gradual, though certain, march of improvement'[218]:

> European skill and capital have been applied to its manufacture, and European superintendence and energy to its cultivation; and in spite of many drawbacks, the result has been that the quality has been brought to a high state of perfection; the Native manufacturer has been almost entirely superseded by his European competitor.[219]

Yet an Act of 1846 intended to protect 'the home refiner and (the) West India proprietor from the effects of the full development of skill in the manufacture of the East'[220], followed in 1851 by the abolition of preferential duties, fully crushed Robinson's hopes. Subsequently, export trade collapsed, and when next the question of developing the Indian sugar industry arose, it was no longer a question of reviving an export trade but of meeting a greatly enlarged internal demand.[221] Ulbe Bosma wrote that in the 1850s, 'it became clear that attempts by European planters to transfer Caribbean methods of sugar production to North India were faltering'.[222] Subsequently, till around 1900, at least, European planters preferred indigo not in the least as this was 'the only tract in which native manufacturers had not, by that time, succeeded in establishing themselves in competition with Europeans'.[223] During the next fifty years, sugar in Bengal had thus to do without (much) European capital, knowledge, and manpower. Historian Chandra Prakash N. Sinha concluded that

> the priorities of a rising imperial power did not permit such a free play and the cultivators of sugar-cane and the manufacturers of sugar in Bihar and Bengal were effectively barred from developing this industry (i.e. for production of export quality sugar) and the hands that sweetened the lives

of Englishmen were made to cover their faces to conceal their tears and agony.[224]

For the time being, these 'Englishmen' stopped 'colonising' sugar cane in Bengal, that is trying to manufacture 'industrial (white/crystal) sugar' and efforts to improve cane. Consequently, as Ulbe Bosma researched, the downfall of industrial sugar 'left the door open for the (Indian) *khandsari* manufacturers to supply the European market with Indian sugar'. All was thus not lost for Indian sugar cane growers at this point, and rather different from Chandra Prakash N. Sinha, Bosma concluded that till the early 1860s,

> the khandsaris were not only favoured by British refiners, but could also rely on a well-established market and distribution system in South Asia. Sugar traders had been going in and out of Bengal at the northern borders for centuries. The East India Company and its successor, the government of India, never controller the trade of sugar within South Asia. Indian traders retained control of the export from Bengal and Bihar.[225]

The Opium Monopoly of the East India Company in Bihar (1773–911)

Even before the formal takeover of the EIC in Bengal, sugarcane, tobacco, indigo plants as well as the poppy plant all figured in its trade and manufacturing systems. Poppy was manufactured into opium, and in fact, opium had been a major commodity in an expanding intra-Asian trade ever after the mid-sixteenth century, Alfred W. McCoy described. Indeed, under the reign of Akbar (1556–605), when tobacco had just been introduced in India, the Mughal Empire had relied upon opium land as a significant source of revenue. McCoy also explained that although cultivation covered the whole of the Mughal Empire, it was concentrated in two areas: upriver from Calcutta along the Ganges Valley there was the so-called Bengal opium and upcountry from Bombay in the west the 'Malwa opium'.

The earliest European expeditions to Asia also show, McCoy continued, 'their (European) involvement in the Asian's opium trade'[226], and poppy became one of the first plants to become fully 'colonised' by the English in Bengal. When the company's rule effectively had started in 1757, one of the first measures taken by the British governor had been the abolishment of the Indian opium syndicate at Patna (in Bihar) and the establishment of a monopoly over the opium produce of Bengal on principles that operated for the next half of a century. Initially, this was in the hands of company's servants in their private capacity, but in 1773, Warren Hastings declared the opium manufacture and trade as a government monopoly and introduced the system of contract or 'exclusive privilege' for the annual supply of opium to the EIC.[227] This official monopoly was extended from Bihar to Banaras–Ghazipur and other opium-producing areas in the Ganga region.

In 1797, the company introduced a policy under which all the opium produced in these territories in eastern India became directly appropriated from the peasants (*raiyats*). Poppy cultivation now was strictly regulated through the grant of licences to these producers. EIC servants procured opium in its raw, semi-liquid state and further processed it in the company's own establishments in Patna in Bihar and Benares, which is in present-day Uttar Pradesh. The bulk of this opium was intended for export and mainly to China. As it is described in detail by other scholars, the EIC's export opium was auctioned at Calcutta to private dealers who then took the risk of smuggling it into China.[228]

By 1797, the EIC had eliminated the local (Indian) opium buyers in Bengal and controlled poppy cultivation, processing, and export. From its factories at Patna and Benares in the heart of the 'opium country', British officers in senior positions directed some 2,000 Indian agents, we learn from McCoy, who circulated through the poppy districts, extending credit and collecting opium in its crude form. Richards informs that nearly all cultivators in Bihar who engaged for opium with the colonial authorities had been from the *koeri* caste, which specialised in intensive market gardening and 'irrigated cultivation of high-value cash crops'.[229]

McCoy estimated that opium provided 'six to fifteen per cent of British India's tax revenues' and 'remained a staple of colonial finances' throughout the nineteenth century.[230] The district of Tirhoot (hereafter Tirhut) in Bihar,[231] at the time part of Bengal and situated at the bank of the river Ganga, was one major supplier of poppy plants apart from being famous for its 'luxuriant crops' of indigo, tobacco, grain, and sugar cane.[232] Opium remained a monopoly in the region even after 1857 when the Indian government had evolved a systematic, bureaucratic structure of licensing to administer the production process of poppy and the sale of opium as Richards detailed.[233] This opium monopoly yielded huge revenues to the colonial government.[234]

Yet all was not well with the British opium trade in Bihar. To begin with, this opium trade with China had been under attack. Moreover, from the late 1830s onwards – and with increased frequency and force – this opium trade had been attacked by people in England, who wanted this trade to stop quoting 'moral' reasons. In particular, clerical men had been arguing against this 'iniquitous traffic'. In 1839, one of them wrote in an article on the subject that it was 'abundantly evident, that the effects produced on the nervous and animal economy by the habitual use of opium in any shape – even in the most popular and most innocuous forms, the sulphate, nitrate, or muriate of morphia – are of the most destructive kind'. The writer concluded that it was 'therefore, to our minds abundantly clear, that opium is altogether interdicted by religion, morality, medicine, and experience, as a luxury'. He also added that the effects of opium 'are a thousand times worse than those of alcohol; and its narcotic powers, if such *luxuries* are indispensable, may be secured by snuff and tobacco – a Scotch "sneeshin mull" and an aromatic Havannah'.[235]

Yet during the nineteenth century, at least, British opium traders were confronted with more urgent problems in the nature of competitors.[236] The company's monopoly on Bengal opium, in particular, faced strong competition from Turkey. Americans also became very resilient rivals in this regard, yet the chief threat came from 'Malwa opium' grown in the princely states of western India, as Amar Farooqui described.[237] Besides, when China finally had been forced by Lord Elgin in 1858 to legalise opium imports, Chinese officials began to encourage local poppy cultivation, and increasingly, cheaper China-grown opium began to supplant the high-grade Bengal brands. Consequently, after a peak in 1880, Indian imports (from China) declined slowly, in particular after the 1911 Treaty of Tientsin between China and Britain that provided for simultaneous suppression of illegal poppy cultivation in China and India and was accompanied by reductions in Indian exports.[238]

Apart from the competition from China itself, Englishmen propagating 'free trade' remained reasoning against the monopoly system.[239] However, unlike tobacco, for instance, in this case government did not change its mind, and the profit from opium – as long as it lasted – made it less necessary for the government to colonise other plants in the region in the same way as they did with poppies. This allowed non-official Englishmen, around 1860, to try and colonise plants producing indigo, sugar cane, and tobacco in Bihar if and when they so desired.

Colonisation of Indigo[240] in Bengal (1780–834)

Before the declaration of the Permanent Settlement of Bengal by Lord Cornwallis in 1793,[241] Gujarat, Rajasthan, Lahore, Oudh, and Agra had been centres of indigo cultivation and export in India. The indigo from those regions had also drawn the attention of European traders during the sixteenth and seventeenth centuries, but by the eighteenth century, this branch of the Indian trade had dwindled down as the Dutch, too, had succeeded in raising very large crops of indigo in Java and other islands. Bal Krishna, who analysed the indigo trade during those centuries, therefore concluded that in doing away with the necessity of buying indigo in India, it was 'evident that the foreign markets for this commodity had practically been closed in the beginning of the eighteenth century'.[242]

However, in 1788, the directors of the EIC had identified indigo in Bengal as 'an article which, considered in a political point of view, ha(d) every claim to attention, as having a tendency to render the company's possession in Bengal more valuable'. In 1792, the Board of Trade in its commercial proceedings guessed that probably, 'the bounties in favour of the colonies in North America and the West Indies' had caused 'the trade from this country (India) to decline'. Though, it was added that the English and Dutch, till about 1740, annually still exported a quantity of 'Agra Indigo' from Surat. Yet this 'petition of indigo manufacturers' of 23 January 1792 added that 'the troubles which ensued in Hindustan upon Nader Shaw's Invasion put an end to this branch of commerce'. During the last two decennia of the eighteenth century, however, indigo from India once more entered European wish-lists and this time much was expected from the plant in Bengal. Yet at the time, the EIC did not desire private European planters but rather 'the natives' themselves to bring these plants to utmost perfection. In the words of the directors of the EIC, the 'improvement' of indigo would be possible 'by creating from the soil and labour of the natives and export commerce, capable of being carried to a very great extent'.[243]

Though efforts had been made before to resuscitate the indigo trade in India, it was, in particular, after the loss of trade from St. Domingo that indigo from the 'East Indies' received a real chance.[244] The EIC servants had started their investments in 1779–80, and by 1795, Bengal had become the chief source of supply to England, and around 1802, when exports from the American states had almost ceased, those states began to import indigo from Bengal. In short, by the end of the eighteenth century, the entire indigo production of North America encountered almost ruinous competition from Bengal, and by the beginning of the nineteenth century, the latter had all but wrecked the production from America. For a long time afterwards, colonial Bengal had no rival in the indigo trade except for Dutch Java.[245]

This was an interesting fact as Bengal had not had much prior experience in the commercial production of indigo.[246] Yet during those decades that there had been an immense home consumption in Great Britain and as the supply of indigo from the USA and Guatemala had diminished considerably, Bengal was seen as an alternative supplier. Besides, West Indian planters had switched from indigo to crops like sugar cane, which seemed more profitable at the time. Indigo's growth and manufacture in the British 'settlements in the East Indies' was therefore greatly encouraged by the Court of Directors of the EIC. With some experimentation 'in the mode of preparing and managing Indigo', it was not only hoped that its quality would equal that of 'the finest Guatemala Indigo' but also that in time Bengal could supply such an amount of good indigo that would 'render any importation thereof from foreign countries unnecessary'.[247] Though neither having indigo manufactories of its own nor 'any power to impose terms on the proprietors', during the last two decennia of the eighteenth century, the EIC did everything to ascertain the lowest price at which indigo could be procured. The best method to do so the company felt was that of investing general sealed proposals of contract, and the same method appeared to them also 'the best stimulative to improvement in the quality, by making success dependant on it'.[248]

In short, it was thus resolved that 'East India' could 'furnish every kind of Indigo wanted in Great Britain'.[249] The EIC servants saw in indigo also 'a regular means of remittance to transfer their wealth and pay for imports'.[250] Indigo could also replace the export of valuable textiles from India as a basis of profits and remittances for the EIC as the latter had been sharply undermined by the beginnings of industrialisation in Britain.[251] The EIC now greatly interested in this 'important article of Bengal' believed that the stimulation of its 'quality and cost' was required not only in 'the interest of the company' but also because it concerned 'the welfare of this country'.[252] Accordingly, treatises on indigo had been published that contained accounts 'of the culture and preparation of that important article of commerce'.[253]

Yet the EIC government officials did not think the 'monopoly model', which had been applied in the case of poppy, would be suitable for the 'improvement' of Bengal indigo. Actually, the directors of the EIC was not involved in the business directly but had contracted Indian cultivators to supply them with a certain quantity of indigo, for 'this trade could afford the company's servant a legal, ample, and we hope advantageous mode of remitting their fortunes to Europe'.[254] Advances were provided by the EIC for the manufacture of indigo to these local 'planters', and the EIC guaranteed purchase. Apart from 'natives' and EIC servants, non-EIC parties sometimes, already involved in sugar cultivation, manufacture, or its trade, had also become interested in becoming such 'planters', 'making Indigo' and 'realising a fortune'. Consequently, between 1770 and 1800, several non-official Europeans had come to Bengal to try their luck with indigo often introducing the so-called West Indian system of manufacturing indigo. In their turn, these early 'indigo planters', as they were known from 1786 onwards, drew the particular attention of the governor general to the possibility of making indigo a most 'valuable article of production' and begged 'his strict attention to the subject'.[255] However, in general, these early (European) planters were seen as mere 'adventurers' and till 1833 had not been entitled by the EIC government to hold property in their own name.[256] The *Calcutta Review* looked back in 1858 and wrote about these early 'settlers':

> We see that the British settler, one of the race that had conquered the country, could not possess in his own right even the land on which he erected his house. An isolated adventurer – liable at any moment to be deported, subject to the caprice of the Company's civil servant, who was the king in the district under his control – opposed by the wealthy and influential zemindar; – this man, under every disadvantage, by the force of his energy and determined perseverance, succeeds in founding a factory.[257]

After 1834, as Bose argued, a large extent of Bengal's economy prospered or decayed according to the fluctuations in the London market.[258] Moreover, by this time, it was these European planters who had succeeded in taking a great part of the indigo industry out of the hands of the 'natives'.[259] Such indigo planters were almost the sole white *mofussil* settlers in the EIC's possessions, and the *Calcutta Review* concluded in 1858 that 'of late years they have become one of the most important classes in British India'.[260] In other words, by 1860, these indigo planters had become powerful agrarian colonisers.

The Indigo Industry: A Risky Business

Though the indigo industry could be very lucrative, it was a risky business. 'A peculiar feature in Indigo is that', the *Calcutta Review* of 1858 had mentioned, 'most of the items of outlay are certain, whereas the outturn is very uncertain.'[261] Many 'factories' (or concerns) were in debt, and indigo planters 'do sometimes hope against hope'.[262] 'So uncertain is Indigo', it was added, 'that it has become an object to divide the risk with some other business', like silk or sugar for instance. Yet this required, of course, 'considerable capital'.[263] Competition among planters but also between these European planters and 'natives', that is *zamindars* in Bengal, had added to this uncertainty. There had also been competition between the British planters in Bengal and 'native' producers in Upper India. In 1800, the former had, therefore, demanded a tariff protection on the grounds that indigo, being new in Bengal (including Bihar), had necessitated a larger investment and operating costs. Besides, these planters alleged that the 'inferior quality of Upper India indigo would destroy the reputation of Indian indigo in the world market'.[264]

In other words, 'British subjects engaged in the manufacturer of indigo' within Bengal and Benares wanted 'preferential treatment' in order to compete with indigo trade 'carried on by foreigners and others in the districts of Agra and Delhi'. The latter was indigo manufactured by 'natives and sold by them to European Dealers [. . .] at a rate so much below what the article can be made for within the Company's Provinces, that the difference would be deemed a fair and reasonable profit'. This indigo was exported from Calcutta under the name of 'Bengal Manufactured Indigo', these planters alleged, 'having been previously marked with European Characters'. These planters were sure, however, that this indigo manufactured by the native manufacturers was 'not equal in quality and purity to ours, nor have they we presume any knowledge of the theory of an art the perfection of which depends so immediately on science', and these British planters in Bengal feared that their 'own' indigo 'may be brought into disrepute by the introduction of inferior indigo under the denomination which those produced within the Company's Provinces are exclusively entitled to'. Moreover, the increased importation of this 'foreign indigo' could not 'but be productive of the most serious apprehensions that the market in Europe will very soon be overstocked'.[265]

Early European settlers in Bengal had other complaints too. Alexander Nowell, an indigo planter settled in Tirhut (Bihar), had complained, for instance, that both the system of public loans to the planters to manufacture indigo as well as the EIC policy to purchase indigo should be abolished as this 'forced unnatural expedients' caused 'overstocking the markets' and was thus against the interests of the indigo planters as well as that of the government. This planter stated in his petition to the 'Honourable the Court of Directors of the United Company of Merchants of England trading to the East Indies' that he preferred taking loans from 'the houses of agency', as the EIC loans had comparatively been small, and 'consequently, the scale of manufacture, though hitherto invariably sufficient for the demand' was confined. He preferred 'to place this branch of commerce upon a better footing ultimately than the measure so extensive in its operation as the present loan'. Instead of such an EIC loan, this planter requested the government to 'temporarily reduce the heavy duties it (indigo) at present labours under'. If the government really wished to promote 'this very valuable branch of commerce', the removal of these 'oppressive taxes' would be 'in the true interest of his commerce, which interests are inseparable from those of the company and of the empire at large', Nowell had argued. Wishing the government to withhold loans to the planters, he wrote a petition to the Honourable the Court of the Directors of the EIC in 1801, stating that

> with you, Sir, so conversant in the unparalleled capability of these provinces, as well from uncommon fertility of the soil as comparatively low price of labour, to afford any of their natural or manufactured products, there cannot exist a doubt that we must undersell the whole world! That by nature, we are entitled to the exclusive supply of all Europe

with this valuable article of commerce. And if we have not already attained this desirable situation, it has been owing to embarrassments which the measure in question cannot remove, but on the contrary, as we know from experience, must increase.[266]

When the company indeed stopped advances to contractors operating in the indigo business in 1802, it became the Agency Houses that started providing capital for the manufacture and trade of indigo. Having not much capital themselves, these contractors (the indigo 'planters') now borrowed from these houses which raised capital locally. Till 1834, it was the capital supplied by these Agency Houses, accumulated by ex-servants of the EIC and (native) merchants,[267] that made the increased export of indigo from Calcutta to London possible.[268] In his erudite style, Sugata Bose explained how such Agency Houses possessed 'monopsonistic control' of indigo production, with a few giant houses of Alexander, Colvin, Cruttender Mackillop, Fergusson, Mackintosh, and Palmer dominating the scene. Yet due to regular withdrawals by partners, these houses were hampered in the process of capital formation. Moreover, Bose described:

> The susceptibility of eastern India's regional economy to crises at the centre of the capitalist world economy in Britain was manifest in the 1820, early 1830s and late 1840s. The state of demand in remote European markets increasingly determined price levels and the volume of credit of Bengal. The peak of a boom in the indigo market was reached in 1823. As signals of the trade depression in Britain reached Indian shores, the market in indigo began to wobble in 1825–6 and collapsed with the leading Agency Houses between 1830 and 1833.

As a result, agricultural prices in Bengal went into a steep decline although volumes marketed and exported did not contract sharply. Bose continued that the 'want of capital, the loss of credit, the destruction of trade, and contraction of currency' could be identified as the key features of a bleak scenario.[269] The Agency Houses had now given way to a new type of trading organisation which came to be known as the 'Managing Agency System'. The company's scheme of hypothecation, which had already emerged in 1829 as another way of facilitating remittance from India to Britain as well as the Union Bank of Calcutta, became 'the financial plank on which the indigo system of eastern India rested'.[270] The Union Bank of Calcutta started in 1829 with the object 'to replace the private banks of issue by a public one'. Its capital was 'Indian' (i.e. natives and Europeans residing in Calcutta), and it was under the direction of 'the merchants of India', native and European.[271] However, in 1847, the Union Bank 'deeply enmeshed in the indigo mess' closed. Bose concluded:

> If there were structural weaknesses inherent in financing the indigo operations with borrowed capital, these were exposed and exacerbated by the downward fluctuations emanating from the centre of the larger economic system to which the region was now closely tied.[272]

The EIC Government and British Indigo Planters till 1834: Ambiguous Relations

The position of 'European' planters in Bengal was also insecure as down to 1833 no Europeans had the power of holding land in their own name. Instead, they had been obliged to take estates in the name of an agent or something of that kind or under some subterfuge. As a result of this uncertainty, these 'planters' complained in 'a letter from Bengal' that 'innocent and unoffending individuals' had been 'ordered away from India'. An example was given of a Mr Reid, a clerk in Mr Nowell's indigo factory, 'a quiet, faultless young lad, without reproach of any kind' whose 'only crime' was the fact that he had been 'found in India without the Company's licence!' The letter concluded that surely this was wrong as 'the settlement of Englishmen ought above all things to be encouraged, as the only means by which improvement of India can ever be effected'.[273] More in general, therefore, British planters objected to the settlement policy of the EIC at the time, and they claimed that indigo was 'the sole production of the Indian soil which receives anything like adequate benefit from European capital and direction' and therefore was 'also the sole exception to the inferiority of Indian productions'. Yet 'the exclusion of European settlement' hindered the further progress of indigo in Bengal:

To say, however, that it does not suffer, would be most be most untrue. The prohibition to hold lands, or take security on lands – a tax equal to half the gross produce of the land imposed upon those who hold it – the precarious and dependent footing of Europeans living beyond the protection of the King's Courts; the imperfect administration of justice in the interior – and the hostile leaning of the Government and its agents towards all the private enterprise of British subjects – are most serious obstacles to this branch of industry.[274]

In similar fashion, James Peggs, a late missionary of Cuttack in Orissa (also part of Bengal at the time), had proposed in 1832 that 'native growers' of 'the most important of all tropical commodities' had to be replaced by Europeans. Above all, Peggs felt that the great indigo trade had demonstrated how 'enlightened colonisation in India' had promoted the improvement of the produce of the country. The best indigo, Peggs had argued, was that 'created solely by the skill, capital, and enterprise of British-born subjects living in India' as the 'miserable peasant without skill and without capital makes no attempt to improve the variety of the plant'. He asked: 'What chance can such barbarous child's play as this have, even in the fairest and most open competition, with the ingenuity, the judicious economy, the enterprise, the skill, the capital, the machinery, and, what is not less potent than these, the commercial probity of the European colonist?'[275]

While these European 'planters' kept on emphasising their importance for a general improvement of the agricultural scene in Bengal, the EIC did not want to antagonise the 'natives' however. As detailed in Chapter One, EIC authorities had forbidden the involvement of these Europeans in 'inland trade' of commodities like tobacco but had themselves monopolised that of opium. Moreover, in the latter part of 1829, agents and merchants in Calcutta came to know that the Court of Directors in England had transmitted secret instructions to the governor general in Bengal, directing an inquiry to be made 'into the conduct of the British planters and other settlers in the provinces, in reference to their relations with the native inhabitants'. As a result, the agents and traders requested 'their correspondents' (i.e. the indigo planters) to 'defend' themselves. Nearly forty European planters thus wrote letters 'to counteract the injurious effects of *ex parte* statements transmitted by their opponents'.

Many of the planters argued that their indigo factories had greatly increased the extent of ground cultivated and that if all factories were shut up, the native landholders *(zamindars)* would find it difficult to pay the revenue demanded now from them by the EIC administration. Moreover, if 'Europeans' would be allowed 'to hold lands free from transmission at will, the cultivation of the country would', these planters were convinced, 'improve by their taking lands into their own hands'.[276] They also felt that without their factories, the land would relapse into 'its former condition of wildness and poverty'.[277] They trusted that

> the day is not far distant when they will be lawfully permitted to hold lands in their own name; when decrees of the local courts will be rendered more prompt and effective; and when means will be afforded them of holding, under legal securities, such lands as they fairly and justly rent.[278]

Somewhat contradictory but in order to strengthen their demand, these European planters stressed their close connection with 'natives'. They knew their language, whereas EIC administrators, though 'well-educated' with 'good intentions', were characterised by their 'unavoidable ignorance as strangers and sojourners'.[279]

European Planters as East India Company Partners in the Agricultural Improvement Project (1833–57)

The year 1833 was one of celebrations among the British planters' families in Bengal. The Charter Act of 1833 not only wrested the monopoly rights from the company, which it had possessed over the China trade, but also declared 'complete free trade'. What is more, all restrictions on the settlement of British nationals were withdrawn, and as Subbhas Bhattacharya lucidly described thereafter, 'British capitalists were allowed to invest capital freely in plantation crops' and could freely turn Bengal into 'an agricultural colony of Britain'. Clauses 81–86 of this Charter Act of 1833 dictated, Bhattacharya informs us, that 'it was now permissible for the "natural-born subject of His Majesty to proceed by sea to the Company's possessions, to reside therein, to acquire and hold lands or to make profits out of such residence without licence".

These natural-born subjects were authorized to acquire and hold lands for any number of years.'[280] The EIC could no longer say to the planter: 'you shall not establish a factory.'[281] Therefore, the planter had 'held his own' and no longer remained a 'tabooed adventurer'.[282]

What is more, these planters were now even taken in by the EIC government as partners in its great agricultural improvement project. Not a 'native' but also not a 'stranger' anymore, he had become 'an Anglo-Indian planter', interested in the 'varied produce of the soil' but particularly in indigo- and sugar-producing plants, which provided his living.[283] These planters now saw themselves as:

> To all intents and purposes, merely a farmer cultivating one kind of crop. He pays his rent to his landlord: his ploughing, weeding, and other agricultural operations give employment to the lower orders of the peasantry and their families at a time of the year when their own crops require no attention whatever; and the manufacturing season the planter keeps in constant employ many hundreds of day labourers.[284]

Such self-ascribed 'farmers', though more like 'farm managers' or their assistants, also argued that the 'poorer class of peasantry' looked upon 'the European planter' as a 'protector and supporter in their little difficulties and distresses', and these planters would advance money ('without even taking interest') to the cultivators when they were in distress.[285] Yet these planters were not unaware of criticism from 'the natives'. Mr Hampton, one such a *Nil Saheb* in 'Lower Bengal', also known as 'Bengal proper', explained his position and behaviour to a *Times* correspondent. 'In the first place', he said to his English visitor,

> They hate us and our race. We are surrounded here by fierce Mohammedans and a very stubborn race of Hindoos [. . .] Next, as a man of business, while I discharge my own obligations, I try to keep them to theirs. I never exact one farthing more than the rent reserved by the perpetual settlement; a native zemindar would probably double it, and besides that make perpetual demands under all sorts of pretences. He would never help them in sickness or famine, and never advance them a price, but would leave them to the

native money-lender, who charges from 30 to 60 per cent. I am
only too glad to advance them money without interest to buy
me buffaloes or seed, or to keep them if the rice crop fails, for
these advances enable me to make them cultivate indigo. Yet
the native prefers the native zemindar. In prosperous seasons
he has a better chance of bribing his servants. There is always
chance of cheating, and the native loves that chance. In bad
seasons they die off. It is the nature of the natives to love a
loose grasping oppression, with which they are constantly at
war, rather than a plain matter-of-fact debtor and creditor
account [. . .] The proportion I require is never more than
one-eight [. . .] *However, no Indian ever grows it by choice.*
[emphasis mine]. [. . .] You must put this single requirement
against all we do for them, all the capital we expend, and all
the cultivation you see about you, for every begah reclaimed
from the desert was reclaimed by our money.[286]

In an article that appeared in the *Calcutta Review* of 1847 on 'Indigo in
Lower Bengal', which was based on the *Report of the Committee of the House
of Commons, 1828–29* and the *Report of the Superintendent of Police of the
Lower Provinces for 1844–45*, government's opinion and expectations of these
British planters are exposed. The article wants to provide a balanced view of
the 'planter' in Bengal, who was involved in 'either sugar cultivation or indigo
cultivation'. It endeavoured to give a sketch of the system pursued by Indigo
planters, of their dealings with 'zemindars, middlemen, and ryots', 'of the
manifold temptations to which they have been exposed, of the excuses they
may plead, and of the *degree* of condemnation they must incur'. The article
ends, however, expressing the expectation that

as the Planters spread over the country and the opprobrium
hitherto attached to their name passes away, visions now dim
and distant, will be realized in their brightest colours. It may
be that energies at present devoted only to the clearing of jungle
and the increase of cultivation in land, from purely personal
motives, may be turned to the clearance of that equally dense
jungle of ignorance in which the native population are buried.
We may hope to see Schools, the rule and not the exception,

medicines doled out to the Ryot with as much regularity as the seed at sowing time; bridges built; roads laid down, embankments raised to prevent the encroachments of rivers; swamps drained; tanks dug; and physical, intellectual and even moral energy imparted by the master and eagerly received by the subject.[287]

By the end of the 1850s, therefore, administrators hoped the planters would prove genuine partners in their 'improvements projects' and in empire building and preservation and had therefore decided to take them in.[288] For some more years, a somewhat suspicious mode towards them remained however.

Melee in the Indigo Lands of Lower Bengal or Bengal Proper

Planters, 'backed by English capital and guided by true Christian principles of conduct', thus had a great task before them: they had to prove that 'indigo may benefit the hut as well as the factory, the ryot as well as the sahib'.[289] Yet planters in Lower Bengal, now virtual landlords or *zamindars* themselves, had difficulties fulfilling this 'great task before them'. The *Calcutta Review* explained in 1858:

> The beating is the most difficult and important part of the process. Only a planter can know the annoyance and loss caused by its being performed by tired or sulky men; supposing sufficient of them to be in the factory. But how often are a planter's hopes blighted, and the produce of many fields of fine plant lost, by a number of the coolies, with advances only half worked out, decamping. Coolies moreover are becoming more and more scarce and wages are rapidly rising. As railroads and other public works are extended, this difficulty will be still more felt.[290]

The latter, that is the rise of the wages of *coolies*, was even more worrying the planters as 'the low rate of wages has been one great cause of indigo being made at a remunerative price'. A new line of the Eastern Bengal Railway Company was also in the planning and would run through some of the principal indigo districts of Lower Bengal, and in that project, the *Calcutta Review* of 1858 cautioned the planters, 'every coolie in those districts will find work'.[291] An anonymous writer in the *Calcutta Review,* therefore, felt that the planters should pay more 'attention to the comfort of the coolies'.[292]

By the late 1850s, while the planters indeed looked upon themselves as 'the father, the protector, the banker, and the physician of his people',[293] increasingly the relation between this 'indigo planter' and his workers in Lower Bengal, in particular, was perceived in a different light by others. Descriptions of this relation contained the 'abuses and evils' caused by the existing indigo system in Lower Bengal. A compilation by 'A. Ryot' was published in 1858, and though it was agreed that naturally the planter had done some good to the country, this 'ryot' emphasised that 'the indigo planter, by reason of his coercive and oppressive acts, is extremely unpopular with the community'.[294] Importantly, it was believed that the evils were *only* related to 'indigo planting', which was 'a losing game or barely remunerative for the trouble and expense it costs'.[295] The system worked as follows: in ordinary years, indigo cultivation would yield a profit of 25 per cent, without oppression or injustice to 'the ryots'. But much higher profits were aimed at, and it was therefore that hardships were inflicted upon the 'ryots'. Moreover, in bad indigo years, things were even worse, though indeed there were 'honourable exceptions'. The problem also was that, and still according to this 'ryot' (possibly an Indian landholder himself), the indigo planter put all the blame on the (Indian) *zamindars*.[296]

By 1858, many more 'native' *zamindars,* different types of *raiyats*, that is actual cultivators and possibly agrarian landless labour too, plus some English officials and most British missionaries had argued that the worst characteristic of indigo growing was its 'forced nature' caused foremost by the system of advances which the planter 'himself pressed for money' pressed 'upon a half-unwilling ryot, without ever satisfying himself what parcel of land he is advancing for, or even whether it is in the possession of the recipient of the advance'.[297] In his introduction, 'the ryot' had also asked:

> Anyone with tolerable insight into human nature will allow
> that no race-hatred, or any other feeling or motive will induce
> a man to sacrifice his self-interest, especially when he belongs
> to the genus which labours but to live, and lives but to gain. If
> Indigo cultivation were really so paying as the planter insists,

why in the name of goodness does the ryot seize the first chance to fly the factory and resort to the cultivation of rice?[298]

The compiler of this treatise (i.e. our 'ryot') emphasised that even where the land was not favourable to rice cultivation, the ryots were 'unwilling cultivators'. It was perceived that this forceful character, *the taking away of choices from ryots,* was solely associated with the indigo system and set the indigo planter apart from other European planters who had come to India and who had succeeded everywhere in India and had 'lived with confidence and esteem among the natives', though they too had had to deal with 'the lower orders of the natives'.[299] In not a few instances, these planters had even attained prosperity through the aid and goodwill of their 'native friends', and the 'indigo planter' was almost invariably the 'territorial lord' of the soil, 'which he sows with indigo seeds. The ryots, as a social and political necessity, are completely at his mercy'.[300]

In 1858, our 'ryot' believed, however, things could still change for the better in Lower Bengal.[301] He had noted that missionaries – *zamindars* who were he thought 'as a class not ill-disposed against the planter' and even some planters themselves 'who heartily regret these constant collisions which generally end in bloodshed and misery' – were all 'anxious to settle the causes of quarrel and to establish a general harmony'. Yet this 'ryot' thought a conference like the pre-Christian missionaries had organised in 1855 in Bengal would not serve the purpose, and he instead proposed an 'official commission of enquiry' conducted by the 'authorities', that is by the EIC administrators.[302] Our 'ryot' indeed got what he had requested for, and in 1860, the 'Indigo Commission' made inquiries in the 'blue mutiny' of 1859–60.[303]

Possible Alternative: Bihar (Upper Bengal)

Given the changing political economy of indigo in Lower Bengal, one might have expected the indigo manufacturers/managers to respond to this new state of affairs by diversifying their enterprises, shift to a different 'great staple', or just quit 'Indigo land' altogether. Some did the latter and went into tea in Assam. Some chose the former, and jute was one commodity that sometimes replaced indigo in Bengal proper. Yet there was another alternative: reallocation in the indigo business to Bengal's hinterland Bihar (Behar).[304] Indeed, Sugata

Bose described: 'The planters were defeated in Bengal (proper) but regrouped to fight another day in neighbouring Bihar'.[305] Prakash Kumar explained that the agitation by native growers against unjust wages had continued to simmer through the 1850s and erupted into open rebellion in the early 1860s. This had driven out most planters from Bengal proper, and thereafter, the plantations in Bihar were first populated as an overflow from the Bengal districts and grew rapidly from the mid-century as the industry retracted from Bengal.[306] Wynne Wright also concluded that the structural and historical conditions of the region had engendered a 'culture of indigo production' that did not peter out after the collapse of indigo in Bengal but was simply reproduced in Bihar.[307]

Indigo manufacturing by European planters had not been absent from Bihar before 1860. In fact, Tirhut[308] in north Bihar had been a 'great seat of the indigo industry',[309] and twenty-five factories had been established there with the help of the EIC government by the year 1803 already. Some of the 'planters' who had managed these early factories had come from the West Indies though they had adopted a local form of indigo manufacturing mainly and not the one in use in the Caribbean. Tirhut comprised the same region, which also had relatively large outputs of poppy, sugar cane, as well as tobacco crops, and 'indigo concerns' there, in fact, often also supervised growing of sugar cane apart from growing some wheat or rice, and some tobacco, vegetables, and fruit trees for own consumption were grown on *zeerat* land, that is the private land of the 'planter', which was held on perpetual lease.

According to a report of 1810, the collector of Tirhut estimated that the district sent 10,000 maunds of indigo to Calcutta every year. The abolition of the trade monopoly of the EIC in 1833 had also proved an impetus for indigo entrepreneurs (including managers and their English assistants and their British 'clerks') to settle down in Bihar.[310] In fact, as Ranjan Sinha concluded, next to the opium industry, which 'was a good source of emolument to the members of the Patna Provincial Council', the indigo industry was one of the most important (colonial) industries in Bihar by 1830 already.[311] Moreover, by the late 1850s, although indigo was introduced in Champaran nearly thirty years later than in Tirhut proper, the area under cultivation was much greater there than in Tirhut proper.

Violent clashes involving European planters and cultivators or landholders like those that had occurred in Lower Bengal had not been absent in Bihar. Mohammad Sajjad described how by 1829 already, 'the peasant' (*kisan*, i.e.

landowners as well as tenants and subtenants)[312] of Tirhut had started their fight against the European planters in the law courts established by the colonial regime. Indeed, Sajjad continued that the indigo planters in Bihar 'quite mercilessly oppressed the peasantry', and discontent among the latter had first been noted by the government in 1830. In 1856, thirty-eight cases had been filed by the *raiyats* of Tirhut against the planters, and Sajjad even contented that this 'accumulated discontentment of peasantry, combined with those of the Indian soldiers of the British East India Company, resulted into the upsurge of 1857' in that region.[313]

Like in Bengal proper, the relationship between planters in Bihar and government administrators, in particular before 1834, indeed had not always been cordial. In a memorial, James Hay, an indigo planter in Poorneah (Purnea) in Bihar, had complained against W. Wollen, who had been appointed as judge of the district. Hay had explained his case to the EIC directors:

> I had followed the business of an Indigo Planter for many years, in the district of Poorneah, in a peaceable and lawful manner, according to the system established in that country, sanctioned by the Government regulations, as well as long custom and the habits of the people. This, as well known, is for the Planter to make certain pecuniary advance to the Ryuts, or cultivators, to furnish them with seed, and enable them to bear the expenses of culture; which advances are liquidated by the quantity of plants produced, estimated at a certain stipulated rate. Such an outlay of capital by European planters gives a new stimulus to native industry, multiplies the valuable products of the country, and enable the Zumeendars to pay the public revenue, as well as greatly improves the condition of the people, who would otherwise be destitute of the means of employing their fields in such valuable cultivation, and left entirely in the hands of native money-lenders, who are in the habit of supplying their necessities on the most usurious terms.

James Hay went on stating that he had been encouraged by these favourable prospects, and in the year 1824, he had purchased some new factories, named Simelbarry, Hussen-Domreahm Soontah, and Gurwah all located in the same district, in the hope of still farther expanding his indigo cultivation. Yet at that point of time, Mr W. Wollen had been appointed to the important position of judge of the district. Hay was furious as

> this gentleman, of his own authority, took it upon him completely to subvert the established regulations of the Government, by at once annulling the contracts entered into between the Planter and the cultivators of Indigo, besides encouraging the latter by extra-judicial means, to retract from their agreements, and combine to defraud me of my just rights.[314]

Therefore, though the EIC administration had, since the Charter Act of 1833, taken in these 'indigo planters' as partner in their agricultural project in Bengal, in practice relations between officials and non-officials, also in Bihar, could be strained, to say the least. It remained to be seen, therefore, whether Bihar would really entice indigo planters from Lower Bengal after the latter had been driven out of that region.

Developments in Bihar after 1857

Several scholars have noted the fact that the so-called Mutiny of 1857 fundamentally changed the relations between indigo planters and the government in Bihar. Bengal in general was thoroughly reshaped after 1857. One contemporary Englishman reiterated that 'the terrible Mutiny of the Bengal army in 1857' also announced 'the real beginning of the history of British India as an autonomous empire'.[315] In this new empire, the planters of Bihar earned themselves a privileged position and had a well-described task. S. K. Mittal, for instance, maintained:

> The attitude of the Government became much more sympathetic towards the planters after 1857. The Mutiny was more serious in Bihar and the planters proved to be strong props of the Company's rule. They fought against the mutineers, guarded Muzaffarpur and other places and helped the Company restore its submerged authority from the waters of the mutiny.

Mittal also quoted B. B. Misra, who earlier had asserted that the 'experiences of the Mutiny and the motives of imperial interest' had 'dictated the expediency of creating pockets of European population intended to support the Empire in times of emergency'.[316] The happenings in 1857 indeed provided the planters with an opportunity to prove their loyalty to the rulers.[317] The *Calcutta Review* printed:

> As it is, Great Britain is indebted to her Indian 'adventurers'. How many did good service in the Upper Provinces! Foremost among them Mr Venables, the indigo-planter, who held a station after it was deserted by the civilians, and who regained a district from hosts of rebels. In Tirhoot, the firm front of the planters, when the civilians vanished, kept that large and important district in order. In Bhaugulpore and the adjacent districts, the planters again were instrumental in preserving the country from rapine and plunder.[318]

Afterwards, planters in Bihar had demanded their reward of course:

> It would be well if the Government of India would ponder over these events before it is too late. If they read them rightly they will probably see what a suicidal policy they are pursuing, not only in a financial but a political point of view, and may discover before it is too late that it is only by the free introduction of free European settlers that India can be held. They not only cost nothing but contribute largely to the exigencies of the State, but they and they only are a class that can ever take root in the soil.[319]

The new administration that replaced the EIC did not fail the planters in Bihar as Her Majesty's government made quite a lot of them honorary magistrates. Though the government had been instrumental in ending indigo in Lower Bengal, this was now projected as a 'temporary hardship' only as now Bihar had become a real alternative. The government also promised improvement of infrastructure in Bihar. The latter had been asked for as indigo industries in Lower Bengal had had to incur only small amounts of transport costs as compared to factories in Bihar as Calcutta being the main market and port of sale of the dye and its export was further away now. The government, therefore, transferred capital to Bihar for a 'post-Mutiny programme' of intensive railway building, and even though the primary aim had been military, this investment had made Bihar far more attractive for English settlement as well as for English 'at home' interested in Bihar's exports or Bihar's buying capacities of British exports.[320]

Many planters indeed preferred Bihar above Lower Bengal as it was thought that 'the Tirhoot district is far in advance of the lower one in its system of cultivation. The lands are thoroughly prepared by repeated ploughing and harrowing; the soil is thus pulverized and the moisture retained. The seed is sown by means of the drill-plough.'[321] But above all, many planters must have chosen to stay on in Bihar as, Sugata Bose explained, indigo planters could enter in a partnership with Bihari landlords (*zamindars*) who would supply coercive power, whereas the planters would provide the necessary finance. In Bengal proper, such a partnership had become virtually impossible as moneylending landlords had emerged since the late 1840s as rivals of the planters in the credit market. Bengal proper had also developed a larger intelligentsia, Bose argued, which enabled indigo peasants to count on a broader range of support from other social classes than their counterparts in Bihar as had become evident in 1860.[322]

Moreover, besides these British planters, the new GoI seated in Calcutta had identified this landed aristocracy in Bihar as another government ally. Therefore, like the British planters, these *zamindars,* too, were made partners in the 'Great Agricultural Improvement Project' that further evolved after 1860 in Bihar. Ram Swaroop put this somewhat differently and had concluded, 'Thus during the latter half of the nineteenth century, a "triple" alliance was formed in the Bihar countryside to exercise control over tillers of the soil.'[323]

CHAPTER THREE

Changing Hierarchy of Tobacco Tastes and Colonial Demands

During the nineteenth century, developments in sugar cane, poppy, and indigo cultivation and manufacture overshadowed all other plant colonising efforts of the government and/or its partners in Bihar's agricultural field. Whereas poppy had become a 'government plant', indigo and sugar cultivation and improvement had been farmed out to British planters and/or *zamindars*. Within this constellation, the tobacco plant had been placed betwixt and between these commodities. In this chapter, I illustrate, however, that though tobacco remained in the shade of these other plants, colonial authorities had not given up on tobacco improvement in Bengal. On the contrary, factors extraneous to the sugar, indigo, and poppy developments, described in the previous chapter, resulted in the colonial gaze being directed towards Bengal in matters of tobacco improvement schemes as well. The tobacco plant shows a great variety of forms, leaves, colour of flowers, and texture. Each kind has some peculiar feature or quality not found in another. One plant variety will have large leaves while another small ones. One kind possesses pink, and another has yellow flowers. Some plants come with black greenish or brown leaf and yet others with yellow, green, or dark red. Different cultivation methods influence this variety. What is more, once the plant is harvested, one can choose from different curing/drying practices. Finally, storing and transportation affects tobacco too. What is considered a 'good-quality' tobacco depends on tastes (i.e. some people prefer a 'mild' or 'strong' type of tobacco with more or less nicotine content) but more particularly on tobacco's deployment (i.e. whether for smoking, snuffing, or chewing). In addition, if tobacco has to be preserved for a long time or transported overseas, tobacco's requirements will be different than the tobacco meant for local consumption; all this points to the subjective nature of quality definitions. In Bengal, smoking tobacco in *hookah* had been popular among Europeans as well as Indians, and accordingly, this tobacco variety was cultivated and cured. In this chapter, I show that after 1860, tastes and corresponding demands not only changed among the British in colonial Bengal but that it was in particular markets in England that increasingly defined the character of tobacco experimentation in Bengal directed at its 'improvement'. Bihar became the centre of these government experiments during the last quarter of the nineteenth century. Yet by 1905, after decennia of such experimentation, Bihar had still not developed into the cigar-tobacco supply region, which colonial authorities had desired it to become.

A Century of *Hookah* Smoking among Indians and Europeans in Bengal (1750–60)

Whereas in England people smoked tobacco in pipes or preferred the inhalation by nose of pulverised tobacco leaves (snuff), till around 1860, many Europeans in Bengal used tobacco in the same way as Indians did in that region. When tobacco consumption had spread in Bengal, it was either chewed with lime or smoked, and the latter prevailed during the first half of the nineteenth century.[324] Tobacco flavoured with molasses was put at the top of a small earthen bowl with a tube and kept smouldering with burning charcoal. When the smoker puffed, the smoke would pass down through the tube (pipe) and then through a jar of water before being inhaled. The kind of tobacco leaf considered good for chewing and *hookah* smoking varied from brown to dark brown, and the plant was cut along with its stalk and sun-cured thereafter. The cured leaves were thick-bodied, and this was the kind of tobacco cultivators grew. Many households in nineteenth-century agrarian Bengal grew some tobacco for their own consumption. There also were cultivators who grew tobacco for the local markets, and relatively, good quantities had been exported to Burma, where it was made into *cheroots* ('Indian cigars'). Lower Bengal was in particular known for its *cheroot* tobacco, whereas Tirhut in Bihar (Upper Bengal) specialised in *hookah* tobaccos.

These had been the types of tobacco that had been part of the 'inland trade' that had flourished so much during the latter part of the eighteenth and early decennia of the nineteenth centuries, as described in Chapter One. It was also this tobacco trade that all sorts of traders shipping under the British (EIC) flag had desired to colonise.[325] During the first half of the nineteenth century, the preparation of this tobacco as well as the manufacture of *hookahs* also was a flourishing business. George A. Grierson, in his book on *Bihar Peasant Life* of 1885, described how shopkeepers used to buy tobacco leaves from cultivators or middlemen, pounded them at home, mixed spices, kept the mixture steeped in some sweet liquid in earthen jars, and sold this preparation to consumers after some time.

Grierson also provided a detailed description of the 'pipe maker' and the 'the pipe-stem maker', who made 'pipes' *(hookahs)* of various kinds.[326] This Indian version of a water pipe, the *hookah* or a variety of it, remained popular among most Indians till the end of the nineteenth century, though Europeans in Bengal stopped using it some fifty years earlier.[327]

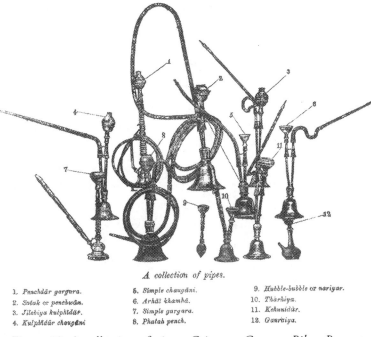

A collection of pipes.

1. *Panchdár gargara.*	5. *Simple chaugáni.*	9. *Hubble-bubble* or *nariyar.*
2. *Satak* or *penchwán.*	6. *Arhál khamhá.*	10. *Thárhiya.*
3. *Jilehiya kulphídár.*	7. *Simple gargara.*	11. *Kehunídár.*
4. *Kulphídár chaugáni*	8. *Phatah pench.*	12. *Gauraiya.*

Figure 10. A collection of pipes. Grierson, George. *Bihar Peasant Life*, 1885 (courtesy New Delhi: Cosmos Publications, reprint 1975).

The *hookah*, an Arabic word, literary meaning 'a round casket', became in particular known all over the world because of its 'curious compound of tobacco, spices, molasses, fruit, and so on' that was smoked in it. This *hookah* was very much part of social life in Bengal during the first half of the nineteenth century. There were many *hookah* varieties, and the kind of *hookah* used also was a definer of etiquette and status. Thomas Williamson, in 1813 in a book on the *European in India,* described, for instance, the *goorgoory* which was formed on the same principles as the *hookah* but 'for the sake of convenience' had in lieu of a long pliant snake a curved pipe of bamboo, at the end of which the mouthpiece was fitted. This smoking instrument had been used by European planters in Bihar, for instance. The 'lower classes among the natives' also smoked the *goorgoory* but used a coconut with only a straight bamboo pipe, serving as a snake, and without any mouthpiece. 'This apparatus', Williamson maintained, was 'an indispensable part of the travelling baggage of even the poorest among them'. Native women were, Williamson had added, 'very skilful in preparing tobacco'.[328]

Figure 11. A native gentleman smoking a goorgoory, or hookah, in his private apartments, attended by his dancing girls. Drawing by Charles Doyley and description by Thomas Williamson, *The European in India,* London: Edward Orme, 1813, plate xix (courtesy New Delhi and Madras: Asian Educational Services, reprint 1995).

Figure 12. Hookah smokers in Calcutta. Williams Jackson, A. V. (ed.), 'The European Struggle for Indian Supremacy in the Seventeenth Century', in Hunter, W. W, *History of India* (Volume VII), London: The Grolier Society, 1907, photograph between pp. 262–3.

In the *mufassil*, the *hookah* was still in use during the second half of the nineteenth century, among the 'natives' that is to say. William J. Wilkins, a missionary with the London Missionary Society, described its social function in Bengal in 1888:

> As we sit and talk to the people in this friendly style, their pipes are brought out, and pass from hand to hand – those belonging to one caste of course being allowed to use only the pipe of men of the same caste. We should certainly not have a lengthened conversation if we were to attempt to prohibit the use of the pipe. Perhaps here a word may be said about the use of tobacco in India. It is almost universally 'drunk' by the Hindus – for that is the idiom [. . .] With the Bengali smoking is a business that absorbs his whole attention for the time. The ordinary pipe, commonly known as the Hubble-Bubble, from the noise made by it when in use, is a cocoa-nut shell filled

with water. To this are fixed two tubes, the longer of which goes to the bottom of the water; and on the other end a clay cup is attached, into which the tobacco and burning charcoal are put: the other, which goes inside the nut above the water, is the one that is put into the mouth.[329]

It was not only among 'the natives' that the *hookah* was popular in Bengal. Till around the 1850s, the *hookah* was used by Englishmen in Bengal though its popularity had progressively decreased from the 1840s onwards. But in 1840, the *hookah* was still very common at Calcutta dinner tables, as well as regimental mess tables, and its sound (bubble–bubble–bubble) was heard from various quarters before the cloth was removed, the latter being a custom at the time. John Crawford, in an article on the *History and Consumption of Tobacco* published in 1853, believed that *hookah* smoking was popular as it was a much 'cleaner habit' than smoking an ordinary pipe, cigar, or using snuff as it purified 'the smoke by passing it through water'. Besides, the tobacco leaves used for *hookah* smoking needed not to be so strong as those used in other pipes and for cigars which used the 'strongest and, therefore, the most offensive varieties of the plant'.[330] At the beginning of the nineteenth century, *hookahs* even appeared in England, where it was used by EIC servants who had returned from India.[331] Indeed, 'most men who had resided any length of time in India had become addicted to them', 'Asiaticus' had commented in 1774.

Figure 13. A gentleman with his sircar or money servant. Drawing by Charles Doyley and description by Thomas Williamson, *The European in India*, London: Edward Orme, 1813, plate ix (courtesy New Delhi and Madras: Asian Educational Services, reprint 1995).

In old Calcutta, the *hookah,* thus, was 'the grand while away of time', and even 'Indo-British ladies' (i.e. British women residing in India) were said to have been 'much addicted to its use'.[332] Such women had replaced the Indian 'concubines' with whom many a British settler had spent his life during the previous century. These women appreciated the mixture of tobacco and other ingredients as well as the fact 'that the smell of the smoke never remained in their clothes or in the furniture of the rooms'. Besides, the highest compliment these women could pay a man, it was said, was 'to give him preference by smoking his hookah'. In this case, it was 'a point of politeness to take off the mouthpiece he is using and substitute a fresh one, which he presents to the lady with his hookah, who returns it'. This compliment was not always of a trivial importance; it sometimes signified 'a great deal to a friend and often still more to a husband'.[333]

In particular, after 1765, when the English had procured the *dewani* for Bengal, Behar, and Orissa – the real beginnings of the 'empire of British

India' – Suresh Chandra Ghosh argued, 'the use of the richly ornamented hookah and the employment of a hookah-bardar became a ritual, almost a sign of status'. Instead of their perusal of a paper 'furnishing the head with politics and the heart with scandal', these 'gentlemen' now indulged themselves with the *hookha's* fume. A 1792 advertisement of a European firm in Calcutta offered for sale: 'Elagant Hookah bottoms – urn shaped, richly cut, with plates and mouthpieces' were offered for sale.[334] The *hookah* also was popular 'upcountry' where many 'gentlemen' among the European community had taken to this smoke.[335]

Using travellers' tales, Pran Nevile depicted life of some English gentlemen in eighteenth-century India, who 'lived in grand bungalows, surrounded by the luxuries of oriental splendour' and among the 'troops of dusky white-clad servants' that stood near their master, *hookah-bardar* was always present with 'perfumed tobacco from a jewelled hookah'. Nevile explained that during those days, there was 'no colour prejudice, and marriages with native women were common and even encouraged by the East India Company'. In the field of recreation and amusement, this meant 'the British became more Indianised', Nevile argued in his chapter entitled 'When Sahib Was Hooked to Hookah'.[336]

Though some never lost the taste for it, during the first decades of the nineteenth century, the use of it gradually became looked down upon among the European community. Moreover, even at its height, among the European community in Bengal, the *hookah* had competed in fashion with 'ordinary pipes and cigars'. First, Englishwomen in Bengal were dissuaded to use the *hookah,* and later, the idea developed that their presence inhibited the smoking of their husbands.[337] In a *vade mecum* for the public functionary, government officer, private agent, trader, or foreign sojourner in British India and published in 1825, it was explained that the *hookull, kalean,* and *goorgoory* were in general use among 'the natives' and even among the 'ladies of Hindoostan' who smoked their *goorgoories* 'in high style'. Though the Englishmen had become reconciled to this sight of females smoking, the *vade mecum* did, however, not recommend this for Englishwomen who resided in Calcutta: 'however delicate may be the preparation of the tobacco and however elegant the apparatus, still, when we see a European lady thus employed, a certain idea, not very conformable to feminine propriety, possesses the mind'.[338] However, among English gentlemen in Calcutta, the *hookah* was still popular during this time and much more preferred than *cheroots.* The *vade mecum* explained:

> The lowest classes of Europeans and of natives, and, indeed, most of the officers of country-ships, smoke *cheroots*, exactly corresponding with the Spanish *segar*, though usually made rather more bulky. However fragrant the smokers themselves may consider *cheroots*, those who use *hookulls*, hold them to be not only vulgar, but intolerable. Hence, sometimes a whole company has been driven away by some unlucky visitor, who, either from ignorance, or from disregard to the feelings of the more delicate, mounts his *cheroots*; thus abrogating in a trice, all distinctions of musk, cinnamon, rose-water, &c.[339]

Indeed, the *hookah* was still so popular among most European 'gentlemen' in Calcutta during the first few decades of the nineteenth century that those who could afford it retained a *hookull-burdar* or preparer of the *hookah*. This was, according to the *vade mecum,* 'a domestic of great consequence', and some gentlemen even had one for the night and one for the day. Regarding the tobaccos used for smoking, the *vade mecum* mentioned, several places in Bengal from which it was procured and called their quality 'absolutely to be admired'. Besides, as the tobacco used for the *hookull* was often chopped and mixed with ripe plantains, apples, molasses, or raw sugar, together with some cinnamon and other aromatics, the fragrance of the tobacco was effectually superseded, and the *vade mecum,* therefore, implied that this gave ample scope for the *hookull-burdar* 'to serve up rank *mundungus*', as bad tobacco was termed, in lieu of the supposed good-quality tobacco. Natives also mixed musk, *ganjah* (hemp plant), and even opium with tobacco, but the author of the *vade mecum* was happy to state that he had known 'only one or two English gentlemen' indulging in this 'objectionable practice'.[340]

Increasingly, however, Englishmen abandoned the *hookah* and even criticised the quality of the tobacco used in it. Suresh Chandra Ghosh explained that when during the first decades of the nineteenth century, the British in Bengal became – and increasingly so – alienated from the 'natives' among whom they resided; they also rejected some of the Indian customs earlier adopted. Thus, one could notice, as Ghosh himself described, 'a decline from favour the habit not of smoking but of smoking the hookah',[341] and by 1860, the habit had been entirely abandoned and had been replaced by cigars, *cheroots,* and cigarettes at the beginning of the twentieth century, as will be detailed in later chapters.[342] Consequently, these English residents in Bengal demanded a different tobacco variety than that could be obtained in Bengal at the time.

Increased Internal and External Demands for Improved Tobacco from India

In 1859, F. W. Fairholt (FSA), in his book on *Tobacco: Its History and Associations,* explained that cigars were of comparatively recent use in England, reasoning that the heavy import duties of both ready-made cigars from foreign countries as well as unmanufactured cigar tobaccos combined with an absolute prohibition of tobacco grow within the United Kingdom had 'helped to keep a knowledge of cigars out of the country'. Indeed, tobacco imports from Virginia and Maryland had considerable diminished after England had lost these colonies. Yet after the so-called Peace of 1815, when twenty years of war against France had ended and Napoleon had been defeated, ports in the United Kingdom had been thrown open for foreign cigars which had increased the cigar trade of Britain. Nonetheless, around 1860, Fairholt maintained that in England, cigars still had been 'an aristocratic luxury then'.[343]

Around fifteen years later, however, when E. R. Billings wrote his treatise on tobacco, cigar smoking had become most popular among king and pauper.[344] Billings enumerated some principal tobacco varieties that were cultivated at the time and all over the world. Among others, he mentioned: Connecticut seed leaf, New York seed leaf, Pennsylvania (Duck Island), Virginia and Maryland (Pryor and Frederick, James River, etc.), North Carolina (Yellow Orinoco and Gooch or Pride of Granville, etc.), Havannah, Yara, Mexican, St. Domingo, Brazil, Arakan, Greek, Java, Sumatra, Japan, Hungarian, China, Manila, Algerian, Turkey, Holland (Amersfoort), Syrian (Latakia), French (St. Omer), Russian, and Circassian. All these varieties were divided into three classes, Billings further explained, viz., cigar and cigarette tobaccos,[345] snuff, and cut-leaf tobaccos (used for smoking and chewing purposes). During his days, South American tobaccos were almost exclusively used for the manufacture of cigars, whereas European tobaccos (as they were 'milder in flavour') were used for snuff, and tobaccos of the East were 'well adapted for the pipe' (including the *hookah*). Billings ended his enumeration with the remark that 'many of these varieties are well known to commerce, and others are hardly known outside the limit of their cultivation'.[346] Fairholt had classified cigars into white tobacco (*Tobacco blanco*), made from Havannah and Virginia leaf, and black tobacco (*Tobacco negro*), made from Brazilian leaf. Quality of cigars differed not only because of the variety of leaf used but also, according to Fairholt, because of the place of manufacture, and in his opinion, the 'Havannah cigars have been justly famed as the finest made'.[347] The studies by Fairholt and Billings thus clearly indicate that both authors very well realised that tobacco was an engineered commodity and quality a quite subjective matter.[348]

For long England obtained its (new) requirements of cigars, in particular, from Manilla. Yet by 1884, the Manilla supply had been lost, and England was in search of an alternative region that could both supply ready-made cigars as well as raw tobacco that could be used for cigar manufacture. By that time, Europeans in India had also exchanged their *hookahs* for cigars, and cigar smoking had even gained ground 'with the better classes of natives all over the country'. George Watt, formerly professor of Botany Calcutta University and now, among others, reporter on economic products to the GoI, for instance, mentioned in this huge compilation on the *Commercial Products of India* of 1908 that in South India and Burma, cigar smoking had been a popular habit during the last quarter of the nineteenth century.[349] In any case, while in Bengal the *hookah* and chewing had become the main form of tobacco consumption, in the Madras Presidency and to some extent in the southern part of Bengal, too, *cheroot* smoking had become popular among the local population. Not only had *cheroot* manufacture started, but it also flourished in the Dindigul and Tiruchirapalli areas of Madras.[350] This *cheroot* had been popular among the European community in Bombay, too, yet during the last three decennia of the nineteenth century, these Europeans complained about the quality of leaf used to manufacture these 'cigars'.

In fact, the most important part of the cigar was its wrapper, and the quality of this cigar-wrapper tobacco was supposed to be much more inferior in the whole of British India if compared with anywhere else where it was grown.[351] As a result, better-quality leaf for manufacture of *cheroots* and cigars in British India had to be imported from outside the country. An article on smoking in India in 1888 mentioned: 'about 1,500,000 pounds (tobacco) have been imported into India, mostly for consumption by the Europeans, who are accustomed to tobacco of a better cut and curing than can be had in India'.[352] However, increasingly, this European community in India and even more people in England itself perceived that the *cheroots* from 'any part of southern India, Lower Bengal, or even Trichirapalli itself' could replace the cigars from Manilla if the quality of wrapper tobacco in India would be 'improved'.

This demand for tobacco improvement had not been new. Since the 1830s, it had been advanced that though in India tobacco was grown in abundance and very much liked by the Indians themselves, who used to smoke it in their *hookahs*, its quality was not sufficient to please European merchants trading for the London markets. In 1832, James Peggs, the late missionary of Cuttack in Orissa, had, for instance, complained that tobacco in India was 'the very worst in the world':

> We have in vain looked for an article of *Indian tobacco* in the prices current of Antwerp, Rotterdam, Amsterdam, and Hamburgh. Even in the London prices current we discovered it but only occasionally. In fact, only a trifling quantity scarcely worth naming, has now been imported for trial, in the urgency and difficulty of finding remittances [. . .] In short, the commodity reaches Europe in an unmarketable state, wholly unfit for the competition with what has been grown, prepared, and brought to market by a more intelligent and skilful industry. The very lowest quality of American tobacco is worth in the London market 20 per cent more the best Indian tobacco.[353]

Writing on the history and consumption of tobacco, John Crawford explained, in 1853, that tobacco could be grown almost everywhere in the world, but that 'qualities' differed. According to him, 'The valuations of an ordinary price current afford a good criterion by which to judge of the quality of the different sorts of tobacco, as far, as they are presented in our markets'.[354] The London market did certainly not value the Indian tobaccos, and since the 1840s, when the demand for cigar tobaccos was on the increase in England, more and more Englishmen started arguing that, therefore, Indian tobaccos should be 'improved' so that it could get a fair price in the London markets. In his celebrated *Essay on the Productive Resources of India*, J. F. Royle – late superintendent of the Hon. E. I. C. Botanic Garden at Saharunpore, the Horticultural Society of London, and now professor of materia medica and therapeutics at King's College, London – in 1840, surveyed the quality of tobacco varieties throughout India and even argued that some specimens of tobacco in India had been pronounced of good quality by the 'best judges in London'. He, therefore, concluded that India was capable of producing tobaccos of much better quality than what the London market had normally obtained from India. These results were even more remarkable, Royle felt, as such tobaccos had been grown 'by the natives themselves, and without aid of any foreign seed, and are of yet greater consequence, if we consider the very distant situations, and the very different climates of Arracan, Bengal, the Northern Circars, Nagpore, and Guzerat, in which they were produced'.

Yet Royle agreed that even this 'good' tobacco from India was good if used for smoking 'in the hooqqa, after being beaten up with conserves or molasses' but not liked by dealers and manufacturers in London who wanted tobacco that could be used as snuff, cigars, and for smoking in ordinary pipes, *viz.*, Havannah, St. Domingo, and Amersforth tobaccos. Royle, therefore, recommended the continuation of experimentation in India with 'American seed' according to the 'American method' as he hoped that if cultivators in India would pay attention not only to the selection of the soil and of the seed and of a careful culture but also to the subsequent preparation and packing of tobacco, cigar tobacco 'may be grown in India with as much certainty of success as any other crop in any other country'. Royle had emphasised, however, that Indian cultivators, in order to produce quality cigar tobaccos, should be taught how to cultivate the plant properly as if one compared 'this careful culture and preparation' (in America) with that practised in India, one should not be surprised that the 'tobacco of the latter country should bear so little comparison with that of the former, where so much pain is taken with every part of the process'.

Besides, Royle recommended that Indian cultivators should send their produce to the open markets of England – instead of reserving this improved tobacco for the limited competition of the presidencies – where 'it would obtain the highest prices'. He concluded that the EIC government should help the Indian cultivators to realise these better prices by increasing the schemes of tobacco improvement experiments in India as it must never be forgotten that 'American tobacco did not attain its pre-eminence until after years of unremitting attention both on the part of the government and of the cultivators of Virginia'.[355]

Twenty years later, some progress seemed to have been made through the application of some 'European skill and capital', and hopes were still high. In his *Manual for General Use,* Montgomery Martin argued, in 1862, for instance, that 'a fair remuneration for one or more articles will encourage rivalry in the cultivation of other crops, and in time Hindoostan may supplant Virginia in supplying *tobacco* for the English market'. Martin explained that though the plant was extensively grown throughout India and even was of 'good quality', little care had been given to its curing and preparation for export.[356]

Ten years later, J. E. O'Connor, in his very important report on tobacco in India in 1874, still reported that though a lot of experimentation had been done all over India, 'the general complaint against Indian tobaccos has been that they are either received mouldy and fit for nothing or so high-dried and brittle as to be fit only for snuff'.[357] O'Connor summarised the state of affairs in India as his officials had perceived it around 1874 and stated that 'so little' was known about Indian tobacco in the English market that it was not even quoted in some of the best mercantile returns of current prices, though to O'Connor's horror, 'they quote China, Japan, and even Java tobaccos'. Like Royle in 1840 and Martin in 1862, O'Connor again a decade later decided that this condition really had to change and attention had to be given to the improvement of tobacco's quality 'by careful cultivation and preparation'. Yet O'Connor warned:

> As long as there is no demand for Indian tobacco in the European market, and its consumption is wholly confined to the natives of the country, so long may we expect to find India produce nothing superior to the coarse, rank, ill-flavoured tobaccos for which it has already acquired an unfortunate reputation. The natives of the upper classes disguise the natural flavour of the tobacco they smoke by the admixture with it of perfumes, such as patchouli, or conserves of roses and apples, and other confections. The lower classes take their tobacco *au naturel,* and the stronger and ranker it is the better they like it.

It would take some time, O'Connor agreed, before such an extensive demand would arise even after Indian tobacco had been improved, and this improved tobacco would thus only be for export to England as it would not suit the local tastes. Yet since the actual extent of tobacco cultivation in India was very great, though it was impossible to say with exactness for, there 'are yet no trustworthy agricultural statistics in India nor does any agency exist for their collection', it was, in O'Connor's opinion nevertheless, 'desirable to consider whether efforts might not with great advantage be made to improve the quality of tobacco now produced in this country up to the standard required by European taste, as well as to increase the yield of the cultivated area'. O'Connor reasoned that such well-directed effort was advisable as it 'must *pro tanto* react upon the general agriculture of the country':

> Tobacco is essentially a crop which requires high cultivation, and the example given by successful growth of tobacco in accordance with sound principles, will of necessity, have most beneficial effects upon native agriculturists [. . .] If it is considered that tobacco cultivation, to be successful, essentially requires high manuring, deep ploughing, and constant attention in keeping the soil loose, clearing away weeds, searching for and removing worms, removing suckers, topping the plants, and a hundred other small matters, which can be neglected only at the risk of losing the crop, it will be easily understood, that not only will the land be in an excellent state to receive another crop, but also that the agriculturist is taught habits of care, foresight, and attention which cannot but be of the highest service to him in every point of view.

O'Connor also recommended such 'a well-directed scheme of tobacco improvement', as the production of better tobacco in India would make it unnecessary to import tobacco from elsewhere. This import was meant entirely for 'the European population of the country, including its armies', and would 'almost altogether cease' if good cigars were manufactured in India itself using quality tobacco cultivated within the country. O'Connor conceived that 'well-directed action on the part of "the officers of Government and of non-official European gentlemen engaged or interested in agricultural pursuits [emphasis added]" would remove India's tobaccos "inferiority" and change "ignorant and bad methods of cultivation and curing"'.[358] Success of such an improvement scheme, O'Connor concluded in 1874, was 'quite possible'.[359]

Tobacco Improvement through a Government-Supported Scientific Agricultural Scheme

Even after more than fifty years of experimentation, in 1878, John Forbes Watson, 'reporter on the products of India' at the India Museum in London, recognised that the 'movement for agricultural improvement' was 'barely at its commencement'. So far, all experiments had been 'fitful and unsystematic'. Watson ascribed the lack of improvement to 'attachment to tradition, want of enterprise, want of capital and smallness of farms in particular in Bengal and other obstacles'. He, therefore, proposed that the agricultural enterprise of the GoI should not be left to land-revenue officers like in the EIC days but should become the task of a separate department with specialists. Yet the most important problem was, he confessed, that

> as yet Europeans have next to nothing to teach the natives in matters of agriculture except general ideas; that before Government attempts to direct the native agriculturist to better methods, those methods must be discovered; that wholesome importations of English methods, tools, and machinery, and of ready-made scientific rules, can meet with nothing but failure; and that a long series of experiments, conducted by specially qualified men, is necessary, in order to find out the specific manner in which the general scientific ideas or empirical results of European agriculture can be applied to the vastly different conditions of soil and climate in India, and in order to realise what improvements are suited to the economical position of an Indian ryot. There is no such thing in existence as a science of agriculture which can afford, without further trouble, infallible guidance to the Indian cultivation. It is not abstract science which is wanted, but men with habits of scientific observation of agricultural phenomena. Such men, versed in the principles of the sciences referring to vegetation, and brought into contact with actual agriculture, as carried on under Indian conditions, will in time, by patient investigation, discover rules for practical guidance, based on scientific principles, and suited to Indian

conditions. *The advantage of science is not that it would enable them to dispense with Indian experience, but that it will supply them with better methods of observation, and enable them to profit more quickly by experience, and to derive from it more practical conclusions than could be derived in the same time by men not possessed of previous scientific training* [emphasis added].[360]

However, this 'science' had to come from Europe, and Watson had recommended that

there exists in Europe an extraordinary amount of agency available for the universal introduction of agricultural improvements, side by side with establishments for the further scientific development of agriculture. No time should be lost in trying to provide India with a nucleus at least, of a similar organisation, having in view both sides of the question – the development of new agricultural methods, and their rapid dissemination, without which success in the first part of the task will only remain a sterile scientific acquisition.[361]

Such an establishment of a scientific scheme for agricultural improvement was extremely important because, Watson had summarised in 1878,

cultivation of sugar-cane and the extraction of sugar has considerably advanced in most of the colonies, but the formerly considerable export of sugar from Bengal has fallen off to a mere fraction of what it has been. There is no staple which may not be threatened in the same manner. America is vigorously trying to develop the growth and production of indigo and jute. The Burmese rice has to encounter competition from Java, from Siam, and from Cochin China. India's monopoly of opium is attacked from both without and within, by expanding cultivation, and by a blight threatening the Indian crops. Nothing but improved agriculture can preserve and develop the position already acquired by India in regard to these staples.[362]

The tobacco improvement scheme that developed during the 1870s in Bihar has to be analysed keeping this general agricultural enterprise of the (new) GoI in mind. Tobacco improvement was important for the government as it was, like other plants, a commodity that produced revenue.[363] Indeed, in particular, during the 1870s, it was argued that tobacco should get 'imperial attention' as 'a source of gigantic revenue' could be created, which 'if its success may be prejudged by the results of the same industry in America, would enable our finance ministers to watch unmoved the increase of Chinese or American opium cultivation, and even to laugh at cotton'.[364]

However, not only India had been selected for the dissemination of tobacco improvement schemes in the British Empire. In fact, around the same time that India had been chosen, other British colonies had been mentioned, too, as potential suppliers, and Jamaica, which had become a crown colony in 1866, was among these.[365] Yet for the time being, all hopes were on India, and during the 1870s, tobacco improvement in India was a subject of utmost imperial importance and, according to O'Connor, was considered more important than either tea or rhea and not less important than cotton and cinchona. Moreover, these products 'were all new industries', whereas 'tobacco has been grown in India for 250 years. Its cultivation is widely diffused.' The improvement of tobacco was, in fact, O'Connor had reasoned, 'the improvement of Indian agriculture generally'. He had further elaborated:

> No crop so speedily and so largely repays the care bestowed on it; no crop is more profitable when due attention has been given to its growth. But it should not be forgotten that tobacco demands the most constant and persevering attention, from the selection of soil and seed to the packing of the cured leaf, and no experiment should be considered to have been thoroughly carried out unless at least as much care and attention has been given to the curing of the leaf as to the growth of the plant.[366]

Tobacco improvement meant that colonial officials during the 1870s agreed making Indian tobaccos fit for the London market. In other words, tobacco colonisation implied bypassing Indian tastes and demands, except those of Europeans in India and a few English-educated urban Indians perhaps. Dr Forbes Watson of the Product Department clarified:

According to the unanimous statements, the chief desire of the native cultivators is to obtain strength, which implies a high percentage of nicotine in their tobacco. But the Havannah tobacco is exactly that which contains the smallest known amount of nicotine, whilst on the other hand it is distinguished by richness of aroma; therefore, in all experiments with new seeds, *it is not sufficient to choose what are considered by the ryot good tobacco soils, proper cultivation, &c., it is essential to use other soils and a different culture, to develop qualities different from those at present esteemed in the native commodity* [emphasis added]. What are considered favourable conditions for the culture of tobacco by the native farmer in India, are in no way an indication of the conditions necessary for ensuring the successful culture of varieties for the European market, and therefore the new trials ought to be made without too much deference to Indian experience.[367]

O'Connor agreed and stated that though tobacco grew almost everywhere in the world, tobacco that commanded the European market and that sold for high prices therein was produced in only three or four places in the world, namely, Havannah, Virginia, Cuba, and Manilla. Therefore, what 'we are attempting to do in India, as so to improve the quality of Indian-grown tobacco, by culture and by improved processes of curing', was intended 'to excite an export demand for it, such as exists for the American varieties'.[368] It was for this reason, for instance, that O'Connor had proposed 'model farms' should engage 'the services of experienced curers from America or from the Philippines for the purpose of teaching a number of selected intelligent natives'.[369]

Having contributed this much, the important question for consideration now became, as O'Connor posed, 'how far the government can and should encourage and sustain the well-directed efforts of individual or associated capital and energy in working out and extending an industry which has taken deep root in the country'?[370] Indeed, the government had already experimented extensively in the past, yet most of these experiments failed, according to O'Connor, due 'to the mistaken selection of agents and to the misdirected zeal of these agents than to any inherent difficulty in the task'. Yet he hoped:

Now that the local Governments have been entrusted with the immediate charge of the model farms, their close supervision and constant, repeated, and well-directed efforts will prove to native farmers how much they have to learn and unlearn in the methods now pursued by them.

The establishment of such 'model farms' in 1873 had convinced many other officials involved in government's great agricultural project that it was 'a year of small beginnings in great subjects of administration'.[371] A year later, O'Connor ruled that among other things, the cultivation of tobacco should have 'a prominent place' in these model farms. However, it was useless to undertake tobacco cultivation in tracts like the Benares and the Central Provinces, where the climate and the soil alike were, in O'Connor's opinion, 'unfavourable to tobacco' and where the tobacco yield was poor and its quality was 'bad'. Instead, he felt that more promising tobacco-growing tracts of India were in Burma, a large area in the Bombay and Madras Presidencies, the native state of Travancore, many parts of Bengal, and some small scattered tracts in the north-west provinces. In these provinces, O'Connor suggested, 'the cultivation might be spread and the quality of the produce very greatly improved'.[372]

The area under tobacco cultivation in Bengal was 'very large', the *Report on the Cultivation and Curing of Tobacco in Bengal* stated in 1874, and most of the tobacco was, as in most other provinces of India, cultivated in garden plots and small bits of land adjoining the villager's house. The largest tobacco-producing districts in Bengal were Rangpur, Tirhut, Purnea, and Kuch Behar. Rajshahi and Rangpur districts (both in present-day Bangladesh), along with those of Patna, Shahabad, Tirhut, and Sarun, were moreover mentioned as regions that at least attempted any curing process whatever as 'in every other district the leaf is simply dried in the hut or in the shade or in the sun'.[373] The *report* described the many experiments that had been carried out all over India, for a very long time now. Between 1786 and 1871, numerous experiments had been conducted in various regions of Bengal as well in order to improve the 'indigenous tobacco' in such a way that it could 'compete with that grown in America for the foreign market', and the *report* concluded that though most of these experiments had ended in failure, it also had been 'conclusively proved that tobacco of very superior quality can be grown in Bengal'. Yet the best means of fostering and developing the cultivation and preparation of the best kinds had still to be discovered.[374] The government fully accepted its responsibility in this regard.

Transforming a Horse-Breeding Stud to a Model Farm at Pusa (Tirhut)

During the beginning of the 1870s, the GoI was thus extremely optimistic over the chances that cigar tobacco cultivation and consumption had within India. Forbes Watson had written:

> The very wide scope of the question is evident. It involves nothing less than the reform of a considerable branch of agriculture, a reform not only profitable from an agricultural point of view, by raising the value of one of the Indian staples, but also salutary from hygienic considerations, by substituting the more aromatic and enjoyable varieties of tobaccos for those of which the strength lies in their nicotine, a substance which cannot fail to exercise a deleterious action on the system.

Yet the reform had to be brought out gradually and by the force of example and thus also involved changing tastes in India. Concerning 'gradual' improvement in cultivation, Watson had argued, this had been the only manner in which agricultural reforms had ever been introduced. The possibility of growing superior varieties of tobacco had to be demonstrated practically and not only in a few garden experiments but also on the same scale and in the same manner as it is to be conducted by the producers. Watson had continued:

> I need only allude to the success with which the same means have worked in the case of the cultivation of tea, and are now being applied to the cultivation of cotton and other commercial plants. Tobacco belongs to exactly the same category, and the general scheme followed in the efforts made in introducing and improving the cultivation of other staples applies equally to it.

The tobacco 'colonisation scheme' through model farms encompassed the improvement and selection of species, including seed farms for placing within the reach of the agriculturist the seed of the most favourable species. It also encompassed improvement of soils and the tending of plants in order to obtain the maximum of yield, and importantly, it meant the improvement of the different curing processes as by these the raw natural produce would be converted into a (highly) saleable commodity even within the country, but only of course if 'tastes' would change too. If the commodity was meant for overseas export, improvements in storing and packing practices were needed. The scheme, Watson was convinced, was not merely tentative or promised only a 'problematic success'; on the contrary, it was only thought necessary to follow a known track and apply principles which had already succeeded in the case of other commodities such as tea. Yet tea was 'an entirely new culture', whereas 'thousands of acres' were already devoted to tobacco cultivation and 'a vast mass of people' were already thought to be interested 'in everything which affects the commerce in one of *their own chief articles of production* [emphasis added]'. It now only remained for government 'to open to them the prospect of an advantageous export trade by showing the preliminary conditions which must be satisfied in view of this prospect'. According to officials, this all could be accomplished by means of model farms under the charge of foreign specialists who could give the subject the full care it required. Such 'goal farms', as Watson called them, were sure to 'afford special facilities for the organisation of experiments for the successful cultivation of tobacco and other products'.[375]

In 1874, after 'mature consideration of the subject' about which 'considerable diversity of opinion seems to exist as to the benefits likely to accrue from such step', the lieutenant governor finally recommended the adoption in Bengal of 'a systematic course of experiments for improving both the growth and curing of the plant under state supervision in the districts of Rungpore[376] and Tirhoot'. As far as Tirhut was concerned, the lieutenant governor directed that the 'Poosah stud lands', south of the Gunduck, which the GoI had made over to the Bengal government in 1873 for the purposes of experimental cultivation, would primarily be devoted to the tobacco scheme as outlined by Watson and other colonial administrators. It had been confessed that 'the tobacco of Tirhoot would not seem to be equal in quality to that of Rungpore, but the cultivation has laid firm hold of the district and the large area therein already devoted to its growth (40,000 acres mark it out as, after Rungpore, the most eligible field we can try)'.[377]

By the end of the eighteenth century, the EIC Court of Directors had decided to finance and control a horse-breeding stud in Bengal. A proposal to this end had been formulated with the primary object to breed an improved variety of horses for the company's army and with a secondary aim 'to encourage and excite the natives to breed horses of a proper size'.[378] For this purpose, a good location had been sought, and Frazer, who had authored the proposal, had, in 1795, gone off on an extended tour throughout Bengal to identify a suitable site for the new stud farm. His final choice, for soil, situation, and climate, was a 1,500-*begah* (approx. 1,300 acres) site located in the bed of the Burhi Gandak River amid rich agricultural land near the villages of Lodipur and Pusa in Bihar, some 40 miles north-west of Patna and at the time about ten days journey by water from Calcutta. The company had accepted his choice, and during the next decade, the 'empty' Pusa site had been transformed into an expanding institution for horse breeding. Moreover, besides the enclosed pastures and paddocks for the horses and the experimental breeding herd of oxen and prize cows, a nursery had been established for young trees, an orchard, coffee and cotton 'plantations', and fields of various experimental grasses, clover and grains all tilled, sown, and harvested with 'the latest European scientific ploughs, harrows, hoes, drills, and winnowing machines, and the whole under the control of a specially recruited agricultural expert'.[379]

Yet as it turned out, Frazer's choice for Pusa proved wrong, at least for horse breeding. The damp and low-lying Pusa neighbourhood proved itself to be far from ideal as a centre for horse-breeding operations, and in later years, the breeding operations had progressively been transferred to the drier soils further west up the Ganges. Yet it was only in the 1870s that horse breeding stopped altogether at Pusa. From the very beginning, however, the Pusa stud had been intended to be a vehicle for general agricultural 'improvement' as well, on British lines, of course. Alder analysed:

> Its original inspiration in the 1790s came in part from that contemporary intellectual movement in Britain which, combining aggressive evangelical Christianity with humanitarianism and scientific agriculture with machine-based industry, eventually provided the dynamism and

confidence to export not merely British goods and capital to India but the whole cultural and technological baggage of European civilisation as well.[380]

Pusa, moreover, was in the midst of indigo fields, which was more closely located to the bungalows of indigo planters and their indigo vats. It had been these indigo planters, in fact, who mostly had bought the horses bred at Pusa. Therefore, Pusa constituted an ideal site for tobacco colonisation. Indeed, while the horse-breeding experiment was abandoned in 1872, the site was selected as a model farm in which experimentation could be conducted, aiming at the production of first-class tobacco suitable for the manufacture of cigars in England, elsewhere in Europe, or in southern India and Burma. At that juncture, Pusa's history as a centre for agricultural development had just begun, and next to some poppy experimentation, S. C. Bayley, the commissioner of the Patna Division, was convinced, in 1874, that the Pusa model farm should be devoted 'in a great measure' to tobacco growing, adding that Tirhut was such a tobacco-growing district in his division that if skilled curers were appointed at the farm at Pusa, it would turn out 'a good and useful experiment'.[381]

The Bengal government along with the GoI convinced that the 'ordinary native system' would do little towards carrying out the object which these governments had in view as this 'local method of cultivation was entirely wrong' (for the production of an export crop that was). Experiments with new methods of cultivating and curing of the tobacco plant had to be carried out, which for the time being should be under government supervision. Lieutenant governor of Bengal Richard Temple in his *Minute* of the 1st of September 1875 wrote:

> It becomes, therefore, important to make an experiment, which shall be conclusive as to whether the plant can be successfully cultivated according to this other way, so as to rival the American and West Indian culture, and whether the leaf will admit of being cured in the best known manner. Such an experiment ought to be made, if undertaken at all, in a precise and scientific manner; and if it be of consequence (as I think it is), that while the matter is in an inchoate, novel, and dubious position, the Government should be satisfied of the conclusiveness of the experiments scientifically and practically,

then it would follow that such experiments ought to be made under the direct administration, or at least under the direct control of Government. *The object of Government is not of course to make any particular profit pecuniary* [emphasis added], but to prove or disprove a scientific theory, *and to solve an economic problem* (of the British) [emphasis added]. No doubt this sort of work as a general rule can be done better by private persons than by Government officers. Still if Government is to be satisfied as to the effect of an experiment, it must work with its own means. For this reason, I am for undertaking the experiment as a Government measure on the Poosah Estate in the first instance. *If it shall succeed, then the further carrying on of the work can be left to private enterprise hereafter* [emphasis added].[382]

Yet even if methods were discovered by which the Indian tobacco plant could be improved, the next problem would be, it was anticipated, how to convince 'the natives' of the usefulness of such new methods of cultivation. Lieutenant governor of Bengal Richard Temple, therefore, added in his *Minute* that there was a need for 'education of the natives', and he thus proposed to make the Pusa farm an appendage to an agricultural college in Bihar.

I do not think that the fine estate which once belonged to the Government Remount Service at Poosah in Tirhoot should be converted into a Government Model Farm as regards general agriculture. Experience shows that we cannot succeed in making such experiments as will induce the people to adopt any essential changes in the existing modes of culture. This is indeed much to be regretted, but the fact cannot be overlooked. If model farms are to be of use to the country, they must be managed in a manner different from any that we have yet been able to adopt. Moreover, it is clear that the mere sight of improvement does not induce imitation on the part of the people of Behar. The indigo planters have cultivated superior products other than indigo; yet this circumstance does not seem to have had any effect on the native agriculture of the neighbourhood. One reason, among several, of this indifference on the part of the people is the want of education. It seems to me that if there is to be a model farm at all, it should be a training ground attached to a technical school for agriculture. I quite share the opinion entertained by many that instruction in scientific agriculture ought to be made a branch of our public education. And to the establishment of an Agricultural School or College, the addition of a model farm would be essential. If the Poosah Estate could be used in this way, that is, if it could be made an adjunct to an Agricultural College of Behar, I should be glad to consider the question of maintaining it, though I should be for abolishing it as an ordinary model farm.[383]

Pusa, as I will detail in later chapters, certainly did not become 'an ordinary model farm'. As we will see, Lord Mayo, a viceroy of India from 1869 to 1872, had repeatedly tried to get through his proposal for setting up a Directorate General of Agriculture who would take care of the soil and its productivity, formulate newer techniques of cultivation, improve the quality of seeds and livestock, and also arrange for imparting agricultural education. It was, however, only during the reign of Lord Curzon, as viceroy from 1898 to 1905, that Pusa became a full-fledged agricultural research and educational institute, as we will see later on; the latter meant as evidence here for education of the 'natives'. Till 1905, however, the only experiments in Pusa aimed at the production of acclimatised varieties of tobacco fit for European markets. Government had hoped that 'by force of example', the 'whole native cultivation will be brought to a higher degree of excellence'.[384] Yet there was a need of 'experts' who, 'by force of example', would assist government officials in successfully implementing the tobacco improvement scheme at Pusa, Tirhut. Importantly, the government was not any more interested in colonising the internal tobacco trade only by becoming a dominant player in it but now also desired a change of direction of this trade, that is export to London. Collaborators would thus have the task to teach Indian cultivators new methods in cultivation and curing that would produce better tobacco suitable for cigars and cigarettes. Besides, by providing the good example, such collaborators along with the government were also expected to change local tastes.

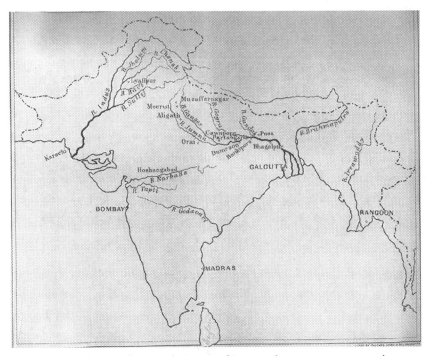

Figure 14. Map showing location of Pusa and environment in early twentieth-century India. Taken from *Memoirs of the Department of Agriculture in India*, Botanical Series, Vol. III, No. 4, Calcutta: Thacker, Spink and Co, April 1910, n.p. (after p. 218).

CHAPTER FOUR

Taking in the Private Capitalist: European Planters in Tirhut

The decision to make Pusa the centre of Bengal's tobacco experiments was based on more than the simple fact that colonial administrators considered the Tajpur subdivision of Tirhut in which Pusa was located a most promising tobacco region. The government had first leaned on Tirhut for its saltpeter and later its opium requirements. Pusa had also been made the centre of horse-breeding activities. After 1857, moreover, though Tirhut also was well-known for its *gur* (unrefined sugar), the region became most referred to because of its indigo production. The happenings between 1857 and 1860, as described in this chapter, did not only make Tirhut more prominent as indigo region but also cause Tirhut to become a 'safe heaven' for European planters. What is more by 1860, government officials trusted these planters could be beneficial to the general agricultural enhancement in the region and in particular helpful in matters of tobacco improvement, that is colonisation. Indeed and also explained in this chapter, by the end of the century, a close though not unproblematic relationship had developed between these two different classes of Englishmen in Tirhut. After a century of experimentation, these government officials along with private capitalists such as the 'indigo planters' were now finally prepared to work together to further plant colonisation in the region.

European Planters in Tirhut till 1857

The Tirhut district, lying between the boundaries of Nepal towards the north and the Ganges in the south, had Muzaffarpur as its main city. It comprised an area of 6,343 square miles and had a population of around 4,389,250 by the mid-1870s.[385] This region in Bihar produced crops such as rice, oats, linseed, pulses, and the castor oil plant but also sugar cane, tobacco, poppy, and indigo-producing plants. Till 1857, apart from a handful of EIC civil servants and army personnel, most 'white settlers' in Tirhut comprised of so-called indigo planters. In fact, most of these 'planters' had been proprietors of indigo concerns (the actual 'factories') where indigo plants were manufactured into cakes or more often had been mere assistants of factory owners and managed these factories with their Indian clerks basically supervising the workers in indigo vats, either in the main concern or in its so-called outworks. Besides, they visited the indigo fields to supervise the cultivators there on horses. There was office work too.

Figure 15. Horses played a big role in the life of British indigo planters in Tirhut, Pandaul Concern, 1908 (courtesy Charles Allen and BASCA, The British Association for Cemeteries in South Asia).

Many owners actually did not even live in Tirhut but in Calcutta or even in Britain. The Tirhoot Indigo Association of London owned many concerns, for instance. Importantly, till around 1850, taking Tirhut as a whole, many European planters had remained 'growing' sugar cane as well as some other crops for own consumption or by way of experimentation. Among the former had been kidney beans and 'English' vegetables and among the latter tobacco and cotton. Only poppy cultivation was not tried by them as it had become part of a government monopoly. Some of these concerns also produced refined sugar cane and had, in fact, been started as 'sugar factories' only.[386] Sugar cane cultivation in this region had attracted European settlers when and as long as profit could be made.[387]

Indigo-producing plants had been cultivated, and indigo had been manufactured even before the arrival of European settlers in the region. This indigo cultivation and its manufacture greatly expanded, however, after the foundation of a Dutch concern by Alexander Niel at Kanti in the district of Muzaffarpur in 1778. Moreover, when Francois Grand had arrived in 1782 as the first revenue collector in the 'Sarkar Tirhoot' (comprising then the districts of Darbhanga and Muzaffarpur), he had simultaneously taken interest in indigo cultivation.[388] 'Native' indigo concerns remained, however, and new concerns were even established, and the European planters used to call these 'interloping' factories arguing that these 'natives' produced indigo of inferior quality. Increasingly, however, Indian factory owners often employed Europeans as managers of their indigo concerns. By 1850, the indigo business had thus established itself as a 'European business', and consequently, indigo plants became looked upon as 'foreign' plants. By that time, indigo could, therefore, be said to have been fully 'colonised'. Yet this had been the result of a more-than-fifty-years process during which 'indigo planters' had had to fight for their place in the Tirhut landscape.

After having abandoned the indigo business, William Huggins, who had been an indigo 'planter' in Tirhut till then, described the situation in 'indigo land' in 1824, mentioning that in Tirhut, the indigo factories had all been of 'a respectable size'. Those 'petty establishments' common in Jessore and that part of Bengal proper did not exist in Tirhut, Huggins argued. According to him, in Tirhut, the average factory had around eighteen pair of vats and planters cultivated around 3,000 *beghas* of land. Huggins further mentioned that a proprietor – sometimes a Calcutta agent or an indigo planter himself – would own four to five factories, and a concern was superintended by a person who received a salary and a 'share for his trouble'. This person would have assistants who were in charge of one factory each. These assistants, too, would be European but under them 'a large establishment of native servants' worked with the *amlah* as head. The latter kept an account of expenditure in Persian and 'informed their master', Huggins further explained, 'respecting local matters and customs necessary to be observed'. This *amlah*, in fact, also did the overseeing of labourers. Therefore, these *amlahs* could be called the real 'men of business'. Yet whereas the European assistant in charge of the factory would earn around 150 or even 200 rupees per month, the *amlah* would receive from 7 to 30 rupees per month.[389] In order to conduct his business properly, according to Huggins, an indigo planter had to be acquainted with farming, able to speak Hindostanee well, and have a competent knowledge of the laws and customs of India. He also should have 'a good constitution, no prejudices, and great activity, so as to ride sixteen miles in the morning without inconvenience'.[390]

Figure 16. Indigo cultivation, Tirhoot, Bengal in 1881. Ploughing print (courtesy www.old-print.com).

During Huggins's time, there had been two ways in which European indigo planters had a right in the soil. First, by taking a lease of villages from a *zamindar* in an *amlah's* name and holding these villages by this subterfuge as Europeans at that time (i.e. 1824) had not been permitted to own land in their own names. Second, by giving money in advance to a *zamindar* and getting an engagement from him to cultivate a stipulated number of *beghas*. In that case, *zamindars* or rather his tenants would do the planting. Huggins commented:

> The first is both more agreeable and more beneficial, for by it the planter acquires a landlord's power over his tenants; so that his business is carried on without trouble, and he can select good land for his own purposes: at the same time there is a risk of the *omlah*, claiming real instead of nominal possession, so that he should be under a bond that would prevent this; the latter is often attended with difficulty and inconvenience; for, after a *zemindar* has received his advances, perhaps he refuses to prepare his lands, importunes the planter for more money, and, in some cases, will not cultivate at all; so that, beside the disappointment, it is necessary to commence a lawsuit against him.[391]

The cultivation in lands around the factory was known as *zeerat* cultivation, and labourers working on this land were very lowly paid, and that was, Huggins explained, the reason why expenses attending indigo factories could be kept low.[392] Huggins agreed that 'the natives are naturally averse to indigo cultivation, both on account of the trouble it is attended with and on account of the trifling profit, which is not a sufficient recompense for their labour'. Yet he said, 'They are forced to it by their necessities', and in Tirhut, Huggins judged, this business was 'carried on *more through the necessities of the people, than regard for itself*' [emphasis added].[393]

Generally, the 'Tirhoot planters', Huggins summarised, were a 'hard-working, healthy class of men, who inhabit one of the finest districts of Lower India, and are generally addicted to field sports and the pleasures of the table'. Interactions among planters took place only at particular times and seasons as their factories were distant from each other. The *amlah* was, therefore, the most important person in the day-to-day life of the planter, and the former could make 'a handsome fortune' through his master but also through the 'natives' employed at different factories. Huggins further elaborated that most planters remained unmarried and found it 'more agreeable, or more convenient, to keep native mistresses, who have been all prostitutes'. 'To conclude', Huggins wrote in 1824, 'these country gentlemen of India, during the cold season, hunt and give parties, at which mirth, plenty, and hospitality prevail; Bacchus is lord of the ascendant, and they indemnify themselves for the many dull, heavy days they have to pass during rains and manufacture'.[394]

Yet it had not always been party time, and early settlers in Tirhut had commented upon the insecurity they had experienced especially as indigo entrepreneurs. E. Fletcher along with twelve other proprietors of indigo concerns explained in 1801, for instance, that in the case of other commodities there was less insecurity.

> The principle articles of commerce in which Europeans are engaged in this country are cloths, sugar, and indigo. A merchant trading in the two first articles is not obliged to diminish this trading capital by laying out part of it in dead stock, but can have the whole actively employed in the trade in which he is engaged, and if it should not answer his expectations, can leaf off, after selling his merchandize, without embarrassment.

The case of indigo was very different, however, Fletcher explained, as the indigo planter 'is under the necessity of laying out a large part of his capital in buildings'. He was obliged to make this outlay 'a long time before he can begin to manufacture indigo', and if he was prevented supplying his works with indigo plants because he had chosen 'an unfavourable situation in respect to soil, from the country being liable to inundation', his buildings 'unfit for any other purpose than that of manufacturing indigo are rendered useless and unsalable'. Yet these men complained to the governor general of council, Fort William, that the worst problem the English indigo planter faced was the 'interference of others with his cultivation':

> We have, my Lord, erected large expensive buildings in different parts of the Company's provinces for the purpose of manufacturing indigo, and have had the satisfaction to observe considerable tracts of land brought into cultivation

that were formerly waste. But we find our property liable to be rendered unproductive and unsalable from there being no rule to retain individuals from building new works so near to ours as to interfere with the cultivation necessary for supplying us with the indigo plant.

These English indigo entrepreneurs – as they better could be called – had thus pointed to 'the precarious and uncertain state' in which their property fared and solicited for protection from the government being 'fully sensible of your Lordships to promote the commerce of this country, and to encourage indigo trade, which has been depressed for some years past'. They argued that 'when indigo works are built too near to each other, there is no remedy but one of the parties abandoning his works and entirely giving up the capital laid out in them – a sacrifice that cannot be expected to be made'. They also said that this 'interference' was fixed and lasting and could 'only be prevented by a restrictive regulation of government'. Moreover, such protection would not only benefit them, but they also declared that 'experience has proved the situation of the ryots where the interference we complain of has occurred to be much worse than that of other ryots where there has been no competition, both in regard to their circumstances and their morals'.[395]

This particular competition complained of had existed among Europeans, with the English claiming more rights than the 'foreigners', and competition had also existed among English themselves between old settlers and 'new comers'.[396] Yet foremost competition had been between Europeans and the 'country-born', the 'natives'. Though, things had been a bit more complicated as some European planters were employed by a 'native agency'. The Tirhut collector wrote in 1828:

> Indigo cultivation has been extended so greatly in this district that I am of the opinion, for the benefit of the district some restrictions should be put upon it. From the good understanding which has prevailed and still prevails amongst the European planters, disputes one with another are not of very frequent occurrence. Disputes have, however, of late occurred through descendants of Europeans embarking in indigo cultivations chiefly, if not entirely, on native agency.

This revenue collector for the EIC, therefore, decided that

> for the peace of the district and welfare of the established
> planters, it therefore appears highly desirable that the
> Government restrictions regarding the erection of factories by
> Europeans shall be extended to the descendants of Europeans,
> and power be vested in the Magistrate to prevent engagements
> for the cultivation of indigo by other than the proprietor or
> proprietors of an established factory.[397]

Actually, during the first few decades of the nineteenth century, the government in
Bengal had chosen 'natives' rather than these European planters as collaborators
in their plant colonisation activities. Till 1857, the EIC government grappled
with the reality of governing Bengal and of having to extract resources from
this 'the richest country in the world'. In this Bengal that had been described
by the Mughal Emperor Aurangzeb as 'the paradise of nations', officials had
to manage the highly productive agricultural sector in such a way as not to
waste the 'wealth of England' or rather that of the EIC. This 'corporate state'
had been curtailed somewhat by the beginning of the nineteenth century yet
retained, as Nick Robins researched, its administrative 'responsibility' in return
for the annual dividend the EIC servants could distribute among themselves.[398]
In order to get that dividend (taxes), the government, in 1793, had defined
a 'permanent' revenue system in Bengal called the *zamindari* system, which
determined the structure of land tenure. From 1793 onwards, the revenue was
collected by the *zamindars* entitled as such by the EIC government.[399]

EIC administrators believed that this proclamation of the Permanent
Settlement, as it was called, had opened 'a new era in the history of our
government in the East and must be considered by the natives as the greatest
blessing conferred on them for many years'. It was claimed that 'by these
measures, a permanent revenue is secured to government, property to
individuals, and a prospect of wealth and happiness is opened to the natives,
coextensive with the industry and capital they shall think fit to employ in
the cultivation and improvement of their lands.[400] Due to this system, some
native landholders had, indeed, become powerful as legitimate owners of the
land with the *raiyats* as their legal tenants. At the same time, these newly
entitled landholders had also become 'mere officers' for the EIC. In 1846,

Augustus Prinsep had analysed the change after the introduction of Permanent Settlement in Tirhut and had concluded:

> Under the new system then, the raja of Tirhoot fell from the condition of a sovereign to that of a zemindar; and being confirmed in the possession of the lands already forming his khalsah estate, he continued to be, in every sense of the word, their proprietor. The heritage of this zemindari having fallen into the hands of Chhutur Singh, the present incumbent, without a single flaw in the succession, we know that the proprietary rights of the family have withstood every public change. The same revolution that reduced the Raja from his character of sovereign to that of a mere proprietor, raised up his jagirdars or under-tenants, by whatever name they may have gone, to the same rank. The treasury of Delhi being now the place for depositing their jumma, they became released from all the ties of vassalage, and at the same time, from all superior authority in their tenures. Their new sovereign, content with the fixed portion of the produce, left them the free disposition of their interests or estates.[401]

It had, therefore, been these *zamindars* and not the English planters that were favoured by the EIC, and it was this structure that had been objected to by the English planters not because of the adverse effects it had on Indian cultivators or not even because of its impact on agriculture in Bengal but because within this system *they* had no rights in land. It was this structure, too, that had made EIC civil servants wary of these Europeans who had claimed their share in the lands of Bengal, which might upset the 'native' *zamindars*. Many administrators agreed with missionaries, therefore, who had feared that 'an augmentation of the number of such settlers would obstruct the executive authorities in the administration of the laws, retard the general prosperity of the country, and injure the condition of the labouring poor'.[402] The relation between administrators and Europeans planters in Bengal during the first three decennia had been frosty therefore, to say the least.[403]

Yet with time, the outlook of the administrators had been changing. Increasingly, these administrators felt that in order to realise their aims in the agricultural field of Bengal, the 'native *zamindars*' had not been very helpful, neither forthcoming with the expected 'industry' nor with the 'capital'. Moreover, administrators felt these 'natives' did not possess the right skills that were needed to improve the useful plants in Bengal. 'Improved' seeds had been distributed among them but had not produced 'better' crops. The Agricultural and Horticultural Society of India had printed the opinion of some of these Englishmen who had felt that 'there is, however, much room for improvement if we could overcome certain prejudices fixed and strengthened by mercenary considerations, which bias the in favour of quick and small returns in preference to future permanent and solid advantages requiring time and a little sacrifice to attain.'[404]

Officials' experiences with European planters had been much better than those with natives in this regard. Improved seeds had also been given to them, and hope was in the air that through these planters the aims of the administrators could be realised. Lord William Bentinck, for instance, who had been appointed as governor general of Bengal in 1827, had written in a dispatch to the Court of Directors that these European planters had greatly contributed to the progress of civilisation, the development of the resources of the country, and the prosperity of its inhabitants. On these grounds, Bentinck had urged that 'it would be a wise policy to afford Europeans every facility and encouragement to settle in India'.[405] Indeed, some concessions had been given to these European planters in 1833 already, but their status in Bihar, in the eyes of the government, that is, genuinely changed from 1857 onwards.

Changes in Bihar after 1857

The Edinburgh Review in 1866 published a review of 'The History of the Sepoy War' by John W. Kaye (1814–76), the founder of *The Calcutta Review*. *The Edinburgh Review* denied the allegations of Kaye that the acts of violence against the British in many places in India during 1857 had been part of a 'rebellion', a rise against the EIC government. It went at length to show that the outbreaks of violence in Bihar – that beautiful and fertile province that lies between Bengal proper and the province of Benares – had not been a proof of the dissatisfaction of Indian landholders against the new fiscal measures that had recently been introduced in province. Kaye's take on it had been different, however, as he had explained that many *zamindars* in Bihar, who previously had been exempted from paying land revenue now had been compelled to do so in order to bear 'their fair share of the public burdens'. This had caused disaffection among them, or so Kaye had alleged, which had been displayed during the outbreaks in Sarun and Tirhut. In Muzaffarpur, Arrah, and Gaya, Kaye had argued that the 'law and order' situation had been worst during 1857 as 'natives' had tried – assisted by equally dissatisfied 'sepoys' – to murder or expel the English authorities from the country.[406]

Whatever it was – and scholars are still debating this issue[407] – the 'Great Indian Mutiny of 1857' had seriously challenged the authorities in England to reflect on their policies in India. Not long after 1857, the EIC was extinguished as a governing body.[408] The Secretary of State now replaced the old Court of Directors and whatever power was exercised in England in regard to the internal administration of India was in his hands. Moreover, this secretary was unlike the EIC, directly responsible not only to the crown but also 'to the people of England for the mode in which he administers his authority'.[409] Now 'these people of England' intensely debated the reasons for the 'unsettling' happenings all over British India in 1857. While some defined these happening as the 'Indian Mutiny of 1857' or 'Sepoy War', many others used the term 'Indian Rebellion' to define the same. The latter attributed the happenings in 1857 to the 'civil misgovernment' during EIC rule in India.[410] However, only a very few in England felt India should be 'given up'. Most Englishmen, during the 1860s, argued that the GoI had to be improved so that '1857' would not be repeated. The general consensus was, moreover, that the field that needed such improvement most was agriculture.

Yet no such consensus existed regarding the means to be applied to effect such an 'agricultural improvement'. One important debate was related, for instance, to the role of *feringees* (outsiders, the white officials, and non-officials) in this development. The other debate concerned land reforms and related revenue matters. The 'problem' of the role of 'private Englishmen' in the development of India was thus debated by the new colonial administrators as well as by these private English settlers themselves, and most felt that in the past, wrong decisions had been made.

> How to rule an empire like India, which is at the same time both a military dependency and a colony. The principles on which it would be desirable to govern a colony of the ordinary kind, and a foreign dependency inhabited by a conquered

nation and a half-civilised race, are obviously very different. The motto of the old Company was: We rule for the benefit of *the people of India*; and when they found the interests of the people of India clash with those of the colonists, they sacrificed the latter.[411]

This should now change, however, and the interest of the 'colonists' should be taken into account. Yet around 1862, it was generally agreed upon that India could never become 'an English colony'. It was explained that two things had been essential for the success of colonisation in 'proper' colonies, and that had been 'labour and land'. The English settler in Canada or Australia had found these plenty, and as a result, they had gone to those countries with the purpose of making them their own home and that of their descendants. In those places, the English settlers had been able to 'rear a healthy, vigorous, energetic offspring'. In India, everything was different, however. First of all, land was either already occupied and could not be theirs. Second, the available 'wastelands' needed labour to clear and cultivate them. The latter demanded not only capital but also time, and 'time is always grudged by the European settler' in India:

> If he goes to India, he does so with the determination not to live a single day after he has reached the precise number of pounds sterling which he considers necessary for the London house or country villa. He can neither rear nor educate his family in India [. . .] With such feelings, the Indian settler lives a life of irritation and impatience against everybody and everything that delays the day of his return. He hates alike both the population and the Government, for the interests of the former and the scruples of the latter retard his object.[412]

Nonetheless, the new government agreed that there were different settlers too. These were 'English zemindars, farmers, and talookdars' who had 'held their position with equal advantage to themselves and to the people on their estates'. They had studied the native character, the native language, and the native interests.[413] After 1857, it was decided that this kind of settlers should get all the support they needed, provided this Englishman would enter India 'with a deep sense of his responsibility, not only to those among whom he is about to reside but to his country'.[414] The settlers in Bengal had been satisfied with this change of mindset among administrators and had proclaimed:

> We believe, with almost every independent man in this country, that the introduction of the European element in India is one simple solution of all our political problems [. . .] that a policy, diametrically opposite to the one that has been pursued by the East India Company, is necessary. We hail with delight the abolition of its name, and the transfer of the Government to that of the Queen.[415]

Nevertheless, government officials in Bengal, ever after 1857, remained concerned about another group in the agricultural landscape, that is 'the people of India'. In order to attract more settlers to India, the government had passed two measures during the early 1860s – the redemption of the land tax and the sale of wastelands – which should the government hoped to 'do much to increase the wealth of India and the prosperity of England and to strengthen our hold over our Eastern empire'. Yet it was realised that these objects 'must ever depend on the extent to which we carry the immense population with us'.[416] Lieutenant governor of Bengal, J. P. Grant, had, therefore, concluded that

> as to the advantage of having English gentlemen, with the loyalty, courage, energy, perseverance, and skill, which is their patrimony, scattered over the country, it is impossible in general terms to rate the political and social value of this too highly. But it *is only when these Englishmen are in relations of mutual benefit with the people of the country that their residence is of social and political advantage* [emphasis added].[417]

The Blue Mutiny, the Sepoy Mutiny, and Indigo Planters in Bihar (1857–60)

Between 1857 and 1861, the cracks in the indigo system of Lower Bengal had become more visible to a wider public, also in England. In particular, the publications of the missionaries working in indigo regions in Bengal had a huge effect on the 'public opinion' regarding indigo planters.[418] Moreover, 'evidence' published in the *Indigo Commissioners' Report* of 1860 was widely commented upon.[419] Indigo cultivation had since long been a source of contention between the English planters and 'the natives', yet the resistance in 1860 was referred to as 'the Indigo Disturbances' by contemporaries and was later on described by scholars as the 'Blue Mutiny'.[420]

Lt. Gov. J. P. Grant mentioned in a *Minute* of 1863 that unlike other trades, indigo had '*always* been a remarkable exception'. Already in 1810, the governor general had issued orders to the magistrates to look into 'the gross ill-usage of the natives' as they compelled the *ryots* 'against their will to enter into engagements to sow indigo'. Four planters had even been expelled from India because of this 'habit'. Several missionaries had continuously been reporting on the 'secret murmuring and discontent among the people' and had also helped in making the contents of *Neel Darpan* or 'Indigo Mirror' widely known. The latter book was a Bengali play published by Dinabandhu Mitra with the planters' atrocities as its theme.[421] The final collapse of the system in Bengal 'proper' had come in 1861. What 'brought the matters to a crisis', *The National Review* of 1862 explained, was the fact that within the last three years, all agricultural produce rose in value to double its price. 'What, then, must have been the feelings of the ryots, in their hand-to-mouth poverty', *The National Review* had asked, 'when they found themselves deprived to a great extent of the golden prospect which this opened to them?'[422] Besides, the slump in the London prices of indigo between 1839 and 1847, the fall of the Union Bank of Calcutta, a consequent credit squeeze, and the takeover of smaller concerns by larger 'indigo seignories', scholar Ranajit Guha added, increased the pressure on the *ryot* and his misery still further. These *ryots* had now refused to cultivate the plant and later to pay their rents in protest against the oppressive practices of some planters. When the authorities had interfered in favour of the planters by making the non-fulfilment of indigo contracts a criminal offense, riots had raged and 'bloodshed had been the consequence'.[423] Clearly, this 'Blue Mutiny' had been more than *ryots'* protest against planters. During three years, as *The National Review* had described in 1862, a 'social revolution' had been going on 'in our oldest Indian possession – the districts of Lower Bengal':

> In course of this movement, almost every great Indian
> question has been at issue – the relations between the natives

and our English settlers and planters, the relations between the latter and the Indian Government and officials, the relative position of the cultivators and their so-called landlords, and the extension of European enterprise in India.[424]

As all this turmoil in indigo land had been going on during the time that the 'Indian Mutiny' had passed – and some even argued they were interrelated – it had challenged the new government to take firm decisions in this regard. Professing to do 'justice to all classes' and to aim at 'prosperity of all', officers of government hoped to restore 'the peace and order [. . .] in this fertile and populous territory by endeavouring to do justice to both planter and ryot'. Yet, in order 'to discourage a state of things which was a disgrace to the administration and to the English name',[425] at the end of 1860, administrators ruled that 'growing of indigo could not be imposed against the will of the cultivators'.[426] This decision predicated the rapid outflow of planters, if not the decline of the indigo system in Lower Bengal (Bengal proper).

The two described political processes (i.e. the Blue and the Sepoy Mutinies) had many changes in the offing for indigo planters in Tirhut[427] in Upper Bengal. The collapse of the indigo industry in Bengal proper had led to an influx of capital and planters to Bihar, where indigo cultivation had continued without much more uproar than usual.[428] The production of indigo in Bihar was concentrated in only a few regions when compared to Bengal proper. Most of the indigo in Bihar was produced in the Tirhut region.[429] By the mid-1850s, indigo in Tirhut had superseded sugar cane as the prime industry of the English planters in the region,[430] and the Champaran region had in particular been popular among English planters.[431] By that time, indigo plants had been fully 'colonised' by the later to the expense of Indians.[432] Indigo, in fact, the 'original product of Hindostan', as John Forbes had explained in 1840, now had been colonised 'by the application of European skill and energy, as well as to the culture of the plants as to the chemistry of the manufacture'. Europeans had been able to win the competition with Indians, Royle explained, as they, and not the 'natives', had been supplied with 'accurate information' and 'specimens of the quality of drug it was desirable to rival'.[433]

Moreover, the new administrators also knew that all the efforts of the European planters in Bengal proper would 'hardly have suffied had it not been for the extensive purchases made by the EIC', as well as by the losses the EIC had sustained and by the advances they had continued to make. During the 1860s, the new government decided no longer to provide this kind of support to 'foreign indigo', however.[434] Yet this did not mean that the new government would abandon English planters too. To the contrary, the happenings during the 'Great Mutiny' in Bihar had made this government decide that these English planters should stay put.

Sir Hastings D'Oyly, who had worked in Bihar for many decades in various capacities, remembered at the end of his life how for some years after 1857, English administrators in Bihar had remained feeling quite insecure. Having been appointed as assistant magistrate of Tirhut, just after the Mutiny, D'Oyly remembered, for instance, how he and his wife had started for Muzaffarpur. The first 100 miles had been by train to Raniganj, but as the railway by then had not been completed, the rest of the travel of 400 miles had to be carried out in a *dak gharrie*, described by him as a kind of large *palankeen* on four wheels, in which one could lie full length, with sliding doors each side. Normally, these carriages would have been drawn by small horses, but as these all had been commandeered for transport work during the Mutiny, D'Oyly narrated, 'Our carriage had to be drawn by native coolies, relays of whom were placed at stages along the Grand Trunk Road'. It had been a 'very tedious journey', D'Oyly remembered, but even more so as:

> This road passes through a corner of Chota Nagpur, a hilly and jungly tract, and we learnt that these jungles were the full of 'Bhagees', or fugitives, remnants of the rebel Koer Singh's army which very shortly before had been thoroughly beaten and dispersed by Sir Vincent Eyre at Sasseram, a little further north on the other side of the Sone River. At night we both woke up as the carriage stopped suddenly, to find that our coolies had deserted us and left us stranded in the jungles. This was by no means a pleasant situation for us in a dense jungle full of our savage enemies![435]

It was the indigo planters in Bihar that the handful of administrators posted in Tirhut now relied on for more 'security'. These planters were swelling the numbers of 'whites' in Bihar after the happening in Bengal proper. What is more, as indigo planter, Minden J. Wilson detailed, when in 1857 the 'native army broke out into Mutiny', a body of some forty men, principally planters and officials belonging to the districts of Tirhut and Darbhanga, had assembled in Muzaffarpur. During those trying times in Tirhut, this bunch of men had wanted to 'protect' the English against possible attacks from the side of the 'natives' but had realised the complete lack of drill and arms 'in case of necessity arising at any future period'. In 1861, a meeting had, therefore, been arranged during which the government was requested to allow the formation of a 'Mounted Volunteers Corps' to be called the 'Soubah Behar Mounted Riffles'. This had been sanctioned by the government in 1862. It was later renamed the 'Behar Light Horse'.[436]

Scholar Girish Mishra has reasoned that the Mutiny of 1857 had been more serious in Bihar and that the planters in north Bihar had proven strong props of the company's rule: 'They (planters) fought against the mutineers, guarded Muzaffarpur and helped the Company restore its rule.' Consequently, Mishra argued, the attitude of the government had become much more favourable to the planters, and Mishra had added that after the Mutiny, 'The hands of the planters were strengthened, and they were given magisterial powers and posts in the army'.[437] Indeed, the relation between officials and planters before 1857 had been frosty, and generally, there had been a mutual dislike between these two species of English plant colonisers. During the 1860s, however, the new officials started looking with somewhat different eyes to planters:

> The magistrate of an Indian district lives often for months together beyond the reach of any one speaking his mother-tongue, surrounded by native subordinates, who he knows are leagued to deceive him at every step, without a soul to speak to who has one thought in common with himself. As he travels through his enormous district, he now and then comes across a 'factory', with its English comforts, its 'home-like' garden or park. He finds a hearty welcome from the jovial inmate, and an excellent dinner, over which they discuss the politics of the district, and he hears of all the rascalities of his host's rivals and enemies. The next day the fellow-exiles join a number of planters from other factories to engage in a tiger-hunt or pig-sticking expedition, which ends in another dinner, and still more confidential revelations of native rascality.

'Indeed', this official concluded, 'to have a planter in a district, if he is an honest man and a gentleman, is of greatest possible advantage.'[438] Apart from their work in cultivation, these English planters could, for instance, keep a watch over the 'natives of Tirhut' as well as 'safeguard' colonial officials posted in the region. Indigo planters had thus become 'volunteer aides', helping officials in delivering 'good governance' as co-workers rather than foes of officials in the rural settings of Bihar. Yet there had been a spoiling element in this cordial relation; though the government now openly had favoured the settlement of these planters in Bihar, in 1860, officials had declined open support to their indigo business.

Competition *Wallahs* and Indigo Planters in Tirhut

During the second part of the nineteenth century, colonial agricultural policies in Bengal changed fundamentally, influenced by recurrent and severe famines in the region. Not only could these famines, floods, and droughts and general poverty among Bihar's rural population provide reasons for even more turmoil in the region than during the Mutiny, but it also would cause less agricultural outcome and therefore meant less revenues too. In order to enhance this sorry-and-'dangerous' situation, the subject of introducing an improved system of agriculture in Bengal was considered in the early 1860s, and as some officials felt that the Mutiny had partly been caused by the alienation of the Indian landholders, its main feature had been 'to secure the assistance of the zemindars'. Yet the opinion of some revenue officers also was that 'no advantage was likely to be derived from them', and the steps proposed for improvement in this way, that is the engagement of Indian *zamindars* only in this agricultural improvement project, did not justify a grant of public money being made for that purpose.[439]

Yet a famine in 1866, which had been particularly severe in Tirhut, changed policy makers' ideas. Though structural changes had still to wait, grants were released, committees formed, and relief operations gradually undertaken. But clearly, apart from *zamindars*, administrators now looked upon the indigo planters to help them to relieve 'the general distress amongst the lower classes' by providing employment in indigo factories[440] and support construction of roads and wells, tanks and canals for irrigation and by setting an example in this way to 'native zamindars', who 'have practically ignored their obligations and responsibilities in this crisis'. At times these officials had even argued that indigo – like opium – could provide the cultivating classes, with the much-needed cash to buy, for instance, rice that had become so expensive. Indigo planters were, however, requested to give fair prices to indigo cultivators like government officials did; it was alleged in the case of poppy.[441]

Significantly, all relief operations undertaken by the government were having their centres at indigo factories. Indigo planters also assisted with the distribution of food it was reported and often officials left the choice of food to be supplied, and the quantities of the daily ration to be given to each applicant entitled to receive relief, to these indigo planters. The latter made themselves useful in other ways too. As the magistrate collector had no subordinate agency working in the interior of the districts, through which 'he can keep himself regularly informed of such important subjects as the state of the crops, the increase or decrease of area under cultivation, the state of trade, and the conditions and prospects of the people generally', the information provided by indigo planters was more than welcome and thought of as much more useful than that obtained through the 'irresponsible agency of the (Indian) landholders'.[442] Yet though administrators and indigo planters, during the last four decades of the nineteenth century, generally displayed such demonstrations of 'mutual support', administrators remained somewhat wary of the indigo these planters grew.

Unlike the previous half of the century, life in rural Bihar or *mofussil* life, as it was called during the second half of the nineteenth century, had required a strict separation between the 'natives' and the 'whites', and the only interaction English officials had with 'native society' was as employers.[443] At the same time, however, the interaction between such officials and 'non-official' settlers such as the indigo planters greatly increased. Besides, in one family, it could happen that the father was deputy collector or civil surgeon while the sons were indigo planters.[444] An 'ex-civilian' narrated, for instance, that 'the station society' of Muzaffarpur in Tirhut around 1878 consisted of the judge and additional judge, the collector with wife and some young children, the doctor 'with a very charming wife' and no children, the clergyman and his wife, a planter with his wife and family, the deputy magistrate, and deputy opium agent with large families and the planter's doctor. Besides, 'many planters were frequently coming in on business and had leased a bungalow in the station, which they had formed into a club'. There, further, was the manager of the estate of the 'young rajah of Durbhungah', which had been taken under the care of government, who was supposed to reside in that place but who actually passed the greater portion of his time in a 'palatial mansion at Mozufferpore, called Secundrapore', and who was 'of great importance in assisting the station festivities'.[445] Consequently, during the 1860s, the relation between the English 'competition wallahs'[446] and the indigo planters, generally, was cordial if not fantastic. D'Oyly remembered, in 1920, that by 1860,

> the district of Tirhoot was famous for its numerous indigo factories, and large fortunes were then made by many of the planters. They were all most hospitable and jolly good fellows. They had a Planters' Club at Mozufferpore of which dear old Minden Wilson was the President. He is still alive though very old. He wrote a most amusing book about the Tirhoot indigo planters.[447] I will give one or two tales which I heard about them. Paddy Cox, of Dooly, fifteen miles from Mozufferpore, was a cheery, merry Irishman, and his house and table were always open to any visitors, to whom he always gave a hearty welcome. Once [. . .][448]

There had been prejudices between the two classes of Englishmen, no doubt.[449] Had, for instance, the indigo planter been proud of his 'superior sportsmanship', the *wallah* emphasised his 'superior culture'.[450] But the *wallahs* had been lonely. . . Nonetheless, this 'civilian' had always to be 'on his guard against creating wrong impressions in the minds of the natives', and 'it was only in very few cases that friendship could be free and restrained'. Besides, from the planters' side, there had been hesitations too, and some of them believed that 'civilians' just 'act as troublesome buffers'. There was friction between the two English classes in Tirhut,[451] in particular, arose when *raiyats* refused to grow indigo and the 'civilians' knew who was at fault.[452] It was, in particular, during the later part of the 1870s, when planters' feudal rule was frequently challenged by 'natives' in Tirhut, that the relation between official and non-official Englishmen became really sour. Indeed, not only had the relation between indigo planters and English administrators changed after 1857, but also the relation between the former and the 'native cultivators' was changing too.

Unlike Bengal proper, many of the planters in Bihar had not been dealing in just one (and a very uncertain) commodity but also grew other crops apart from indigo. The indigo system itself, however, remained basically the same as that which had existed in Bengal proper before the 1860s and was based on a certain amount of 'unwillingness' among the cultivators to grow it. One 'artist in India' wrote to his sisters in England:

> Now the crops commonly sown by the Ryuts *on their own account* [emphasis mine], are rice, tobacco, sugar-cane, rye-soorsa (two kinds of mustard), moosnea, or linseed, chillies, turmeric, jeel, or sesame, wheat, barley, peas, kulâee-chunna-urrah, and a variety of other dalls or pulse [. . .] and this brings me to a few remarks upon indigo cultivation, as effecting the interests of its cultivators the Ryuts.[453]

Clearly, indigo was seen as a colonised plant, whereas peasants still cultivated tobacco and sugar cane 'willingly'. The commissioner of the Bhagalpur Division explained why the 'unwillingness' to grow indigo had only increased during the early 1870s:

> Day by day the old style of relation between planter and ryot, which can best be described in a single word as a feudal relation, is dying out, and with it disappears the best security for kindly feeling and mutual respect. While, on the one hand, the people are more difficult to manage, as with the spread of knowledge (especially of law) they become increasingly independent, on the other hand the occupation of factories by their proprietors who, from long residence amongst the people, could exert real influence over them, is becoming more and more rare; and with a constant change in the management, it is not to be considered strange if sometimes an unwise or unscrupulous hand, is seeking to extend the profits of the concern, places a strain upon the system, which it cannot bear.[454]

Indigo, unlike, for instance, tobacco, chillies, or sugar cane, was not only unpopular among the cultivators but also considered a 'foreign' crop, *not their own* but of the English planters. During the 1860s and early 1870s, 'petty differences' had occasionally arisen between planters and *raiyats* which had worried officials. Initially, competition *wallahs* argued that 'none of that universal disaffection and discontent, which prevailed for years in Bengal', was seen in Tirhut.[455] Yet in 1877, when ten years of continuous tension and occasional outbreaks of violence in Tirhut had been completed, the commissioner of the Patna Division had concluded his annual report:

> In concluding my remarks on the indigo question, I may express my opinion that the viciousness of the existing systems is due to two principal causes [. . .] and that the combined effect of all these circumstances has been to enrich a few hundreds of Europeans and some thousands of zamindars, to impoverish the peasantry of the district, and to cast a dark blot on British administration.

'But', this commissioner agreed that all the 'evils' related to the indigo system were not entirely caused by the planters but also due to the approval they got from local administrators who in this way perpetuated 'policy that is rotten to the core'.[456] The indigo system, he explained, consisted of either 'zerat', 'assameewar', or 'khooshgee'. *Zeerat* was, 'when the land is in the planter's sole possession and the ryot employed on it is a mere hired labourer'. *Assameewar was*, 'when the land is in the ryot's possession and when he is compelled to grow indigo on it at fixed rates per beegha'. *Khooshgee was*, 'when the ryot, under no compulsion, grows the plant as a remunerative crop'. Most disputes, the commissioner had judged, arose in connection with the *assammewar* system of indigo cultivation, and exactly, this system had been most popular among planters as it guaranteed labour to the planter which the *zeerat* did not.[457]

But even in regions where *zeerat* cultivation dominated, disputes between indigo planters and cultivators were reported.[458] Already in 1867, tenant cultivators of the huge Pandaul indigo concern in the district of Tirhut had shown open disaffection. They had refused to sow indigo and, according to government reports, also committed acts of violence.[459] These cultivators had claimed ownership of many of the lands that had been claimed to be *zeerat* (homestead) and part of the indigo factory. The government had argued that unlike other indigo-growing regions, this protest in Tirhut was new and that prior to the cold season of 1866–67, 'any disturbances in connection with Indigo cultivation were unknown'. Before 1867, the system of indigo cultivation that existed in Tirhut had been judged in much more favourable terms than that pursued in Lower Bengal. Moreover, the problems in that year had been confined to the Pandaul indigo concern in the northeast of Tirhut where the manager had allowed the factory *amlah* to grow up a system of sublease in the concern under which, 'whilst the planter demanded his full share of indigo from the ryot, he sublets his villages to his factory servants, who on their side, endeavoured to exact the highest rent they could obtain'. Such leases were known as *kutkina* leases.[460]

J. C. Gale, the manager of the factory at the time, had been convinced of his rights, however, and decided violence could be used if the tenants would not yield to his stipulations. Tension and protest spread to neighbouring indigo concerns. Many cultivators in the region united and formed a body to continue their struggle, and subscription was raised among them: 'each man paying according to the number of cattle he held'.[461] They complained against forced cultivation of indigo on their lands, forcible conversion of their best land into factory *zeerat*, seizure of their bullocks, ploughs, and carts during sowing seasons, and demanded immediate governmental interference to protect them from the oppression of the planters. Gale denied such charges and complained that some 'mischievous persons' had been inciting the cultivators against planters. Government officials had been reluctant to interfere and argued they could not do more than 'to keep peace, settle questions of disputed possessions, and punish trespass and mischief'. They also advised the planters to make some concessions to the tenants as this would make them willing to cultivate indigo. Meanwhile, these government officers would ascertain 'the feelings of all parties'.

In 1868, a full report was submitted to the GoI in the Home Department 'on the subject of the reluctance shown by the ryots of the Districts of Tirhoot and Chumparun to grow Indigo in fulfilment of their contract'.[462] Once more the government emphasised that compromises between cultivators and planters would be the best solution, that is increased pay to the *assamees* (cultivators) so that they would be willing to resume indigo cultivation and also to keep the *amlahs* satisfied. Direct interference on the part of the government was definitely not advocated by the lieutenant governor as the immediate consequence of such a course would be a wide-spread rumor that the Government had prohibited the cultivation of indigo, followed by immense losses, if not entire ruin, to the majority of those who invested their capital in this interest. The very reasonable and moderate conduct of the body of Planters in Tirhoot and Chumparan during the late events has certainly not deserved such a fate.[463]

Yet such 'amicable settlements' between planters and cultivators did not work very well, and 'unrest' remained. In 1873, differences between indigo factories' managers or owners and cultivators/*zamindars* and/or *amlahs* in Tirhut were again brought into the open.[464] After that, though there had been 'quiet periods', indigo cultivation was left 'in as insecure and unsound a footing as before', some government officials admitted.[465] Government often agreed that the indigo cultivator often was 'no better than a serf' and that indigo cultivation was being carried on 'under a system of pressure and terror'. One official, Lawrence, conveyed to William Grey, the lieutenant governor of Bengal at that time, that since the cultivators had asked for an enquiry, the government was 'bound to give them a fair hearing' and a commission should, therefore, be established 'to enquire into the relations generally between planter and ryot in Tirhoot'.[466] However, the lieutenant governor had advocated a policy of *laissez-faire*. Not only was the latter afraid to hurt the interests of the planters, but he also pointed out that 'the indigo system was so much interlinked with the rent questions that it had become a highly complicated system'. Though Lawrence protested, he finally shrank back from taking decisions, and no enquiry committee was established.[467]

Lawrence had also disliked the increased power of private companies in Bengal, which presented 'large amounts of capital' and were composed of 'many and influential persons in England', as the agents and officials of these companies had 'strong tendencies to look to their boards in England rather than to the local government', and in this way, Lawrence feared, powerful corporations grew, which the government found difficult to control. Lawrence had concluded, 'So long as the Government goes with the agents in India all plain sailing; but the case becomes very difficult when we exhibit desire to control or check them'.[468] The next lieutenant governor agreed that, beyond doubt, the want of definition and record of rights in land and the unsatisfactory character of the civil courts by which alone these rights could be determined were 'great evils'. Sir George Campbell also admitted that the Bihar indigo system was not an 'altogether healthy one, fairly based on free trade'. It had, he acknowledged, 'elements of quasi-feudal compulsion'. He, nevertheless, repeated that 'the agriculture and indigo manufacture, which is carried on by Europeans in Behar, is a great and important business, which in the hands of a most enterprising body of men is productive of much wealth, and which has been and is in the main beneficial'. Thus, the commissioner of the Patna Division stated that

> his Honor gladly acknowledges that most of the planters do credit to the British name and increase rather than derogate from the popularity of our rule. It is only because looseness of system has given rise to temptations to abuse that His Honor thinks that both the credit of the administration and justice to the people call for the interference of Government to check occasional abuses, and require that it should exert all its influence to bring the system into good lines, and to establish parties concerned. Sir George Campbell hopes and believes that the indigo industry will go on and prosper.[469]

It did not remain quiet for long, however, and again in 1875, the Judicial Department reported an 'indigo riot case' in Muzaffarpur. Metcalfe, the then commissioner of the Patna Division, informed the secretary of the government of Bengal: 'Breaches of the peace connected with the cultivation of indigo in Behar have for so many years happily been so scarce, that I the more regret to have to report a case which occurred on the 14th ultimo.'[470] This again was a case of the manager of an indigo factory trying to take 'forcible possession' of land to grow indigo which was disliked by a cultivator and protest had cost him his life. The European manager was accused of the act of criminal trespass and unlawful assembly and ordered to pay a fine of Rs. 1,000 or in default to undergo two months simple imprisonment. Had he been 'a native zemindar', the joint-magistrate judged Rs. 100–500 would have been a sufficient sentence yet upon a European rests 'the moral obligation', 'to set an example of keeping the law and not breaking it', and therefore, it had been decided to give Mr Manners, the manager of the Belsund factory, the heaviest fine that the law allowed. Contemplating the case, the lieutenant governor earnestly hoped that good sense and the right feeling of the indigo planters will be exerted in order to prevent any collision arising with the ryots, an occurrence which would cause great regret to the Government; on the other hand, the ryots must understand that they can expect no support nor encouragement in resisting whatever demands may be just and lawful.[471]

In 1877, the Bihar Indigo Planters' Association had been established with its headquarters in London and its local headquarters at the 'Tirhoot Planters' Club' in Muzaffarpur. The association 'promised', among others,

> that if it be brought to the notice of the Committee by any member of the Association or Government official that the conduct of any manager of a factory in respect to his dealings with his maliks, ryots, or coolies, is injurious to the planting interest, the Committee shall call on such manager for an explanation of his conduct, and after investigating the matter shall, if necessary, recommend such alteration in his system of management as the Committee may consider expedient for the general welfare. Should the manager decline to observe the suggestions of the Committee, the case shall then be placed before a General Meeting.

The association was most desirous to meet the views of the lieutenant governor regarding indigo planting and stated that 'the forcible seizure of ploughs, carts, and cattle and enforcement of labour' had no existence in 'any well-managed factory in Behar' and that the association pledged itself 'to prevent their occurrence by every means in its power'. The government commented that it looked that the association had shown a sincere desire to reform the system and improve the relations between planters and native cultivators. The lieutenant governor had, therefore, no intention to interfere in its business as long as the law was strictly obeyed, and indigo planting was carried on like any other commercial enterprise 'without the frequent complaints and the necessity for executive interference which have hitherto characterised it'. Yet the government also recognised that 'even in quiet times, indigo brings a good many cases to the criminal courts', and the lieutenant governor, therefore, decided that 'whether manifest or not, the discontent is such as to require very close watching and very strong officers to deal with it'.[472] The 'dilemma' faced by officials is evident, therefore, and just as had been the case in Bengal proper as scholar Raaj Sah pointedly put it: the administration's policy towards British planters in Bihar, too, 'displayed a multilevel schizophrenia between protection and competition, mercantile adventurism and administrative caution, and long-term aims and short-term expediency'.[473]

Offering an Alternative for Indigo Planters in Tirhut: Tobacco

In the Muzaffarpur and Dharbhanga districts of Tirhut,[474] however, things had somewhat been different than in another important 'indigo land'. In Champaran district, opportunities for planters had seemed better as Girish Mishra explained:

> Hitherto the planters had been able only to secure temporary leases of land, but circumstances then arose (in Champaran) which gave them a more permanent and secure hold on the soil. By 1876, the Bettiah Raj, owing to the extravagance of the Maharaja and the mismanagement by his employees, had become heavily involved in debts, and Mr T. Gibbon was appointed manager to set the affairs of the estate right. One of the first steps of Gibbon was to ensure financial equilibrium. In 1885, in order to pay off the debts, a loan of £ 2,45,000 was negotiated in London with Guilliland House, bearing interest of 5 per cent on a sinking fund, a sum of £ 28,000 was to be paid annually to the loan trustees in liquidation of the debt, which was to be paid off by 1925. Thus, the Guilliland House floated a sterling loan of nearly Rs. 95 lakhs, on the sole condition of substantial European security. To satisfy that condition and cover the interest on the loan, permanent leases of villages were granted to the planters.[475]

Permanent leases known as *mokarrari* being assured in Champaran not only did existing planters extend cultivation of indigo there but planters from outside also came to try their luck in Champaran. However, those planters who remained in the Pusa region of Tirhut had to cope with administrators who remained somewhat uncomfortable with indigo as well as that they still suffered from insecurity of land leases.[476] Indeed, W. W. Hunter had concluded in 1884 that though, in general, at least in the districts of Darbhanga and Muzaffarpur (which by 1875 had been separated from Champaran), most disputes had 'amicably' been adjusted, 'the relations between capital and labour and land in overcrowded tracts, almost entirely dependent on the local crops raised, are, however, always apt to be strained'.[477]

After the Pusa Stud in the subdivision of Tajpur in Tirhut had been converted into a tobacco experimentation farm, the government had started suggesting tobacco could be an alternative investment for these 'private capitalists with skills and energy' in Darbhanga and Muzafarpur. This would be a solution to both the problems of tobacco improvement and the 'indigo problem' in these tracts. Government's call to British planters in this subdivision to exchange indigo for tobacco became even more audible after 1878 when Dr Adolf Von Baeyer in Germany successfully invented an artificial dye that could replace the natural product. Especially after the year 1897, when the artificial dye made its first appearance in the market, civil servants in Bihar proposed tobacco could 'save' the British planters in this part of Tirhut at least.[478] For Champaran, sugar cane was proposed instead.

During the first part of the 1860s in Bihar – and like sugar cane[479] – tobacco was (still) seen as a commodity of the 'native *ryots*', whereas indigo was associated with the English (foreign) indigo planters. During the colonisation process initiated by the government along with English planters, the indigo plant itself had been 'alienated' from the people, whereas tobacco was seen as a plant 'of the people'. Tobacco was sewn by them along with other plants such as wheat, oats, barley, mustard, chillies, and linseed, for instance. Moreover, tobacco land was getting special treatment, and though 'the Tirhoot farmer', Huggins wrote, 'never manures any lands', he made an exception for 'those which lie adjacent to the village and are appropriated for the production of tobacco'.[480] F. M. Halliday, collector of Tirhut, wrote in a report to the commissioner of the Patna Division that tobacco cultivation was carried on all over the district, 'but the most extensive cultivation, as well as the best tobacco, comes from the Tajpore subdivision in pergunnah sareyasa, which is famous for the good quality of the plant'. A study by Mr Wace had been included in this report, and the latter had found that even tobacco trade had also largely remained uncolonised.

The more high land there is in a village the more tobacco is grown [. . .] The tobacco of the Sereysa pergunnah is considered better than that of those surrounding, and is, I am informed, famed through India. The soil of the villages bordering on the Gunduk is considered to be especially suitable for tobacco cultivation [. . .] The crop is now and then sold standing; as may readily be imagined, Babhuns and others do not care to undertake the constant tending of the plants after they are cut [. . .] and so sell the crop off as it stands to some koeri or hardworking man [. . .] All ryots cultivating tobacco, except those of the higher caste and more independent character or position, pay an extra cess to the malik or ticcadar [. . .] The last call on the ryot is the percentage of the 'dalal', who helps to drive the bargain between the ryot and the trader who goes about the country buying up tobacco for exportation [. . .] Information as to the export of tobacco, which is very largely carried on, is as difficult to give as information as to the area on which tobacco is grown. Tobacco leaves the sub-division in various ways. Some of the ryots themselves export it in carts to Nepal, others take it to Hajeepore, and there dispose of it; while a considerable quantity is taken in the same way to a mart names Islampore in the Behar sub-division. Many thousand maunds are bought up by the travelling merchants and transported by river and rail to the Upper Provinces and Bengal. It is exported in bundles tied up in straw [. . .] (Yet) if by manufactured [. . .] is meant prepared for smoking (cigars), the question as to its exportation in that state should be answered in the negative.[481]

Till around 1860, therefore, tobacco – and unlike indigo – had been a 'native branch'. Yet not all cultivators in Tajpur could grow tobacco. It was only the 'well-to-do' among them who could afford the cultivation of this crop. Hunter's report mentioned that

in Tajpur, it is said that a *rayat* has to pay as much as Rs. 15 per *bigha* for good land and even where the land is held at a fixed rent, or the tenant has a right of occupancy, the actual payments are much in excess of those shown in the rent-roll. All *rayats* who cultivate tobacco, unless of independent character or of high caste, have to pay an extra cess.[482]

Report after report mentioned that the decision to cultivate tobacco was taken by the *zamindars* but that the actual cultivation was carried out by *koiris* described as 'industrious, peaceful, and contented cultivators' who were 'in great demand among zamindars' and who were 'always glad to settle lands with them'.[483] Lieutenant Pogson in his manual of agriculture in India of 1883 also described how the green tobacco leaf was converted into marketable leaf tobacco and how it was cultivated by the 'zemindars'. Yet he remarked that this all was according to the 'Indian' plan, and the landholder 'has no means to prepare leaf tobacco on the American plan'. But Pogson was convinced, 'If he was supplied with good seed (all varieties of American tobacco, including the Cuban, Maryland, Kentucky, Virginia, and Orinoco as well as the best kinds of country tobacco) and grew the tobacco on properly manured land and sold the crop as cut to European or native capitalists, who would undertake the proper preparation of the leaf, India would soon be able to produce large quantities of first-class leaf tobacco'.[484]

Indeed, by the mid-1870s, in this part of Tirhut, tobacco was projected as the most promising, alternative plant to be colonised apart from indigo, and if found successful, it could even replace indigo. John Forbes Royle had already pointed out that the 'history, culture, and manufacture' of indigo plants in Bengal 'afford most useful lessons for the means to be adopted for ensuring success in other cultures, which at first appear equally unprofitable but are not more hopeless'.[485] In 1780, indigo, sugar cane, and tobacco had been suggested by Mr Prinsep as 'objects of introducing into Great Britain from the East Indies' and 'Europeans bred to different arts and sciences as well as the most intelligent mechanics and planters of the East' should assist in this scheme.[486] Indigo and to some extent sugar cane had had their fair chance in 1870, and almost a century later, it was decided that it now finally was tobacco's turn. The 'Pergunnah Sureysa' in Tirhut was selected for the purpose. This region was famous for its tobacco that was exported as the revenue surveyor had reported in 1854, 'In large quantities to Patna and the East-ward, both for smoking and chewing'.[487] The question before the administrators had been:

The present cultivation of tobacco is regulated by the taste of Indian purchasers. The latter prefer coarse and strong kinds, the growers consequently produce such tobacco. The effect of improving the flavour of tobacco, as we would consider it, would be a fault in the estimation of the native consumer. While this improved or Manilla tobacco would be unsaleable here, would it suit the European markets? I fear not. The conclusion I arrived at is, that we should either stimulate the present cultivation so as to produce the best and largest crop for an Indian market, or induce a separate cultivation for European consumption by offering prices and buying up the improved kinds that would otherwise be unsaleable.

The government decided in favour of the latter. In other words, around 1870, administrators decided Tirhut tobacco should be (fully) 'colonised'.[488] English capital, skill, and manpower had to be applied in order to produce the cigar (wrapper) tobaccos that could be exported to England or be locally manufactured into *cheroots* and cigars for the use of the Europeans in India or the 'native elites' who all had abandoned the habits of tobacco chewing or smoking it in the *hookahs*.[489] What is more, the new government in Bengal now hoped that indigo planters residing in the region would assist them in this grand tobacco improvement scheme.

Like in Bengal proper and as already detailed, Englishmen in Bihar, too, had started experimenting with 'Virginia' tobacco, since 1790 already.[490] As a result, there now were two kinds of tobaccos in Bihar, that is the *deshi* and the *belatee*, the latter secured through the introduction of Virginia in the region. Indigo planters had played their part in this experimentation.[491] Related to the situation in 'the continent', which made it difficult for British factories to get its raw tobacco supply from there, it was around 1870 that these initial often private experiments in India now also received full support even from Imperial Britain.[492] Accordingly, it was decided that tobacco in Tirhut could be brought 'to almost any state of perfection by careful cultivation and proper curing'[493] but again (only) with the help of information provided by indigo planters. Pusa had been selected for the purpose of 'expert' experimentation and had been preferred above other model farms.

Seeing [. . .] that no benefit to the State is to be obtained by continuing the cultivation of tobacco on the (Ghazipur) farm, as leaf of equally good quality, and in sufficient quantity for our requirements, can be grown at Poosa and elsewhere, it might possibly suit Government to sell or otherwise dispose of the Ghazipur property.[494]

Between 1870 and 1880, the government, however, increasingly realised that apart from soil and climate, labour was an essential factor in tobacco improvement. By this, colonial administrators did not mean 'mechanical work' done by the cultivators but 'labour' referred

to the higher, more artistic, and more intelligent efforts of the European planter and his assistants and overseers, who direct and instruct the native labourers in their duties, and are absolutely responsible for the cultivation of the plant throughout all its successive stages, commencing with the hoeing of the land and the selection and sowing of the seed and concluding with those infinitely more delicate operations – the sorting, fermenting, and preparing the tobacco for the European market.

Such policy makers involved in the tobacco improvement scheme had also stipulated that

a good tobacco planter requires not, to be a man of brilliant parts or high intelligence [. . .] On the contrary, those gifts of intellect which are needful to a brilliant statesman, or journalist, or a successful man of business, would in all probability be a stumbling-block in the career of a tobacco planter. A tobacco planter, unlike a poet, is made – not born. Sound common sense, the power to observe and draw accurate conclusions, a knowledge of mankind, the ability to govern all sorts and conditions of men, and at the same time to retain the respect and esteem of those you govern, the gift of organisation, the moral strength to enforce discipline: such are the attributes of the successful tobacco planter. Monotony, exile, solitude, the absence of any necessity for great mental exertion, the concentration of one's thoughts and faculties on one object, and that nothing more than a tobacco plant, and the constant and enforced intercourse with men of like singleness of ideas, to all these disadvantages the planter must submit [. . .] and it is, therefore, that common sense, practicalness, and a sound constitution are more likely to produce successful planters than those more ordinary attainments – great learning and intelligence.[495]

The indigo planters in Tirhut were best equipped to become such 'tobacco planters', administrators judged. The lieutenant governor of Bengal had observed that 'the relations between planters and the ryots are somewhat more feudal and less mercantile than might be desired'. Having thus witnessed that indigo had not been 'very popular with the ryot', the government had, therefore, decided that 'in matters of pure merchandise, things may most properly be left to find their own level', but where it was 'feudal and not wholly voluntary', government officers in charge of wards' estates 'should not give direct facilities for an extension of the system by letting fresh villages to indigo planters'.[496] Yet indigo planters had been flexible, officials had also observed. They had first converted their sugar refineries into indigo concerns, and now in eastern Bengal, 'indigo has a good deal given way to the spread of jute and other cultivation'.[497] Therefore, after Pusa had become a tobacco experimental farm,[498] the government called upon the 'professional hands' of the indigo planters who should replace 'amateur supervision'. Yet indigo planters did not get the full charge.

> The farm has been placed in the charge of a Mr J. Paterson, an Indigo planter (on a salary of Rs. 200 a month), who has had long practical acquaintance with native agriculture [. . .] The soil must be analyzed at the outset to ascertain whether it is really adopted to the growth of tobacco of good quality. A competent Resident Superintendent (Dr E. Brown) must take the conduct of the experiment, with an assistant thoroughly versed in the models and resources of native agriculture below him, such a man, in fact, as, it is hoped, we have already secured at Poosah in Mr Paterson.[499]

Indigo planter Paterson had arrived with good feelings about the place, and he thought no more suitable spot or better climate could have been selected. He also proposed that before tobacco, which started only in October, paddy and Indian corn could be sown for sale and for straw. Cattle could be kept not only for ploughing but also for milk and manure. In this way – and 'with God's help' – he was sure that even with limited means, 'our anticipations will be fully realised'. He even felt that as labour was very cheap, a private person could take up the task of farming from government.[500] Yet after some trials, the results even in Pusa proved disappointing, and the government concluded:

> It was soon discovered that cake tobaccos and smoking mixtures made entirely of Ghazipur and Poosa leaf could not compete with those of English and American manufacture, and American leaf had to be imported as wrappers for the cavendish, and for use in mixing in the case of the cut tobaccos. This added considerably to the cost of the manufactured tobaccos and, although the quality of these has been improved, so that there is now a limited sale for them, progress has been slow, and the quantity disposed of has not hitherto been sufficient to make the business profitable.[501]

Therefore, as in 1878, the curing of tobacco by a government agency on a small scale at Pusa had thus proven a failure, and 'practical difficulties' had arisen in the way of giving effect to proposals for 'scientific experiments connected with physiological botany and agricultural chemistry', the government decided to withdraw and give the task 'to teach the Indian peasants physiological botany and agricultural chemistry and a system of cropping based not on the experience of years and seasons but on theory and science of Europe' to private enterprise. Thereafter, Messrs. Begg, Dunlop & Co., to whom the Ghazipur stud lands had been let by the government of the north-western provinces for tobacco, was granted a lease of the Pusa lands and buildings for seven years 'for the establishment of a bona fide factory for the manufacture and cure of tobacco' as 'these gentlemen have secured the services of experienced curers' and had been 'prepared to lay out a sufficient amount of capital to make the project a success'.[502] The Bengal government still had great faith in the eventual success of tobacco in India, and would afford every encouragement to bona-fide pioneers in this enterprise. There can be no doubt of the honesty of Messrs. Begg, Dunlop and Co's intensions to do their utmost to make the production of tobacco for European Markets a success (Mr Buck from N. W. P also strongly recommends them). At the same time, it is essential that the Government should entirely withdraw from any seeming competition; and if we wish to improve Indian tobacco, we can best do this by assisting private traders in their efforts, and not by going into the open market ourselves as cultivators and manufacturers.

Importantly, however, by transferring the Pusa farm to Messrs. Begg, Dunlop & Co., indigo had been bypassed. Earlier, Gisborne & Co. had wanted to purchase the government interests in the Pusa estate on account of their clients Messrs. Studd and Macintosh, who owned the Dhooley indigo concern, which surrounded the Pusa estate. The latter had been anxious that 'no outsiders should gain admission within the limits of their cultivation'. Yet the government of Bengal had decreed that the estate should not be sold to indigo planters unless the latter would give up indigo and start tobacco cultivation.[503] Mr Eden of the government of Bengal had, therefore, preferred Messrs. Begg, Dunlop and Co. (who also had invested in indigo[504]) as 'they want the land, and especially the buildings, for tobacco only, and offer the fullest guarantee that they are engaged in a bona fide endeavour to establish a tobacco enterprise'.[505]

During the next ten years, this private British firm, backed by government support, grew tobacco in Bihar according to the 'American plan' and manufactured it for the European market. For the purpose, five English/American curers had been employed. Indeed, one new scheme of the 'Imperial Agricultural Improvement Project' had now been rooted. 'In tobacco', the late secretary to the GoI in the Department of Revenue, Agriculture, and Commerce reported in 1879, 'but little more remains to be done by the government, an energetic European firm having undertaken the cultivation and manufacture of it on good principles in farms made over to the firm for the purpose (they were old stud farms) on very favourable terms by the government'.[506]

In that year, the report on the internal trade of Bengal also stated that a considerable impetus had been given to the tobacco trade by the establishment of a tobacco farm by Messrs. Begg, Dunlop and Company in lands at Pusa made over to them by the government. In this way, trade had been diverted, and instead of tobacco being sent to Patna or eastwards, it was now sent to Calcutta from Tirhut from where it could possibly be further shipped to England if quality would suffice.[507] In 1886, Hunter concluded that 'the enterprise may now be said to have passed beyond the stage of experiment'.[508] By the end of the nineteenth century, when indigo in Tirhut seemed to government, as detailed in the next chapter, 'not so remunerative as other crops which might be grown on the same land', the total switch from indigo to tobacco by European planters had looked all the more likely.[509]

CHAPTER FIVE

Colonisation of Plants through British Scientists

During the last quarter of the nineteenth century, recurrent famines and unfavourable market conditions had resulted in agricultural stagnation if not deterioration in Bengal. It was, therefore, feared that Bengal would not generate the requisite surplus to meet the food and raw material requirements of 'the motherland' as well as that of the region itself. A new Department of Agriculture, Commerce, and Industry was therefore established to inaugurate and stimulate improvements in cultivation and to direct industrial pursuits. This department was, in fact, the first organised accomplishment after more than half a century of individual activities and haphazard institution building in Bengal working in the same direction and also with government's support. It was now believed that a more centralised direction of scientific exploration and research could better capitalise on government investment in science. Though in many aspects the individual activities of EIC men who manned the botanic garden near Calcutta widely differed from activities by 'scientific men' or institutions established in Bengal during the end of the nineteenth century and the beginning of the twentieth century, they all had shared a 'scientific optimism', that is the idea that the application of (British) science to agrarian policies would automatically translate into agrarian improvement. Yet with the advance of empire building, imperial interests were also increasingly reflected in policies and programmes formulated in or for Bihar. Indeed, such agricultural engineering policies were not only intended to remedy specific agrarian problems in Bengal (still including Bihar), or in the whole of British India for that matter, but it was also expected that the knowledge which resulted from such 'scientific' engineering could be applied elsewhere in the British Empire as well. Yet for this to materialise, new committees, commissions, boards, and institutions (also in England) were called for, which could provide scientific advice to the newly created departments and institutions in India. Additionally, a new class of men in the Indian Civil Service 'with superior technical and scientific knowledge of practical agriculture' (i.e. scientists) was also to be nurtured in order to assist the government in India in their great agricultural improvement project. This chapter bears out that by the beginning of the twentieth century, therefore, not three but four agencies, that is government officials, indigo planters, *zamindars,* and scientists, had been readied to improve tobacco's quality in Bihar.

Figure 17. The Agricultural Research Institute and its laboratory unit at Pusa before the earthquake of 1934 that destroyed this building. Taken from Playne, *Bengal and Assam, Behar and Orissa,* 1917, p. 695 (courtesy New Delhi: Asian Educational Services).

Institutionalisation of Agricultural Science at Pusa

In 1871, a Department of Agriculture had been established to take cognisance of all matters affecting the practical improvement and development of agricultural resources of the country. In 1878, a 'Famine Commission' had been sent out to India at the instance of the British Parliament. Consequently, apart from introducing in Bengal a few of the 'most visible accomplishments of Western technology'[510] such as railways[511] and public works such as irrigation schemes, land systems and police administration were also reviewed 'with a view to give security of possession to cultivators and to obtain correct statistics and prompt information regarding agricultural conditions and agricultural depressions'.[512] Somewhat later, dictionaries of the economic products of India were published by the GoI with the double purpose in view that something was done, Thavaraj analysed, 'to advance the material interests of India and to bring the trade and capital of the West into more direct contact with the resources of the empire'.[513] Likewise, the GoI around the turn of the century desired to bring a valuable collection of species of Bengal products held at the Provincial Economic Museum in Calcutta into 'scientific order'. Imperial and provincial lists and collections were subsequently enlarged and arranged, and the result was exhibited in the Economic Court at the Calcutta Exhibition.[514] Meanwhile, the Department of Agriculture was revamped into the Revenue and Agricultural Department. What was new in such efforts was the open willingness of the GoI to accept the view that decreed in England that India's 'critical resources' should be tapped through the use of scientific knowledge and techniques. Indeed, in British India between 1870 and 1914, at least, 'applied science and technology' was considered 'indispensable tools in the creation and consolidation of Britain's economic hegemony'.[515]

Importantly, in 1889, a British 'expert' Dr J. A. Voelcker had been brought over from England to India to advise as to the best way of applying chemistry to Indian agriculture. After an extensive tour throughout India, the latter concluded that agricultural improvement was possible in India, and an extensive scheme was designed by him in this regard. In fact, the again revamped Department of Agriculture and Revenue, manned of course mainly by British officials and scientists, was willing to implement his 'scientific advice'. Chemists were followed by other 'men of science' such as mycologists and entomologists who not only came on a visit from England to Bengal but even got employed in its agricultural department. Scientific advice would still come from England of course from existing institutions such as the India Office, the Royal Society, and the Imperial Institute, but commissions such as the Indian Advisory Committee and the Board of Scientific Advice were newly established for the same purpose.[516] Subsequent governments in India, thus, asked advice from one of these institutions in England as a general administrative instrument. The advice requested could concern appointment matters of scientists for their departments but also concern questions of botanical classification and systematisation.

Indeed, by the turn of the century, Bengal was converted at last, as Peter Robb concluded, 'to the cause of agricultural development' on scientific basis. Moreover, Robb added that the time was now ripe 'for, and more ambitious, proposals, expressing each official's view of the importance of his field'.[517] The establishment of the (later imperial) Agricultural Research Institute, Pusa, was the outcome of such a 'more ambitious proposal'.[518] This proposal had been made by the Viceroy Lord Curzon in whose hands scientific research in India 'was brought more closely into imperial government'.[519] Confronted by reports on the appalling famine of 1898, Curzon prepared a plan for the appointment of experts, the construction of experimental farms, and the foundation of agricultural colleges to ameliorate the situation. Step by step, this cumulated into the Indian Agricultural Research Institute which is now located in New Delhi,[520] but was founded in 1903 at Pusa in Bihar, Tirhut.[521]

This, indeed, was the very same place that the EIC had selected as the location of a stud-breeding farm which could ensure the indigenous supply of horses.[522] Yet as the Pusa stud farm had not proven successful, it had eventually closed down.[523] As shown in the previous chapter, it had remained as a government estate, however, but till 1897, it had been leased out to a British concern named Begg, Dunlop (Sutherland) and Co.[524] with the sole aim being tobacco improvement. After some years, the concern had backed out, however, and when, in 1898, Lord Curzon had taken over as the viceroy, Pusa, thus, became the centre of agricultural engineering of the imperial government.[525]

As described in the previous chapter, around Pusa, there were many British (indigo) planters, and by the beginning of the twentieth century, the place, in fact, had become a kind of 'mini British Kingdom' and therefore thought to be uniquely suitable to carry out crop experimentation through application of British government capital, skills, manpower, and importantly now also 'science' (including the introduction of this science-based technology). Curzon believed that agricultural research had received a too limited financial encouragement from the government since the creation of the Department of Agriculture and Revenue in 1881.[526] He, thereupon, decided to use a gift of US$ 30,000 he had received from an American millionaire named Henry Phipps, who had toured India in 1902–3, for the purpose of scientific agricultural improvement and selected Pusa as the most suitable place for the establishment of a full-fledged agricultural research institute and college. Indeed, within a few years, a magnificent college and well-equipped institute arose on the bend of the river Gandak, surrounded by 640 acres of land (later increased to 1,300 acres), devoted to experimental cultivation and demonstration.[527]

The actual foundation stone of the Agricultural Research Institute and College was laid by Lord Curzon himself on the 1st of April 1905. In his opening speech, he expressed his hope that Pusa would become the nucleus of agricultural activities, research, and education that would benefit Bengal (including Bihar) and the whole country and indeed the entire British Empire that would attract the best talents from abroad and India.[528] Yet though Pusa was, thus, Curzon's brainchild, this viceroy had been forced to leave India that same year but for different reasons however.[529]

When, in 1906, the Imperial Department of Agriculture produced its first annual report (1905–6), W. T. Thiselton-Dyer, assistant director (and later director) of the Royal Botanic Gardens, Kew, described the establishment of the institute at Pusa in *Nature* as an 'epoch-making' development. Pusa was called the 'Rothamsted of the East',[530] putting agricultural research in India on a new footing:

> Hitherto fitful and uncoordinated, and always at the mercy of uninstructed and unsympathetic officials, whose one cannon of criticism has been the solvency of the annual balance-sheet, agricultural research could now proceed in a directed fashion.

Others agreed that India needed 'the application of modern scientific methods and knowledge to pressing economic problems', and at Pusa, it was argued by others in *Nature*, research was directed 'to practical problems that require early solution and is not wasted on inquiries which are only of importance from the theoretical standpoint'.[531] In order to solve the 'pressing economic problems' of India, it was also decided that experimentation with new crops was not really necessary. Lieutenant governor of Bengal, Sir R. Temple, had already written in 1882, 'To introduce new and foreign stables which may or may not prove suitable to this climate (was) a very difficult task, for the successful accomplishment of which the best talent procurable from Europe would be needed.' Temple had, therefore, devised another plan: 'To examine scientifically and botanically the physiological characteristics of all our principal indigenous staples and the chemical properties of properties of our soils, with a view to improving the fertility of our fields and the yield of our produce.'[532] When Pusa developed into British India's first and leading agricultural resource centre, it indeed emphasised such research, education, and outreach programmes covering, on paper, 'all crops in India'. In practice, however, not all plants received government's equal attention. The commercial potential of plants remained the most important criteria for their inclusion in research schemes.[533] Besides, these economic reasons, moreover, the GoI also provided imperial, ideological, and political grounds to justify scientific experimentation at Pusa.[534] As will be shown below, it was this mixed *raison d'être* that prompted the government to simultaneously support 'scientific schemes' at Pusa, aiming at indigo, sugar cane, and tobacco improvement.

Agricultural Science in Service of the British Empire[535]

Pusa also housed the headquarters of the central (all-India) government's Agricultural Department. The Pusa estate, which had been given to the Bengal government for tobacco experiments as detailed in the previous chapter, therefore now became an 'Imperial Centre' for general agricultural research.[536] A magnificent two-storeyed gigantic structure with a flat roof surmounted by a massive dome known as Phipps Laboratory came up in 1907. In 1905, three scientists of the Imperial Department of Agriculture in London were transferred to Pusa, and additional positions of director of the institute, agricultural horticulturist, and economic botanist were created for this purpose. After Curzon's departure, Pusa also housed sections of botany,[537] chemistry, mycology, entomology, and one library. Research findings were made available through the institute's and the agricultural department's numerous types of publications.[538] In 1911, the institute was renamed as the Imperial Institute of Agricultural Research and as Imperial Agricultural Research Institute in 1919. Accordingly, positions changed into 'imperial agriculturist', 'imperial economic botanist', 'imperial agricultural chemist', 'imperial mycologist', 'imperial bacteriologist', and 'imperial entomologist'. These name changes were not immaterial.

This whole exercise at Pusa seemed to have been the empire's response to growing disapproval by 'nationalists' within India (British and Indian), regarding the manner in which Britain ruled India. Under the regime of 'men of science' (from Britain), there would be abundance even for the poorest classes, and as one of the British politicians formulated it at the time, 'all classes might join in a prosperity that would make INDIA A HAPPY COUNTRY [capitals in the original]'.[539] In 1901, William Digby had written a sarcastic book entitled *Prosperous British India* in which he argued that the great mass of the Indian people lived in extreme poverty. Digby felt that the English meant well, but the GoI was too ignorant and too proud to listen to others, including Indian nationalists. Administrators' answer had been 'science'. It was expected that scientists, as scholar Michael Worboys argued,

> would be catalysts of development by discovering economic opportunities, making the tropical environment safe, solving technical problems in production, processing and distribution, directing and improving the productivity of investment, and generally *demystifying the tropics and their people* [emphasis added].

Worboys had concluded that 'science became a major factor largely by default, when more conventional but expensive and contentious alternatives failed'.[540] In any case, policy makers, including some Indian scientists, around 1910, contended that if India would make common cause with England, India would be recognised as an integral part of the empire, 'with equal rights and privileges with England in the matter of colonial expansion'.[541] Pusa had been an outcome of such an ideology, too, and research in this institute was thought to be in the interest of India as well as the rest of the British Empire, including, of course, Britain itself. Indeed, as the Botanical Garden in Calcutta had been established more than a century before on the pattern of Kew Gardens in London,[542] in similar way, the Pusa Institute was connected to the Imperial Institute in England. The Imperial Institute had been erected at South Kensington as the National Memorial of the Jubilee of Empress Victoria, by whom it had been opened in May 1893. The principal objective of the institute was to promote the utilisation of the commercial and industrial resources of the Empire by arranging comprehensive exhibitions of natural products especially of the Colonies and India,[543] and providing for their investigation and for the collection and dissemination of scientific, technical and commercial information relating to them.[544]

The Scientific and Technical Department of the Imperial Institute worked in cooperation with the Agricultural and Mines Department in the colonies, whose operations it supplements by undertaking such investigations and inquiries as are of special scientific and technical character connected with agricultural or mineral development, as well as inquiries relating to the composition and commercial value of products (vegetable and mineral) which can be more efficiently conducted at home in communication with merchants and manufacturers, with a view to the local utilisation of these products or to their export.[545]

Consequently, research at Pusa did not only relate to plants but to the whole plant industry, that is their manufacture into and export of as commodities. Besides, through the connection of Pusa with this Imperial Institute as well as with Kew and other imperial advisory committees that had been established, results from experimentation carried out at Pusa were disseminated to other colonies and the 'motherland' or indeed made available to the whole (scientific) world. In this way, 'the whole world was in Bihar and Bihar was in the whole world'. In other words, if considered useful, research outcomes of experimentation in Bihar could be used elsewhere in India or in other colonies and in the homeland but also the other way around. In short, plants selected for colonisation schemes at Pusa were also truly globalised.

The indigo, sugar cane, and tobacco experiments conducted at Pusa were, therefore, not only related to each other but had not materialised in a 'policy vacuum'.[546] At Pusa, plant colonisation of the past (through trade or otherwise) was replaced by a 'benign kind of agricultural imperialism', as Galloway formulated it.[547] No doubt, there was a genuine concern of British imperial policy makers for the welfare of peasants in Bihar's rural society in which the Pusa Institute happened to have found itself as, after all, famines did not only affect 'law and order' but also affect the land revenues. Yet not only the interests of cultivators in Bihar or even not only those of cultivators in the rest of British India had to be taken into consideration. At Pusa, the newly formulated Imperial Agriculture Project functioned in the interest of the whole British Empire of which India was an integral part. This condition was reflected in, among others, the kind of plants chosen for research, which plant varieties were (not) wanted, and in other research specifications. Most of all, it affected the direction of plant 'improvement'. This condition was also reflected in the attitude of the imperial government towards (English) scientists employed at Pusa. When these agricultural officers arrived (from England) in Bihar, a director of the Pusa Institute explained in 1916:

> They found in nearly every crop they studied an extraordinary number of mixtures. The cultivator whose interests were limited to his village saw no harm in this; but when the demands of outside trade set a standard, the disadvantage was brought home to him and was reflected in reduced prices.

Such enthusiastic and often still relatively young scientists who freshly arrived from England to become employed at the Pusa Institute or in the Department of Agriculture situated in the same building had therefore (been) stipulated that 'improvement' of such 'crops of commerce' was needed to make them better equipped for the export market.[548] Scientific research methods had to be applied to 'improve' plants with that aim in mind, that is the transformation of cultivated plants into profitable export commodities. Four methods could be adopted to accomplish such a transformation: (1) the method of improvement by selection, (2) improvement of plants by cross-breeding or hybridisation, (3) the introduction of and acclimatisation of new plant varieties of the same plant from elsewhere, and (4) improvement in agricultural practice (including cultivation but also the after-process). In Baber's words, scientists at Pusa were thus required to 'deploy scientific expertise to expand the empire' while at the same time they were 'seeking to take advantage of the opportunities to develop their careers as scientists'.[549] However, while developing their careers at Pusa, scientists found it difficult at times to work within these boundaries dictated by empire.

Indigo Improvement Scheme at Pusa

In Bihar, officials ruled that such scientists newly arrived from England should not replace the 'amateurs' on whom they had depended thus far to carry out their plant improvement schemes, that is indigo planters and Indian *zamindars*. Instead, these scientists were, in fact, required to 'serve' the former in trying to cope with the 'indigo crisis'. By the end of the nineteenth century, as shown in previous chapters, English planters in Bihar had fully 'colonised' indigo,[550] and though colonial administrators had not openly supported the industry, the planters had been welcomed ever after 1857 to assist them in their great agricultural project. Since planters had, indeed, done this during the decades that followed, officials by the turn of the century had decided that these planters needed a 'reward'. Walter Scott Seton-Karr, who had been the president of the Indigo Inquiry Commission earlier, stated the following during a session of the Royal Society of Arts in 1900:

> It must be recollected that though we *never can colonise the plains of India, factories, whether indigo, cotton, or jute, represent property and wealth that can be transmitted to heirs for generations* [emphasis added]. I now desire to add my testimony as to the value of a great industry to the views emphatically and clearly expressed by Sir Steuart Bayley. Indeed, all Indian administrators whose opinion is worth having, within my knowledge and observation, have invariably set a high value on the residence in the interior in the country, of Englishmen and Scotchmen engaged in agriculture or commerce. Before the Mutiny, during the Mutiny, and after the Mutiny, the planter had been looked upon as an element of strength and a source of prosperity. In time of famine the factory supplies a readymade organisation for relief and the supervision of works, and if at any time there is any friction between the Englishman and the native, between capital and labour, as there is in many other countries (England included), the result has lent animation and earnestness to Government and its administration. The presence of Englishmen in factories scattered over large districts furnishes a guarantee for the detection and redress of grievances. Natives will often endure a good deal in silence;

the Englishman makes his voice heard; and when we are told that, in three large districts in Northern Bihar, there are no less than 700 Europeans serving as volunteers, coming in daily contact with all classes of natives and conversant with their feelings, interests, and wants, it is easy to understand the value of such a body in troublous or peaceful times, in the development of natural resources, and in epochs of scarcity, sedition, or discontent.

This body of English planters in Bihar was too useful, the GoI was convinced, to allow it to perish. When, therefore, synthetic indigo was put on the market in 1897 and the indigo industry in Bihar was about to collapse,[551] Curzon reserved a special grant spread over a number of years 'to defray the cost of scientific inquiry into the methods of production of natural indigo'.[552] Moreover, though the indigo industry in Bihar continued to decline, scientific research sponsored by the government continued. This research sought ways to produce indigo cheaper as both government as well as indigo planters knew that 'synthetic indigo can only compete with them by being sold at a fraction above the cost of production'.[553] Besides, in 1904 Bernard Coventry, an indigo planter in Bihar who had carried out experiments with indigo as well with other plants, had been made director of the Pusa Institute and remained there till 1916. Clearly, therefore, scientists had to join this 'holy trinity' between indigo planters, the GoI, and Indian *zamindars* who existed during the first two decades of the twentieth century in Bihar.

In 1914 – just before the start of the war with Germany – this government agreed that 'a quarter of a century ago, indigo was one of the most prosperous industries in India'. Yet then had come 'the German chemist and his synthetic dye' and the planter of Bihar who once constituted 'a large and wealthy community' now was 'the greatest sufferer'.[554] Yet it was decided that, and in particular during the war which had shut out the German dyes and 'brought a new spell of prosperity' to the planters, advantage had to be taken of the 'present prosperous conditions to make further efforts to place the industry on a sound commercial basis and, by scientific research, to produce natural indigo in such a form that after the war it will be able to compete on a footing of equality with synthetic products'.[555]

Administrators' best wishes were, therefore, with the planters, and it was thus decided to employ scientists[556] who had 'at heart the welfare of our Indian Empire' and were in for 'a good fight' in the battle against the 'coal-tar rival'.[557] Already in 1915, these government officers feared that the progress of the synthetic dye had been so rapid that it was not likely that the indigo-growing industry would survive.[558] Yet it was still hoped that 'the evil may be put off for a time' (by the introduction of the Java/Natal variety and superior methods of oxidation for instance).[559] Besides, even when after the war almost everybody knew that the days of 'Tirhut indigo' were numbered, administrators still employed scientists who had recognised that 'from a scientific point of view, the production of artificial indigotin is undoubtedly a grand achievement', but at the same time, they declared that 'if it can be produced in large quantities at such a price as to render indigo planting altogether unprofitable, it can only be regarded by Englishmen as a *national* [emphasis added] calamity'. Not only scientific research at Pusa continued, therefore, but government extended help in other ways as well.[560]

Sugar Improvement Scheme at Pusa

An old official, a collector, a judge, and afterwards a commissioner in Tirhut, who had 'learned to appreciate the value of the English gentlemen planters in north Behar', described Tirhut around 1900:

> It was not an English colony exactly, but it was the nearest to it in India. There were some 700 Europeans employed, and a capital [. . .] estimated at £4,000,000, with an annual expenditure of £300,000. There were 300,000 acres under indigo, and an enormous population who were dependent upon it for their living, and that in an a district where the pressure of population was greater than in any other part of agricultural India [. . .] You could not ride ten miles in any part of those districts without coming across a planter's bungalow [. . .] and each such bungalow was really an oasis of civilisation. It meant a higher standard of honesty and of justice; in various ways in progressive cultivation, in helping the ryot with money, and in all his trouble giving him just that

assistance which you expected in England from an English squire. And it meant that the planter was unconsciously a sort of policeman; the very fact of his presence prevented a considerable amount of fraud and oppression, especially, amongst subordinate officials, which otherwise go on.

Clearly, government's perception of non-official Englishmen in Tirhut had changed tremendously within the span of a century. Had they been 'interlopers' or 'speculators' by the beginning of the nineteenth century, around 1900, they were called 'gentlemen planters'. Sir Stewart Colvin Bayley, who had served most of his time in Bihar amongst the older planters and among whom he 'could number many intimate friends', had always believed in a government policy that assisted the planters in their battle 'not so much from the chemical or commercial side, or even from the side of old friendships, as it was from the administrative side'. Bayley had added that from the point of the official, this all should not be allowed 'to be swept away' as the importance of these gentlemen planters 'could not be overestimated'. In case they would depart from the region, the 'government would have to increase both its administrative and military machinery in those parts'. This body formed 'a most efficient ready-made organisation, an unpaid administration', ready to the hand of administrators and who 'could be implicitly trusted and who, from their knowledge not only of the people at large but of individuals, could be of more assistance than any imported official machinery'.[561]

Such administrators like Bayley had, therefore, hoped that the application of science and employment of scientists at Pusa would assure that this body of gentlemen planters[562] would stay put in Tirhut. Importantly, however, at the same time that scientists at Pusa had been asked to do indigo research, they and others had also been directed to carry out sugar cane and tobacco research.[563] As it happened, in an order of 1900 by the Department of Revenue and Agriculture of the GoI regarding the legislation for protection of the indigo industry in India, 'grants for loans to planters for the revival of sugar trade of Bihar' were also discussed. In fact, Sir W. B. Hudson, while still an indigo planter in Bihar, himself had asked in a letter to the government for such a simultaneous support. In his letter, Hudson had suggested that 'for permanently improving the present unsatisfactory condition of the industry carried on by indigo planters in Bihar', he wanted to obtain the government 'aid for the purpose of introducing the cultivation and manufacture of sugar'. He defended his request in the following way:

> There are many suggestions as to the form this assistance or protection might take. Many of these may be dismissed as impracticable or as inconsistent with the interest of Government, as the guardian of the subjects of the Empire, generally; but it cannot be said that one of the primary duties of Government as paramount Land lord of the soil of it and dependent in a large measure on the revenue derived from it, is to foster and protect its agricultural products, and all industries on which their welfare and stability immediately depend. I am therefore confident that my subjects will in any case receive attention, and in the similar circumstance perhaps sympathetic consideration.[564]

The latter was indeed the case. The lieutenant governor of Bengal decided that 'the scattered community of English gentlemen has been a source of notable information and help to the administration' and that their 'disappearance would be, in his judgement, a serious political loss'. They had 'embarked a very large amount of English capital in this (indigo) industry', and 'for all these reasons', the lieutenant governor decided that 'any assistance that government could give, either towards improving the method of indigo cultivation and manufacture or in seeking a substitute for it in the shape of other more profitable crops, should certainly be given'. Of these 'more profitable crops' than indigo, many of the gentlemen planters, indeed, chose sugar and received ample government support from 1900 onwards when the lieutenant governor decided that there were 'grounds for believing that it may be possible for the indigo planters of north Bihar to take up the cultivation of the sugar cane and the manufacture of sugar, either growing the cane as a rotation crop in alternate years and keeping up the growth and manufacture of indigo or even abandoning the latter industry altogether for the manufacture of sugar'. The lieutenant governor of Bengal knew that even in the past, English planters in Bihar had made attempts to grow and manufacture sugar, yet the end of these attempts had 'undoubtedly been failure'. But now (1900) the circumstances had changed:

In the first place, as the Government of India are aware there is evidence that there has now grown up amongst the people of this province a considerable demand for the cheaper kinds of refined sugar. Till recently this was supplied by the importation of bounty fed sugar, and it is now being satisfied by larger importations from the Mauritius. Again, in the past, the manufacturers did not possess such machinery for the manufacture of sugar as is now available to diminish the cost of refining while greatly improving the quality of the outturn. Further, in the past, the planter who manufactured sugar was often ruined by the absence of communications. His produce was weighted with freight and transport charges, and he suffered severely from delays in transit. These defects have, through the opening of railways, now to a great extent disappeared.

The lieutenant governor added that there were many other reasons which favoured a revival of the sugar industry. Sugar cane in north Bihar was largely grown by the *raiyats,* where irrigation was rarely required, and as the *gur* produced by these cultivators was said to be in considerable demand for the use in refineries in other parts of India, owing to its superiority for refining purposes, it appeared to the lieutenant governor 'that there is some prospect of making sugar cultivation and manufacture in Bihar a profitable industry'. Importantly, the lieutenant governor decided that since the planting community had large areas of land available for the cultivation of the crop and had already commenced experiments on a small scale with it and since labour, which was so costly in the sugar plantations of Mauritius, was abundant and cheap throughout north Bihar, the planters should be assisted by the government in their efforts to make sugar a profitable industry in Bihar. However, in order to avoid 'mistakes which handicapped the planters in former times', 'further independent enquiry' was necessary.[565] In other words, science had to be applied, and scientists appointed by the government in order to find out what were the 'prospects of making sugar cane cultivation in Bihar a profitable industry'.[566] Thus, colonisation schemes were started, which could 'improve' the quality of *gur* in Bihar.

Moreover, around 1917, when the government had more or less given up on indigo improvement, it was decided to provide full support to experimentation of sugar 'on scientific lines' as, though Bihar and Orissa, Bengal and Assam[567] along with the United Provinces constituted the largest sugar-producing area in British India and 'considering the fact that India was probably the original home of the sugar cane', the sugar industry did not occupy the position which the demands of the country warranted. Facilities for the growth of the sugar cane had already been provided but had to be improved upon as the cultivation of sugar in India had, during the previous thirty years, shown a declining tendency. The explanation given was that this was partly due to 'the absence of scientific and up-to-date methods of cultivation and manufacture'. The decline in 'local cultivation' had been most marked in Bihar and Bengal, but 'the knowledge of the possibilities of India as a sugar-growing country' had led the GoI to devote special attention to the industry, and 'experimental farms and factories' had been, therefore, been established.[568] Indeed, from around 1920 onwards, indigo research at Pusa was more or less abandoned, and scientists concentrated, among others, on sugar cane.[569]

The indigenous sugar industry had to be revived, and the government felt, 'These attempts may not be limited to the encouragement of improved and scientific methods of cultivation and refining'. It was hoped that such methods as well as measures of protection would restore the sugar trade of India to such a position that it will be able to provide the needs of the country and export the surplus. India, 'which once exported sugar to Europe', indeed, became 'a field for European commercial enterprise in the possession of cheap refined sugar',[570] and Bihar became one of its centres, thus revived another project of plant colonisation.

Tobacco Improvement Scheme at Pusa

Meanwhile, tobacco experimentation in Bihar had never stopped. In 1897, the Company of Begg and Dunlop had given up hopes that tobacco in Bihar would ever improve in such a way that it could be used as cigar wrappers or improve the quality of Indian *cheroots*. Yet by the turn of the century, the GoI had renewed expectations of Bihar tobacco. By 1905, when Curzon had opened the Pusa institute, policy makers (still) hoped that they could 'colonise' the 'native tobacco industry', and when growing Chinese sentiment for reform as well as a revival of poppy cultivation in China itself[571] lessened the importance of opium in the GoI's budget and growing anti-opium pressure within England itself, in India,[572] and even from elsewhere[573] contributed to the gradual phasing out of this monopoly,[574] authorities pointed to tobacco as an alternative plant that could possibly replace the poppy as an alternative source of revenue.[575]

What is more, the humble *koeris*, who were known as the 'hereditary high priests of the poppy-cult' in the land of 'the white poppy', as G. Levett-Yeats described in 1897, would now be free to engage himself in 'tobacco improvement'. A centuries old tradition has it that this caste was associated with the farmingprofession and casted its members as 'market-gardeners'. Levett-Yeats had described how 'watched over by Government with a paternal care' this Koeri had 'through hard work', reaped the 'reward of their labour a hundred fold, for they bring in great earthen pots full of opium to the weighing centre every year, and return to their villages rejoicing, with many bright rupees tied up in their waistcloths'.[576]

Even more than the diminishing of importance of the poppy, it was the indigo crisis that made British administrators in England and in India look for alternatives. Rising competition from other colonial powers had urged for decision making. Alfred Lyall, in his overview in 1891 of the *Rise of British Dominion in India,* had already warned that the 'danger' that the British Empire faced was coming not only from within India but also from outside:

> Not only is it certain that Asia lies at the mercy of the military strength of Europe, but in all the departments of thought and action she is far inferior. In these circumstances European civilisation is never likely to suffer a great repulse at the hands of Oriental reaction; and European dominion, once firmly planted in Asia, is not likely to be shaken unless it is supplanted by a stronger European rival. Henceforward the struggle will be, not between East and West, but between the great commercial and conquering nations of the West for predominance in Asia. In this contest I believe the English will hold their ground.[577]

The decision at Pusa favoured tobacco research, and administrators were happy to note findings of scientists who had carried out indigo research at Pusa and who had discovered that instead of impoverishing soils, the growing of indigo actually made the land better fitted not for indigo itself but for growing *rabi* crops such as tobacco. Such scientists had argued that if the British (indigo) planters would rotate indigo with such crops like tobacco, they would come to know that 'indigo refuse is one of the best fertilisers there is'.[578] Such administrators, therefore, ruled that scientists had to carry out the task of research which previously had been assigned to self-made men such as English planters. Yet while earlier only demands from England had determined tobacco experimentation, it was now also 'local demand' that justified new policies in this regard.

Times had changed, and one significant development had been that Indians and only a handful of British within Bengal had, since 1905, argued that 'purely Indian enterprise' financed 'by Indian capital' should get government's attention. Indeed, by the beginning of the twentieth century, the political mood in Bengal had changed drastically. For one, many residing in the country, non-British as well as some British, wanted a fairer deal for India in relation to its 'wealth'. They, in particular, believed that the existing fiscal policy, imposed on India by England, was solely in the interest of the 'motherland'. As a part of so-called *swadeshi* (my own country's products for me), which was reigning in Bengal proper in particular,[579] 'nationalists' not only had proclaimed a boycott against 'foreign goods' like imported liquor, garments, and cigarettes but also argued in favour of protective and even prohibitive duties on all imports from England. Within India, even some English subjects of King Edward, therefore, supported an 'imperial preference' policy. This would be, in their opinion, the only way to 'save the empire' as well as that it would benefit India and Indians. Imperial preference would be beneficial for India, it now was argued, as it stimulated the development of the 'nascent industries' of India.

In these circumstances and as a result of Bengali enterprise, among others, many so-called *swadeshi* firms dealing with cotton goods, drugs, soaps, chemicals, leather goods, shipping, and marches had been started. Importantly, as Amit Bhattacharyya researched between 1900 and 1920, fourteen cigarette and cigar enterprises had also been started mainly in Calcutta but also in Murshidabad and in Rangpur.[580] The GoI believed in the possibilities of a revival of such 'indigenous enterprise' and envisaged the commercial as well as ideological and political benefits of such an endeavour. Though the GoI did not think of an Indian tobacco industry fully managed by Indians, administrators, nevertheless, saw nothing wrong in state promotion of a tobacco industry within India. These English administrators in India felt that tariff reform and imperial preference might enable the Indian government 'to raise more money without appreciably adding to the burdens of the people':

> If England adopts tariff reform, then inclusion of India (as nationalists had campaigned for) is not likely to do it any harm, and may perhaps be of some advantage to it. It would at least go some way to meet the views of the small educated class (the Indian *swadeshi* leaders). Their opinions on the question, if not identical with 'the considered wishes of the Indian peoples', who have never heard of the matter, can no longer be met by a blank refusal to consider it.[581]

In fact, this policy matched the (new) preference in England for 'empire-grown tobacco'. D. H. Moutray Read had defended:

> Turkish, Egyptian, American, Cuban – these we know – but Empire-grown? After some such fashion the matter usually is dismissed by the average stay-at-home Briton. Yet, even after allowance is duly made for the staunch conservatism of the smoker, the very general ignorance of the English public is in this respect surprising, for, let alone that India grows over a million acres yearly, the British Empire has few places where the plant is not raised to some extent, and fewer still where it could not be. Artificial conditions, largely a matter of prejudice moral and financial, are the chief deterrents to its cultivation.

Time had come to start tobacco cultivation afresh, and tobacco growing within the empire, including India, was now stimulated.[582] Yet it was argued that the 'old-fashioned type' of the tobacco industry in India (i.e. *hookah* industry) had to be placed on a new footing, and apart from the sugar industry, as shown above, the tobacco industry was thus yet another 'indigenous enterprise' that could be face-lifted through the appliance of (western) science, manpower, and capital.[583] Durant Beighton, an Indian Civil Service officer, was one such a supporter of protectionism in the case of tobacco in India. Tobacco, he believed, was a plant that could be grown to advantage over a very large area in India, both in the north and in the south and also in Burma. It could be produced at a price that would defy all competition, and the improvements that could be effected in the quality of the Indian product through scientific manufacture and more careful cultivation could and had already produced better tobacco second to none in the world. But for a 'decent treatment' to be accorded to this nascent industry in India, this improved Indian tobacco would even do very well in the export trade which could grow, Beighton speculated, to 'gigantic proportions'.[584]

In 1909, H. B. Lees Smith, professor of public administration and lecturer of economic and political science at Bristol, also had great expectations of Indian tobacco and favoured 'preference'. Yet he felt that there was a want of uniformity and a low grade of the crop, and these facts combined with a heavy duty in European countries on both unmanufactured (raw) tobacco and the finished product had caused the export trade to the UK to remain insignificant. Lees Smith, therefore, aimed at the improvement of tobacco in such a way that it would answer the needs of an expanding home consumption. Yet, like in England, consumption patterns in India, too, had changed. Lees Smith deduced:

> Indians, in many parts, smoke from early youth, but the 'hukka' is gradually being abandoned for cigars and cigarettes. These are imported in great quantities, and the prospects of the Indian tobacco industry depend largely upon its success in taking their place. The exports to Great Britain are, at present insignificant, a fact which is of importance in the discussion of preferences.[585]

Therefore, had a private firm thirty years before (unsuccessfully) attempted to introduce at Pusa the manufacture of improved pipe and cigar tobacco, what authorities even those in England now demanded from scientists was they studied ways in which way to improve tobacco for the use in cigarettes.[586] In order to produce good cigarettes in India, the right type of tobacco leaf had either to be imported or, more economically, to be cultivated within India, and the GoI, therefore, kept on emphasising that improvement of 'native tobacco' through science or the acclimatisation of Virginian tobacco in Indian soil was needed:

Enough has been said to indicate the transitional stage of modern research into tobacco manufacture and the complete lack of knowledge that prevails in India. It is no matter for surprise, therefore, that the Government of India should have deemed a tobacco expert imperatively necessary. Rapid and satisfactory though the progress has been in certain directions of the Indian trade, skilled supervision and definite research locally conducted seems almost certain to effect improvements calculated to place India in the foremost ranks of the tobacco-producing countries of the world.[587]

Engineering Cigarette Tobacco at Pusa

In seventeenth century, Spain considered a 'poor man's cigar', using leftover tobacco from the cigar industry, the spread of (hand-rolled) cigarettes to other countries had been slow but steady.[588] In the UK, cigarette smoking only increased somewhat after the 1850s. Yet the invention of a machine in 1880 by James Albert Bonsack, the son of a plantation owner in the United States, in which shredded tobacco was poured into one end of the machine and a single long tube of paper-covered tobacco came out the other, announced the birth of the 'cigarette century' during which cigarettes' global spread seemed guaranteed. Indeed, by 1910, in the UK and the United States that was, chewing and evening cigar smoking definitely faced a big competing form of tobacco use, namely cigarette smoking.[589]

Interestingly, the imperial *Gazetteer* of India mentioned, in 1908, that there were two tobacco varieties in India. The first one was '*black* [italics added] tobacco', 'used for smoking in the *hukka*'. This tobacco was procured through sun/ground curing. The second tobacco type was 'yellow tobacco, prepared differently'. The result from an alternative curing process was that 'the leaves assume a bright yellow colour'. This had been possible by 'perfecting the native methods of curing and manufacturing tobacco'.[590] With the increased popularity of cigarettes in the UK, the demand for this 'yellow' tobacco leaf had increased considerably there as well as among the Europeans and Indian elites within India. Naturally, therefore, when at Pusa it was decided that the tobacco improvement project should continue, it actually meant that black *deshi* tobacco in Bihar should become 'bright yellow'. In other words, the black-cured tobacco variety that was so much in demand for chewing and *hooka* preparations in Bihar had to be made yellow as it was now perceived by merchants and manufacturers in the UK and the United States alike that a combination of a light golden-coloured leaf grown in a light-coloured soil and the adaption of lighter curing methods were responsible for the 'mild taste' of 'bright tobacco' and made it, therefore, prefect as cigarette filler.[591]

Between 1905 and 1924, tobacco research at the Imperial Institute at Pusa was carried out by two scientists, namely the British (Sir) Albert Howard and his originally German wife Gabrielle Louise Caroline Howard-Matthaei and Kashi Ram, the Indian third assistant to the imperial economic botanist. Albert, son of a farmer in England, had got the charge of the Botanical Section of the Pusa Research Institute and became the 'imperial economic botanist'. He and his wife, who became the second Imperial botanist, stayed at Pusa till 1924. Albert approved of the tobacco project given to him (besides other projects) as he had had 'little time for flora with no economic consequence'.[592] During most of the time that the couple worked for tobacco's improvement in Bihar, they busied themselves with isolating, testing, classifying, and describing the biology of tobacco seeds/plants. In particular, Mrs Howard was occupied with genetic research and methods of inheritance and pollination and used the Mendelian scheme of genetics.[593]

Actually, Mrs Howard had learnt from the failures of experimental work with exotic seeds and experiments with foreign tobacco curing methods that had been carried at the Pusa Model Farm before her time. During those early days of experimentation, it had appeared logical to direct attention to the establishment of practices found successful elsewhere. Mrs Howard soon learnt, however, that this line of advance was not likely to yield fruitful results in Bihar. She, therefore, decided to concentrate on existing tobacco varieties as well as exotic ones and try to improve *deshi* tobacco through hybridisation and cross-fertilisation.

Mr Howard did more 'applied research' and was interested in the introduction of new cultivation methods (such as topping and spiking) and curing practices. Yet like his wife, Albert also recognised soon that he 'was dealing with soils and systems several centuries old' and that research should concern itself more with the existing 'country methods' of curing and improvements on these. At the same time, however, Mr Howard was also interested in marketing issues and believed that in order to be able to compete with 'the highly organised and heavily capitalised American export market', 'local cultivation practices' had to be changed.[594] During his absence in England, Albert had even 'studied the trade requirements for improved Indian wheat and tobacco'.[595] The outcome of their and other tobacco research at Pusa was published in the institute's numerous journals, memoirs, scientific reports, monographs, bulletins, and articles.

In 1910, the Pusa Agricultural Research Institute published the first two out of three huge tobacco studies carried out by the Howards while employed at Pusa.[596] These studies concerned Indian *deshi* tobaccos and emphasised that tobacco 'improvement' also meant adopting the 'right' methods of cultivation and proper curing[597] so as to produce a finished leaf that could be used either as wrapper, filler, or blender in cigarettes.

Figure 18. Furrow irrigation for tobacco as propagated by Scientist Gabrielle Howard at the Imperial Institute of Agricultural Research at Pusa in Bihar (Howard, A. and Howard, G. L. C., 'Studies in Indian Tobaccos. No. 1. The Types of *Nicotiana rustica*, L. Yellow Flowered Tobacco', *Memoirs of the Department of Agriculture in India. Botanitical Series*, Calcutta: Thacker, Spink & Co, Vol. III, No. 1, March 1910, Plate I).

Figure 19. The effect of green manuring with *sann* on tobacco. The plot on the left was green manured with *sann* and the plot on the right with old tobacco leaves and stems. *Memoirs of the Department of Agriculture in India. Botanical Series*, Calcutta: Thacker, Spink & Co, Vol. III, No. 3, April 1910, Plate III.

Figure 20. Pure line culture of *N. tabacum* at Pusa, 1909. (Howard, A. and Howard, G. L. C. 'Studies in Indian Tobaccos. No. 2. The Types of *Nicotiana tabacum*, L.' *Memoirs of the Department of Agriculture in India. Botanical Series*, Calcutta: Thacker, Spink & Co, Vol. III, No. 2, March 1910, Plate II.)

Experimentation with newly compiled tobacco seeds in combination with ground/sun and rack curing, as was the tradition in Bihar, was therefore done and green manure soil treatment was tried. During this period, both 'pure' races of *Nicotiana rustica* or 'yellow-flowered tobaccos of India' as well as *Nicotiana tabacum* or the 'pink-flowered tobacco' were isolated and studied at Pusa, and on that basis, a botanical survey of 'Indian tobaccos' had been compiled by Mrs Howard. The method of growing tobacco by furrow irrigation was also tested and improved upon. Research, furthermore, concentrated on the height of the plant, time of flowering, number of leaves per plant, leaf shape, leaf margin, size, and colour of corolla.[598]

Figure 21. F$_3$ generation of cross type 1 x type 16. (Howard, G. L. C. and Ram, K. 'Studies in Indian Tobaccos. No. 4. Parthenocarpy and parthenogenesis in two varieties of *Nicotiana tabacum* L. – var. Cuba and var. Mirodato. No. 5. The Inheritance of Characters in *Nicotiana rustica* L.' *Memoirs of the Department of Agriculture in India. Botanical Series*, Calcutta: Thacker, Spink & Co. Vol. XIII, No. 1, June 1924, Plate XV.)

In the course of their work, the idea was dispelled that 'variation in type arose with difference in environment, as currently suggested by many American investigators'. Thereafter, Mrs Howard embarked in a project of cross-fertilisation and the 'study of the extension of Mendelian laws to characters not qualitative but recognised by measurement only'. Yet this work consumed too much of their time, and the Howards decided to get involved in more useful work that promised immediate outcomes. 'The most attractive aim' for the Howards perhaps was, Gabriele's sister Louise had written later on, 'the evolution of a good cigarette tobacco'. They could not get good results with 'American varieties' however, and then surprisingly enough, one indigenous variety was isolated which did not, too, badly compare in flavour, texture, and colour – the three important points – with other good cigarette tobaccos. By 1915, this seed was baptised as Pusa 28.[599] Meanwhile, Albert Howard had also decided that the existing curing and cultivation practices of the growers had to be changed as these were 'about the worst possible'. He believed that for cigarette tobacco cultivation, the way tobacco growers looked after their fields was 'particularly defective'.[600]

Seed research continued, however, as even this Pusa type no. 28 'could not be cured to a really bright colour' and possessed 'a flavour which makes it unsuitable for use in any but the lowest grade of cigarettes'.[601] Finally, just before their departure from Pusa in 1924, the Howards found that the 'exotic Adcock leaf' did very well in Bihar, provided that certain relatively simple changes in cultivation methods were adopted. These changes were made after the couple's departure, and one *Pusa Report* mentioned that after more trials with Adcock and Burley, it had been found that 'these exotics can be grown successfully in Bihar and that it may be possible to produce a bright cigarette tobacco with the curing methods devised'.

Encouraged by this result, tobacco research continued, in 1927, and now conducted by F. J. F Shaw and K. Ram, who tried out flue-curing in the newly established barns at Pusa after which research on the ratio of cost to price showed a satisfactory profit to the grower of the improved tobacco. However, after having been manufactured, the cigarettes proved very disappointing in burning and aroma qualities. This was due to the effects of the climate on fermentation processes in Bihar or so it was believed. Next year's batch, however, showed that 'cigarette tobacco leaf of a quality superior to any produced in India before' could be obtained by flue-curing Adcock tobacco, and now special attention was paid to the economics of the flue-curing. By 1930, a kind of tobacco leaf was produced at Pusa that seemed ready for export to England: 'the best we have seen so far of Indian growth, being the nearest approach to the corresponding American type'.[602] The plant's seed was distributed among 'cultivators' (*zamindars* and British planters) around Pusa who surely would make black *deshi* tobaccos yellow bright in Bihar, scientists predicted.

Subsequently, now that scientific research at Pusa had produced the 'right' type of tobacco plant as well as that scientists had shown its 'proper' cultivation and curing methods, it had become time, colonial administrators decided to reflect on its 'takers'. In fact, though the GoI had wholeheartedly supported the tobacco experiments at Pusa, administrators had wondered whether Tirhut itself was ready for it. Science had indeed engineered a tobacco variety of sufficiently high grade for the manufacture of cigarettes yet had also pointed out to policy makers the problem of cultivators' unwillingness to accept this 'improved' tobacco variety in Bihar.[603] Policy makers knew it would be difficult to assist men of science to change the cultivation and curing practices of the 'natives'.[604] Yet they hoped or rather expected private English capitalists would turn their attention to the production of cigarette tobacco, which they now knew could be produced in Bihar if sufficient capital, skill, and organised labour were utilised in a scientific manner.[605] As the 'gentlemen planters' faced an acute crisis in the indigo industry, it appeared to the government there was no want of 'trusted leaders of industry, of trained managers, and of efficient workmen' who would direct this nascent industry in Tirhut.[606]

CHAPTER SIX

Cigarette Tobacco in Bihar
till the Early 1920s

Though from 1905 to 1920 tobacco colonisation was accompanied by other plant colonisation schemes, in particular that of indigo and sugar cane, tobacco improvement was a most important point on the agenda of empire builders. Pusa in Tirhut had been selected as the central stage where such an improvement had to happen. As shown in Chapter Five, 'improvement' actually meant the engineering of cigarette tobacco, which scientists had indeed faithfully generated. We, therefore, could call the period between 1905 and 1920 'the cigarette age of Bihar'. Not only scientists at Pusa were required to engage themselves in tobacco improvement, however. Along with them, private capitalists – in particular indigo planters – as well as *zamindars* and (other) tobacco cultivators were expected to collaborate with state authorities to make this tobacco endeavour work. However, in this chapter, I show that rather than indigo planters, another category of private capitalists took the lead. In 1902, two of the biggest tobacco firms in the world, the American Tobacco Company and Imperial (encompassing Great Britain and Ireland), had agreed to end their decade-long price wars. Under the terms of an agreement, the companies decided to utilise each other's brands in their exclusive areas of dominance and had set up a third entity called British American Tobacco (BAT) to handle trade outside the UK and the United States. Apart from being active in other countries like China, India during the first two decades of the twentieth century, it had been Bihar that became a prominent centre in which

BAT concentrated its activities. As detailed in this chapter, between 1905 and 1920, in Tirhut, a quadruple, that is the government, scientists, British private capitalists (including BAT and indigo planters) as well as the Indian tobacco cultivators (including *zamindars* and other 'cultivators' in Bihar), now collaborated in a bit to make the tobacco improvement project successful in Bihar, that is to spread the taste for cigarette tobacco and its cultivation.

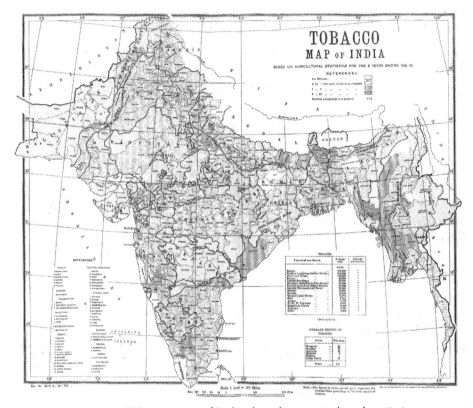

Figure 22. Tobacco map of India, based on agricultural statistics for the five years ending 1918–19. (Commercial Intelligence Department (Calcutta), Calcutta: Government Printing, 1923, courtesy Forum Library (Special Collections), Wageningen University, The Netherlands.)

Deshi (Country) Tobacco among Other Plants in Tajpur/Samastipur (Bihar)

Colonial authorities had selected Tajpur, encompassing, among others, Pusa, as centre of tobacco improvement activities. The Tajpur subdivision of Darbhanga District now is part of the separate Samastipur District.[607] The region displayed a great alluvial plain with rivers (i.e. the Ganges, the Little and Great Gandak, and the Kamla-Tiljuga groups of rivers) flowing on raised beds.[608] It was rich in all sorts of crops, mainly rice but also bamboos, groves of mangos, and *sisu*. The Little Gandak had been an important local transport river that connected Champaran, Muzaffarpur, Darbhanga, and north Monghyr with many large bazaars and marts on its banks and was navigable practically throughout the year for country boats of fair size. It entered Darbhanga near Pusa, and its offshoots reached Monghyr, Muzaffarpur, Bhagalpur, Hajipur, Patna, and Nepal. Yet around 1907, its importance was somewhat diminished due to the railway that had been constructed. It was a level plain but with a belt of fairly highland along the bank of the Ganges in particular. The alluvial soil contained saltpeter and some limestone. There also was dense submontane forest, and there were 'open park-like jungle' and 'flexible bushes' with tigers, deer, gazelles, and 'small game'. A great part was under cultivation around 1907, yet the density of population in those parts was very high. 'So close, in consequence, is the tilth that', it was explained in the *District Gazetteer of 1907*, 'throughout whole districts field is conterminous with field, and the cultivated land abuts so closely on wayside and watercourse as to leave no foothold for those species that form the roadside hedges and fill the weedy waste places so characteristic of Lower Bengal'.[609] Yet in some areas, there was plenty of 'field weeds' such as *Indigofera*. There were many lakes but regular floods too, and the region was earthquake prone.

The region featured low-lying lands fertilised by silt deposits of rivers as well as uplands. Uplands were supposed to be most fertile and especially fitted for the production of 'cold weather' or *rabi* crops (such as tobacco and poppy), crops harvested in spring, and *bhadoi* crops (such as indigo) reaped in August–September. Other *rabi* crops such as wheat, barley, *arhar (dal)*, oats, other pulses, oilseeds, and edible roots also grew well on such lands. The main food crop was rice (mainly an *aghani* or winter crop) that because of the 'teeming population' depended mainly on the soil for its subsistence. O'Malley of the Indian Civil Service had remarked in his *Gazetteer of 1907* that the area which could be devoted to such crops was, therefore, necessarily limited, and he had added that 'as it is, a considerable proportion of the area is given up to indigo raised by European capitalists'. Apart from indigo, which O'Malley still considered the 'most valuable of all the food crops', in 1907, sugar cane was defined by him as the second most important 'non-food crop'. He also remarked that the cultivation of sugar cane had been extended of late, owing to the decline of indigo:

> In earlier days the cultivation of sugar-cane was very considerable, and it is a somewhat remarkable fact that many indigo concerns were originally started as sugar factories, the manufactures of sugar being given up when indigo proved to be more profitable. The reverse process is now taking place, as indigo is in many places being replaced by sugarcane; and the area under the latter is steadily expanding.[610]

After sugar cane came poppy, in this government official's view, as a non-food crop of great importance as though the area occupied by it (12,180 acres) was not large, the price obtained for the crude opium rendered it a 'valuable crop'. As mentioned before, (the production of) opium was a government monopoly, and no person was allowed to grow poppy except on account of government. The best soil for poppy was loam, so situated that it could be highly manured and easily irrigated, and for this reason, homestead land was generally selected. Yet like indigo, O'Malley had noted in 1907:

> There is a tendency for the cultivation of poppy to decrease, as year by year it is becoming less profitable to the ryots. The plant is delicate; a thoroughly favourable year come only at uncertain intervals; and the cultivators have had to contend with a number of bad seasons. There is accordingly a marked tendency to withdraw from an industry so precarious and to substitute the more robust cereals or such paying crops as sugarcane, potatoes, chillies and vegetables. This movement has been quickened by the fact that the value of cereals has increased of recent years, while the price paid for the crude drug remains stationary.[611]

Oilseeds were also considered 'very important', but it was unusual for them to be sown singly, and they usually were mixed with other *rabi* crops such as tobacco, which came next in importance in the government's opinion. This Indian Civil Servant even suggested that for the 'native' cultivators, the cultivation of tobacco was very profitable. Tobacco occupied 17,400 acres or 1.12 of the net cropped area in 1907, and O'Malley described:

> It is grown on an appreciable scale only in some limited tracts on the borders of Darbhanga, *but the high price obtained for the produce makes it a very valuable crop, to which the cultivators look to pay their rents, clear off their debts and obtain a few luxuries* [emphasis added]. The fame of the tobacco of *pargana* Saraisa, in which these tracts fall, has spread far beyond the limits of North Bihar, and purchasers come from distant districts every year and buy large quantities of it. It is largely consumed also in the district, being either smoked in *hookahs* or chewed with a little lime.[612]

The *Darbhanga District Gazetteer* of 1907 also informed that 'non-food crops' predominated in the Samastipur subdivision, which at the time was part of the Darbhanga District and where they occupied 22 per cent of the total cropped area, whereas in the other two subdivisions, this was only 14 per cent. It was furthermore recorded that in Samastipur, the major portion of this large non-food crop area was devoted to indigo and tobacco and described as 'two very valuable crops, which are unimportant elsewhere'. 'On the other hand, the area under sugar cane is mainly found in the north of the district, particularly in the Madhubani subdivision, where it has recently been substituted largely for indigo'. But, as whole, the *Gazetteer* concluded that 'the more valuable non-food crops are grown mainly in the Samastipur subdivision'. In Samastipur, tobacco, thus, occupied a 'large area' (29,800 acres) and was 'probably the most paying crop in the district' as far as the villagers were concerned:

> Five-sevenths of the total area is found in the Samastipur and Dalsingh Sarai thanas, and most of the rest is in Warisnagar and Benipati. The latter, though mainly a rice-growing tract like the rest of Madhubani, contains a considerable stretch of high land which is used for more valuable *rabi* crops.[613]

Though as detailed before, tobacco was not 'native' to the soils of Bihar; during the 1870s and 1880s, the tobacco that was found in this region had appeared as *deshi* or 'country tobacco' in the various British reports and treatises on tobacco published in Bengal as well as in Britain around that time.[614] After a presentation of a voluminous paper on tobacco in India by J. E. O'Connor, presented to the House of Common, Britain, an inventory of the prevalent cultivation and curing of tobacco in various districts in Bengal was published in 1874 under the aegis of the GoI. Tobacco cultivation was found in almost every district of Bengal (Bihar included).[615] S. C. Bayley, commissioner of Patna, had reported to the secretary of the government of Bengal that the Bihar division possessed numerous varieties with each region having its local name for a particular type of tobacco. However, in Tirhut, it was generally known as 'desi tobacco' according to Bayley.[616]

This 'desi tobacco' was then compared with tobacco elsewhere in Bihar that had already been subjected to improvement efforts by these indigo planters. In the above-mentioned paper on tobacco in India, O'Connor did, for instance, quote an indigo-concern manager in the *Sarun* (Saran) region of Bihar who had reported on 'exotic' tobacco seed trials with 'Virginia and Havannah', which had failed as the 'natives' had said that 'the flavour was much stronger than the common *dési* tobacco' and therefore refused to buy it. O'Connor did, however, not go much into the details of local appellation and divided 'Indian tobaccos', also described by him, as 'indigenous tobacco' according to their regional origin. Accordingly, there was 'Bengal', 'Guzerat', and 'Madras' tobaccos, and so on. The 'Behar' tobacco was again categorised on regional basis, and accordingly, '*Tirhut* tobacco' received a few special paragraphs.[617]

A decade later, (Sir) George Abraham Grierson, fellow of the University of Calcutta at the time, specified the tobacco found in Tirhut as '*Nicotiana tabacum*' and said the locals called it *tamaku* or *tamakul*. According to Grierson, only the variety found in north-east Tirhut was known as *desi* or *barki* tobacco, whereas in Champaran and north-west Tirhut, it was called *bilaeti* or *kalkatiya*. In his book *The Bihar Peasant* of 1885, he also mentioned that Bihar possessed a third tobacco variety known as *jethua*, which was sown in January–February and cut in *jeth* (May–June).[618]

Around this time and ignoring all these local appellations, colonial categorisation increasingly divided various tobacco types in northern India (including the north-western provinces and Oudh) into two groups: (1) those plants grown from 'exotic' seed (imported from outside India, the '*bilaeti*', or from Kolkata, the *kalkatiya*) and (2) those plants grown from 'local seed' ('*deshi*').[619] Moreover, at that point of time, the difference between the two varieties was regarding taste, with 'country' (i.e. local) tobaccos found to be less strong than the exotic. In 1881, J. R. Reid had written, for instance:

> Two kinds of tobacco are cultivated in Azamgarh – the *desi* and the *vilayati*: and of the former there are two varieties. The *vilayati* is of recent introduction, having come into the district from the eastward. [. . .] but neither of the desi varieties is so pungent as the vilayati. That is too strong for some native smokers, and has to be mixed with the desi. It is said not to keep so well in the manufactured state as the desi.[620]

Indigenous tobacco appellations, thus, were on their way out, and what remained by the beginning of the twentieth century was colonial botanical knowledge which set '*deshi*' against 'exotic'/'foreign' tobacco. Sir George Watt, member of the Royal Horticulture Society of England and former professor of botany at Calcutta, in his momentous work on the commercial products of India, for instance, believed, in 1908, that the tobacco commonly produced and cured by the 'natives of India' was of two types: one was known as *deshi* and the other as *vilayati* (foreign). Importantly, the colour of the tobacco leaf did not figure in his chapter on tobaccos in India.[621] Yet, though taste, thus, was an important way to categorise and value *deshi* (country or 'native') and *vilayati* (foreign) tobacco during the last quarter of the nineteenth century, 'indigenous' tobacco in India had also been classified on basis of its uses and the two had been connected. Accordingly, Grierson had divided *tamaku* into chewing tobacco (*khaini, surti,* or in Patna *dokhta*), snuff (*nas*), and smoking tobacco (*piani*), which again was subdivided into many local varieties with different tastes, smells, and make-up.

During the latter part of the nineteenth century, the 'germ theory of infection' had changed the course of chewing in other countries. This public outcry had made chewing tobacco a socially unacceptable behaviour and even unlawful in some of US cities.[622] Yet this had had no impact in Bihar. Chewing tobacco there possessed great sociocultural value, and some people had called it *kal jug ke amrit* or the ambrosia of the *kali* age. In fact, the older practice of consuming betel quid had accommodated tobacco, and so-called *paan*, as it was locally known then as well as now, was commonly prepared consisting of betel leaf, areca nut, slaked lime, and tobacco. Various other tobacco preparations were also used in unprocessed, processed, and manufactured forms. Tobacco was, for instance, used raw, sundried or in roasted form, finely chopped or powdered, and scented. Alternatively, tobacco was boiled, made into a paste, and scented with rosewater or perfume, the final product placed in the mouth and chewed.[623] Grierson had provided one example of the many proverbs on chewing tobacco that according to him existed in late nineteenth-century Bihar. It was about a man who had mixed tobacco with lime (for chewing) and had offered this mixture to others without having been asked even. By this virtuous act, people said this man surely would conquer 'heaven, earth, and the lower regions' (gain immortality).[624]

The *biri* (hand-rolled 'Indian cigarette'[625]) had also existed as one 'Hindoo', describing 'native' ways of tobacco use in India, had mentioned in 1888 that 'some improvise a cigar by rolling the green leaf of a tree into the form of a cone and filing it with tobacco'.[626] But as explained later on, in Bihar *biri* smoking became really only popular during the 1920s. In fact, after around 1860, oral uses of smokeless tobacco became more popular than smoking tobacco in *hookahs*, a consumption pattern that even more reduced during the twentieth century to be replaced during the 1920s and 1930s by *biri* smoking. At the same time, the oral intake of tobacco remained, and by 1950, Bihar was not only identified as a 'chewing and *hookah*-producing state in India' but also associated with *khaini* (raw chewing tobacco) consumption and *biri* smoking.

Even by the early 1870s, some of the *deshi* tobacco found in Bihar and used in *hookahs* and for chewing was still praised for its excellent yields and taste. Mr Wace, a district officer, in a report submitted to F. M. Halliday, collector of Tirhut, mentioned that he had been informed that 'the tobacco of the Sereyasa pergunnah is considered better than of those surrounding, and is, I am informed, famed throughout India. The soil of the villages bordering on the Gunduk is considered to be especially suitable for tobacco cultivation'.[627] Nevertheless, by the beginning of the twentieth century, it was this 'valuable tobacco plant' and its cultivation and curing methods that had to be 'improved' upon as colonial authorities had deemed that this country tobacco was not suitable as filler in the newly manufactured 'little white salver',[628] that is, the cigarette. The London markets now demanded cigarette tobacco, and authorities even hoped that once improved, this *deshi* tobacco of Tajpur could also be used for the manufacture of cheap cigarettes within India.

Zamindars and Tobacco Cultivators in Tajpur

Though British self-proclaimed and professional botanists had termed the tobacco cultivated in the Tajpur region of Bihar as 'country' tobacco, generally tobacco growing, it must be realised, could only have been an option for the somewhat better-off tenants or the small *zamindars,* thus 'people with a little money to invest'.[629] Tobacco, like poppy, needed first-class highlands close to the village as well as an irrigation source. Yet tenants or proprietors of such high-lying lands had to pay high rents/revenue too. Importantly, rates of rent in Bihar varied not only according to the character and situation of land but also according to the caste and position of the cultivator. Thus, a high-caste man paid less than a lower-caste man, for instance.[630] Though many others must have been involved in its cultivation as (landless) labourers or otherwise, only intermediate agricultural caste groups such as *koeris/koiris* (in Bihar also known as *kushwahas),*[631] *goalas* and in stray cases *kurmis* as well as a few better-off Muslim *raiyats* (*sheikhs* or *jeths*) along with the upper-caste *babhans* or *bhumihars*[632] were involved in decisions regarding tobacco growing in Bihar.[633] Most of them were, however – like the indigo 'planters' – not directly involved in the cultivation process, and though most cultivators used family labour, such *zamindars* hired lower-caste landless labourers (*coolies*) from the neighbourhood to carry out the actual cultivation work and lower castes to do the harvesting of the crop.

Colonial accounts confirm that, in particular, *babhans* and *koeris* had taken to tobacco growing. The former was the most numerous of so-called intermediate castes in Bihar with a lower ritual/social status than *brahmans* or *rajputs* but enjoying a higher rank than the *sudra* castes. These *babhans* or *bhumihars* were found in great numbers in south-east Tirhut and the adjacent district of Monghyr.[634] Importantly, officer Wace had added in his report of 1873 that the tobacco crop was often sold standing as 'may readily be imagined, Babhuns and others do not care to undertake the constant tending of the plants after they are cut [. . .] and sell the crop off as it stands to some koeri or hardworking man, at rates varying from Rs. 2 to Rs. 4 per cottah'. But Wace had added that 'the best quality could fetch from Rs. 5 per maund'.

Though, the price had hardly been constant as could have been expected 'from there being such a large demand for the article'.[635]

During the nineteenth century, over a million of *raiyats* had received government licenses to grow poppy with intensive cropping techniques each year on lands totalling 500,000 acres or more in Bihar.[636] The organisation of the opium monopoly had been supervised by the Benares and Patna Opium Agencies.

The latter consisted of eleven subagencies of which one was Tirhut. Nearly all the *raiyats* who cultivated poppy for the colonial government had been *koeris* – those under the Patna Agency at least – who were said to have had specialised in intensive market garden and irrigated cultivation of high-value cash crops. The *koeris* were *sudras* and not of so-called high ritual status,[637] but high rates of savings seemed to have enabled a number of them to purchase lands and become revenue-paying proprietors for either all or part of the lands which they used. Based on stereotypes that suited the British[638] but also on the fact that such caste groups paid higher revenues,[639] these *koeris* had thus been qualified as 'worthy' cultivators of poppy by the British, and it was maintained that they could be distinguished from other cultivating castes such as the *kurmis* by their skill in rearing tobacco, poppy, and other special produce requiring more careful cultivation than the staple crops.

What is more, this stereotyping had become a self-fulfilling prophecy it seemed, and the peasant castes most closely associated with poppy cultivation had indeed been the *koeris* in Bihar, according to most scholars. The members of this caste had acquired poppy licenses, access to plots of the first-quality loam of village lands, and access to water for irrigation. Apart from poppy cultivation, another specialty of this caste, supposedly, was tobacco cultivation, and it was in particular members of this caste – though not all of them and not only *koeries* – who had turned to (even more) tobacco cultivation in 1911–12 with the abolition of the Opium Department in Bihar, though some also had 'chosen' indigo in exchange for poppy cultivation.[640] Significantly, the *First Report of the Royal Commission on Opium* reported that during the early 1890s, the cultivation of poppy in the region was not widely practised, 'its place being taken by its rival, tobacco'.[641]

Peter Robb reminds us that cultivators' crop choices take place within a value system and that crops are part of a social as well as an economic hierarchy.

For instance, according to Robb, rice was associated with power in the land, and its numerous varieties compared with the clans of the Rajputs or the *babhans*, the dominant castes. Yet millets were associated with poverty and lowliness. Robb argued that the value attached by many a *raiyat* to plants such as poppy and indigo was 'subjection', and he offered the example of poppy. Yet Robb qualified that this 'subjection' in the case of poppy was not absolute and not directly related to the opium department. This 'subjection' was also not uniform, and mounting protest against, for instance, poppy chiefly reflected the extent to which 'opium was less advantageous to the khatadar than other crops'.[642] Robb added that the same arguments could be made about the opposition to indigo cultivation in Champaran in Bihar which had culminated in Gandhi's intervention in 1917.[643] Robb concluded that 'if food were a major and visible illustration of status, cropping decisions could hardly be socially neutral or easily imposed by outsiders'.[644]

Like sugar cultivation in colonial Bihar, as Robb elsewhere described, and unlike poppy, tobacco, around 1905, was neither a monopoly nor a product manufactured wholly by modern factory methods and for export, like *indigo*. Like sugar, tobacco, too, was grown on a large number of small holdings, 'within', as Robb explained in the case of sugar cultivation, 'a complex system of indebtedness and dependence' and to 'benefit the profits of intermediaries'.[645] In other words, though tobacco, around 1905, could still be considered a 'native' or 'uncolonised' plant (and thus was considered an 'own crop'), it was not free from an association with 'subjection' for many.[646]

This truth should be kept in mind. Yet I nevertheless argue that around 1905, when scientists started their colonising activities at Pusa, 'cultivators' in Tajpur (including *zamindars*) attached a different value to indigo and poppy on the hand and sugar cane and tobacco on the other. Around that time, the former two were associated with the Raj and seen as 'colonised' plants manufactured into commodities that were in demand in England and not locally consumed. In marked contrast stood sugar cane that was still valued as an 'indigenous' plant, though (revived) attempts to 'colonise' this plant, too, had started around 1900, as will be shown in more detail in the last chapter.

The same applied to the tobacco plant in Tirhut. *Zamindars* and richer tenants such as *koeris* involved in tobacco cultivation considered tobacco as a 'native' crop. What is more, even the colonial administration attached this value to the tobacco plant in Tirhut. Though, this did not mean, it again should be emphasised, that tobacco cultivation was free from exploitation.[647] The challenge before the authorities, therefore, was to get the collaboration of *zamindars* and the richer tenants such as *koeris* so that 'country tobacco' would change into a 'foreign' commodity, that is cigarettes through the use of foreign science that would alter the cultivation and curing methods now applied for the 'native' product.

Hugh Martin Leake and Hesitation among Planters to Experiment with Other Plants

Authorities had also looked upon indigo planters as collaborators in their tobacco improvement venture. In his stirring *Indigo Plantations and Science in Colonial India,* Prakash Kumar described how the 'indigo culture' in Bihar became more 'modern', 'science-based', and 'expert-driven'. In fact, when a cheaper and purer synthetic indigo had become available by 1897, the planters had themselves supported, albeit a little late, the establishment of laboratories to find ways to cheapen the cost of indigo manufacture and improve the quality of the blue dye produced in Bihar.[648] In its turn, the government had sponsored research by scientists at Pusa into plants capable to produce indigo. By 1913, the Bihar Indigo Planters' Association had, for instance, spent eight *lakhs* of rupees on research work carried out by Messrs. Rawson and Bergtheil, and although the planters did not feel that these scientists had succeeded 'in obtaining any important results', their labours, nevertheless, had 'guided the industry in its effort to reduce the cost of production'.[649] Moreover, these scientists had been very sincere workers for 'the cause' of these indigo planters. From their side, too, planters had put trust in these scientists and had even established the Indigo Defence Association in 1898, which reflected, according to Prakash Kumar, 'the planters' desire to elicit pertinent information and develop the ability to intervene directly in the key London market in the face of synthetic's threat'. What is more, this company had been mandated to initiate scientific investigations, to buy patents relating to improvement, and to pursue matters of interest with the national government.[650]

Apart from tobacco improvement, scientist at Pusa, Albert Howard, had also been requested to undertake indigo research. Consequently, he had, for instance, tried to solve the problem of paucity of seeds attacked by wilt disease in Bihar. Howard's operation at two government farms at Pusa and Dholi had resulted in the procurement of a huge amount of seeds, though he had not been able to accurately pinpoint the root cause of wilt. Instead, he recommended better cultivation practices as well as proper drainage of the soil through the 'Pusa method of drainage', which, in fact, had been developed during his tobacco research at Pusa. His advice did not solve the problem, however, and though the Bihar Planters' Association had given its full backing to biological experimentation, it did not offer immediate results that the planters could apply. Nevertheless, planters had been grateful to Howard that he had solved their immediate problem of seeds.[651] As far as Howard was concerned, he had considered this indigo experimentation 'useful' as it had enabled him to experiment with the 'selection method' for the improvement of plants in general.[652]

Not all scientists who had been called upon to work for the indigo planters and help them to 'save' the industry were liked by the planters, however, and the dislike was mutual in the case of, for instance, Dr Hugh Martin Leake, Albert Howard's close friend. Leake had been called upon to help the planters even before the Pusa Institute had been established. However, not only he appeared to have been quite cynical regarding the task at hand, but also he actually did express not much of willingness to help these private capitalists in Tirhut with their indigo problems. After his graduation as biologist from Cambridge in 1900, Leake had come to India to work for the Bihar Indigo Planters' Association which he, indeed, did from 1901 to 1904. Reflecting on this time, Leake wrote much later in life in *An Historical Memoir of the Indigo Industry of Bihar*:

> A certain sympathy must be extended to a community which, brought up in the assurance that its source of income was unassailable, suddenly finds that source so rapidly eroded that mental adjustment to the new conditions is impossible. That was the position in which the indigo community found itself. It had adapted itself to a life of sport with frequent visits to England and well-lined pockets. It was the victim, too, of that human weakness which makes no provision for the rainy day so long as the sun continues to shine.[653]

First of all, Leake felt that the planters could have foreseen 'the blow which hit the industry' as the chemical methods by which indigo could be produced had been but in the final stage in 1880 already. Under such circumstances, the indigo planters had had two alternatives: (1) to attempt to restore the indigo industry or (2) to seek an alternative source of income in a change of crop, such as sugar cane or tobacco. Leake thought that the first alternative which most of the planters had initially preferred was a 'foredoomed course' however. He rather supported the second alternative that urged the planters to exchange indigo for tobacco or sugar cane. Nevertheless, when planters had asked for a biologist – not a chemist – to help them to save the industry, Leake had applied for the post as after having spent a year on research under the professor of botany, Marshall Ward in England, he had 'come to realise that it was time to think of earning a living'.[654] Leake remembered much later in life:

> Learning of the post of Biologist to the Bihar Indigo Planters' Association I submitted an application only to receive the reply that the post was already filled. Little more than a month later, a further letter came, asking if I was still available as their nominee had died of cholera on arrival. As I had close connections with India – my grandfather had commanded the Punjab army in pre-mutiny days and several of my relations were still serving in India – that did not worry me and I accepted. I arrived at Mozuffarpur, the Head Quarters of the Indigo Planters' Association in the late autumn of 1901. The President was away and no planter had been detailed to meet me but a room had been booked for me in the Planters' Club and I spent several days in the verandah studying the planters, whom I can only describe as a very disgruntled body, and gathering what little information I was able about my future position.

Later on, Leake met the president, however, but the latter had not had the slightest idea about 'the function of a biologist'. Even when at the planters' research station at Sirsiah, Leake remembered he had not done much more than 'rough shooting' along with the planters. Yet he had become restless, and then he discovered that there was another research station at Dalsingh Sarai 'which was financed by a group of Calcutta businessmen interested in the indigo trade' (i.e. Begg Sutherland and Company, which had also had its stint in tobacco experimentation at the Pusa Model Farm as shown). The president of the Planters' Association readily had agreed that Leake would go there as 'here was a nuisance to be got rid of as soon as possible'. Leake had been much happier with the 'atmosphere' in Dalsingh Sarai, where the planter B. Coventry had been in charge at the time and who, 'though completely lacking in scientific training', had been 'a real live wire'. Coventry's 'receptive mind' had given the biologist 'a free hand', and this is what Leake seemed to have been looking for. Along with a planter named C. W. Spencer, who had been in charge of the outwork, Leake had started his research buying a pony and riding around with Spencer on some of his morning trips, a thing he had never done before. He thus embarked on his 'programme of biological research'.

Yet as he realised after some time, the planters had refused to pay him as 'I had broken my agreement – the nature of the break was not mentioned'. It was then that Leake had severed his connection with the Planters' Association at Sirsiah and entered in a new agreement with 'Coventry's group' in the Pemberandah/Dalsingh Sarai research station, which had been administered by the Agricultural Department and received a Bengal government's grant. In due course of time, the research carried out at this station had become part of the 'more grandiose scheme', that is implied though the Imperial Agricultural Research Institute of Viceroy Lord Curzon which had been under the control of Central Government at Pusa and where, incidentally, Conventry had become its first director. Leake had been offered a position at the Pusa Institute, too, but by that time, Leake wrote, 'It had already become clear that the indigo industry could not be saved', and he decided to leave India in 1904. Leake had been satisfied with this decision as after his departure 'the indigo industry came to play a smaller and smaller role until, like the Bellman's nephew in the *Hunting of the Snark,* it softly and silently vanished away'.[655]

Yet this had not at all been the end of Leake's career in British India as in the same year he had joined the Indian Agricultural Service and was posted as garden-in-charge at Saharanpur, in present-day Uttar Pradesh. He later on became the head of the Botany Section of the research station there and thereafter till 1915 the economic botanist and geneticist of the United Provinces. Between 1915 and 1919, he was the principal of the Cawnpore Agricultural College and director of Agriculture of the United Provinces in Lucknow between 1919 and 1923. During his second stint in British India, Leake made a 'significant contribution to agriculture science in India' by improving poppy and cotton plants through genetical means.[656] It was with these plants that Leake found his academic freedom at last. In the United Provinces, Leake had also been allowed to appoint his own staff, and he selected two Indian assistants: Sri Ram Prasad Singh and Mune Ki Kabir Khan. The former had been selected by him, 'less on account of his practical knowledge but because of his high standard of intelligence' and the latter 'as one with a good knowledge of agricultural procedure'. What is more, in the United Provinces, Leake did not have to do indigo research which he always had considered 'a futile business'.[657] Instead, he conducted research with wheat plants which had made him feel very 'useful'.[658]

Yet though Leake had expressed minimal interest in indigo research, he had not disliked all indigo planters though as his friendship with Conventry indicates. Leake had, however, not been surprised that these planters had taken no action after he had presented his research findings in a meeting before the Bihar Planters' Association as this 'probably' was 'because it was envisaged that the death of the indigo industry was inevitable'.[659] His main problem had been with planters in Bihar who – unlike him – stuck to indigo (only) and had been unwilling to change crops or experiment with other plants along with indigo. Leake had also been highly disappointed when he experienced that these planters did not pay attention to one of his research outcomes which actually 'has left an enduring impression' and which is an aspect 'even now (1975) overlooked'. In his *Memoir*, Leake had detailed:

> I will draw special attention to it. The residues of the fermentation vats – 'seet' as they were called – was spread onto the land and worked into the soil. It was really amazing the health and vigour of the subsequent crop of whatever nature it was. It was a striking example of the importance of the role played by humus and the micro-flora of the soil – a lesson our agricultural institutions, brought up on NPK theory, have not fully learned.[660]

This finding, Leake had emphasised, should have even more pushed planters into shifts away from indigo only and to the inclusion of tobacco or sugar cane cultivation in Tirhut along with some indigo cultivation for the production of *seet*.

The British American Tobacco Corporation in Bihar

By 1907, the imperial tobacco improvement scheme had all been set in place at Pusa. The Imperial Institute had selected tobacco as an important economic plant, and scientists had been appointed to carry out tobacco research. Furthermore, government officials had encouraged private capitalists such as the English indigo planters to experiment with (new) tobacco seeds, provide capital and also 'manpower' as managers and supervisors of Indian cultivators. In this way, authorities had envisaged that these planters could act as intermediaries between (government) scientists and cultivators and actually 'teach' the latter how to 'improve' tobacco. The desired outcome was 'empire tobacco' that included a cheap cigarette tobacco variety that suited the local Indian market. Clearly, therefore, the task at hand was the colonisation of the whole indigenous tobacco industry (including now manufacture too) on modern scientific lines for the sake of empire, India now included.

Yet still too busy with rescuing 'their' indigo or with new sugar cane experiments initially, neither were many planters interested in the findings of scientists such as Leake's, who had pointed to the use of indigo *seet* for improved tobacco cultivation nor those of the Howards and their research into cigarette tobacco and tobacco diseases. The government could not induce them to invest much capital in tobacco improvement. Instead, an altogether different private capitalist had entered Bihar, who welcomed scientists' tobacco research as well as government's imperial tobacco improvement scheme. Speaking of the 'modern cigarette trade', J. E. O'Connor had observed in 1903 that within the last three or four years,

> a singular modification of popular taste has been witnessed, one which hardly have been possible in such a country and amongst such a people. Some enterprising firms in Europe thought they saw an opening in India for the Native consumption of American tobacco in cigarettes in supersession of the *hookah* (or water-pipe) still commonly used by the people. Acting on this idea they imported cigarettes in increasing quantity at lower rates bringing them within the reach of the masses, and in a very short time the arrangements made for bringing the cigarettes within the easy reach of the consumer had a very manifest effect.

O'Connor had wondered, however, 'why should the supply of these things (cigarettes) be allowed to come from abroad?'[661] Indeed, this 'enterprising firm in Europe' had also spotted the opening in Bihar. Though as detailed in the previous chapter, the period between 1905 and 1914 saw the rise of some indigenous or Indian-managed cigarette factories in Bengal (proper),[662] no such *swadeshi* enterprises had been started in Bihar. There, instead, a British American 'enterprising firm' made a niche for itself. The British American Tobacco Company under the name of 'Imperial Tobacco Company of India Limited' (ITC) had started first in a leased office in Kolkata. This remained the centre of the company's existence till 1926 when the company bought a plot of land and established 'Virginia House', which became one of Kolkata's most venerated landmarks. ITC thus was a BAT affiliate,[663] and from trading, it had quickly graduated to manufacturing of cigarettes, setting up a cigarette factory at Monghyr[664] in Bihar in 1907 through 'Peninsular Tobacco'.

Figure 23. ITC in 2011 in Munger (previously Monghyr). No permission to enter its premises. Photograph by Masoom Reza.

Figure 24. Indian Leaf Development Company, Ltd. Taken from Playne, *Bengal and Assam, Behar and Orissa,* 1917, p. 350 (courtesy New Delhi: Asian Educational Services).

The company also pioneered in the cultivation and development of leaf tobaccos in India through its Indian Leaf Tobacco Development Co. (ILTDC). Significantly, once the ITC had taken the lead, planters had also come forward, and in fact, the two groups of private capitalists mingled well in the end. In fact, most of the British and American ITC employees also became Bihar Light Horse members. Some ex-indigo planters even became ITC employees.

Through its various business houses and factories, ITC limited now (2014)[665] is the largest buyer, processor, and exporter of leaf tobaccos in India, serving customers in forty-eight countries across more than sixty-nine destinations. It buys nearly 50 per cent of all tobacco types grown in India. ITC possesses green leaf processing plants at Chirala and Anaparti in Andhra Pradesh, which now can be said to be the 'tobacco hub' of India where it links cultivators to the global market.[666] This shifting focus from Bihar in northern India to the state of Andhra Pradesh in southern India is followed and explained in the next chapter. Yet during the period from 1910 to around 1920, Bihar was the centre of ITC's activities when it still was known as the ITC and Peninsular Tobacco in Bihar.

In September 1902, two of the biggest tobacco firms in the world, the American Tobacco Company and Imperial (Great Britain and Ireland), had agreed to end their decade-long price wars across the Atlantic on each other's soils, which had been eroding each other's margins. Under the terms of an agreement, the companies decided to utilise each other's brands in their exclusive areas of dominance and had set up a third entity called BAT to handle trade outside the UK and the United States.[667] Compelled by the terms of its constitution, BAT quickly began to explore world markets, and as Howard Cox unearthed, although the company supported the growing of tobacco in other parts of its international organisation, notably in China, Brazil, and parts of Africa, India became 'the apple of BAT's eye'.[668] Soon after BAT had entered India, it established a unified separate entity[669] named the Peninsular Tobacco Company (later known as the ITC). The latter moved ahead to establish as BAT's manufacturing arm, which had its first cigarette factory, opened in Monghyr in Bihar.[670] Champaka Basu wrote in her commissioned history of the ITC (1910–85) that Monghyr had been selected because a factory established 'closer to the UK' as Karachi had proved a failure and the ample supply of water also played its part in the choice of Monghyr as a suitable location for the factory. The river itself provided an effective means of communication with the north and east, an important consideration when one remembers that Nepal, a thriving market for cigarettes, lay to the north and Calcutta to the east. Timber that was necessary for case making grew in abundance all around and could be floated down the river. Skilled workmen were readily available, nurtured as they were on the traditional cottage industry of gun making. And though the people who live there at present may find it difficult to believe, Monghyr was then considered to be something of a resort town to which people journeyed up to the Ganges.[671]

Yet to these reasons as to why Monghyr had been selected by the ITC as the ideal place to set up a cigarette factory, we have to add some more, however. Not only had Monghyr been a centre for the ironware industry, some saltpeter manufacturing, and quite some indigo factories in the Begusarai subdivision,[672] it had also become – and therefore – a major centre of British rule. Importantly, the same rulers had called private capitalists to the region and had asked them to support a modern tobacco industry that would manufacture cigarettes that could be exported to England or other countries that formed the British Empire, if needed with the help of protective tariffs.[673] In return, the GoI would receive handsome taxes, of course, paid by this private company.[674]

When the ITC had come to Bengal (proper), the so-called *swadeshi* movement had been in full swing and a boycott against 'foreign cigarettes', that is those made from 'foreign' leaves and/or manufactured outside Bengal/ India, had been called for.[675] An assistant collector had reported in 1905 that a European firm had complained that in particular soap, perfumery, boots, and foreign cigarettes had been targeted by this movement but that a distinction had been made between 'English' and 'continental' goods and that the protest had been directed towards the former only. This collector furthermore stated, in 1905, that 'sales of cigarettes have stopped so far as Bengalis are concerned, and the effect of the movement is even said to have been felt in the Delhi market, owing to Bengalis residing upcountry having ceased to buy'.[676] Therefore, considering this environment and adding to this the fact that the prices of import of unmanufactured tobaccos from outside India had drastically increased, it is not difficult to understand why BAT had chosen to set up a cigarette factory in Bihar at that point of time.[677]

After the establishment of the factory, Peninsular Tobacco Company turned its attention to the procurement of the raw material with which to feed its factory. In 1908, as the Monghyr district itself did not have much of tobacco cultivation,[678] three men (Murdoch, Ashbury, and Graves) arrived in Shahpur Patori in Samastipur to buy tobacco for the newly established factory in Monghyr. However, these three men soon realised that procurement of local tobacco and processing it to make it fit for cigarette manufacturing was cumbersome and operationally intensive. One of the most problematic issues was the fact that the ground-cured Bihar tobacco, when brought in for sale by the cultivators, carried such a high moisture content that had proved impossible to pack without it going mouldy. This tobacco had to be transported as the Monghyr cigarette factory needed it there, and therefore, it was decided to dry it out again locally after purchase from the cultivators and before transport to Monghyr. For this reason, the ILTDC (hereafter just company) was established in the tobacco-growing regions of Tirhut, where it placed its first redrying machine in the Shahpur Patori that same year to be followed two years later by one in Khajauli. Importantly, disused indigo factories had lent themselves to this operation. The Shahpur Patori machine was installed in the old Abbott Indigo Factory, while the other one at Khajauli was put into the Bhakwa Indigo Factory, which was owned by the maharaja of Darbhanga, a powerful and well-known pro-British *zamindar*. Yet another redrying factory was established in Dalsingh Sarai, the centre of indigo research at the time and which became the largest unit of the three.[679]

Figure 25. Railway station at Dalsingh Sarai in the early twenthy-first century. Photograph by author.

Thus, as C. R. Fay rightly remarked in 1936 already, 'the British American Tobacco Company, through its associated companies, is something more than a merchant and manufacturer in India, yet it is not a planter'. Fay meant by 'planter' the actual tobacco cultivators, I described as *raiyats*, those who worked on the field carrying out the different tobacco operations. This work was, of course, not done by the ILTDC, but it had entered into contracts with these cultivators to get them grow cigarette tobacco and sell it to the company. Fay described how ILTDC did this in Chirala in the Guntur District of southern India, where the company had also started operations since 1915.[680] In Tirhut, too, the ILTDC bought 'large quantities' of tobacco leaves from the cultivators,[681] which thereafter were further processed, and a small 'cigarette factory' had even been started locally by the ILTDC for the production of a cheap type of cigarettes for local consumption only.

Figure 26. Advertisement for Capstan Navy Cut Cigarettes in *Advance*, Calcutta, Sunday 29, 1936.

The remaining of the redried tobacco leaf was sent to Monghyr and made into a somewhat better type of cigarettes going by brand names such as Maypole, Capstan, and Gold Flake, which were in turn transported to Kolkata for regional consumption, and if of very good quality, they were repacked and transported overseas, though only an even smaller quantity of this lot reached the London markets.

Tobacco Improvement through a Professional Private–Public Partnership in Tirhut

The ILTDC and the Peninsular Tobacco Company not only heavily depended on the Indian cultivators for the required supply of the right kind of leaf, but a close and necessary direct relation also existed between them and the Agricultural Department of the imperial GoI located at Pusa as well as between them and Pusa's scientists involved in tobacco research.[682] This interdependence is more than evident when the various *Reports of the Agricultural Research Institute and College at Pusa from 1907–21* are scrutinised.[683] A report of the Pusa Institute in 1909, for instance, mentioned that 'arrangements have been made with the Peninsular Tobacco Company of Monghyr to conduct experiments at Pusa to ascertain the best varieties and the best means of growing tobacco suitable for the manufacture of cigarettes'.[684] Importantly, it was also mentioned that this 'work will be conducted in collaboration with one of the experts of the company'.[685] Curing experiments at Pusa were also done 'in conjunction' with Peninsular.[686] Another Pusa report in 1911 added that arrangements had been made with the ITC in London for Pusa scientist Albert Howard to visit two of the best factories in London to inspect the type of leaf required by British factories. These visits proved 'of greatest use' to the scientist, and some of the knowledge obtained had been applied during the next year at Pusa.[687] What is more, when cured, the new hybridised results from Pusa experiments by the Howards had been sent to Peninsular at Monghyr and made into cigarettes in order to check their burning capacities and see which of them fetched the highest price. Subsequently, it was planned 'if possible to repeat the results amongst the cultivators'.[688] By 1912, it was clear from a report that had followed Pusa's achievements over the year that the Peninsular could neither do without the Pusa Type 28 seed as produced by the Howards and their Indian assistants nor without these Pusa scientists themselves:

> The only type of Indian tobacco found suitable for cigarettes in Bihar, when cured by the country method, is one known as Type 28. This was grown on a fairly large scale on the Dholi Estate (previously an indigo concern) during the last tobacco season and the crop was cured on the ground – an assistant being lent from Pusa to show the factory staff how

to proceed. The yield of cured leaf to the acres was very satisfactory and the product was taken over by the Indian Leaf Tobacco Development Company at Dalsingh Serai. This year (1911–1912) a larger area is being grown on the Dholi (ex-indigo) Estate. The spread of the cultivation of this kind is now a matter of price. If the growers are able to obtain a premium for this kind from the Company to repay them for the extra care required in the curing process the area will expand. On the other hand, it must be remembered that there is no competition on the part of the local trade for this tobacco when grown for cigarettes and at present the Company can to all intents and purposes make its own terms.

The ILTDC also needed the advice provided by Pusa scientists in other matters of cultivation. Around that time, the ITLDC realised that though the main 'problems' faced were caused by the 'wrong' curing methods of the cultivators – and the Pusa Indian assistant scientists had to 'teach' them the 'right' ways – it was also thought that 'the growers suffer a large amount of loss of crop and waste a good deal of labour'. The Howards involved in tobacco research at Pusa at the time were asked for help. Albert Howard had been of the opinion that both could be avoided as 'these losses are due to the primitive methods of growing the seedlings to the frequent loss of the majority of the first sowings and the numerous casualties after transplanting, resulting in a very uneven crop'. Therefore, the Howards started experiments 'with a view to remedy this state of affairs'. Soon, a paper appeared that dealt with the results obtained from research on the inheritance of characters in the tobacco crop. It had been cowritten including Albert's 'personal assistant' (i.e. Mrs Howard) and 'undertaken with a view of obtaining some general idea of the best method of attacking the problem of the improvement of the quality of the Bihar tobaccos – more particularly from the cigarette tobacco standpoint'. The paper marked 'an advance in the application of modern methods of plant breeding to crops of economic importance'. Meanwhile, the production of new varieties by selection and hybridisation was continued, as well as the testing and curing of the varieties already isolated.[689] During this period (1912–20), the ILTDC also faced the problem of loss of soil moisture, and accordingly, Pusa had started its experiments with indigo refuse (*seeth*), as already discussed above.

Importantly, the ILTDC had desired the quality of leaf that could match the Virginia (Golden) tobacco, which was yellowish in colour after flue-curing. The *Report on the Administration of the Territories now Included in the Province of Bihar and Orissa (1911–12)* had explained that 'the quality of tobacco grown in north Bihar is much liked by the natives, and tobacco has been a staple of these parts for at least a century past', but 'what is most wanted at present is to introduce improvements in the curing process'. Experiments with 'rack curing', instead of the usual 'ground-curing' method, were, therefore, also initiated by the Howards at Pusa, and the Pusa report of 1912 even stated that 'it now remains to be seen whether the planters in Bihar are prepared to take the trouble necessary to grow and cure this tobacco. If they do, it will be possible to consider whether not fire curing in some simple form in earth-built barns can be undertaken in Bihar with any prospects of success.'[690] Later, on demand from the ILTDC, these experiments were extended in a big way when the first assistant to the imperial agricultural chemist, the Bengali J. N. Mukherjee, had realised that

> ground curing produces tobacco of a dark brown hue and generally of leaves of small elasticity. For cigarettes, this dark brown colour is undesirable and the more this develops, the lower is the value of the product. For the Indian market, colour is of very little importance and no care is ever taken to produce tobaccos of a light colour. Since ground-curing does not produce tobacco of a suitable kind for cigarette manufacture and since flue-curing in barns does not suit the local conditions prevailing in this country, the Peninsular Tobacco Company suggested the process known as 'rack-curing' which consists of the following operations [. . .]. In March 1917, a number of plants from one large plot were rack-cured and the rest from the same plot were ground-cured by the ordinary country method. A sample of the rack-cured and one of the ground-cured tobaccos of one and the same variety and grown in the same field were obtained from the Indian Leaf Development Company, Dalsingh Sarai.[691]

During this period, the Agricultural Department in Pusa also reported that 'the demand for seed of the cigarette tobacco, Type 28, continues to increase and a large quantity was distributed during the year', and the ILTDC was its main taker:

> Evidence of the popularity of Type 28 for cigarettes and its suitability for widely different soils and climates continue to increase. The Bihar ryots who are growing leaf for the various branches of the Indian Leaf Tobacco Development Company, are demanding the seed of this type in larger and larger quantities, the distribution being carried out by the Dalsing Serai Branch [. . .] If still larger quantities of protected seed are asked for, the expense involved will be considerable and it may be necessary to ask Government to increase the annual grant for this section.

The ILTDC 'demanded' even more from Pusa scientists as they wanted the production cost to be lowered. The two chief items in this expenditure were, first, 'the labour involved in the management of the monsoon fallow which precedes tobacco' and, second, 'the cost of manure required'. Thus, 'both these matters' got the attention in the Botanical Section of the Howards. Regarding the latter, the Pusa research report of that year stated:

> Proceeding in this manner, namely, by green-manuring on drained land containing *thikra* (broken tile), a crop of cured cigarette tobacco weighing 24 maunds to the acre was produced, which was sold to the Indian Leaf Tobacco Development Company at Dalsing Serai for fifteen rupees a maund.

Yet one more problem stared the ILTDC in the eyes and that was the feared tobacco disease, and thus did Pusa embark on research on the serious tobacco parasite (*tokra*). Importantly, around this time (1920), finally, several 'indigo' planters also openly began joining this professional private–public partnership that existed in the tobacco fields around Pusa and Dalsingh Sarai. After a short revival of their indigo business due to the world war that had prevented indigo supplies from Germany to England and some other European countries that required the dye as well as increased demand from England related to soldiers' uniforms, after the war most planters finally accepted they had lost the battle.

Consequently, those who stayed put in the region embarked on other ventures, and 'indigo' was dropped from their appellation. Some of such 'planters', many of whom, in fact, had been mere 'assistants' or engineers and not planters at all, in particular the fresh arrivals from Britain that till around 1920 had continued, not only closely collaborated and acquired friendships with ILTDC employees in the region but also started growing tobacco on their *zeerats* that was sold to the ILTDC. Some did this next to sugar cane and even kept on having some indigo production.

Figure 27. Dalsing Serai (Dalsingh Sarai) concern for crop experimentation with, in particular, indigo but also tobacco and rhea. It was managed by Bernard Coventry, among others. Proprietors of the concern were Messrs. Coventry, Dalgleish, Harington, Hollway, Spencer, and Strachan's estate. It was known in the indigo world as the 'colour factory' using the method of manufacture known as the 'Coventry' process. The tobacco of the concern was also highly valued, and the very 'fine' tobacco sold to the Indian Leaf or the British American Tobacco Company. Taken from Playne, *Bengal and Assam, Behar and Orissa*, 1917, p. 291 (courtesy New Delhi: Asian Educational Services).

Louise Howard, Albert's second wife and Gabrielle's sister, had later on concluded that

> by 1924 enough seed was being distributed to cover one-quarter of the areas devoted to tobacco in India, namely, some 250,000 acres, and thus to maintain a supply of needed material for the cigarette factories which were springing up and catering for the new fashion of cigarette-smoking which was beginning to displace the hookah.[692]

For some time, this network seemed to have functioned well with all parties involved satisfied. Indeed, the whole enterprise was very successful in BAT's opinion at least as in 1917, it was reported that 'the local manufacture of cigarettes is developing rapidly'[693] and 'the handful of Europeans posted at these factories' appeared to have been 'content with their lot'.[694]

Figure 28. Dowlutpore concern. C. G. Atkins was managing proprietor, and other partners were Miss E. MacDonald, Mrs T. A. Robertson, Mrs E. N Swire, and Miss D. MacDonald, for whom Atkins was trustee. It started as a sugar concern in 1800. Fifty years later, it switched over to indigo, which was given up in 1914, and the land reserved by the owners, known as the 'Home Farm', was subjected to intensive cultivation, including manuring with green hemp, tobacco stalks, cow dung, and oil cakes, and this was followed by growing of very considerable quantities of tobacco and chillies. Some was purchased locally, but in addition, tobacco was rack-cured annually in an old (indigo) cake-house on the estate. The river Gandak was nearby and provided water for irrigation (and crocodiles, 'good for shooting', T. R. Filgrate of the Planter's Association had added). The concern had outworks too. Importantly, the concern was part of the Dowlutpore Central Co-operative Bank, which was one of the largest of its kind in the whole of the province and first founded by the then managing proprietor, C. R. MacDonald. This was a scheme for cultivators with little or no capital to sell their produce to advantage. The agricultural land was lent to these cultivators on the *zamindari* system, and perpetual leases had been granted in a few instances. Taken from Playne, *Bengal and Assam, Behar and Orissa,* 1917, pp. 298–99 (courtesy New Delhi: Asian Educational Services).

CHAPTER SEVEN

End of Cigarette Tobacco Cultivation in Bihar

Compared to the beginning of the nineteenth century, British Tirhut looked very different between 1920 and 1950. British officers and even some planters now drove cars instead of mounting horses; they smoked cigarettes instead of cigars or pipes and played tennis and golf instead of hunting tigers and pig-sticking. Besides, their houses now had electric fans, and some even used tractors in the fields. Civil servants had passed exams and knew some Hindi. Yet in Tirhut, the number of these Englishmen had greatly been reduced. Many (indigo) planters had left, replaced by Indian *zamindars* and British civil servants by Indian government officers (*sahibs* and *babus*), scientists and peons who smoked cheap cigarettes, *biris*, or chewed *pan* instead of using the *hookah*. The few English planters who had stayed put – the 'interlopers' of the past – had become 'gentlemen planters/farmers'. What is more, indigo battles (litigations) in civil courts were now things of the past as was indigo itself and so did poppy. Instead, there were labour unions and disputes. Some planters had exchanged the now 'monotonous alluvial plains' of north Bihar for 'industrial planting' in the collieries of Chota Nagpur in the southern part of the state. Others had gone for tea in Assam, though the majority just went 'home'. What remained of the indigo planters of 'those days' were their cemeteries and memorials, empty indigo vats and semi-ruined planters' houses, or those converted into *dak* bungalows. The Planters' Club had now changed its name into Muzaffarpur Club and also allowed some *zamindars*, but Indians had also set up their own clubs such as the Muslim Club, the Town Club, and the Orient Club for Bengali-speaking residents. Even the Pusa Institute was not 'imperial' anymore. It had lost this status after the earthquake of 1934. Bihar, which had been separated from Bengal in 1912, was, in 1936, also separated from Orissa. 'Natives' had become Indians, and the British Empire was shaking, the rise of India being the main cause. As a result, though temporary at the time, the ITC had to shut down its redrying 'factories' in Bihar. This chapter analyses the period between 1920 and 1950 in Bihar, which witnessed the end of a whirlwind in which a cigarette tobacco variety had not only been contrived but also been introduced to the *raiyats*, planted, sold, and made into cheap cigarettes through a network that had involved: (1) an affiliate of British American Tobacco along with a few British planters, (2) Indian landholders and cultivators as well as (3) Imperial Pusa, and (4) its scientists.

Figure 29. Grave of little Winifred Jennie, the infant daughter of Bernard and Ella Coventry, who died in 1893. Such sad experiences were also part of a planter's life such as that of Bernard Coventry, who later had become Imperial Pusa's first director. Photograph by author.

Figure 30. Society established for British planters exclusively. Photograph by Masoom Reza.

Figure 31. Society established for Bengalis in Bihar as a reaction to the Muzaffarpur club that did not allow them to become member at first. Photograph by Masoom Reza.

Figure 32. Old indigo vat in Samastipur. Photograph by author.

Precarious Dependency amongst the Quadruple

BAT's first trust in India had been the promotion of sales of imported cigarettes. Yet as described, due to unfavourable tariff as well as a national upsurge in Bengal (proper), better known as the *swadeshi* movement, during which Indians (at the time British subjects) but also some Englishmen in India (at the time called 'Anglo-Indians'[695]) had demanded trade protection, the import of 'foreign' cigarettes had been tabooed. This combined with a growing demand for cigarettes in India itself had stimulated a call for the production of 'Indian cigarettes' made out of 'Indian leaf'. The subsequent establishment of the cigarette factory in Monghyr (Peninsular Tobacco) had been the result. The projected aim of the factory was to produce cheaper brands of cigarettes, which mainly used indigenously grown tobacco. As the Monghyr factory was situated next to the tobacco-growing areas in Tirhut,[696] it was logical that the cigarette factory in Monghyr should be supplied with this tobacco leaf from the Samastipur and Darbhanga regions. When Monghyr started manufacturing cigarettes in 1907, it was perceived, however, as I detailed in the foregoing pages, that there had been something amiss not only with the tobacco grown in this region but also with the curing methods of the cultivators.

Around 1905, the GoI also believed that improvement of tobacco grown in Bihar was urgently needed for an Indian tobacco industry to flourish within the country. This fitted nicely with the freshly formulated agrarian policy of the British Empire that sought improvement of the agrarian wealth of India not only for the well-being of Britain and the empire but also in the interest of the 'Indian population'. However, in order to realise such an agrarian improvement, the application of European capital and science was considered a *sine qua non*. As described, the Pusa model farm, therefore, was destined to grow into a major agricultural research institute of the empire with tobacco research propagated as one of the most urgent needs of the day. Within a few years, scientists at Pusa succeeded in developing a tobacco variety with corresponding rack- and even flue-curing methods that also suited demands from Peninsular in Monghyr. In fact, the cigarette factory at Monghyr became the great taker of the seeds developed at Pusa. However, for the purpose of converting the plants that had sprouted from these seeds into the desired commodity (i.e. cigarettes), Peninsular that later became ITC had established several so-called redrying factories in Tirhut through its ILTDC. What is more, as indigo had failed the English planters in Tirhut, they increasingly diversified their concerns. Some who had had their concerns in the Samastipur region or the greenhorns, who had taken them over, even started supervising the cultivation of cigarette tobacco plants in fields that once had been preserved for the production of the blue dye only or on *zeerat* land around the factory. The imperial government along with imperial tobacco, BAT's branch in Monghyr, seemed the great winners. Yet success of this great imperial tobacco improvement scheme that aimed at a self-sustainable cigarette industry in Bihar was only guaranteed as long as English planters would supply the right tobacco leaf and/or the ILTDC could procure the desired plants directly from the cultivators.

For some time, things worked out well for the ILTDC, which had three buying depots in Bihar and later on even experimented with flue-curing at Imperial Pusa. Planters and the ILTDC obtained the right seed variety through the Agricultural Department located within the Imperial Agricultural Research Institute in Pusa, and Indian cultivators (*raiyats*) stimulated by free seeds and advancements, indeed, brought forth the so much sought-after raw material, that is tobacco leaves which they themselves, middlemen or the *zamindar*, sold to the ILTDC which processed (redried) them and transported them to be used for cigarette blending at the factory in Monghyr. These new tobacco varieties could only be grown on highland which was, in particular, available in Samastipur or the old Darbhanga and Muzaffarpur districts of Tirhut. In this region, poppy and indigo cultivation had decreased considerably, and some of this land was now used for the cultivation of tobacco, mostly the 'traditional' chewing and *hookah* tobaccos but also some cigarette tobacco for the ILTDC. The situation seemed thus a happy one for all four categories involved as the scheme not only served the imperial government and the private capitalists but also served part of the Indian population by providing employment in the factories and on the land and cheap cigarettes and a guaranteed sale for the cultivators.

Yet as well can be imagined from the above, this whole imperial tobacco improvement/development (i.e. colonisation) scheme had created 'dependency'.[697] By dependency, I do not mean so much addiction to the smoke, but the dependency of the Indian cultivators (and even the Indian factory workers) on English (private) capital, skills, and science. At the same time, the imperial government at Pusa not only needed the ITC/ILTDC but also its scientists, and the latter two were dependent on the collaboration of *zamindars* and British planters. Additionally, the imperial government (GoI) at Pusa needed support of the provincial government, that is the Bihar government, and the Monghyr factory needed (cigarette) consumers. Besides, in order to manufacture this commodity, the ITC/ILTDC needed cultivators and labourers in fields and factories. Lack of this labour would mean the discontinuation of its operations. Consequently, cultivators would be bereaved of (free) seed provision, drying, and curing facilities and would also suffer the loss of their sole buyers. A 'Note on Indian Tobacco' had already cautioned:

> The marketing of flue-cured tobacco in India is however, subject to a very definite limitation. After curing and bulking is completed, it must be passed through large and expensive plants of 're-ordering and drying machines' few of which exist at present in India. Therefore the sole market for flue-cured tobacco is with the commercial organizations which maintain such machines in India and for this reason agriculturists who wish to attempt the production of flue-cured cigarette tobacco, should come to an agreement, with the possible purchasers of their leaf before commencing operations.[698]

Pouchepadass's unpublished paper on 'Peasant Protest in a Global Setting' that refers to indigo cultivation in Champaran in Bihar is imperative in this context. He described the agricultural context in which cultivators operated, which to a large extent was characterised by 'agrarian dependence'. His model can well be used to describe the situation in Samstipur as well as there, too, the cultivation of cigarette tobacco was, like indigo and poppy before and sugar cane later on, as Pouchepadass explained, 'produced within the framework of pre-capitalist relationships of power and dependence', which had insulated the cultivators from the market. *Deshi* tobacco grown for *hookah* and chewing tobaccos had partly been grown for own consumption and partly for the local/regional markets and mostly had been loaded on bullock carts and brought to these markets by the relatively not-so-poor tobacco cultivators themselves. The cigarette tobacco cultivator, however, had no direct contact with or were only partially integrated in the market and dealt with the ILTDC that gave him free seed and possibly an advance of the price of the crop against an agreement to grow and deliver the same to the company.[699] In this way, the cultivator had been hooked up to (long-distance) tobacco markets which workings (culturally as well as in economic sense) had been unknown to him and which politics he could not understand or in which he simply possessed not much power to play politics.

What is more, the drawback for the cultivators of cigarette tobacco was not so much that they depended on a commercial organisation, but the fact, as Howard Cox skilfully analysed, that though Bihar had now been 'endowed with the basis of a modern cigarette industry', it had been one that 'lay under the control of British rather than Indian capital' as the GoI as well as the government of Bihar had been unwilling or unable 'to help mobilise local capital in the Indian cigarette factory' and local capital had not been forthcoming by itself in Bihar.[700] This dependency of the cultivators on outside and alien capital, knowledge (science and even scientists[701]), tastes, and manpower proved disastrous for the final and permanent embedding of cigarette tobacco cultivation if not consumption in Bihar. As I will show in this chapter, this was not the only reason for 'failure' of tobacco colonisation in Bihar, but the other dependencies outlined above also proved fatal, and a slow disintegration of the collaborative network, as described in this chapter, meant the death knell for cigarette tobacco in the state.

Figure 33. Remains of tobacco redrying factory near Dalsingh Sarai. This room must have housed redrying machinery as well. Photograph by author.

Figure 34. Remains of tobacco redrying factory near Dalsingh Sarai. From this room, most of the redried tobacco was transported to the cigarette factory at Monghyr. Photograph by author.

Figure 35. Abandoned ILTDC office near Dalsingh Sarai. Somewhat ironically at present it houses a labour union's welfare unit for *bidi* workers. Photograph by author.

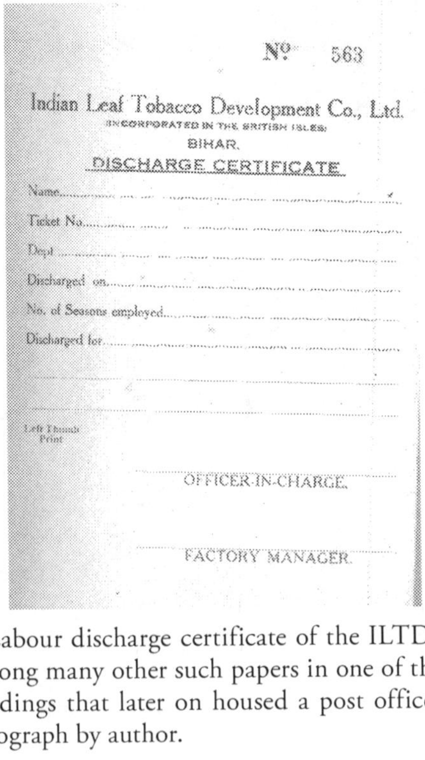

Nᵒ 563

Indian Leaf Tobacco Development Co., Ltd.
INCORPORATED IN THE BRITISH ISLES:
BIHAR.
DISCHARGE CERTIFICATE

Name...

Ticket No..

Dept...

Discharged on..

No. of Seasons employed...............................

Discharged for..

Left Thumb
Print

OFFICER-IN-CHARGE.

FACTORY MANAGER.

Figure 36. Labour discharge certificate of the ILTDC, found on the floor among many other such papers in one of the abandoned ILTDC buildings that later on housed a post office (also closed down). Photograph by author.

Imperial Science under Attack and Scientists' Warnings vis-à-vis Tobacco Improvement

Research into plant improvement that had previously been conducted in botanic gardens, stimulated by agrihorticultural societies, thereafter had been carried out in experimental and model farms. During the whole of the nineteenth century, however (amateur), scientists and subsequent government officials had not always been in agreement with each other, and projects had been unconnected and somewhat idiosyncratic. The founding of the Imperial Agricultural Research Institute at Pusa in Bihar, in 1905, had changed this situation altogether. Actually, this institute fully embodied the belief in Imperial science both in Britain as well as among officials working in India. Subsequently, this science swiftly and hugely developed at Pusa, where 'sub-sciences' of economic botany such as plant genetics, agricultural chemistry, and mycology also matured.[702] In fact, as David Arnold detailed, 'confidence in the transforming, modernising power of science climaxed with the viceroyalty of Lord Curzon (1899–905), when the doctrines of high imperialism were echoed in the rhetoric and institutions of India's "imperial science".[703] In other words and as illustrated in the previous chapter, plant colonisation was at its imperial high at this time, and tobacco improvement research at Pusa was dictated by the imperial demands. However, not only did such demands change over time, but also it increasingly had incorporated demands from the GoI, and even demands from 'the better classes of natives' all over the country had been taken into account as reflected in tobacco research at Pusa. Till the end of the nineteenth century, European markets had desired tobacco leaf that could be used for the manufacture of cigars or used as snuff. Yet around 1905, 'the habit of cigarette smoking' had not only picked up in Europe but also 'invaded the social life of various races and peoples of India.'[704] Expecting increased revenues in this way, these changing demands had been taken in by the imperial government as reflected in the nature of tobacco improvement research conducted by scientists at Pusa.

As shown in the previous chapter, during the first period of Pusa's existence from 1905 to 1935, in which Pusa had become an Imperial Institute under the GoI,[705] most of the botanical work was carried out under the guidance of scientists Sir Albert Howard and his wife Gabrielle L. C. Howard.[706] Unlike his first wife Gabrielle, Albert Howard (1873–947), an English botanist, has become world famous and is now considered by many as the 'father of modern organic agriculture'. After Albert Howard and his wife Gabrielle Louise Caroline Matthaei (1876–930) left Pusa and started working in Indore, the two of them had commenced research on the connection between a 'healthy soil and the Indian villages' healthy populations, livestock, and crops'. Albert also became interested in composting, and all this research in Indore resulted in a book published in 1940 entitled: *An Agricultural Testament,* which now considered a classic organic farming text. Later on, he published even more on the subject, and in this way, he inspired many farmers and agricultural scientists who furthered the so-called organic movement. Albert devoted the last half of his career to studying the forest in order 'to farm like the forest', presaging contemporary ecologists' interest in the relation between ecology and agriculture.[707] Albert's output while in Indore and later on was huge. Besides, most of that work is easily available, republished, quoted, admired, reviewed, but also severely criticised.[708]

Yet the number of publications authored by Albert and his wife Gabrielle while in Bihar – and I think her contributions are hugely undervalued –was also considerable, though much less circulated.[709] Only Albert's research on Indian wheat, which he conducted while still working in Bihar, received some attention later on. However, work on Indian tobaccos is completely absent from contemporary lists that enumerate the Howards' accomplishments. The reason for this seems rather obvious. At a time that tobacco cultivation as well as consumption is considered to be health enemy number one, not many of Albert's followers, who love his book on *Farming and Gardening for Health or Disease* (later republished as *The Soil and Health: A Study of Organic Agriculture*), would like to admit or just do not know that the Howards' initial experiments were almost exclusively devoted to tobacco improvement. What is more, they were successful, too, as shown in the previous chapter. By the early 1920s, when the Howards left Pusa, the couple had contrived a tobacco variety that was in high demand all over India if not in other parts of the world.

Accounts that explain the emergence and final dominance of the cigarette on a global scale are manifold and not only describe the use of new methods of production and new methods of marketing but also describe the adoption of flue-cured tobacco, which was of such great importance for the global history of the cigarette. Such narratives emphasise that though the switch to the cigarette was relatively slow, after 1950, the pattern in most countries in the world was one of increasing consumption of manufactured cigarettes, on the one hand, and on the other hand, a decreasing use of both local tobacco leaf and curing methods as well as of traditional methods of consumption. In short and notwithstanding recurrent anti-cigarette protest movements, which already started in the late 1890s in the United States itself, cigarette smoking spread all over the world elsewhere, and 'the cigarette', indeed, became a quite 'global' commodity in the long run as we know.[710]

Hobhouse described that in the fifty years between the Great Exhibition of 1851 and the death of Queen Victoria in 1901, tobacco was industrialised, and in England and the United States, the cigarette began to replace snuff, chewing tobacco, pipe, or cigar. In these fifty years, the making of cigarettes became one of the most profitable manufactures in the world.[711] However, in England itself, older forms of tobacco consumption such as the pipe smoking continued to be proportionately larger than manufactured cigarette smoking until the outbreak of World War II.[712] Nevertheless, when the importance of cigarettes grew in England, 'Virginia' or 'Bright-cured', as had developed in North Carolina, came to dominate leaf exports to England, and it was this tobacco that was desired to be developed at Pusa. Seen in this light, the experiments conducted by the Howards in Bihar between 1905 and 1920 were pioneering, and potential outcomes expected to be of great value not only for Bihar or British India but for the whole of the British Empire and even beyond.

Albert,[713] son of a farmer in England, had expressed his doubts however. Not only he had doubts regarding the direction of tobacco improvement, but also he, in fact, had questioned 'imperial science' at Pusa as a whole. Before Pusa, Albert had been employed in Barbados as mycologist and agricultural lecturer at the Imperial Department of Agriculture for the West Indies. Looking back, he wrote about his time there: 'In Barbados I was a laboratory hermit [. . .] but my tours of various islands [. . .] This contact with the land itself and with the men practically working on it laid the foundations of my knowledge of tropical agriculture.'[714] After a stint in Kent, working with hop growers, Albert got the charge of the Botanical Section of the Pusa Institute in 1905. Yet he later on remembered, 'On arrival the new institution only existed on paper.' He, nevertheless, got an area of about 75 acres of land at one end of the Pusa Estate. On this land, Albert used to experiment with various crops, in the beginning, in particular with tobacco, which it had been his duty to 'improve by modern plant-breeding methods'. In this way, he was expected not only to improve the plant but also to produce new valuable varieties.[715] Louise Howard, Albert's second wife (and sister of Gabrielle), later noted that Albert had 'little time for flora with no economic consequence' as 'the true farmer does not care for flowers'.[716] Economic considerations thus inspired Albert to take up tobacco research, among others, and the 'improvement of the crop' was the job at hand. Albert Howard later in life wrote:

> My main duties at Pusa were the improvement of crops and the production of new varieties. Over a period of nineteenth years (1905–24) my time was devoted to this task, in the course of which many new types of wheat (including rust-resistant), of tobacco, gram, and linseed were isolated, tested, and widely distributed.[717]

While at Pusa, Albert conducted numerous tests regarding soil aeration, irrigation, pollination and cross-fertilisation of species, growing cycles, manuring of crops, harvesting, processing, and packing of crops and applied these measures to a number of crops. Apart from tobacco, Albert undertook research in fruits, vegetables, hemp, wheat, sugar cane, various oilseeds, and indigo. He or rather his wife carried out systematic surveys of tobacco varieties that grew in Tirhut and selected the most promising 'country types' and isolated them. This was followed by hybridisation of the improved new variety via crossings that did or did not conform to Mendelian principles. Finally, there was the genetic stabilisation of hybrid varieties that would come true from seed.[718]

Interestingly, though the Howards were, as detailed in the previous chapter, very successful in the field of tobacco 'improvement', later in life Albert never referred to his tobacco experiments in Pusa nor did he count the engineering of the so-called Pusa 28 tobacco variety as one of his achievements. Though towards the fag end of his life, he did refer to his research on wheat plants and fruit growing carried out during the same time; this remarkable achievement at Pusa in the field of tobacco improvement was not mentioned, not even by Albert himself. For one, this might have been caused by the fact that anti-smoking campaign in the UK had gained strength by that time.[719] Yet, more than this reason, I comply that Howard's silence later on was caused by the fact that he himself must not have considered his tobacco experimentation to have been 'successful'. In fact, the kind of experimentation with cigarette tobaccos in Tirhut did not fit well with the kind of definition the couple had of 'improvement'.

Albert later on, indeed, agreed that the time he had spent at Pusa had provided him with a wisdom that had been 'incidental to my main work' during that period.[720] To be precise, while at Pusa, Albert, 'assisted' by Gabrielle – though, in fact, it was more the other way around according to Gabrielle's sister[721] – started redefining the function of agricultural science in (colonial) India.[722] When questioned by the Indian Industrial Commission in 1916, whether Howard thought an agricultural college in India would 'improve agriculture', Howard had answered:

> Agriculture I might explain is an art. It depends upon the personal fitness and aptitude of the man. Many of the best agriculturists in Europe know no science at all, and I do not think that teaching them or their sons, science would help at all. Science is an instrument, by which new knowledge can be applied to industries for producing results which the people engaged in those industries can use. If you wish to put a thin veneer of science over the population of India in the hope that this would make them better for anything then I disagree.

The commission's reply was that the commission's members were 'not talking of the population of India' but about 'a few men who would do better than the general mass of cultivators'.[723] According to the Howards, however, plants could only be called 'improved' if they had become more 'useful' to the people who grew them. His definition of 'usefulness' still clearly defined in economic terms, however. In other words, a new tobacco variety such as the Pusa 28 could only be said to be an improvement in comparison with the 'country tobacco', if by growing cigarette tobacco cultivators' profits were higher than if growing chewing and *hookah* tobaccos in Tirhut.

This 'wisdom' that Albert gained through his tobacco research at Pusa seemed to have been, too, threatening for authorities at Pusa, however, as it had pushed the Howards into the experimentation with 'country' varieties too. It had also raised the Howards' interest in the cultivation methods of the 'natives', some of which they considered very 'useful'. As a result, Albert was remanded by the authorities to return to his 'main work' at Pusa, that is his duty to improve tobacco by modern plant-breeding methods aiming at better quality cigarette tobacco. Albert's ability to be able to communicate with the 'tillers of the soil' (though they must have been *zamindars* mainly[724]) and take their knowledge into account in matters of agricultural policy formulation made him, according to the scholar M. G. Jackson, a 'pioneer of an entirely new way of thinking about agriculture', that is that agriculture should be studied as 'a whole', including plants, soils, climates, insects, as well as people.[725] Albert Howard's 'whole' even encompassed 'labour'[726] and 'socio-economic' issues. Dr H. M. Leake, a close associate of Sir Albert Howard, his 'loyal friend' in fact and considered an authority on 'tropical agriculture' at the time, remembered in 'An Appreciation' written a year after Howard's death:

> It was in 1906, when Sir Albert Howard arrived in India and visited me in Saharanpur, that there commenced that association and friendship, which lasted uninterruptedly till his untimely death in October last. At that date, the Agricultural Department had only recently been established and official views as to the function of the different technical officers was in a state of flux [. . .] Thence arose that broad vision of agriculture as an essential unity and not as a series of disconnected subjects, to be studied in water tight compartments.

During his Pusa days, 'loyal friend and colleague' Leake continued, Albert had asked why plants failed 'to develop their intrinsic merits when placed in the hands of the Indian cultivator?' The answer had been provided by Albert himself:

> The answer is that that close inter-connection between the plant and its environment, which it was Howard's life work to demonstrate, was not recognized. The response of the plant to its environment is direct; man is the adaptable organism. A social organization which places man's requirements first and into which a plant must be fitted, offers an example of placing the cart before the horse. That is the position in India; a heavily indebted peasantry, with the family holding averaging five acres or under, is not in a position to provide

these essential conditions which will enable the plant to give maximum response.

Leake explained that this had been 'the atmosphere'[727] in which Howard evolved what in later years became his fundamental thesis. Yet Leake had added that 'it was not his function at that time to follow his conclusions to their logical end – the reform of the land-tenure system; that no agricultural officer could do, since land-tenure was intimately linked with the administrative problem of land revenue'.[728] Albert Howard thus never really questioned the 'political'. This is why he later on in life still became 'Sir' Howard, even though he had questioned the basis of 'colonial science'[729] as it was on unequal and exploitative (land) relations. Nevertheless, Howard did suffer from the boundaries imposed by the Imperial Institute, as described in the previous chapter, and which had restricted his personal academic freedom as his second wife later on wrote: Albert Howard had 'felt suffocated' at Pusa, 'with its conventional research traditions'. He, therefore, gradually tried to shake himself free from the influence of his colleagues at Pusa, and while doing this, his popularity there decreased. Finally, Albert and Gabrielle left Pusa and started a new life in Indore. Louise, his second wife, narrated:

> Neither Sir Albert Howard nor his wife, were finally satisfied that the *fundamental question of relations with the population* [emphasis mine] was being handled with sufficient vigour and enlightenment. They determined that transfer to their own Institute at Indore should be made into an opportunity for unique developments.[730]

Therefore, though the Howards had carried out path-breaking tobacco research at Pusa with the desired outcomes as well, a general lack of (scientific) freedom finally compelled them to leave Pusa and set up their own institute in Indore.[731] In 'A Criticism of Present-day Agricultural Research', Albert mentioned: 'It is the exception rather than the rule to find an investigation in the hands of one competent investigator, provided with land, ample means and complete freedom.'[732]

There was another scientist at the time paying more attention to 'the fundamental question of relations with the population' than (only) heading to imperial or British interests. In a scientific article, Albert's close friend Leake made a very interesting observation. He first explained that 'pure cultures' required very great care, and there was 'no doubt that mixed cultures are best adapted to a primitive type of agriculture for they provide a form of insurance'. He had observed that 'in the precarious tract of Bundelkhand (now in Uttar Pradesh), the common mixture of wheat, barley, mustard, linseed, and gram offers an extreme case in which, whatever the season, the cultivator is likely to reap one'. The 'pure' culture had no such flexibility, and 'control' to check disease was doubly important where 'pure cultures' had been widely introduced. Besides, 'quality as well as uniformity' was products 'of other causes than purity of the crop'. Leake explained that 'where the primary product requires preparation for the market, the quality of the marketable form may depend on the care exercised in the preparatory processes'. He gave the example of tobacco, where the curing process involved chemical and biological reactions, which required skilled manipulation if a satisfactory product is the result; otherwise, the loss of quality was permanent. Importantly, Leake concluded: 'The conduct of such processes by small and independent units must react detrimentally on the price received, for market prices tend to adjust themselves to the lower quality (of tobaccos) and the smaller producer of good quality will with difficulty secure the intrinsic value of his produce. Again, control is necessary if this source of depression of quality is to be avoided.'[733]

Leake's finding is essential to understand the 'failed' outcome of tobacco experiments with Virginia tobacco in Tirhut around 1873 by, for instance, an indigo planter of the Shahpore, Undi concern and other such tobacco experiments. The indigo factory had got some Virginia tobacco seed from the Agricultural Society at the time, and this had been distributed in the nearby villages too. It had been 'only sown on the best lands' and 'gave a larger yield per beegha and was readily bought up by the merchants before the *deshi* (Indian variety)'. Yet the collector of Tirhut at the time, F. M. Halliday, had reported: 'I am informed that in defiance of all the rules of political economy, though thus so far sought after, it (*belotee/*'foreign' tobacco, needed for cigars at the time) never commanded a higher price than the *deshi* (tobacco needed for chewing and *hookah* preparations).' Halliday had remarked: 'There must be something in this assurance, however, for the cultivation of Virginia tobacco in these villages is very small. The area under tobacco cultivation is estimated at 15,600 acres.'[734]

Peninsular and ILTDC in Bihar's Agricultural Landscape till the Early 1920s

The contemporary Bihari agrarian landscape has often been termed a 'semi-feudal' agricultural environment based on unequal power relations and characterised by share-cropping, perpetual indebtedness of small tenants, concentration of two modes of exploitation – usury and landownership – in the hands of the same class (*zamindars*), and lack of accessibility of the small tenants to the markets.[735] Indeed, colonial Bihar's peasantry had been widely differentiated, and 'cultivators' (*raiyats*) could mean anything from the (bigger) landholders or *zamindars* and tenants to crop-sharers and (landless) agricultural labourers. At times, it even signified the (British) indigo planters in the region. Often, it just meant, as Deepak Kumar quoted, 'the half-starved *raiyats*, with their half-starved bullocks, working on a half-starved soil'.[736]

The principal crops in Bihar during the first two decades of the twentieth century were rice (paddy), jute, cotton, indigo, poppy (though the last two both dwindling), sugar cane, chillies, wheat, barley, maize, oilseeds, tobacco, and a few other food and non-food crops. In particular, tobacco cultivation had increased substantially during this period and with it the number of tobacco cultivators. It had, in particular, been poppy cultivators often members of the *koeri* caste that had turned to tobacco cultivation in 1911–12 with the abolition of the Opium Department in Bihar and the establishment of the Imperial Tobacco/Peninsular in Bihar.[737] In disused indigo factories at Shahpur Patoree, Khajauli, and Dalsingh Sarai, the ILTDC had set up redrying machines and distributed Pusa seeds among tobacco cultivators. In turn, these *raiyats* brought their cigarette tobacco in bullock cartloads to one of these redrying plants or had sold it to middlemen. A contemporary report informed:

> This company with its head office in Clive Street, Calcutta, is only of comparatively recent formation, but it has for its object the dealing with *native crops of tobacco* [emphasis added], and especially their *improvement* [emphasis added] both in cultivation and curing by the *ryot*. The efforts made in this direction have already been awarded by considerable success, as there is a marked advance in the appearance and smoking qualities of tobacco grown in the fields where the company has

been interesting itself. The latest type of *American machinery* [emphasis added] has been imported to deal with the crops and no effort has been spared in trying to induce the *ryot*, who has been obtaining better prices for his produce, to improve his methods of cultivation and curing [. . .] Hitherto the bulk of native-grown tobacco has been consumed in the *hookah*, and while the consumption in this form is still enormous, there is a steadily growing demand for cigarettes made of native leaf. It is to the production and curing of tobacco of this latter type that the efforts of the Indian Leaf Tobacco Development Company, Ltd., have been mainly directed, with the result that to-day it is possible to obtain sound tobaccos which meet every requirement of the Indian cigarette smoker.[738]

By 1912, a variety of cheap cigarette brands, such as 'Red Lamp', 'Battleaxe', and 'Madari', was produced at the Monghyr factory based entirely on locally grown cigarette leaf tobacco, and Monghyr's demands increased as cigarette smoking in Bihar had indeed become somewhat more popular during the 1910s. The *Gazetteer* of 1926 had stated that the Monghyr cigarette factory had also got 'a very complete carpentering plant, equipped for converting rough logs of timber into finished packing cases', and the 'whole of the machinery' was driven by electrical power, 'for generating which there are five Lancashire boilers and three sets of high pressure compound engines, each of a capacity of 325-B.H.P', and water for the use of the whole factory had been obtained from the Ganges and stored in three reservoirs, each having a capacity of 100,000 gallons.[739] The *Bihar and Orissa Report of 1925–26* mentioned that the Peninsular Tobacco Company at Monghyr employed nearly 3,000 hands and 'is one of the largest in the world'.[740] Basu added that the factory had imported Bonsack cigarette machines and the 'Unique Fives packing machines' which 'enabled the factory to make and sell cigarettes at five for one piece and thereby compete with the *biri*, a notable milestone on the road to the success of the company'. Local workers who had been 'apt at making guns' were trained in 'the art of handling leaf', and 'illiterate women' were taught 'to hand-pack tens' though they had been 'slow and inept and wasted millions of cigarettes before they graduated from the learners' tables'. Yet 'factory labour was very cheap and readily available, so much so that even in the late 1920s recruitment and discharge were a daily affair'. Champaka Basu explained that 'with farmers having to pay their tithe to the *zamindar*, they were more than willing to seek alternative employment', and 'gradually, the factory's teething problems' had come to an end.[741]

Similarly, the three redrying factories near Pusa had expanded their output and had needed more labour too. By 1921, the redrying plant at Dalsingh Sarai had to employ a local workforce numbering between 300 and 350 to manage its affairs. Besides, quite some cultivators in and around Pusa had accepted several innovations, as proposed by Albert Howard, such as green manuring and furrow irrigation. What is more: 'planters were only too eager to imitate and to buy the improved seed.'[742] Till the early 1920s, therefore, Basu also concluded, there is 'no doubt that the managers, assistants, and foremen, then all expatriates, had a very good time.'

> In the meantime, it was becoming obvious that whether unwittingly or otherwise, BAT had shown great foresight in setting up its factory in India. There were changes in the offing which were to make the indigenous manufacture of cigarettes an economic necessity [. . .] A stimulus for indigenous manufacture had been provided. There had already been some indications that the *hookah* was being abandoned in favour of the cigarette or the *biri* [. . .] By 1924, Peninsular Tobacco Company, with a unit in Monghyr and another in Bangalore, was ready to set up another factory.[743]

Yet this third factory that had, indeed, been established in Saharanpur in 1931 was shut down just five years after the factory had opened. Basu explained:

> Events beyond the control of the Company had begun to take their toll. The national movement was growing from strength to strength and with it there was a deliberate boycott of British goods. Far-reaching changes had been initiated changes that would eventually alter the entire character and organization of the Company.[744]

As Albert Howard had already discovered, 'acclimatisation' of cigarette tobacco in Bihar's socio-economic, political, cultural, as well as biological environment did not only depend on climate, soils, seed, plant varieties, or cultivation and curing methods but also depend even or solely on the willingness and/ or ability of the actual tillers of the soil to accept new tobacco varieties, cultivation, curing, and selling methods. It depended on 'the whole' and, therefore, also depended on the collaboration between these actual cultivators (*koiris*) and Indian estate holders (*zamindars*) and/or British indigo planters and on collaboration between the Imperial Agricultural Research Institute at Pusa on the one hand and Peninsular at Monghyr and ILTDC at Dalsingh Sarai on the other hand. By the end of the 1940s, this network had all but vanished. In the remainder of this chapter, I narrate what all happened during the 1920s and the 1930s that made this network non-functional and therefore brought the cigarette adventure in Bihar to a definitive closure by 1950.

Setbacks for Peninsular and ILTDC (1920s and 1930s)

Cigarette smoking in Bihar had been confined to the richer, educated, and urbanised classes in Bihar, while most others were tobacco chewers and *hookah* smokers. Nevertheless, though never that much in Bihar, numbers had slowly but steadily increased in the rest of India, and by the World War I, BAT had stepped up its investments in India. Its factory at Monghyr, supplying to the whole of India, had been expanded to the point where its output was reported to have exceeded two billion per annum by 1918. During the 1920s, Peninsular also developed its own printing facilities at Monghyr, training locals in the use of the machinery and in this way, 'inadvertently', creating BAT's first industrial dispute by paying these employees higher rates than the tobacco machinery operators, according to Reginald George Baker, chairman of Peninsular from 1935 to 1945.[745]

Historian Ritu Chaturvedi explained this industrial dispute differently, however. She suggested that the problems at the factory should be placed within their wider socio-economic context and pointed to the so-called non-cooperation movement that had been going on during the time of the strike. This nationalist project initiated by Indian Congress leaders had spread throughout India during the 1920s.[746] Indeed, during the 1920s, the political economy – the interaction of economic forces and political choices[747] – had also fundamentally changed in Bihar. One of the agenda points of the nationalist programme of the Indian Congress leaders had been, like other nationalists in

1905 in Bengal (proper) and described earlier, 'boycott' of foreign goods like cloth, glass bangles, rubber, foreign sugar (beet and industrial), and importantly 'foreign' cigarettes. But as Saradindu Mukherji argued,

> 'De-industrialisation and de-urbanisation' are often cited 'as two major corrosive influences of the captive colonial economy, which by destroying the indigenous industries, threw many such uprooted people in agricultural sector for their livelihood, thereby turning them into landless labourers'. At the same time, the establishment of modern industries, like the railway loco-works at Jamalpur, cigarette, and gun factories at Munger and other activities of the Public Works Department created new opportunities of employment.

Not only such modern industries, indeed, had created employment opportunities within factories, but in the case of ILTDC, it also provided an opportunity to *raiyats* to sell their produce. Yet the 1920s and 1930s were the decades, Mukherji also pointed out, during which an important peasant organisation the *Kisan Sabha*[748] had taken the 'decision to pursue the programme of Civil Disobedience Movement, chalked out by the Congress', including their call for the boycott of cigarettes. This, thus, as Mukherji concluded, 'would shelve the solution of the grievances of the peasants for the time being'.[749] The Congress programme was directed against the colonial government (imperial in England as well as GoI and the provincial governments), and most of the Congress leaders who designed the programme in Bihar had been, according to Mukherji, 'either very affluent or middle-class men, and quite a few of them urban professionals'. Some of these 'nationalists' had been 'big *zamindars*' who had organised a *Satyagraha* movement in Lakhisarai in Monghyr for instance.[750] These 'elites' did continue with cigarette boycotts without much thought not only as to what impact this would have on landless labourers and tenants who grew cigarette tobacco on their own fields or *zeerats* of British planters or on lands of other Indian landholders for the ILTDC but equally not as to what did would mean for labourers who had just found new employment in Monghyr or the redrying factories around Dalinsingh Sarai.

Yet Mukherji stated that the 'rural mass also responded wonderfully in boycotting foreign manufactured articles'.[751] He even found that some members of the so-called docile class (the *koeris*) did participate in such actions.[752]

Importantly, and as I have described earlier, Bihari tobacco growers generally belonged to the more affluent sections among the peasantry and therefore, indeed, were likely to have participated in these 'boycott' missions which greatly affected the cigarette industry at the time all over India. Shiri Ram Bakshi, for instance, described:

> Foreign goods were boycotted. Sale of cigarettes was practically stopped. The Imperial Tobacco Company which had an enormous sale of several lakhs in the past desperately wrote to the President, Assam Provincial Congress Committee, meekly pleading that their cigarettes are made in India, out of Indian tobacco and by Indians hands and seeking exclusion from the British goods boycott.[753]

The civil disobedience campaign of 1930s initiated by the Indian Congress once again encompassed a boycott of British goods. This time it was even better organised, and cigarettes were a primary target. Between March and May 1930, the average monthly sales of BAT's cigarettes in India fell from just over 700 million to barely 300 million. The general trade depression had also set back this trade to enormous extent. Only in 1934 did sales begin to recover in earnest, and not until the outbreak of the World War II did they return to the levels of the late 1920s.[754] In a demi-official letter from the director of Industries, Bihar and Orissa in Patna to D. Milne, an agricultural expert, ICAR, Simla, the director mentioned that the Monghyr factory had employed 1,800–2,000 workers but that

> the boycott of European style cigarette had a disastrous effect for a short time on local factories of these and produced quite a considerable boom in *Biri* manufacture. It is expected that a permanent new industry of some importance may result. The leaf that covers *biris* has a peculiar forest fragrance not paralleled in any kind of cigarettes. [. . .] (Cigarette) marketing is very bad owing to boycott and economic condition.[755]

The factory management at Monghyr reacted by closing down departments one by one during three consecutive days and threatened the workforce that it was likely they would stop trading altogether. The workmen were worried, therefore, and refused to work unless they were promised a bonus in addition to the pay they were to receive next day. The manager had refused, and the workmen had reacted by shouting 'Mahatma Gandhi ki jai' (long live Mahatma Gandhi). *Hartal* was observed the next morning too, and finally, the manager had given in. In its report on this strike, the government of Bihar and Orissa judged that 'Peninsular is being ruined by Congress'.[756]

One 'G.D.K' had written in 1932, however, that the 'buy *swadeshi* propaganda', which had been 'on foot in India for about the last two years', had not become 'a permanent feature of Indian life', 'in spite of all this propaganda *swadeshi*'. He agreed, however, that *biri* consumption had tremendously increased in India, but one of the 'real' reasons for the use of *biris* instead of cigarettes was that, G.D.K. had argued, 'India is an extremely poor country' and 'her people cannot afford to buy articles whose price is high'.[757] Indeed, Biharis had had their own 'cigarettes', the *biris*, which were even cheaper than the cheapest cigarettes manufactured by Imperial Tobacco in Monghyr. The number of these *biris* had certainly increased during the 1920s, and that is why Mukherji concluded that the cigarette industry did face a slump 'due to the Civil Disobedience Movement'.[758]

In Bihar, indeed, mini-factories had propped up during the 1920s and 1930s in which a type of 'Indian cigarettes', that is *biris* (tobacco wrapped up in a leaf), were produced.[759] *Biris,* thus, were a typical *swadeshi* product in Bihar, the consumption of which was preferred by nationalists – and sometimes even prescribed by them – along with more traditional ways of taking tobacco, viz., *khaini* (chewable tobacco) and *zarda* (the addendum to betel leaf), snuff, and as smoke in the *hookah*. This resulted in a rising demand for *deshi* tobacco, which suited these *biris,* and at the same time a lower demand for cigarette tobaccos, and consequently, *koeris* stopped cultivating for the ILTDC. However, though alarmed, as both the government as well as the ILTDC had considered *koeris* their faithful collaborators, the commissioner of the division confided to district officers that he was quite sure that all this was just 'temporary enthusiasm' (for the boycott campaign) that would 'gradually wear off'.[760]

Besides, there was another angle too. Again, due to the successful cigarette boycotts in India and the rise of *biri* smoking, cigarette sales went down drastically and naturally the demand for flue-cured cigarette tobacco as well. Reportedly, the ILTDC, therefore, refused to buy the tobacco from the *koeris* under the pretext that the quality was insufficient. The ILTDC faced oversupply of tobacco leaf as the demand for the cheap cigarettes produced by its factory in Dalsingh Sarai had also decreased. The factory even had to close down (temporarily). ILTDC workers and *koeris* felt cheated and organised protest movements in and around the factory premises. Naturally, the Monghyr factory was also affected. Papiya Ghosh, for instance, alleged that during the early 1930s, when the Congress had declared its aim was 'complete independence' and had launched its campaign of civil disobedience, the 'Boycott Movement' had had disastrous consequence for Imperial Tobacco but also for its employees:

> As a result of the boycott of cigarettes in Bengal, Bihar, Orissa and Assam, the Imperial Tobacco Company Ltd., decided to close down its Munger factory. This meant unemployment for 4,000 factory workers. They subsequently formed a union and placed their plight before Congress and the press but apparently with little affect.[761]

The factory never closed down or at least not for long but *Bihar and Orissa Government Report for 1930–31* had confirmed:

> The large tobacco factory at Monghyr had a bad year on account of the boycott of the European style of cigarettes, and had to reduce its staff from about 3,000 to 1,200. The boycott caused a temporary boom in locally-made '*biris*', which may leave a permanent mark on that industry.[762]

Newly established trade unions in Bihar, during the 1930s, provided a voice to the factory's workforce for the first time. The government of Bihar and Orissa had, in 1934, anxiously reported on the deeds of one, Harish Chandra Varma, healing from Monghyr who was suspected to be 'a socialist'. He had caused troubles before at D. H. Railway (Monghyr) while working as a store's clerk there. Varma had now opened 'a labour office' in the tobacco factory under 'the pretext' that he wanted to help the workers who had been dismissed after the earthquake of 1934 when the factory had been enormously damaged following which the management had reduced the number of workers from 3,300 to 1,600. The out-of-job workers explained, however, that they had been removed following the instalment of a new machine in the remodelled factory after the earthquake and not because of 'boycotts' that had hampered the sale of cigarettes. These workers, therefore, welcomed Varma's initiative.[763]

In 1935, the government of Bihar reported on 'socialist activities' in Jamalpur (railway workshop) and in the tobacco factory in Monghyr. In this case, R. N. Sharma had told the tobacco workers that the 'government had given the factory Rs. 50,000/- after the earthquake and that this money had been squandered by the factory and not passed on the labourers'.[764] The government, furthermore, elaborated on a 'trade dispute between Peninsular Tobacco Company, Monghyr, and the workmen of company said' in a report of 1939 and in 1950 after India had become an independent Republic and narrated there had been a dispute between workmen representing the Tobacco Manufacturing Workers' Union at Monghyr and the management because the latter had wished to revert to 'single-shift working', which would mean a 'retrenchment of about 1,600 workmen'. This time BAT took firm steps and permanently closed down all its redrying factories in and near Dalsingh Sarai. Thence, ILTDC was to concentrate on its factories in South India only. From that time onwards, the cigarette factory at Monghyr ordered its flue-cured yellow-coloured tobacco leaf from the town of Chirala in Madras, where a new redrying factory had flourished since 1922 already.[765] The Monghyr factory was there to stay but thus produced cigarettes from leaf acquired from outside the state, and these cheap cigarettes were mainly exported to the rest of India, and a small quantity thereof even went overseas. Its management remained for quite some time in the hands of 'foreigners' and the only Bihari element were its workers.

Thus, in Bihar, the ITC had faced problems that resulted from civil disobedience and non-cooperation movements during which also the *kisan* (peasant) movement and trade unions had gathered strength in Bihar,[766] demanding a better deal for *raiyats*[767] and factory workers and during which protests against cigarettes also played a role, negatively influencing the profits of the cigarette factory in Monghyr. Apart from economics, there, thus, was the 'value' attached to cigarette tobacco during the 1920s and 1930s that should be taken into account. Basu had, for instance, observed that though technically the bulk of the cigarettes manufactured in Monghyr (now spelled Munger) and sold by Imperial Tobacco were, like *Ganja*, not 'foreign', 'the British connection was obvious, and along with all foreign goods, cigarettes manufactured in Monghyr were now shunned by nationalists in Bihar and elsewhere'.[768] The success Imperial Tobacco had enjoyed in its initial years in Bihar had, therefore, eclipsed less most likely due to economic considerations of peasants as to which tobacco variety was more profitable to them (i.e. *deshi* or cigarette tobacco) but more due to the political storm that pervaded the state during the 1920s and 1930s. In this situation, it was difficult for the *Kisan Sabha* to decide on what was the 'better deal for the *raiyats*'. Moreover, besides the boycott movement, the general deteriorating economic situation in Bihar in 1935 had affected, as Mukherji detailed, all 'those growing money crops like jute, chilly, and tobacco', and these *raiyats* 'suffered considerably by the prevailing low prices', which might have induced them to switch to more lucrative crops or to food crops.[769]

Basu likewise concluded that 'the combination of the Great Depression and the boycott was a calamity for the company'. She explained that by 1931, 'the boycott against Imperial Tobacco's cigarettes had reached its peak, and sales were virtually non-existent'. Yet worse was to come. This was the earthquake in Monghyr. J. L. Bowring provided not only a first-hand account but also described how the earthquake had destroyed parts of the cigarette factory. The death toll in Monghyr town had been very heavy amounting to between 2,000 and 3,000 people, yet 'surprisingly, in the factory area, only one death was sustained'. Yet the top of the factory chimney had broken off and had fallen on the boiler house below, severing a main steam-pipe. Besides, in the course of the earthquake, the whole of the company's depot in Khajauli had been demolished.[770] The damage suffered by the Monghyr factory because of the 1934 earthquake only added to the foes of the cigarette factory in Bihar and 'finally competition of so-called *swadeshi* cigarette factories threatened the near monopoly Imperial Tobacco had enjoyed'. Labour agitations at Monghyr as well as at the sides of the redrying factories, in particular the one at Dalsingh Sarai, followed such closures and worker retrenchments.[771] Nevertheless, in the long run, the factory was remodelled and survived, but it was the three buying depots with their redrying machines that paid the price. Basu narrated:

> When the demand for tobacco reduced by 1930 to nil, there was no option but to close down the three buying depots at Dalsingserai, Khajauli and Shahpur Patory. Overhead expenses were further pruned through the closure of the sales branch at Patna, and its transfer to the now surplus accommodation

at the three depots. For these depots the consequences were
to be far reaching.

Though Dalsingh Sarai reopened in 1933, Shahpur in 1937, and Khajauli
the following year in 1938, they were doomed. Already in 1931, Champaka
Basu announced, 'the death knell of the three depots had sounded' suddenly;
however, Basu brings up the 'quality' of the tobacco that was not sufficient:

> However, there was little doubt that *the quality of the tobacco*
> [emphasis mine] was not very satisfactory. Though efforts were
> made continuously to improve the tobacco and to encourage
> the farmers to grow more, the days of the three depots were
> numbered. Their end, *brought about indirectly by various
> political factors* [emphasis mine], was hastened by the fact
> that the Indian Leaf Tobacco Development Company (ILTD)
> had discovered in the intervening years a more promising
> tobacco-growing area and had established itself successfully
> in what came to be called the South India Leaf Area or SILA
> in Andhra Pradesh.[772]

In the last and concluding chapter of this book, I will come back to this
statement by Basu.

CHAPTER EIGHT

New Ventures in Sugar Cane and Tobacco Improvement in Bihar

By 1950, British plant colonisers had all but vanished from Bihar's landscape. Though the Monghyr factory remained and was still under British management, tobacco leaf for cigarette blending was not any longer grown in Bihar. The factory now acquired this from present-day Andhra Pradesh in southern India. Not only had the ILTDC abandoned its plant improvement scheme in Bihar, however. Pusa's Imperial Agricultural Research Institute's slow withdrawal from tobacco colonisation in Bihar had, in fact, started as soon as the Howards had engineered the desired seed that did produce, provided certain cultivation and curing methods were observed, some quite acceptable quality of cigarette tobacco leaf. The legacy these British officials and 'non-officials' such as planters and ILTDC managers left behind was, however, more than abandoned bungalows, ruins of indigo vats, earthquake-destroyed remains of the old Imperial Agricultural Research Institute's premises, tobacco redrying factories, and graveyards. In this concluding chapter, I show that the changes that took places at Imperial Pusa during the 1920s and 1930s announced the beginning of yet another plant colonisation scheme that in the Republic of India continued without the British. Importantly, these changes at Pusa caused the imperial government to look for other places within and outside India where they could continue their efforts at tobacco colonisation. And as analysed in this chapter, the imperial withdrawal from tobacco improvement in Bihar created space for the newly formed government of Bihar to start improving their 'own' *deshi* (country) tobacco in an independent India and for its home market.

The End of Imperial Pusa and Its Tobacco Improvement Project in Bihar

The outcomes of agricultural research conducted at the Imperial Institute at Pusa were meant to be used not only in Bihar but also in many other parts in India, such as Bengal, Punjab, and the United Provinces, in fact in the whole of British India as well as Burma and even in other parts of the British Empire. This implied that what was researched was also dictated by (economic) needs existing outside Bihar or even India. Research at Imperial Pusa could, therefore, be useful to cultivators in the, in 1912, created province of Bihar (and Orissa till 1936) but did not necessarily have to be so in order to be pronounced 'successful'.[773]

Till the end of the 1910s, Imperial Pusa did not face much resistance against this state of affairs from within as well as from outside India. Yet by 1918–19 and under severe political pressure from the provinces in India (including the provinces of Bihar and Orissa), the Government of India Act of 1919 had been implemented. These so-called Montagu–Chelmsford Reforms allowed progressive responsibility to Indians for executive government, and the first steps were, as Peter Robb detailed, 'territorial constituencies' and 'partial responsible government (diarchy) in the provinces'.[774] These reforms had, as David Arnold analysed, 'far-reaching effects on the organisation, funding and political complexion of late colonial science'. As a result of this decentralisation effort, Imperial Pusa, instead of being the apex of agricultural research, found itself out of touch with the provinces that, as David Arnold put it, 'were originally intended to their scientific fiefdoms'.[775]

In 1928, eight years after the governments of Bihar and Orissa had initiated these reforms in the province, a Royal Commission on Agriculture in India under the chairmanship of the Marquess of Linlithgow was formed to 'examine and report on the present conditions of agriculture and rural economy in British India and to make recommendations for the improvements of agriculture and the promotion and welfare and prosperity of the rural population'. Yet it was not within the scope of the Commission's duties to inquire into the existing systems of landownership and tenancy or the assessment of land revenue and irrigation charges or existing division of funds between the Government of India and local governments.[776]

For the purpose, the Royal Commission had invited 'officers serving under the GoI' to give their frank opinion regarding the Imperial Institute at Pusa. The evidence recorded showed that many of these officers had a problem with the organisational structure as it was at the time and even with the very location of the Imperial Institute in Bihar. G. S. Henderson, the imperial agriculturist at Pusa at the time, had been the most outspoken on such matters of 'administration', and in his opinion, 'the stage has now been reached in the history of the Agricultural Departments of India at which the greatest necessity is a thorough revision and reorganisation of the existing administrative system'. He argued that if the 'present state of affairs continues, some of the provinces will have a very large organisation and will completely overshadow not only the other provinces but also the agricultural machinery of the Central Government', which had, since 1912, its capital in Delhi. Henderson recalled that the original idea of the Central Agricultural Department at Pusa, that is for the whole of British India, had been a body of six heads of sections who were 'presumed to be experts of such standing that they carried weight in their branch of agricultural science throughout India' (and not only within Bihar). He added that these scientists had been situated at Pusa as 'a convenient centre or more probably from motives of economy as the Pusa Estate was lying vacant'. The director of Pusa had been the coordinating head, and the department as a whole was represented by the inspector general of agriculture who had kept in touch with the Central Government and 'by means of extensive touring' had been acquainted with conditions in all provinces. However, this post had been abolished, and the director of Pusa and the agricultural adviser to the GoI were, thereafter, 'vested in the one incumbent'. Henderson believed that the time had arrived 'for a thorough consideration of this situation':

> It seems to me that the Department of Agriculture under the Central Government has been too closely associated with Pusa. The name Pusa and the Central Agricultural Department are now synonymous [. . .] hand in hand with the extension which

has taken place in some of the Provinces, there should have been expansion not so much of Pusa, as of the Sections. Some of the Sections should have expanded and establish centres in other parts of India if anything like the original proposition was to have been maintained.[777]

Henderson also pointed to the 'political aspect' under the new conditions following the reforms, which was in his opinion 'all important':

> Where the Directors of Agriculture are in touch with current political affairs, there is a much greater likelihood of getting the requisite financial support and machinery for expansion. In some Provinces the Director is a member of the Legislative Council, in other cases, he deals with the Minister concerned, chiefly through permanent secretaries and undersecretaries. Difficulties may be caused by the situation of headquarters and other factors. These factors have a large bearing on the success of a department. In the Central Government the Head of the Agricultural Department had to be frequently present with the Government in Simla and Delhi while his main headquarters is at Pusa and he has to do a heavy touring to keep in touch with all the Provinces in India.[778]

In Bihar, there were others who had problems with Imperial Pusa yet more as they felt that the Agricultural Department under the GoI (located under the same roof) had too much say in matters that concerned agriculture in Bihar only. Such debates had continued the following year as reflected in the *Proceedings of the Board of Agriculture in India* of 1929. Related to this, the inauguration of the Imperial Council of Agricultural Research at Pusa was applauded upon by all. The Royal Commission had recommended the formation of such a council at Pusa in order to solve some of the problems outlined by Henderson, among others. It was explicitly stated that the 'council has not attempted to interfere in any way with Provincial Departments of Agriculture or the control of these departments', and it was emphasised that 'all the council wishes to do is to supplement the efforts made in the provinces'. Moreover, Sir T. Vijayaraghavachariar in his opening speech on the first day of the board meeting had said that the grants of the council were as open to the provinces as to Imperial Institutions:

> I think we are living in spacious times; the old era of depression is disappearing and it is up to all of us to put up promising schemes of improvement now that we can get the necessary funds for carrying them out. Personally, I feel that in the time to come, whatever political changes may come about, our work will be, if anything, more important than before.[779]

With increased decentralisation, the conflicting interests between the Agricultural Department of the provinces of Bihar and Orissa and Imperial Pusa became even more visible, however. Actually, under the Devolution Rules that had followed the 1919 Act, agricultural research did not fall exclusively either in the Central or in the provincial field. Under item 33 of Schedule 1, 'central agencies and institutions for research and for professional or technical training or promotion of special studies' (such as cigarette tobacco research, for instance) had remained an imperial subject. At the same time, under item 10 of Part II of Schedule II, agriculture, including research institutes, was classified as a provincial subject, and agricultural research was conducted by or under the agricultural departments of the provincial governments, but the lines on which research was carried remained uncoordinated. Consequently, tussles had emerged between the GoI and the governments of Bihar and Orissa and other provincial governments such as that of Bengal which was now separated from Bihar and Orissa.[780]

For instance, there was an ongoing debate as to which path tobacco research should take in Bengal as well as in Bihar and Orissa. N. G Mukerji, a civil engineer employed by the Bengal government, was worried as 'native *chilim* tobacco is unfortunately going out and cigarettes taking its place'. He was aware that for cigarette tobacco, 'the ordinary native tobacco is too much fermented and is too dark and brittle'. In order to produce the 'small-sized leaves with golden colour that make the best cigarette tobacco', 'the whole curing must be altered' and 'the European method of curing' had to be introduced. He had wondered, therefore, whether this was all worth investigation as the costs of flue-curing were much higher than 'the ordinary native method'.[781] Whereas most scientists and bureaucrats at Imperial Pusa were of the opinion that research related to flue-cured Bright tobacco had to be continued at Pusa, others felt that tobacco research should concentrate on dark *deshi* tobaccos as this was the most important commodity of commerce for local cultivators in Tirhut and the cultivation of cigarette tobacco was 'not for the ordinary tobacco cultivators'. G. S. Henderson, now director of Agriculture Department, Bihar and Orissa, described in 1931:

> The Muzaffarpur-Darbangha (Tirhut) area is largely in the hands of the cultivating caste known as *Koeries*. They specialise in tobacco cultivation and their technique is especially good. I have not seen tobacco cultivation in any part of India so well cultivated as is done by these *Koeries*. The plants are gone over individually, all auxiliary shoots and adventitious leaves are carefully nipped off. The *Koeries* grow tobacco without irrigation and the land is very carefully cultivated and a very good tilth is prepared. All cultivation is done by hand. Very heavy manuring is resorted to and 'seeth', i.e. refuse from indigo vats is very highly valued.

Henderson had added that 'tobacco is considered as a specialised crop and generally is confined to *koerie* cultivators and so its extension is unlikely to any extent as capital involved in the cultivation is too large for the ordinary cultivator'.[782] Tension between Imperial Pusa and the provinces remained during the early 1930s, yet the government of Bihar did not have to come to blows with the GoI over the issue of tobacco improvement as the latter left Pusa 'voluntarily'. A powerful earthquake of 1934 was badly felt at Pusa and totally destroyed the massive (Phipps) laboratory.[783] Subsequently, the 'imperial' part of the Pusa institute was transferred to Delhi, the new capital of British India.[784] After this earthquake, the Imperial Council of Agricultural Research was also shifted away from Pusa and accommodated in New Delhi. It was there that the imperial tobacco improvement scheme continued.[785]

Figure 37. A great earthquake in 1934 destroyed major parts of the original agricultural research institute at Pusa. Photograph by author.

In Delhi, the Imperial Institute of Agricultural Research, after having received recommendations of the Imperial Council of Agricultural Research, decided that cigarette tobacco research should be carried out in a tobacco substation located in South India (Guntur)[786] and that Pusa should concentrate on general botanical research. Consequently, Pusa became a botanical substation financed by the Imperial Council of Agricultural Research. However, the imperial botanist remained at Pusa to supervise studies on tobacco diseases such as the leaf-curl disease. Besides, trials with flue-curing tobacco were also carried out which showed 'most encouraging' results, showing that 'definite opportunity exists for flue curing of tobacco in Bihar for people with a little money to invest'. Apparently, not all was lost for cigarette tobacco in Bihar at that point in time.[787]

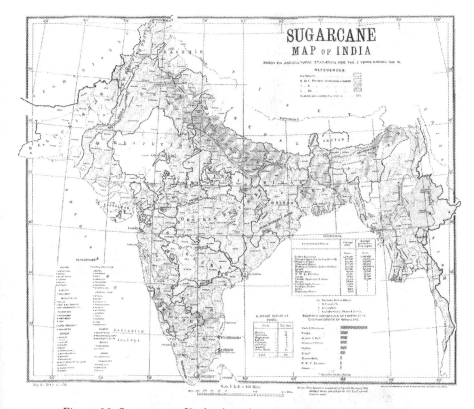

Figure 38. Sugar map of India, based on agricultural statistics for the five years ending 1918–19, Commercial Intelligence Department (Calcutta), Calcutta: Government Printing, 1923 (courtesy Forum Library (Special Collections), Wageningen University, The Netherlands).

Quadruple Unites Again: An Imperial Sugar Cane Improvement Scheme at Pusa

In the first half of the nineteenth century, cane sugar had been an export commodity of many Bihar districts including the Tirhut region. The British EIC had encouraged its cultivation to some extent, yet after 1850, this cane from Bihar had been priced out of London markets by beet sugar. Nevertheless, as the local markets for cane sugar had grown, its cultivation had never disappeared in Bihar. Around that time, sugar cane was used to produce 'impure' sweeteners *gur* and *khand* by local manufacturers. It had remained a '*deshi* plant', and as Ulbe Bosma detailed 'attempts to improve the quality of the sugar by industrial means were discouraged by the differential duties for better-refined sugars, kept in place by the interests of the London refiners who were perfectly happy with the khandsaris'. However, between 1860 and 1900, a British estate-owning company and a few others had improved the small non-industrial refineries (*khandsari*) through, among others, the introduction of the two-roller 'beheea' mill to crush cane, in place of the wooden mortar and pestle.

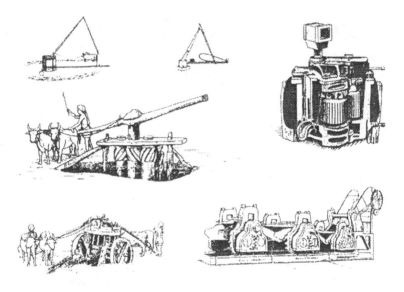

SUGARCANE MILLS—PRIMITIVE AND MODERN.

Figure 39. Sugar mills primitive and modern. Burt, B. C. 'The Indian Sugar Industry', *Journal of the Royal Society of Arts*, Vol. 83, No. 4317, 16 August 1935, p. 922.

Published by: Royal Society for the Encouragement of Arts, Manufactures and Commerce Article Stable URL: http://www.jstor.org/stable/41360530 (courtesy RSA London), last accessed on July 2014.

No efforts had been undertaken, however, to induce *raiyats* to grow sugar cane for a 'modern' factory rather than making *gur*. Actually, it had been decided that no (export) market existed for 'industrial sugar' at the time.[788] Different voices were attended to by the 1890s, however, when India had turned into an importer of European sugar, and agricultural experts in India could finally,

Bosma explained, 'drive home their point that the GoI should do more for the country's agriculture'.[789]

This actually meant that by the turn of the century, the GoI had decided it should revive its colonisation scheme for sugar cane in order to make sugar an export commodity that could compete with sugar from Mauritius, China, and Java on the European markets. At the same time, this would liberate India from its dependence on industrial sugar from those countries and make it self-sufficient in this regard. To realise this aim not only processing methods had to be improved upon but now also the plant itself had to be improved by innovations in planting, by ploughing, or by applying fertilisers. Subsequently, in order to enhance knowledge of how water, soil, manure, and cane varieties influenced the yield, 'model sugar farms' had been started similar to the tobacco improvement model farm that had been established in Pusa in 1870.[790] British indigo planter, Minden J. Wilson, in his *History of Behar Indigo Factories*, wrote in 1908, how the situation in Bihar had in particular changed around 1900 when sugar operations were revived. Wilson himself had also changed his mind regarding sugar cane:

> I have been asked by some planters to give my ideas as to why sugar proved a failure in Behar in 1845–50 and to say what I think of the prospects of its proving a paying industry under improved methods of cultivation and manufacture. My experience of sugar during the early years of sugar manufacture in Tirhoot did not impress me much in favour of its turning out a success, and its eventual abandonment showed that this was the general idea. However, I have had reason after reviewing the faults committed in the growing of cane in those bygone days to change or modify my views considerably [. . .]. The soil of Behar is as a rule light, and a cane crop easily exhausts it. The soil north of the Bhagmattee river in Tirhoot proper is stiffer and better for cane, but the lands there are liable to inundation. In 1854–50 little or attempts at manuring were tried. Most factories grew indigo side by side with sugarcane, but the valuable 'seeth' (refuse) manure was not made use of. In those days saltpetre was a very paying industry and the 'seeth' was used for fuel in the saltpetre

refineries [. . .] who had started sugar were utterly ignorant of what was required to make the industry a success [. . .] That cane will grow in Behar there is no doubt, for I find, in documents of 1793 and after, nearly all the old indigo factories in Tirhoot are spoken of as being sugar and saltpetre, as well as indigo manufactories. In some parts of Behar cane grows better than in others. The reason why the sugar industry was abandoned after 1849–50 was that prices of indigo began to run up and the dye sold at very profitable prices, so men did not bother their heads about sugar. Before sugar was started in 1845 prices of indigo had fallen very low [. . .] Planters who generally grew a few bighas of cane as fodder for their bullocks knew from this experience that indigo grew well in lands where cane had been sown and *vice versa*, and they therefore did not see why cane should not be made a success, and after some study the conclusions come to were that cane to be a paying crop must be grown in new lands. Those lands must be well manured [. . .] Indigo refuse (seeth) must be looked upon as the most valuable of all manures and be carefully guarded and used as well as all bullock, horse and stable refuse [. . .] The new machinery worked by the India Development Co. has been found to make excellent sugar, none of the old defects coming out.[791]

Figure 40. A prize crop of sugar under 'scientific management' in the 1930s in Bihar. MacDonald, B. *India Sunshine and Shadows,* London: BACSA, 1988 (courtesy BACSA, British Association for Cemeteries in South Asia).

Wilson had not been the only planter who had looked towards sugar cane now that indigo was on its way out. In fact, while some indigo planters kept on trying 'to save' indigo, by the beginning of the twentieth century, there were others who had already started looking for alternatives. Such experimentation had been stimulated by the Imperial authorities at Pusa who, as shown before, had looked upon these planters as collaborators in their own Imperial agriculture improvement project. Moreover, as the lieutenant governor of Bengal noted in 1900, the indigo planters

have claims upon the Government. They have rendered valuable services in the past on many occasions of administrative stress, their disappearance would be in many ways a great administrative los, and they have embarked a large amount of capital in the industry. The Lieutenant-Governor considers that any reasonable assistance which the Government can give in inquiries, either towards improved methods of indigo cultivation and manufacture or towards a substitute for it in the shape of more profitable crops, should certainly be given [. . .] Regarding the second point, there are grounds for believing that it may be profitable to the indigo planters of North Behar to take up the cultivation of the sugar-cane and the manufacture of sugar, either by growing cane as a rotation crop in alternate years and keeping the growth and manufacture of indigo, or even by abandoning the latter industry altogether for the manufacture of sugar.[792]

The *Times* correspondent in Simla, who had reported on this 'important step' by the government that had been taken 'to assist the indigo planters of Bihar', also added that a great demand existed among the people for refined sugar, which had been met with by bounty-fed imports until the imposition of sugar duties and thereafter had been satisfied by imports from Mauritius. Yet as labour was cheap in Bihar and abundant available and dear and scare in Mauritius, Bihar had great potential, and cultivation had already begun on an experimental basis.[793] Indeed, around 1903, Bernard Coventry, a British planter who abandoned indigo in 1912, became a 'companion of the most eminent order of the Indian Empire' and also took charge of the Office of Agricultural Adviser to the GoI and even became director of the Imperial Pusa Institute in 1913. He had experienced, for instance, with rhea as 'the decline of the indigo trade induced the indigo planters of Behar to seek new enterprise for their capital'.[794] Importantly, whereas in other Bihar districts in particular in Saran and Champaran, indigo factories either had closed completely or had switched to (industrial/refined white) sugar production only; S. K. Mittal mentioned that 'the (indigo) factories of Muzaffarpur, Darbhanga, and Monghyr stopped work and several took to growing of other crops'.[795]

As many indigo factories had started as sugar concerns a century before, sugar cane was an obvious first option in Tirhut. However, the 'new' gentlemen planters, as they were called, now were interested in the production of 'white sugar' by 'modern factories' and thus started a renewed effort at colonisation of the sugar cane plant in Bihar among them. These planters obviously expected the government to help them with the necessary knowledge as well as capital. Stimulated by such demands for state aid by such planters, the government of Bengal had indeed appointed a committee in 1901 'to inquire into the prospects of the cultivation of sugar by indigo planters in Bihar'. The government of Bengal recognised that

> the cultivation of cane on the methods now employed, and the manufacture of raw sugar there from by the native methods, do not present any prospects of financial success to a European in competition with the native cultivator and manufacturer, and it would be unwise of planters to adopt such methods.

New refining methods had, therefore, to be found for 'the European' to succeed as 'most of the refining is done by rough, inefficient, and expensive processes, the outcome of which cannot compete with sugar refined by modern and scientific methods and appliances'. The Bengal government came forward in this respect, as it was analysed, 'there is no room to doubt that the largest quantity of sugar that can be made by the planters in Bihar will find an expanding and profitable market beyond the limits of Bihar'. The Bengal government, therefore, recommended research as to which methods of cultivation could be adopted by the planters who would be 'susceptible of immense improvement and call for immediate reform' as thus far, 'indeed, nothing whatever has been done in Bihar to improve the cultivation either by rational treatment of the soil, by a rational manner of planting the canes, or by the introduction of improved varieties'. Yet at this historical juncture, GoI did not go beyond recommending 'systematic and coordinated experiments in cultivation' at the Imperial Pusa Research Institute:

> In the course of conversation with the many gentlemen who have spoken to us on the subject of this report, it has frequently been suggested that the Government might give the planters financial assistance towards the cultivation and manufacture of sugar. It seems clear, however, from the terms of the Resolution of the Government of Bengal in which this inquiry was ordered that the Government do not propose to

offer financial aid to individual planters, but desire to limit their intervention to ascertaining through an independent Committee whether the cultivation and manufacture of sugar offer a sufficiently attractive prospect to induce capitalists to invest their money in the venture.

Sugar cane was only one of the alternatives for indigo explored at the time, and the government had stated that

> further, if the government were to aid the cultivation and manufacture of sugar there would be no justification for refusing financial help to persons engaged in other agricultural industries where the product of the field labour needs to be manufactured before it can be brought into use – for instance, cotton, jute, oilseeds, tea.

Therefore, though the GoI recommended research to be carried on other 'country crops' such as tobacco, it was, nevertheless, agreed that the research stations that already were involved in indigo experimentation could also be used for conducting experiments with sugar cane. The government also understood that such

> agricultural experiments must proceed continuously over a long series of years before definite and really valuable results can be secured, and it is possible that private individuals, associations, or syndicates may be disinclined after a time to defray the costs of continuing them when so much of the accumulated experience is withheld.[796]

British officials in Bihar did also recognise that sugar cane was the 'most important crop after indigo' and that its cultivation had been extended during recent years and also 'owing to decline of indigo'.[797] The *District Gazetteer of Darbhanga* of 1907 recognised sugar cane's potential in Tirhut:

> The most important crop after indigo is sugarcane. It has long been grown in the Mudhubani subdivision and in Behera thana, but its cultivation has been extended of recent

years owing to the decline of indigo. In the earlier days the cultivation of sugarcane was very considerable, and many of the indigo concerns were started as sugar factories, the manufacture of sugar being given up when indigo proved to be more profitable. The reverse process is now taking place, as indigo is in many places being replaced by sugarcane [. . .] Sugarcane is one of the profitable crops grown in the district in spite of the labour and expense its cultivation requires. It is a crop, which not only exhaust the soil, but occupies the ground for a long period, extending over a year. As the price of sugar fluctuates considerably, its cultivation is always somewhat of a speculation. One attraction, however, to the ryot is that he can generally get an advance from the person for whom he grows the crop, and this factor almost invariably causes an extension of sugarcane cultivation in a year of drought, when other crops have failed and the cultivator are pressed for ready money.[798]

Though the GoI remained supporting research experiments with other plants such as tobacco for quite some time to come, as shown in this book, it did, indeed, recognise sugar cane as one of the alternatives that could replace indigo, and it was prepared to help British planters (and other forthcoming capitalists) in their efforts to transform the plant into white sugar, so much in demand in Europe. Besides, it was hoped that by improving the quality of sugar within India, needs for importing the commodity would decrease, and India would thus become self-sufficient as far as industrial sugar was concerned. However, during the nascent days of this new industry in Bihar, open state support to planters had been limited less by fulfilling the demand of these planters for aid the government would appear 'partial'.[799]

Subsequent *Reports of the Bihar and Orissa Government* bear out that not only the GoI but also the government of Bihar (and Orissa) favoured the nascent sugar industry in the state, and research in sugar (cane) improvement had been carried out in this regard. The contribution of British planters was highly appreciated in this regard. It was also argued that the cultivation of industrial sugar cane profited the *raiyats*. The *Report of 1923* mentioned, for instance, that special attention had been given to the improvement of sugar cane in the province, and the results of experimental work, both in the laboratory and on the farms, had been successful in introducing a number of improvements.[800] Similarly, B. Abdy Collins of the Indian Civil Service reiterated in his *Report of 1925–26* that indigo used to be an important crop in Bihar, but he was happy to announce that most factories had now switched over to sugar cane. In 1924, a 'Sugar Bureau' had been opened at Imperial Pusa, and Wynne Sayer, the officer in charge of this Sugar Bureau and once the assistant to the agricultural adviser to the GoI, had mentioned that one of the 'contributory factors to the success of the Pusa work had been the presence in the locality of an enlightened set of planters' who had given up the indigo crop and 'were eagerly on the lookout for another to replace it'. He agreed with other members of the *Royal Commission on the Agriculture in India* that such 'enlightened planters like those in the white sugar belt of Bihar are not generally available elsewhere', and these British planters could now help the *raiyats* how to improve their cane.[801]

A scheme for research had been drawn up by the Sugar Bureau that then was taken into consideration by the newly formed Bihar and Orissa Agricultural Committee. Subsequently, it was submitted to the Imperial Council of Agricultural Research for a grant. A similar scheme was proposed for rice as a 'systematic attack on the problems presented by these two crops, the one the most important and the other the most paying crop in the province, is one of the most vital needs of the department'.[802] The *Bihar and Orissa Report in 1931–32* detailed that in northern Bihar, the ready market for the sugar cane crop had lessened the cultivator's difficulties, and white sugar factories were said to have paid him as much as Rs. 80 lakhs in hard cash for the crop. The report concluded that 'this advance in cane cultivation is of the greatest economic value when it is remembered that in 1931 and 1932 sugar cane was the one crop which supplied the cultivator with ready resource of cash'.[803] Finally, the Bihar Department of Agriculture reported in 1932 that the Imperial Council of Agricultural Research at Pusa had indeed sanctioned grants totalling Rs. 3¾ lakhs, to be spread over five years, for rice and sugar cane research. The rice research station was planned at Sabour and the sugar cane station near Muzaffarpur. Muzaffarpur, once the centre of the indigo planters, therefore, now became a 'sugar centre', and the use of improved cane varieties was propagated.

Subsequently, Bihar became 'a storm centre' during which the *Kisan Sabha* and the Congress nationalist party gained strength from 1933 to 1947.[804] In the midst of this agricultural turmoil, though other plants such as tobacco were also considered to be valuable, the Provincial Agriculture Department of Bihar and Orissa decided that a scheme for sugar improvement was the need of day. This department had, furthermore, requested the Imperial Institute at Pusa to support a sugar colonisation scheme in Bihar that also would have the support and involvement of Indians. By that time, it was clear to the GoI that support of sugar cane research had the full support of the provincial government too. Unlike cigarette tobacco, nationalists in Bihar, some of whom had (in 1937) even been installed in the Bihar government, were 'in search of methods of industrial sugar production that did not involve plantations', and 'an equitable order was sought that would reconcile the interests of cultivators and the factories'.[805] By 1933, albeit late, the GoI therefore, because cigarette tobacco seemed to be doomed in Bihar, abandoned their dilly-dally attitudes, and 'sugar improvement' in Bihar now received their total support. A new colonisation project had indeed matured in Bihar that again had united private capitalists (British planters and their sponsors), Indian *zamindars* and *raiyats,* the GoI and government of Bihar as well as scientists.[806] Importantly, 'industrial sugar', unlike 'cigarette tobacco' and indigo in Bihar, had been incorporated as a 'national commodity' that now could be improved upon.

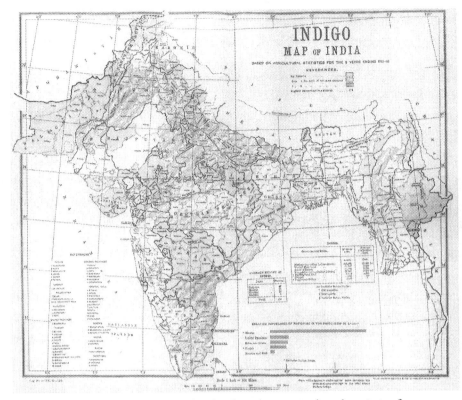

Figure 41. Indigo map of India, based on agricultural statistics for the five years ending 1918–19. Commercial Intelligence Department (Calcutta), Calcutta: Government Printing, 1923 (courtesy Forum Library (Special Collections), Wageningen University, The Netherlands).

Discoloured Indigo, Sugar Cane, and British Gentlemen Planters in Bihar

Indigo cultivation in Bihar not only vanished as a result of the arrival of synthetic (chemical) dye on the markets. For at least two decades afterwards, as shown in this book, indigo planters had had hope against hope that with indigo's improvement, they would win the battle. It was, in particular, the arrival of Mahatma Gandhi to the Champaran District of old Tirhut in 1918 that had caused most planters to finally stop indigo cultivation more or less.[807] Though its cultivation did continue elsewhere in India, in Bihar it had been Gandhi's 'anti-indigo movement' that had really stained indigo beyond return.

Definitely, indigo was associated with the (bad) Englishman and therefore valued negatively. Significantly, though the English concerns targeted in the Bettiah subdivision of the Champaran district around 1910 had been indigo and sugar factories,[808] sugar cane was never discredited in the same way as indigo-producing plants. Indeed, the 'British *zamindar*[809] had learnt some lessons by 1920. Mittal explained: 'In these altered circumstances, planters found themselves reduced to the position of ordinary agriculturists and their imposing investments in factories resulted in dead lost.' Though initially, these indigo planters had 'devised means to transfer their loss on to the shoulders of the tenants',[810] by 1920, they had mend their ways as the government perceived that 'much of what is going on (anti-indigo movements) had every appearance of being a purely anti-European movement'.[811] The altered behaviour in the 1920s was, in particular, reflected in the way these new 'English gentlemen planters' treated 'their' employees. It was, for instance, reported that in the Dalsingh Sarai Concern managed by a family member of B. Coventry of Pusa,

> the rate of pay for labourers is somewhat excessive in this district, but the extra cost is counterbalanced to some extent by the fact that the collies are more enlightened and are of better physique than the average Indian worker. About six hundred daily hands are employed, exclusive of a considerable number who are hired when required.[812]

The old 'indigo planter', who had ruled in Tirhut during the second half of the nineteenth century, was thus replaced by the new 'gentleman planter'. Wilson had described the former:

> Fancy, in your imagination, the manager of Dooria with his sleeves turned up pulling at his *hookah* a hundred years ago putting together his account of expenditure in peace and comfort far away from Europe and the bustle of the French revolution. No trains at Motipore, no worrying telegrams from bothering agents. Probably he never dreamt of the decay of the industry nor the heavy rise in factory outlays.[813]

By the 1930s, this 'old indigo planter', that is the single sole who had stayed put, was treated by the new and also changed government official (the so-called competition *wallah*)[814] posted in Muzaffarpur with slight pity:

> May 18th (1933). Last Sunday my work took me for the first time, bar the visit to Patna, outside the station. It was out at a planter's bungalow about twenty five miles away. I went out with one of the Indian Deputy Collectors in a taxi, which needless to say got a block in the petrol pipe en route. This defect was remedied by blowing down it with the air pump, and so we proceeded on our course dodging cows and infants all the way here and back! The planter was a dear old man who had been in India for 38 years. There were no electric fans and the old-fashioned punkah was kept going by a small boy, who stopped it obligingly, when I put a match to my pipe.[815]

By 1925, most of these planters of the olden times had departed, however. The same government servant described:

> I set forth on a long walk this afternoon down beside the lake at Sikandarpur and along the embankment to Daudpur and back by a new way across ploughed fields and innumerable mango orchards. I passed by what had obviously once been a planter's bungalow in the palmy old days of the indigo industry. It was a fine big building with what must once have been a lovely garden. It was pathetic to see it all so derelict. The picturesque rounded tiles were rapidly falling away from the roof and the stucco was coming away in great cakes from the pillars of the verandah. A public footpath runs through the compound past the old base of a sundial. The forlorn appearance of the house was increased by the presence of a tall and solitary coconut palm before the front door . . .[816]

Besides, the few 'indigo planters' from olden days who had stayed put had to cope with younger blood. T. Woodhouse described his experiences as assistant manager in 'an indigo factory in Bihar' around 1926 and had commented:

While he (the *burra sahib*) dressed for dinner each evening or, more strictly speaking, was being dressed by his bearer, I used to sit in his dressing-room and drink in words of wisdom. Pencil and paper ever ready, I made notes of Hindi words and phrases to learn. These I would commit to memory before getting up in the morning, and later in the day I would try them out on the collies in the fields. The first few pages of jottings I took down were, with the exception of a few commonplace nouns, all imperatives: 'Do this!' 'Come quickly!' 'Work faster!' 'Weigh these oats!' 'Get out of my way!' 'Fine that man two *annas!*' Maybe if I had gone out to the East before the world War, I should soon have fallen in with this point of view. But since I had just spent four and half years myself in hammering and being hammered, my opinions about the efficacy of that particular method of dealing with men had swung, pendulum-like, to the opposite extreme. I was in search of peace, personal if not international, and I was in no mood to resume my cudgel. Fortunately after a month or so my burra sahib, 'big' sahib, went home for a year's vacation, leaving me to look after the concern with a handful of imperatives and an occasional visit from his brother, who ran a factory about thirty-five miles away. Until he left, I hurled shouts and curses at the men in our employ in strict obedience to his orders, but thereafter I was free to follow my own bent toward good fellowship.[817]

Joan Allen also described this 'indigo planter' of former days. Joan had grown up from 'Missy Baba' to 'Burra Mem' on a 'plantation' in Darbhanga. Her father had been a manager of one of the maharaja of Darbhanga's many estates and had been in charge of the indigo production, as well as the cultivation of the plant itself, as this 'planter's daughter' narrated later on in life, 'also that of many other crops grown locally'. She described that between 1896 and 1913,

much of the land was leased out to tenant farmers in small plots, from whom rents needed collection. All this meant many hours in the saddle, in addition to office and factory work. There were no tractors, or other farm machinery then, all the cultivation was done with bollocks drawing ploughs, a pair yoked together. Bullock carts were the only transport, collecting the harvest, and everything else needed, the well-being of the cattle was important. As was that of the elephants kept as well; they were used for the collection of fodder, but principally were for ceremonial purposes.

Figure 42. Joan Allen as an infant in front of her house at Pandaul in 1914 (courtesy her son Charles Allen and Rosie Llewellyn Jones, Honourable Secretary of BACSA, British Association for Cemeteries in South Asia).

Joan Allen continued her narration by describing the change from indigo to sugar:

> During the 1914–1918 War, things for my father did not change greatly, the fighting never reached Indian shores. He was not called upon for regular service, but remained with the Bihar Light Horse, one of the Territorial units kept in India to be called upon for duty to help the civil power, allowing the regular forces of the British and Indians Army to serve in Europe. After the War, the bottom fell out of the indigo

market as synthetic dyes had been introduced. Growing and processing indigo was now profitless, the plants were no longer cultivated, and the simple factories, with their big open drying vats left to moulder. The Maharaja, in conjunction with a firm of Managing Agents in Calcutta, decided to erect a sugar factory on his land only six miles away from Pandaul. My father was made Manager, and given the job of choosing the site. [. . .] My father needed a river to supply water for the factory, and for drainage, but how to find the right spot on which to build, was his problem [. . .] The factory was built nearby and, as far as I know, is still there; to my certain knowledge, it lasted over fifty years at least. Brick bungalows went up, for the manager engineers, chemist, and cane assistants, smaller ones for the Indian clerks, the *babus* so many more staff were now needed. All were considered luxurious because there was now electricity supplied by the powerful new machinery. I was about five when we moved and had my first sight of electric lights, and the coolness from electric fans [. . .] Cars had now appeared on the scene, and, as a manager of a big concern, my father could afford one, it was a Model T Ford, to me a wonder [. . .]

The switch to sugar cultivation had changed these planters a lot it seemed. Yet much remained the same, the difference between 'the Englishman' and 'the Indian', for instance. Joan Allen described that while still a child at Darbhanga,

another sugar factory was also built about twenty miles away and with the help of cars, small social gatherings became more frequent. White children were in the minority, in fact there were only four of us in the district, none living any nearer than ten miles from each other. We all had to learn to amuse ourselves, but I did have a pony, and rose every day, free to go where I liked as long as a *syce* (groom) ran beside me.[818]

Not all the gentlemen planters had behaved differently from the 'indigo planters' of olden days. In 1937, Joan married Geoffrey, who had been made the manager of the Pandaul sugar factory after the previous one had taken to drink. Though the general manager, Gerald, had sent him several warnings, the manager named Paddy did not stop drinking and was given the sack. Though Paddy's 'charming American wife' had tried to stop him, Joan Allen later on wrote, Paddy had kept on drinking 'the local alcohol of poor quality and within a month had drunk himself to death'. Joan commented in her autobiography: 'Geoffrey was distressed but now he had both a bungalow and a better job [. . .] Strangely enough, during almost twenty years between my father being manager at Pandaul and Geoffrey taking over the post, every single manager had died of drink and was buried there'. The difference between the 'indigo planter' and the 'gentlemen planter' was not structural moreover, and basically, the new English gentlemen planter and his family remained on top of things. Betsy MacDonald was the wife of Tommy, one such a 'new' gentleman planter who, among others, had worked as *burra sahib* in a sugar factory near Muzaffarpur. Betsy described her arrival at the factory in 1930:

> A welcoming party appeared: Frank and Babs Barclay, the sugar factory Manager and his wife, and all clerks from Tommy's office, headed by the old Munshi (Head Writer) who had been there forty years and had seen many sahibs come and go. Salaaming with their palms together, touching their foreheads with their fingers and bowing at the same time, the Indians' greeting is charming; [. . .]. There was a large and splendid elephant to transport us home and, as the crowd was beginning to seethe around us, we hastily scrambled into the howdah. Tommy shouted 'Jaldi jao' to the mahout who replied 'Achcha Sahib' and we careered off at a spanking pace scattering children, pi-dogs and dust about us. Tommy pointed out that all his horses with accompanying syces (grooms) were prancing behind us with a priceless 'Fu-Fu' band – all manner of flute-like instruments, drums and cymbals making 'wedding noises'! [. . .] All the servants were lines up to greet us, salaaming deeply. I wondered what they were thinking, poor things – a new memsahib arriving to boss them around [. . .].[819]

Some planters had given up on indigo pretty late. Dholi Kothi, later purchased by the state government of Bihar along with 250 acres of land to establish a new college of agriculture and agricultural research institute, had been the residence of E. C. Danby, an indigo planter at first. In an interview with Prof. Walter Hauser of the University of (coincidently) Virginia on 1 January 1980, Danby explained that when he had first arrived in Bihar, 'a province the size of England with a population of thirty-nine million', there had been more than 400 farms of 200–3,000 acres owned by English people. Starting with indigo and as an assistant in 1919, he shifted to a new industry, that is sugar cane around 1930s, when many other farms had already been sold. Though sugar cane had always been gown in the region, it was on a small scale, and planters such as Danby now imported new varieties from Java and Sumatra; companies were formed, and 'modern sugar mills erected'. Danby spent thirty-five years in India and alleged that when he had arrived in the country, 90 per cent of the sugar domestically consumed had been imported, but when he left in 1944, sugar was being exported. During all these years, he had been collecting rents from more than 400 tenants and also ran agricultural banks 'really to try to save the people from village moneylenders, who charged exorbitant interest'. Besides, he also tried to settle the tenants' 'family or village squabbles' for which a 'superficial knowledge of the law was necessary'. During the horrible earthquake of 1933 (Danby mentioned 1933 but should be 1934 according to contemporary records), which had destroyed all the buildings including the indigo factory and a lot of damage had been done to lands and crops, and three men had also been killed by falling masonry. In 1942, Danby had a 'very unpleasant experience' when the Congress Party, 'the strongest political party in India', took advantage of the situation to stir up 'an agitation against the war', which had involved the imminent threat of 'an invasion of India by the japs' and the occupation of Burmah and 'for independence for India'. Danby described that 'this developed into what amounted to a revolution in Bihar and the neighbouring province'. This experience had made Danby to decide that the time had come to leave India:

> Our Government, in order to keep India quiet for the duration of the war, had promised to give them independence and the Congress Party were pledged to nationalize the land when they came into power. It was with many regrets that I left the place where I had been so long. I had made many friends among the Indians and some still write to me.[820]

This was thus the end of non-official British planters' involvement in plant improvement schemes in Bihar. Over a span of 150 years, starting as 'interloper' he had been promoted to 'gentleman planter' when he left. Unlike indigo planters of the past, these British sugar 'planters' had generally been liked in Bihar and also by the Biharis. By parting from his friends in 1944, E. C. Danby from the Dholi sugar concern was given a farewell address by the managing committee of the local Shree Baliram Higher English (HE) School, Shakra:

> We found in you, Sir, an amiable friend, a shrewd and patient
> judge, a shelter to the weak and the oppressed, an enemy to the
> tyrant and a supreme umpire of the people of the locality.[821]

Surely, sugar cane had not been discoloured by indigo as industrial sugar had been incorporated in Bihar as – and unlike indigo and cigarette tobacco – '*deshi*' (national) commodity.

ILTDC's Preference for Andhra Pradesh (South India)

During the 1940s, planters were leaving, and officials followed suit. A friend of 'Dobbie' (planter Danby mentioned above), P. T. Mansfield had been an Indian Civil Servant and had become a subdivisional magistrate in Sitamarhi in the Muzaffarpur District of Bihar. In 1932, he wrote the general government report on Bihar and Orissa from 1930 to 1931. During his time in Bihar, he had realised, on 24 April 1921, that, penned down in his diary, 'one of the reasons why non-cooperation has had so much success in this district is because the police and some of the old European planters have not realised that times are changing'. On 16 May 1921, he confessed that he did have to say that he had 'a certain amount of sympathy for the labourer. He gets a pretty small way (even our own servants)', and somewhat later, he reported that there were 'a certain number of business people, belonging to Begg Sutherland and Co. who have sugar concerns roundabout and one or two similar firms. These have quite a different point of view from the planter and are naturally a good deal broader minded'. Though, he agreed that most planters had changed their ways as a result of agitation by non-cooperators, and they now did not have much of indigo anymore from which all the disputes had emerged. Dobson's estate 'Belsand', Mansfield wrote on 30 March 1929, grew for instance indigo, oats, wheat, tobacco, and sugar cane. Yet finally even Dobson had left, and at the end of the war, this government official had realised that it was not only these planters who had to leave.[822]

With almost all (whites) gone from Tirhut, the ILTDC also decided to pack and leave. But there had been other reasons too. Besides Bihar, in 1915, the ILTDC had established another unit in the Guntur District of southern India (Madras Presidency), and a year or so later, when the Guntur rack-cured tobacco had been found to be suitable for use in manufacture, purchases had commenced from tobacco cultivators near the Chirala Railway Station. Chirala later on became the headquarters of the ITC in southern India, 'at that time it was merely a collection of small huts grouped round the railway station, flattered by the name Chirala, which means sweet water'. In *A Story of Co-operation in India,* the ILTDC described:

> The village considered itself particularly unfortunate in that four miles away Government had established a settlement of Ericulas – the thief caste of India. For centuries this class of people had lived as roving bandits, son following father in their predestined trade of robbery. In order to give this caste a chance to earn an honest living and break this tradition of crime, Government made a grant of 2,000 acres of land and as these Ericulas were rounded up, they were placed in charge of the Salvation Army whose officers endeavoured to teach the men to cultivate the land and the women to make mats, baskets, ropes and other items.

Yet it was found that the trade of these items had been very limited. Then a few people noted with dull interest, still in the words of the ILTDC, 'the first purchases of tobacco near the railway station, little realising what developments were to follow from this insignificant beginning'.[823] ITC commissioned, Basu wrote, that within a period of fifteen years, a combination of two factors had caused the permanent closure of ILTDC operations in Bihar.[824] Apart from 'socio-economic and political reasons', there also had been the fact that Bihari tobaccos had not been graded very high in London. Basu narrated:

> Early on, in 1920, shipments of Bihar leaf had been sent to Great Britain as samples to find out whether British Manufacturers

could use this leaf. The idea was to attempt to establish an export trade but this effort proved to be unsuccessful. The following year, however, when the experiment was extended to south Indian tobacco, the response was favourable. The samples were found to be acceptable and the Company felt justified in taking measures to establish their business in the south (as well).[825]

Therefore, instead of 'helping' the cultivators in Bihar to further improve upon their tobaccos, the ILTDC exchanged them for the Yerukula community in Chirala in south India. As I have shown in this book, 'push factors' were clearly important for this decision of ILTDC to leave Bihar. Not only had the cigarette (tobacco) in Bihar to compete with the much cheaper *biris* and *deshi* tobaccos for chewing and use in *hookahs*, from the 1920s, they also had to cope with strong nationalist opposition against 'foreign' cigarette and a subsequent (economic or ideological) choice of Bihari *zamindars* and richer farmers involved in tobacco cultivation not to grow cigarette tobaccos for the ILTDC anymore but only to grow *deshi* tobaccos for the regional markets. Besides, the ILTDC must also have realised that British planters as well as the government of Bihar was more interested in industrial sugar cane than cigarette tobacco as an alternative that could replace indigo and poppy. However and additionally, I argue here, 'pull factors' had also been of utmost importance in ILTDC's decision to favour Andhra Pradesh. Basu wrote that 1922 was the year in which the company decided that it would build a tobacco redrying factory at Chirala:

> Chirala was to become an important milestone in the annals of the Company. Simple though its operations were, expansion at this factory was rapid [. . .] Within a matter of a few years the workforce, initially mixed but latterly mainly women, climbed from about 500 people to 6,000. Till 1984, when the factory was closed about 1,500 women and 500 men employed in the Chirala factory came from the Yerucula community, and thereby hangs a tale.[826]

Basu understood this 'Yerukula tale' – and we should remember that she had been commissioned by the ITC itself to write its history from 1910 to 1985 – as follows:

> Nearly a century ago, the British government was faced with the problem of rehabilitating a large number of criminals from all over the country. About 20,000 of these criminals who came to be known as the Yeruculas were settled in a place thirty miles from Guntur that acquired the name of Stuartpuram. They were given 2,000 acres of land here and taught how to cultivate it.[827]

At this point, the ILTDC had come in and still using Basu's wordings:

> In a spirit of enlightened self-interest, ILTD now set about improving matters and their method of tackling the problem was to revolutionize tobacco production in the country. It was a method that was to bring relative prosperity to the *ryots*, to help them become independent and secure, and it resulted in the establishment of an enviable and enduring relationship between ILTD and the farmer.[828]

Meena Radhakrishna narrated the tale of Yerukula women quite differently, however. Hers is a 'dramatic story of pre-colonial trade patterns, of a tribal community engaged in long-distance transport, of the destruction of this means of livelihood by economic changes consequent upon the establishment of British rule, of the stigmatisation of the group as a criminal tribe, of the confinement of families in a penal settlement, of the recruitment of the women for work in a tobacco factory, of their organisation in a trade union under the communist auspices, and of the final success of the employers in splitting the men from the women on a hierarchical basis.[829]

Figure 43. Indian Leaf Tobacco Development Co. at Guntur. A Yerukula tobacco cultivator with cured tobacco leaf for cheroots or cigars in her hand. After tobacco leaves have been picked and cured in the curing barns, they are stacked in bundles called 'hands', which in turn are stacked together into piles. *Indian Tobacco Leaves. A Story of Co-operation in India*, London: ILTDC, 1943, p. 17.

Whatever we conclude about the Yerukula tobacco cultivators in the Madras Presidency, however, Bihari tobacco cultivators were bypassed by them and evidently not because of the better ecological environment in Guntur, the better cigarette tobacco produced by this community, the better soils around the Chirala factory, or the advanced tobacco-growing skills the Yerukula community possessed. In the end, ILTDC preferred to concentrate on cigarette tobacco cultivation in Andhra Pradesh as this community was easier to discipline than the quite independent and better-to-do small-holder tobacco cultivators in Bihar. In the words of the ILTDC, theirs was *'A Story of Co-operation in India'*, and we could add in Bihar, it was a story on 'non-cooperation'. Importantly, the former did not have the alternative of growing *deshi* tobaccos for local markets or any other crops for that matter. Even Basu concluded that in Bihar, in the 1930s, and I repeat and quote fully,

> though efforts were made continuously to improve the tobacco and to encourage the farmers to grow more, the days of the three depots were numbered. Their end, brought about indirectly by various political factors, was hastened by the fact

that the Indian Leaf Tobacco Development Company (ILTD) had discovered in the intervening years a more promising tobacco-growing area and had established itself successfully in what came to be called the South India Leaf Area or SILA in Andhra Pradesh. Indeed, when the Bihar government tried to resurrect tobacco operations many years later (after India's independence) its efforts were thwarted by the fact that locally grown tobacco from Guntur district was not only better but at least 30 per cent cheaper.[830]

Therefore, it was not that the ecological/natural environment such as soil and climate had prevented flue-cured cigarette Virginia (FCV) cigarette tobacco cultivation in Bihar. More than this, it was the socio-economic and political ecology in Bihar that favoured the cultivation of *hookah* and chewing tobaccos and the use of *biris* instead of cigarettes.

Empire Tobacco

Of all the economic plants in Bihar, indigo was really out and sugar cane and tobacco in by the early 1920s. For instance, the *Report of the Bihar and Orissa Government* (1924–25) stated that

just as agriculture dominates the economic horizon of the province, so is its agricultural welfare bound up in the cultivation of rice. Eighteen per cent of the rice-growing area in British India is contained in Bihar and Orissa alone, and in 1924–25 approximately six million tons of this grain were produced in its fields. Not less than half of the cultivated area of this province is given to rice [. . .] Sugarcane, although not so widely grown as several of the other crops, ranks next in importance to rice by reason of its superior value [. . .] More than 10 per cent of the whole area under tobacco in India is contained in Bihar and Orissa, and this valuable crop continues to grow in popularity, particularly in the districts of north Bihar. Another crop which brings in money to the province is chillies, large quantities of which are grown in

Tirhut, whence they are exported all over India [. . .] The cultivation of indigo has been declining now for some years, and this process was greatly accelerated in 1924–25; with the result that is no longer of practical importance.[831]

The *Report of the Bihar and Orissa Government* (1926–27) explicitly stated that though indigo was no longer of practical importance, tobacco, on the other hand, was growing in popularity, particularly in the districts of north Bihar, and more than 60,000 tons of this 'valuable crop' had been produced the previous year.[832] Around that time, the government, indigo planters, and scientists at Pusa had certainly not abandoned the collaborative network aiming at acclimatising cigarette tobacco in Bihar. Yet the protests during the 1920s against cigarettes in India, as described in this book, had not only forced ILTDC to look for alternative regions where they could better pursue their tobacco colonisation scheme. Following ILTDC, in fact, the GoI had also had their eyes on southern India as a suitable region for the further development of the nascent cigarette tobacco industry in India. In the 'Review of Agricultural Operations in India for the Years 1920–21', it was stated that as sugar was the only agricultural product in India in which the balance of trade was decidedly against her, 'there are no two opinions on the necessity of putting the Indian industry on a sound and satisfactory footing'. Yet the GoI had also great expectations of cigarette tobacco and reported that with the recently imposed heavy duties on imported tobacco, 'the prospects for the finer grades grown in India have improved considerably'. Importantly, however, the results obtained from Pusa scientists for the improvement of tobacco in Bihar could also be applied elsewhere in India and even in other parts on the British Empire. In this regard, the GoI had closely followed the steps taken by the ILTDC:

> The demand for the Pusa Selection type 28, which combines yield and quality and is suitable both for cigarette making and general cultivation, has increased more than fourfold during the year when seed sufficient for about 50,000 acres was asked for and supplied. Recent trials of this type, made at Guntur in the Kistna Delta (Madras Presidency) by the Indian Leaf Tobacco Development Company, resulted in the production of tobacco which, according to a report of the Company, will be useful in the manufacture of cigarettes. On account of its

outstanding qualities, this variety is now being tried by the same firm in British East Africa, Kenya and Zanzibar.[833]

Significantly, therefore, though the Imperial tobacco improvement scheme at Pusa had from its beginnings focussed on the 'improvement' of *deshi* tobaccos in Bihar in order to foster a cigarette industry in the province, by 1920, the knowledge acquired from tobacco experimentation in Bihar as well as the successful outcomes (i.e. improved seed varieties) were now applied in the southern part of British India and increasingly also in other countries that constituted the British Empire. A special correspondent of *The Times Trade Supplement* commented around 1922 on the anomaly of an empire possessing millions of acres of land suitable for tobacco cultivation not being able to supply anything approaching its own needs. But though Indian and Burmese cigars and cheroots would always command a certain definite market and though some Indian tobaccos had of late been used for blending, this correspondent sensed that 'for the future it is likely that Africa will provide the most suitable field of development'.[834] In 1926, the Tobacco Committee of the British Empire Producers' Organization posed a series of questions to each of the dominions and colonies, 'with a view to discovering the extent of and the possibilities of development of the Imperial tobacco industry', and the replies proved

> striking evidence of the existence of great opportunities for development, and an unanswerable argument for the preservation, protection, and encouragement of an industry which, as a whole, is still nascent, but which, by wise administration and judicious expansion, might fulfil the highest expectations from the point of view, not only of Empire monopoly, but of world-favour.

Yet here again, though it was recognised that some good research had been carried out in India, England now expected more from Nyasaland and Rhodesia. These British colonies could be stimulated to produce all the tobacco of the Virginia and Kentucky varieties that now mainly was imported from America.[835] During the year from 1927 to 1928, two acres of Adcock tobacco were grown in the Botanical Section at Pusa, and the produce was flue-cured. Special attention was paid to the economics of the process with a view to obtaining an estimation of the cost of flue-curing in relation to the market price of the leaf. The results obtained together with a description of the method of cultivating and flue-curing Adcock tobacco were published as a bulletin. Samples of Adcock leaf produced at Pusa had been submitted to 'expert opinion in the tobacco trade in England' and were described as 'the best we have seen so far of Indian growth, being the nearest approach to the corresponding American type'. Yet it had been added that the market was 'overstocked with Rhodesian tobacco', and consequently, the Tirhut tobacco would never fetch high prices. Moreover, apart from Rhodesia, South Africa was also exporting a considerable quantity of 'quality tobacco', and consequently, English demand for flue-cured tobacco from India had subsided enormously. *The Pusa Scientific Report* for 1927–28 equality had stated that the tobacco market in the United Kingdom 'is at present overstocked with empire grown leaf, and prices are in consequence abnormally low'.[836]

Similarly, in 1927, J. Clinton Cunningham had included tobacco as an important 'product of empire', and among the 'British countries' that sent tobacco to Britain, he pointed to Nyasaland, apart from India.[837] Though India remained on the list of countries from which Britain purchased 'empire flue-cured', the purchases from colonies and dominions such as Canada and southern Rhodesia had been more than three times greater. By 1950, India played only a minor role in this, and Southern Rhodesia had become the most important flue-cured exporter among the empire areas.[838] Clearly, therefore, by 1950, the almost 200-year-old imperial tobacco colonisation project of the British in India, as described in this book, had ended.

Improved *Deshi* Tobacco in Bihar

'Improvement', as Eugenia W. Herbert concluded in her wonderful *Flora's Empire,* 'could be a double-edged sword'.[839] It had not only been British officials who had used the fruits of plant improvement schemes as described in this book. By 1920, there were several old 'indigo concerns' in the Samastipur and Darbhanga regions of Tirhut, which along with indigo/sugar cane or in their place, also experimented with cattle farming, rhea, cereals like Indian corn and rice, and importantly with tobacco. The Dalsingh Sarai, Dholi, Doudpore, and Dowlutpore concerns are excellent examples. The first 'estate' comprised an area of 14 miles by 11 miles in extent and, 'the portion cultivated on behalf of the owners consists of 3,000 acres of indigo, 1,000 acres of tobacco, and about 2,000 acres of *native* [emphasis added] crops'. Rhea had also grown and manufactured 'in the former years'. The last manager of the first concern had been B. Coventry, and in 1916, it was F. M. Coventry. Interestingly, the tobacco crop was

> valued as it stands in the fields, and is purchased by local dealers, although the samples of *fine* leaves are eventually taken by the Indian Leaf or British-American Tobacco Companies. The yield depends very largely upon the quantity of manure worked into the land, but a fair average return is about 20 mounds to the acre.

The Dholi concern was owned in 1916 by Mrs Studd, Messrs. E. B. T. Studd and S. F. R. Studd, Mrs Sutherland Orr, and Mr H. C. Hume-Spry. The total area was about 2,500 acres of cultivated land, including 1,000 acres of indigo, 350 acres of wheat, 10 acres of barley, 225 acres of oats, 25 acres of tobacco, 20 acres of sugar cane, and 50 acres of chillies. It was argued that

> Dholi affords a fine illustration of the generous nature of good land where the practice of scientific agriculture is thoroughly carried out. The successful agriculturist of the present day realizes that, by proper rotation in cultivation, he is able to return to the land those necessary constituents which a succession of exhaustive crops infallibly removes.

Importantly, here again like in the case of the Dalsingh Sarai concern, tobacco was also sold locally, and 'it has always been a special feature of the management at Dholi to have everything of the best, and this applies with force to the agricultural implements and machinery and plant in the factories, which include cultivators, two threshing and other machines and a steam engine of 25 hp.' The permanent staff of labourers consisted of about 600 'coolies', and Mr W. B. Fich was the general manager during the absence 'on military duties' of Mr E. C. Danby.[840] The Dooriah concern covered an area of 208 square miles, of which about 3,490 acres retained and 'cultivated on behalf of the owners' in the following way: indigo 2,700 acres, oats 270 acres, flax 16 acres, and a considerable quantity of tobacco and other crops. The tobacco was grown 'by leaseholders on the estate, and as it thrives remarkably well and gives a return of Rs. 116 to the acre, the area under cultivation, which is now 44 acres, will be shortly increased very considerably'. Mr Mackenzie was responsible for the management of the whole estate and employed about 150 'permanent Indian hands'. The Doudpore concern grew indigo, cane, cereals, and 'other products grown for home consumption', including some tobacco. It was owned by Messrs. F. H. and G. T. Collingridge, who was assisted by 'a European'. Finally, the Dowlutpore concern in Darbhanga had been 'the establishment and successful working of cooperative societies in connection with the agricultural and financial resources of the inhabitants of that portion of the province of Behar'. First, such societies had been founded by Mr C. R. MacDonald. Mrs C. G. Atkins was the managing proprietor. Sugar cane had received attention, but indigo had been given up in 1914. Importantly, 'considerable quantities of tobacco and chillies' were also planted. The leaves of the tobacco produced at Dowlutpore were rack-cured annually in an old (indigo) cake house on the estate, and the price obtained was about Rs. 15 per maund.[841]

As detailed in this book, such 'gentlemen planters' grew tobacco for future processing by the ILTDC. This was, of course, 'cigarette tobacco' that actually still had to become that after redrying by the ILTDC and flue-curing at Imperial Pusa. Yet the above description of the tobacco grown in these planters' lands was also of *deshi* ('native') tobacco grown and improved upon by planters' and Imperial Tobacco's capital and technology through Indian cultivators who grew this *deshi* tobacco on 'scientific' cultivation and manuring lines such as furrow irrigation and employing green manuring with indigo refuse and using new curing practices such as 'rack-curing' as suggested by scientists such as the Howards at Imperial Pusa and by Leake. This improved *'deshi'* tobacco was, as quoted above, grown by 'permanent Indian hands' and bought by 'locals' for 'home consumption' (i.e. for chewing and for use in *hookahs*). Importantly, these 'Indian hands' had planted exactly the same 'improved seed' (such as the Pusa Type 28 and Adcock) that had been freely distributed by the Agricultural Department under the GoI and had been pronounced as very suitable for cigarette blending. When all the three ILTDC depots in Bihar had finally been closed by 1951, cigarette tobacco cultivation came to its final halt in that state. In 1960, P. C. Chaudhury in his *District Gazetteer* testified this death of cigarette tobacco in Bihar:

Previously Virginia tobacco (superior quality of tobacco than *deshi* tobacco utilised in admixture when properly blended with imported tobacco for the manufacture of inferior quality of cigarettes) was grown in Bachchwara police-station but due to the closing of the factory at Dalsinghsarai in the year 1951 owing to some labour trouble, people have left growing of this variety. Proper facilities assured and technical help extended this area may produce better quality of Virginia tobacco.[842]

This cigarette revival never happened in Bihar. But '*deshi*' tobacco was there to stay and was the result of about two centuries of British tobacco colonisation in the state. By 1950, after 150 years of colour-changing, *deshi* tobacco had become fully dark and cigarette tobacco 'bright' in Bihar. It is this dark 'country tobacco' used for chewing and in the *hookah* that remained to be cultivated in Bihari soils with tremendously increased yields. In fact, the area under tobacco cultivation has increased so much that Bihar now is counted as one of the leading tobacco states of India, specialising in 'chewing and hookah tobacco'.[843]

In this book, I illustrated that this sun/ground- and rack-cured dark-coloured *deshi* tobacco only exists because of the introduction of its 'opposite' in Bihar: flue-cured yellow-coloured 'foreign' cigarette tobacco. I also expounded that the characters of this *deshi* tobacco had changed tremendously from, in particular, 1860 to 1950. Moreover, as cigarette tobacco vanished from Bihar, *deshi* tobacco even lost its name and hence was referred to as the 'chewing and *hookah* tobacco type' in independent Bihar.[844]

Not only had *deshi*'s colour changed over the century, but also its seed, taste, texture, and consumption purpose changed besides this tobacco's economic, sociocultural, and political value in Bihar. Cigarette tobacco had consistently attempted to become '*deshi*', that is to 'indigenise'/'acclimatise' or become 'domestic' in Bihar, but failed. However, in the process, though tobacco is not 'native to the soils of Bihar', unlike indigo-producing plants and sugar cane, it was this *deshi* tobacco that became 'truly native'. Yet it was 'not born but made' in the ecological, sociopolitical, and economic context of agrarian Tirhut in a process of negotiation between cultivators, scientists, their patrons, factory workers, government officials, landowners (Indian and British), Imperial Pusa and Imperial Tobacco, and the expediencies of local and international markets.

These political-cultural and economic negotiations also deeply conditioned the production of knowledge regarding differently coloured tobacco varieties in colonial Bihar. In the process of its creation, neither was everything of yellow 'foreign' tobacco fully accepted nor was dark *deshi* tobacco totally belittled. The outcome was the hybrid '*deshi* commodity' that, in fact, had been improved upon through the use of the same seed, technology, science, manpower, and capital as had been used for the improvement of cigarette tobacco as described in this book. Improvement truly was 'a double-edged sword'.[845]

AFTERWORD

Musing Over Failure in Bihar

Consumption of chewing tobacco *(khaini)* is casted as a 'typical Bihari' peculiarity in contemporary India, and the plant that produces this is often thought of as 'indigenous'. In this book, I have shown that the type of tobacco leaf used for the production of this commodity was placed betwixt and between that of the cultivation of other plants in particular that of sugar cane, poppy, and indigo-producing plants. As a result, the history of tobacco cultivation (and consumption) in the state is less known than those of these other plants. Not many people are aware that the chewing tobacco cultivated in contemporary Bihar is, in fact, the outcome of processes that had been engineered by the colonial state and of resistance of Biharis against these. In that sense, one could call chewing tobacco – and for that matter *biri* as well – an authentic *swadeshi* product of Bihar. Quoting one informant in the contemporary tobacco fields of Bihar who remembered a maxim often heard during the nationalist struggle against the British in Bihar:

Inqalab zindabad (long live the revolution)
Khainiwala khaiyga (the tobacco chewer will eat, get food)
Dur hato ai dunyawalo (get rid of this 'man of the world', i.e. 'foreigner')
Hindustan hamara hai (India belongs to us)

I detailed in this book that among the important imperial improvement projects was plant colonisation in British India. Tobacco colonisation had been an important scheme of the 'old' British Empire but had failed in the America once some of these American states had united and posed as an independent nation. The so-called imperial tobacco improvement scheme discussed in this book at length was a revival of that old imperial scheme that this time became centred in Pusa (Bihar), where it had been placed between and betwixt other plant colonisation projects in particular that of indigo and sugar cane improvement. By the end of the eighteenth century, England increasingly looked towards Bengal hoping the input of 'British energy, skill, and capital' could improve tobacco in this presidency in such a way that the commodity would maintain and sustain the British Empire once more. However, this tobacco colonisation scheme had not come to life to improve the so-called indigenous chewing and *hookah* tobaccos[3] in Bihar but to develop 'foreign' (*bilaiti*) tobacco[4] cultivated and its leaf cured on 'modern scientific lines' is such a way that it could be used for production of cigars and later on cigarettes.[5] As described in this book, this imperial tobacco improvement scheme failed in Bihar, however, as 'Indian' FCV tobacco did not get embedded in Bihar's natural, socio-economic, and political ecology, though it did elsewhere in British India and the rest of the British Empire.[6] Ironically, whereas a cigarette factory remained in a workable condition in Monghyr (Munger) and still produces the type of cheap cigarettes

---

3   Though all tobaccos in India originated from 'immigrants from the New World' that had been introduced during the late sixteenth and seventeenth centuries, cultivation spread rapidly in almost all parts of the Mughal Empire and also in Bengal. By the time British 'amateur' botanists or 'plant hunters' discovered tobacco in Bengal, it had acclimatised so well that it was labelled as 'country' tobacco different from the 'foreign' Virginia and Havana tobacco that the British knew of. (Cf. Raychaudhuri, T., Habib, I., Kumar, D., and Desai, M. *The Cambridge Economic History of India: c.1200–c.1750*, Cambridge: CUP, Vol. I, 1982, p. 217.)

4   However, during our field work in the tobacco region near Hajipur in Bihar, we realised that nowadays (this was in 2011) *bilaiti* tobacco is an appellation also used for *biri* tobacco apart from cigarette tobacco and placed against *khaini* (chewing tobacco). This is interesting as this *biri* tobacco is indeed imported from out the state (from Gujarat mainly).

5   Cf. Manogaran, C. 'Traditional Versus Modern Agriculture: A Study of Peasant Farming in Ceylon (Sri Lanka)', *Geografiska Annaler. Series B, Human Geography*, Vol. 56, No. 2, 1974, pp. 68–77.

6   Cf. Mukherjee, A. 'Empire: How Colonial India Made Modern Britain', *Economic and Political Weekly*, Vol. XLV, No. 50, December 11, 2010, pp. 73–82.

so much desired by the agricultural engineers during colonial days, most of these cigarettes are sold outside the state of Bihar. What is more, the flue-cured yellow-coloured tobacco leaves, essential as their fillers, are not grown and cured any longer in Bihar but imported from southern India, in particular from Andhra Pradesh. In the process, however, what remained in Bihar by default as it were was an increased cultivation of improved types of chewing, *hookah,* and some *biri* tobacco.

In fact, in the contemporary tobacco fields of Bihar, the British legacy is only visible through dilapidated indigo concerns, planter bungalows, gravestones, an abandoned 'cigarette' factory (tobacco redrying unit), and a closed sugar factory. British contribution to tobacco improvement in Bihar is (almost) not a part of farmers' memory. As one of our informants worded it, 'the *lal sahib* (red-faced gentleman) was only thinking of *his aphim* (amphetamine) signifying opium and *his nil* (indigo). He did not touch *our khaini* however.' When asked about cigarette tobacco cultivators, they answered that they did not know how to grow it, did not have the seeds, could not afford the extra expenses that it requires to cultivate, cure it, and fertilise the soil, and finally, 'nobody buys it'.

The historical pattern of the failure of the cigarette tobacco plant in Bihar and 'the birth' of a *swadeshi* commodity reflects in the connotation of chewing tobacco (and in similar way the *biri*) not only as a 'typical Bihari product' but also as a 'poor man's smoke', not associated with capitalist or colonial/imperial exploitation or health hazards like cigarette and cigars. Moreover, no or much less taboo exists regarding women or relatively young people using some of these tobacco preparations (such as *gul*) and the *hookah*. This is, I argue, the unintended outcome of the failure of the imperial tobacco improvement scheme as pursued by the GoI in colonial Bihar and as described in this book. Here, I like to muse a bit over this 'failure', however.

James Scott analysed some 'improvement schemes' that are pursued by 'certain kinds of states, driven by utopian plans and an authoritarian disregard for the values, desires, and objections of their subjects' and which, Scott alleged, 'are indeed a mortal threat to human well-being'.[7] In this book, the odyssey of a so-called imperial tobacco improvement scheme was analysed, and it was concluded that cigarette tobacco failed in Bihar. I also argued that this failure

---

7   Scott, *Seeing Like a State*, p. 7.

was indeed caused by what Scott called a 'missing link'[8]; that is, colonial agricultural and industrial engineers of British India had never asked 'the population of Bihar', what plants they wished to 'improve', that is 'colonise'. Instead, they ruled that scientists at Pusa should concentrate on 'tobacco improvement', which in the end meant the development of cigarette tobacco and propagation of its improved varieties as well as improved cultivating and curing practices. With this aim in mind, the GoI provided institutional, regulatory, and research support, but by 1950, there was no capital, price, and market support any longer, and thus, 'FCV' just vanished from Bihar. Yet did this really mean failure of the imperial tobacco improvement scheme?

Lucile H. Brockway, in *Science and Colonial Expansion*, analysed the role of the British royal gardens and quoted Lt. Col. Robert Kyd when he founded the Calcutta Botanic Gardens in 1787:

> Not for the purpose of collecting rare plants as things of curiosity or furnishing articles for the gratification of luxury, but for establishing a stock for disseminating such articles as may prove beneficial to the inhabitants as well as the natives of Great Britain, and which ultimately may tend to the extension of the national commerce and riches.[846]

Clearly, in this sense, the imperial tobacco improvement scheme was, as outlined in the concluding chapter of this book, not a failure for 'the natives of Great Britain' at all. In fact, the scheme proved very beneficial (in economic terms) to Great Britain. First, the scheme provided employment for (young) English scientists at Pusa as well as employment of British capital and manpower. Second, Pusa in Bihar had become the centre of (tobacco) experimentation which outcomes could be used elsewhere in British India as well as elsewhere in the British Empire, in Nyasaland (Malawi) and southern Rhodesia for instance. This indeed was the case to the great benefit of many natives of 'Great Britain'. Analysed from this angle, the imperial tobacco improvement scheme, thus, was a great success. I now return to the benefits for the 'inhabitants', the Indian subjects of the British Empire living in Bihar and those who followed them in the independent state of Bihar.

---

8   Scott, *Seeing Like a State*, p. 307.

Winner by Default

Figure 44. Differently flavoured chewing tobaccos in Bihar. Photograph by Masoom Reza.

Figure 45. Child worker in chewing tobacco-drying shed in Samastipur. Photograph by author.

Once British American manpower, expertise, and capital had departed from the state by default, Biharis had been left with an improved and flourishing 'indigenous tobacco industry' that received and even now receives, though tobacco comes under state jurisdiction, full (though not always open) support of the GoI which promotes production, improves quality, and ensures remunerative prices for tobacco growers. In fact, even the government of Bihar, while at the same time warning consumers for tobacco's health dangers, actively protects the sector. Indeed, national and state governments and many people make (good) money out of the industry. Yet there are costs too.

Like in other places throughout the world, in Bihar, too, tobacco cultivation is facing a declining trend, and increased activity of anti-tobacco lobbies coupled with taxation increments make that some of our informants planned to switch to more paying or less risky/tabooed cash or food crops.[9] Indeed, Bihar is taken over by various other Indian states such as Andhra Pradesh, Gujarat, and Karnataka,, which now constitute the major tobacco-producing states in India.[10] In fact, when I had started my research on the history of tobacco cultivation in Bihar, many around me questioned whether Bihar grew any tobacco at all! Nevertheless, consumption of non-cigarette tobacco products is still high in Bihar, in particular among relatively young people and women.[11] Consequently, the manufacturing industry of these commodities is thriving in Bihar, whereas the production of the now-renamed Indian Tobacco

---

9   Cf. Chauhan, B. R. 'Rise and Decline of a Cash Crop in an Indian Village', *Journal of Farm Economics*, Vol. 42, No. 3, August 1960, pp. 663–66.

10   http://www.ikisan.com/Crop%20Specific/Eng/links/tn_tobaccoHistory.shtml, Accessed on 6 September 2014.

11   Singh, G., Sinha, D. N., Sharma, P. S., and Thankappan, K. R. 'Prevalence and Correlates of Tobacco Use among Ten to Twelve-Year-Old School Students in Patna District, Bihar, India', *Indian Pediatrics*, Brief Reports, Vol. 42, No. 8, August 17, 2005, pp. 805–10; Bhonsle, R. B., Murti, P. R., and Gupta, P. C. 'Tobacco Habits in India', in Gupta P. C., Hammer J. E., and Murti, P. R. (eds.), *Control of Tobacco-Related Cancers and Other Diseases*, International Symposium, 1990, Bombay: Oxford University Press, 1992, pp. 25–45; and Yach, D. 'Commentary: Tobacco Consumption in India', *Journal of Public Health Policy*, Vol. 24, Nos. 3/4, 2003, pp. 246–250.

Company (which now is just ITC) in Munger was reduced in 2003.[12] It, therefore, seems that the 'indigenous tobacco industry' still is a great winner in Bihar – though somewhat threatened – and one could perceive this as the happy outcome of a battle between the 'bad' multinational capitalist industry and the 'good' indigenous, small-scale industry. Can we thus conclude that even in this sense the imperial tobacco improvement scheme has not 'failed'?

Khaini and *Biris* (still) Thrive in Bihar: Costs and Benefits for Biharis

I perceive that there are some problems with this moral landscape in Bihar that depicts the cigarette (and its industry) as the (only) 'beast' and the rest of the tobacco products (in particular chewing tobacco) as 'beauty'. Without 'defending' the cigarette industry,[13] I like to bring in some labour, health, and economic issues associated with these so-called small is beautiful products that are underscored by scholars but not by producers and consumers of these products. It appears that the fact that these commodities are perceived of as 'traditional' or just because they are cheaper – even cheaper than the cheapest Indian-made cigarettes – and therefore have become mass products for the poor in Bihar has saved these tobacco products from any much public outcry against them. I shortly like to refer to scholarly criticism of these products, however, as it belongs to a quite different moral realm which is absent in contemporary Bihar, also among politicians and policy makers.

---

12 'Production in Munger ITC firm reduced, says TU', *Times of India*, June 18, 2003. According to industrialists, this reduction of cigarette production was due to 'exorbitant taxes in the state that threatened the existence of the ITC-owned 96-year-old Munger Cigarette Factory'. Consequently, the ITC had started shifting production to its Saharanpur (UP), Kidderpore (West Bengal), and Bangalore (Karnataka) factories. The Munger Tobacco Manufacturing Workers' Union had protested against such a 'policy of de-industrialisation of the state' and planned launching 'a militant movement' against the Bihar state's policies.

13 How could I? Many studies demonstrate the 'beastly' character of the cigarette industries in particular in the 'south'. (Cf. Campaign for Tobacco Free Kids. *Golden Leaf. Barren Harvest. The Costs of Tobacco Farming*, Washington: Campaign for Tobacco Free Kids, November 2001.)

Figure 46. *Biri* rolling in process. Photograph by
Masoom Reza.

Though *biri* tobacco is not cultivated in Bihar (anymore), the state along with
West Bengal and Orissa – thus the regions that constituted colonial Bengal –
has become the epicentre of *biri* rolling. Labour in these states is cheaper
than that in other parts of India. Though the industry has been affected by
forces of sustained competition and new legislations (like restrictions in child
labour) by the Central Government in New Delhi, the industry has been more
or less stable since the 1980s. Pranay Lal explained: 'The industry wields an
immense local and national political clout and resist any modernization efforts
like mechanization, contributing revenues through taxes and adopting better
labour standards.'[14]

In his study on 'Labour in the Informal Sector' carried out in the late
1990s, Fazal Ahmad concentrated his research on the *biri* industry in Patna,
the capital of Bihar. He recognised that the industry offers employment to
masses of poor who otherwise could scarcely survive in the wake of mass
unemployment and therefore 'proves a boon in some respects for the low-
paid workers'. Yet his study into the socio-economic problems faced by these
workers, which reflected 'the style of life', 'working conditions', 'housing and

---

14 Lal, *Bidi*, p. 1336.

residence', as well as 'the household environment of the bidi workers in the whole of the Bihar state', showed that 'of all types of work in the unorganised sector [. . .] bidi work is one of the most exploited, unprotected, unregulated and unorganised'. Moreover, Fazal Ahmad also found that the health condition of bidi workers was 'very poor', and this was according to Ahmad due to 'the prolonged sittings of the tobacco work'.[15] S. Giriappa in another study on 'Bidi-Rolling in Rural Development' carried out elsewhere in India, therefore, recommended:

> Bidi industry provides an important supplementary activity in Dakshina Kannada. Not only that it is a direct succour to over three lakhs of persons improving their employment and income potential, but also helps to augment government tax resources and indirectly helps agriculture and other sectors associated with it. Hence, it is of paramount importance that the interest of the industry has to be safeguarded and at the same time, conditions of the workers be improved.

Giriappa, therefore, urged that attention in this respect should be directed in particular to the 'condition of child labour' and to 'female labourers'.[16]

A study on tobacco-related cancers and other diseases reported that 'the use of tobacco in any form had been found to damage health seriously'. Yet whereas the health consequences of cigarette smoking have been documented 'beyond any reasonable doubt', many people still are not convinced, according to this study, that other forms of tobacco use, 'including *bidi* smoking, chewing tobacco in any combination, and reverse smoking, habits prevalent in India', poses similar 'extreme danger'. The study had found, however, that 'for example, a *bidi*, which contains one-fourth or less of the tobacco in a cigarette, may deliver as much or more tar and nicotine. Certain forms of chewing tobacco have demonstrated to contain high levels of carcinogenic

---

15 Ahmed, F. *Labour in Informal Sector*, Delhi: Manak Publications, 1999. Similar studies elsewhere in India that also concentrated on growers of *biri* tobacco besides 'factory' (home-based) workers produce same results. See for instance: Efroymson, D. (ed.) *Tobacco and Poverty. Observations from India and Bangladesh*, PATH Canada, October 2002.

16 Giriappa, S. *Bidi-Rolling in Rural Development*, Delhi: Daya, 1987.

tobacco-specific nitrosamines. In India, four of the five leading cancers are tobacco related.' The study concluded:

> Tobacco is a legal agricultural product, and products containing tobacco are legal all over the world. This situation, however, reflects a historical development rather than a desirable state of affairs. If tobacco or any product containing tobacco were to be introduced today, it would not meet existing health and safety standards anywhere in the world and therefore would not be marketed.[17]

Since 2003, Central Government bills and acts on the regulation of trade and commerce, production, supply, and distribution of, as well as on prohibition of advertisement for, tobacco products in India do amend cigarettes as well as other tobacco products. Yet studies on tobacco control in Bihar show that though such measures have some bearing on cigarettes, they have yet to make significant impact on other forms of tobacco use. Interestingly, whereas in 2002, many Indian states banned oral tobacco, such tobacco control policies, though subscribed to by the government of Bihar, too, do not seem to be implemented in the state at all and violated continuously. 'Low motivation' levels are reported at the Health Ministry at state level.[18] In the end, therefore, it is to the reader of this book to decide upon whether the imperial tobacco improvement scheme has failed 'the inhabitants of Bihar' or not.

---

17 Gupta, P. C., Hamner, J. E., and Murti, P. R. (eds.) *Control of Tobacco-Related Cancers and Other Diseases*, International Symposium, 1990, Bombay: Oxford University Press, 1992.

18 Simpson, D. 'India: States Ban Oral Tobacco', *Tobacco Control*, Vol. 11, 2002, p. 291 and Pai, S. A. 'Gutka Banned in Indian States', *Lancet Oncology*, Vol. 3, No. 9, 2002, p. 521. A news item of 1999 stated that 'as a commercial product *gutka* was introduced less than three decades back, but today, there are thousands of manufacturers ranging from small to very large, with a combined annual turnover in the order of several hundred million American dollars'. The same article quoted the words of one of the largest *gutka* manufacturer: 'Yes, *gutka* is harmful, and we have no objection to a ban, but the government should ban cigarettes first.' Gupta, P. 'Gutka: A Major New Tobacco Hazard in India', *Tobacco Control*, Vol. 8, Summer 1999, p. 132.

Figure 47. Somya, aged eighty-five, smoking *hookah* tobacco in Pharota village, Aralia (Bihar). She said her mother also used to prefer the *hookah* for tobacco smoking. Photograph by Masoom Reza.

GLOSSARY

amlah, amla	agent, Indian officer of a judicial or revenue court under the British judge or collector
assami	worker, peasant, tenant
babu	honorific for clerk. Erstwhile landed tenure/title
bataidar	sharecropper
bhit (bhith)	land near homestead, which is better manured, good for crops like tobacco
bideshi, beedeshi	foreign, from outside the country
bigga, bigha/beegha	a measure of land varying in extent in different parts of Bihar
biri, bidi	a hand-rolled type of cigarette with tobacco as filler covered with dried leaf from a *tendu* tree (East Indian Ebony tree)
bhumi	land, soil
cheroot/curuttu (Tamil)	roll of tobacco/a cheaply produced cylindrical cigar with both ends clipped during manufacture
chuna	lime
crore	ten million

dak	post
dak daroga	conveyance of mail or people
dastak/dustuck	pass allowing free trade, which became a matter of serious contention between the Bengal *nawabs* and British EIC servants in the late eighteenth century
dasturi	a customary commission payable on cash transactions
desi/deshi tobacco	country tobacco but also just a local appellation for one of the many *hookah* or chewing tobacco varieties in Bengal/Bihar/Assam. Also used in other ways: *desi chini karkhana* (indigenous, non-industrial) sugar manufactory (refinery machine)
dewani/diwani rights	power to collect land revenue
doab	tract between two confluent rivers
farman/firman	Mughal imperial decree/permission to trade/reside somewhere
feringee	outsider, foreigner, a European in British India
goorgoory/nargile/sheesha	different types of *hookahs*
gul	mixture of tobacco powder, molasses, and other flavouring ingredients; sold as a powder and used as tooth powder, made from the roots and stalks of the tobacco plant

gumashta/gomasta	agent of merchants or landowners or (British) planters, also agent employed by Opium Department to supervise production of opium from poppy in villages
gur	well-boiled undried raw sugar cane juice, unrefined brown-colour sugar
hookah/hooka	Indian pipe for smoking through water (an elaborated hubble-bubble)
hookah-bardar/hooka-burdar	a *hookah* bearer. The servant whose duty it was to attend to his master's *hooka*
katha/cattah	a measurement of land equivalent to one-twentieth of a *beegha*
khainee/khaini	mixture of sun-dried, coarsely cut tobacco leaves crushed into smaller pieces and mixed with slaked lime for chewing. Also chewing tobacco consumed directly
khand	sugar prepared from
khandsari	a kind of sugar refinery machine or its product: white sugar
kothi	actual any residential building but here: indigo concern
kisan	cultivator, peasant
lakh	hundred thousand
maund	unit of weight (40 *seers*)
mofussil/mufassil/mufassal	countryside/remote area
muscovado	unrefined brown sugar

nabob	British man who returned home from the East with fortunes and also just corruption of *nawab*
nawab	The governor of a province under the Mughal Government (deputy to the Mughal emporer)
neel/nil	indigo (blue)
nilhe gaye milhe aaye	proverb in Tirhut: the indigo planters have gone and now we have the (sugar) mills
nus/nas	snuff, dust of tobacco roots which is generally used for inhaling
pan	preparation of betel leaf combined with areca nut and/or tobacco often slaked lime paste is added to bind the leaves
pargana (pergunnah)	revenue/administrative unit comprising a group of villages and forming a small subdivision of a district
raiyat/ryot	peasant, tenant, cultivator
rhea/rami	a flowering fibre plant
tambaku	tobacco
thikadar	revenue farmer, contractor
seer	roughly 400 g
sepoy	Indian infantry soldier in the British EIC army
suba(h)	province in Mughal India
supari	areca nut
ukh	sugar cane

zamindar	a landlord/owner who would collect all taxes on his lands and hand them partly over to the British authorities
zamindari	landed estate
zarda	manufactured from leaves of chewing tobacco. Also known as *kali pati* and used with betel leaf. Flaked leaves are boiled in water with lime and spices until evaporation and then dried and coloured with vegetable dyes (often red).
zeerat/zerat/zirat	own land under direct cultivation of a landowner
zila	a district

Selected Works Consulted

Unpublished Records*
National Archives of India, New Delhi

Government of India, Home (Political), 1929–35.
Government of India, Home (Public), 1790–830.
Government of India, Financial (Accounts), 1861.
Government of India, Home (Port Blair), 1886.
Government of India, Foreign and Political (Internal), 1926.
Government of India, Central Board of Revenue (Land Revenue), 1923–38.
Government of India, Home (Separate Revenue), 1862, Part A.
Government of India, Revenue and Agriculture (Agriculture), 1883, Part B.
Government of India, Revenue and Agriculture (Emigration), 1888, Part A.
Government of India, Revenue and Agriculture (Patents), 1891, A.

Bengal State Archives, Bhawani Dutta Lane, Calcutta (India)

Government of Bengal, *Proceedings of the General Department*
Agriculture Branch, August 1870.
Government of Bengal, *Proceedings of the General Department*
Agriculture Branch, April and May 1873.
Government of Bengal, *Proceedings of the General Department*
Agriculture Branch, February, July, and August 1875.
Government of Bengal, *Proceedings of the General Department*
Agriculture Branch, January and August 1876.
Government of Bengal, *Proceedings of the General Department*
Agriculture Branch, March, May, and June 1877.
Government of Bengal, *Proceedings of the General Department*

---

*   Full details are mentioned only in the endnotes.

Agriculture Branch, March 1878.
Government of Bengal, *Proceedings of the Revenue Department*
Agriculture Branch, April 1870.
Government of Bengal, *Proceedings of the Revenue Department*
Agriculture Branch, September 1872.
Government of Bengal, *Proceedings of the Revenue Department*
Agriculture Branch, July 1886.
Government of Bengal, Revenue Department
Land Revenue, 1869, B File.
Government of Bengal, Revenue Department
Agriculture, 1883, B File.

Bengal State Archives, Writers Building, Calcutta (India)

Notes on the extent to which 'boycott' has at present affected wholesale and retail trade in Calcutta, *Political, (Judicial) Confidential* (J) 86J/1905.

Bihar State Archives, Patna (India)

Government of Bengal, *Proceedings of the Revenue Department*
Agriculture Branch, 1892–903.
Governments of Bihar and Orissa, *Proceedings of the Revenue Department*
Agriculture Branch, 1917.
Governments of Bihar and Orissa, *Proceedings of the Political Department*
Special, 1912–40.

Other Unpublished Works

Pichai, H. and Lakshminarainan, R. 'A Study of Corporate Diversification in the Indian Context: Does Theory Explain Success Stories?', (Unpublished) *Final Report* in partial fulfilment of the requirements for the Contemporary Concerns Study Course in the Post Graduate Programme in Management, Submitted on 21 November 2006 (guided by J. Ramachandran and S. Mukerjee).

Potukuchi, S. 'Controlling Commodity Culture: Indigenous knowledge and Indian Cotton Textile Industry: Andhra Region, 1790–1900', Unpublished paper present at the *2nd Annual Workshop of the Commodities of Empire Project: Commodities in Evolution: Historical Change in Different Ages of Globalization,* 1800–2000, 11–12 September 2008.

Pouchepadass, J. 'Peasant Protest in a Global Setting: The Champaran Movement Reconsidered', Unpublished paper presented during an international conference on *Bihar in the World and the World in Bihar. An Interdisciplinary Workshop on and in Bihar,* organised by the Asian Development Research Institute (ADRI), Patna and the European Science Foundation (ESF), Paris, 16–19 December 1997.

Wilson, N. H. 'The State in Disguise of a Merchant: Extractive Administration in British India, 1784–1834', unpublished paper, Department of Sociology, The University of California, Berkeley, 25 November 2007.

Newspapers, Gazettes, and Reviews[**]

Advance
Bengal Hurkaru
The Bihar Gazette
The Calcutta Review
The Edinburgh Review
The London Gazette
The National Review

Published Reports, Surveys, Minutes, Notes, and Reviews

Indian Industrial Commission. *Minutes of Evidence 1916–1918*, Vol. VI, Confidential Evidence, Calcutta, India: Superintendent Government Printing, 1918.

[**] Full details are mentioned only in the endnotes.

Indian Opium Commission. *First Report of the Royal Commission on Opium: With Minutes of Evidence and Appendices*, Presented to both Houses of Parliament by Command of Her Majesty, London: Printed for Her Majesty's Stationery Office by Eyre and Spottiswoode, 1894.

Milligan, S. *Review of Agricultural Operations in India, 1920–21*, Calcutta, India: Superintendent Government Printing, 1921.

Note on Indian Tobacco. Prepared by the Agricultural Expert to the Imperial Council of Agricultural Research, India, NP, ND.

O'Connor, J. E. *Report on the Tobacco Production in India. Reports on the Tea and Tobacco Industries in India.* Presented to both Houses of Parliament by Command of Her Majesty, East India (Products), Part I, London: Printed by George Edward Eyre and William Spottiswoode, 1874, pp. 139–219.

Proceedings of the Board of Agriculture in India held at Pusa on 9 December 1929 and following days, with appendices, Calcutta: Government of India Central Publication Branch, 1931.

Report of the Bengal Indigo Commission, 1860, with the Minutes of Evidence and Appendix, Calcutta: Printing and Publishing Press Government of India, 1860.

Report on the Internal Trade of Bengal for the Year 1879–1880, Calcutta: Government of Bengal, 1880.

Reports of the Agricultural Research Institute and College, Pusa (Including the *Report of the Imperial Cotton Specialist*), Calcutta, India: Superintendent Government Printing, from 1907–9 to 1920–21.

Report of the Indian Sugar Committee 1920, Simla: Superintendent Government Central Press, 1921.

Report on the Administration of the Territories now included in the Province of Bihar and Orissa, 1911–1912, Patna: Printed at the Bihar and Orissa Government Press, 1913.

Report of the Committee on the Agrarian Condition in Champaran, Vol. I, Patna: Superintendent, Government Printing, Bihar and Orissa, 1917.

Review of the Industrial Position and Prospects in Bengal in 1908 with Special Reference to the Industrial Survey of 1890, Part II of Special Report, Calcutta, The Bengal Secretariat Book Depot, 1908.

Royal Commission on Agriculture in India, *Evidence of the Officers Serving under the Government of India*, Vol. I, Part II, Calcutta: Government of India Central Publication Branch, 1928.

The Argument of the Lord Chief Justice of the Court of King's Bench Concerning the Great Case of Monopolies between the East-India Company, Plaintiff, and Thomas Sandys Defendant. Wherein Their Patent for Trading to the East-Indies, Exclusive of all Others, is adjudged good, London: MDCL XXXIX.

The Cultivation and Curing of Tobacco in Bengal, Calcutta: Bengal Secretariat Press, 1874.

The Imperial Council of Agricultural Research, *Agriculture and Animal Husbandry in India 1937–1938*, Delhi: Manager of Publications, 1940.

Books

Achaya, K. T. *The Food Industries of British India*, Delhi: Oxford University Press, 1994.

Ahmad, F. *Labour in Informal Sector*, Delhi: Manak Publication, 1999.

Ahmed, A. and Salahuddin, F. *Social Ideas and Social Change in Bengal 1818–1835*, Leiden: E. J. Brill, 1965.

Allen, J. *'Missy Baba' to 'BurraMem'. The Life of a Planter's Daughter in Northern India, 1913–1970*, Putney, London: BASCA, 1998.

Amin, S. *Sugarcane and Sugar in Gorakhpur: An Inquiry into Peasant Production for Capitalist Enterprise in Colonial India*, Delhi: Oxford University Press, 1984.

An Ex-Civilian. *Life in the Mofussil or The Civilian in Lower Bengal*, London: C. Kegan Paul & Co., 1878.

Arnold, D. *Science, Technology and Medicine in Colonial India*, The New Cambridge History of India, Cambridge: Press Syndicate of the University of Cambridge, 2000.

Arnold, D. *The Tropics and the Traveling Gaze. India, Landscape, and Science 1800–1856*, Delhi: Permanent Black, 2005.

Axelby, R., Nair, S. P., and Cook, A. S. (eds.) *Science and the Changing Environment in India, 1780–1920: A Guide to Sources in the India Office Records*, London: The British Library, 2010.

Bagchi, A. K. and Bandopadhyay, A. (eds.) *Eastern India in the Late Nineteenth Century, Part I: 1860s–1870s*, Documents on Economic History of British Rule in India, 1858–1947, New Delhi: Manohar, 2009.

Bagchi, A. K. and Bandopadhyay, A. (eds.) *Eastern India in the Late Nineteenth Century, Part II: 1880s–1890s*, Documents on Economic History of British Rule in India, 1858–1947, New Delhi: Manohar, 2011.

Bakshi, S. R. *Advanced History of Modern India*, Delhi: Anmol Publications, 1995.

Basu, C. *Challenge and Change. The ITC Story: 1910–1985*, Hyderabad: Orient Longman, 1988.

Beames, J. *Memoirs of a Bengal Civilian: Lively Narrative of a Victorian District Officer*, London: Chatto & Windus and Hippocrene, 1961.

Beer, G. L. *The Origins of the British Colonial System 1578–1660*, Gloucester, MA: Peter Smith, 1959 (1908).

Benedict, C. *Golden-Silk Smoke. A History of Tobacco in China, 1550–2010,* Berkeley and Los Angeles, CA: University of California Press, 2011.

Beveridge, H. (ed.) and Rogers, A. (tr) *The Tuzuk-i-Jahangiri or Memoirs of Jahangir,* Vol. 2, Delhi: MunshiramManoharlal, 1968.

Bhatia, H. S. (ed.) *European Women in India: Their Life and Adventures,* New Delhi: Deep & Deep, 1979.

Bhattacharya, S. (ed.) *Rethinking 1857,* Hyderabad: Orient Blackswan, 2008.

Bhattacharyya, A. *Swadeshi Enterprise in Bengal 1900–1920,* Calcutta: Sm. Mita Bhattacharyya, 1986.

Bhaumik, S. K. (ed.) *Reforming Indian Agriculture: Towards Employment Generation and Poverty Reduction Essays in Honour of G.K. Chadha,* New Delhi: Sage, 2008.

Billings, E. R. *Tobacco: Its History, Varieties, Culture, Manufacture and Commerce, with an Account of its Various Modes of Use, from its First Discovery until Now, with Illustrations by Popular Artists,* Hartford, CT: American Publishing Company, 1875.

Bloxam, W. P. and Leake, M. H. with the assistance of Finlow, R. S. *An Account of the Research Work in Indigo, Carried Out at the Dalsingh Serai Research Station (under Subsidy of the Government of Bengal) from 1903 to March 1904,* Calcutta: Bengal Secretariat Book Depot, 1905.

Bose, S. *Peasant Labour and Colonial Capital: Rural Bengal since 1770.* The New Cambridge History of India, III: 2, Cambridge: Cambridge University Press, 1993.

Brockway, L. H. *Science and Colonial Expansion: The Role of the British Royal Botanic Gardens,* New Haven and London: Yale University Press, 2002.

Buckland, C. E. *Bengal under the Lieutenant-Governors: Being a Narrative of the Principal Events and Public Measures during Their Periods of Office, from 1854 to 1898,* in two volumes, Vol. II., Calcutta: S.K. Lahiri & Co., 1901.

Capper, J. *The Three Presidencies of India. A History of the Rise and Progress of the British Indian Possessions from the Earliest Records to the Present Time with an Account of their Government, Religion, Manners, Customs, Education, etc., etc.,* New Delhi and Madras: Asian Educational Services, 1997 (Reprint, first published in London by Ingram: Cooke and Co. in 1853).

Chakrabarti, P. *Western Science in Modern India: Metropolitan Methods, Colonial Practices,* Ranikhet: Permanent Black, 2004 (paperback printing used of 2010).

Chaudhary, V. C. P. *The Creation of Modern Bihar,* Patna: YugeshwarPrakashan, 1964.

Chaudhuri, K. N. *The Trading World of Asia and the English East India Company 1660–1760,* Cambridge: Cambridge University Press, 1978.

Chaudhury, P. C. R. *Bihar District Gazetteers. Muzaffarpur,* Patna: Printed by the Superintendent Secretariat Press, 1958.

Choudharym, R. B. 'Lawrence and Indigo Cultivation in Bihar', *Proceedings of the Thirty-Third Session of the Indian History Congress,* Muzaffarpur, 1972, pp. 545–52.

Clinton, C. J. *Products of the Empire,* Oxford: Clarendon Press, 1927.

Colebrooke, H. T. *Remarks on the Husbandry and Internal Commerce of Bengal,* Calcutta: n.p., 1884.

Cox, H. *The Global Cigarette. Origins and Evolution of British American Tobacco, 1880–1945,* Oxford: Oxford University Press, 2000.

Crawfurd, J. *A View of the Present and Future Prospects of the Free Trade & Colonization of India,* Second edition, enlarged, London: James Ridgway, 1829.

Crawfurd, J. *Letters from British Settlers in the Interior of India, Descriptive of Their Own Condition, and That of the Native Inhabitants under the Government of the East India Company. With Notes,* London: James Ridgway, 1831.

Crawfurd, J. *Notes on the Settlement or Colonization of British Subjects in India: with Appendix of Proofs and Illustrations,* London: James Ridgway, 1833.

Crofton, D. H. *Souvenirs of a Competition Wallah. Letters and Sketches from India 1932–1947,* Hythe Kent: Volturna Press, 1994.

Crooke, W. *Hobson-Jobson: A Glossary of Colloquial Anglo-Indian words and Phrases, and of Kindred Terms, Etymological, Historical, Geographical and Discursive,* new edition edited version of book by Col. Yule, H. and. Burnell, A. C., New Delhi: Munshiram Manoharlal Publishers, 1984 (Originally Published in 1903 by John Murray, London).

Curry-Machado, J. (ed.) *Global Histories, Imperial Commodities, Local Interactions,* Hampshire: Palgrave Macmillan, 2013.

Dalziel, N. *The Penguin Historical Atlas of the British Empire,* London: Penguin Books, 2006.

Darrac, P-P. and van Schendel, W. *Global Blue: Indigo and Espionage in Colonial Bengal,* Dhaka: The University Press Limited, 2006.

Darwin, J. *After Tamerlane: The Rise and Fall of Global Empires 1400–2000,* London: Penguin Books, 2008.

Das, P. (editor and compiler) *Report of the Indigo Commission 1860,* Darjeeling: The Registrar, North Bengal University, 1992.

Datta, K. K. (ed.) *Unrest Against British Rule in Bihar, 1831–1859,* Patna: Superintendent Secretariat Press, 1957.

Datta, K. K. *Writing and Speeches of Mahatma Gandhi Relating to Bihar, 1917–1947,* Patna: Government of Bihar, 1960.

Datta, K. K. *Gandhiji in Bihar*, Patna: Government of Bihar, 1969.

De Majumdar, I. B. *How to Improve the Tobacco Crop of India*, Calcutta: Gupta, Mukherjee & Co, 1915.

Dewey, C. and Hopkins, A. G. (eds.) *The Imperial Impact: Studies in the Economic History of Africa and India*, London: The Athlone Press, University of London, 1978.

Dirks, N. B. *The Scandal of Empire. India and the Creation of Imperial Britain*, Delhi: Permanent Black, 2007.

D'Oyly, H. W. *Tales Retailed of Celebrities & Others*, London: John Lane, The Bodley Head and New York: John Lane Company, 1920.

Dutt, R. *The Economic History of British India. A Record of Agriculture and Land Settlements, Trade and Manufacturing Industries, Finance and Administration. From the Rise of the British Power in 1757 to the Accession of Queen Victoria in 1837*, London: Kegan Paul, Trench, Trübner & Co, 1902.

Dutta, A. *Christian Missionaries on the Indigo-Question in Bengal (1855–1861)*, Calcutta: Minerva Associates, 1989.

Eaton, R. M., Faruqui, M. D., Gilmartin, D., Kumar, S. (eds.) *Expanding Frontiers in South Asian and World History: Essays in Honour of John F. Richards*, Delhi: Cambridge University Press, 2013.

Elliot, H. M. and Dowson, J. (eds.) *The History of India as Told by Its Own Historians*, Allahabad: KitabMahal, 1964.

Fairbank, J. K. *Trade and Diplomacy on the China Coast: the Opening of the Treaty Ports, 1842–1854*, Cambridge, MA: Harvard University Press, 1953.

Fairholt, F. W. *Tobacco: Its History and Associations, Including an Account of the Plant and Its Manufacture, with Its Modes of use in All Age and Countries*, London: Chapman and Hall, 1859.

Fisher, C. M. 'Planters and Peasants: The Ecological Context of Agrarian Unrest on the Indigo Plantations in North Bihar', in Dewey, C. and Hopkins, A. G. (eds.), *The Imperial Impact: Studies in the Economic History of Africa and India*, London: The Athlone Press, University of London, 1978, pp. 114–31.

Fisher, M. H. (ed.) *Beyond the Three Seas. Travellers' Tales of Mughal India*, New Delhi: Random House, 2007.

Fraser, L. *India under Curzon & After*, London: William Heinemann, mcmxi (1911).

Freeman, J. *A Reply to the Memorandum of the East India Company or An Insight into British India*, London: Robert Hardwicke, 1858.

Fuller, B. *The Empire of India*, London: Elibron Classics, 2006.

Ganguli, B. N. (ed.) *Readings in Indian Economic History. Proceedings of the First All-India Seminar on Indian Economic History*, Delhi School of Economics, 1961 and London: Asia Publishing House, 1964.

Gaughan, J. M. *The 'Incumberances' British Women in India, 1615–1856*, New Delhi: Oxford University Press, 2013.

Gately, I. *Tobacco: A Cultural History of How an Exotic Plant Seduced Civilization*, New York: Grove Press, 2001.

Ghosh, P. *The Civil Disobedience Movement in Bihar (1930–1934)*, New Delhi: Manak, 2008.

Ghosh, S. C. *The British in Bengal. A Study of the British Society and Life in the Late Eighteen Century*, New Delhi: Munshiram Manoharlal Publishers, 1998 (originally published in 1970 by E. J. Brill, Leiden).

Ghosal, H. R. 'Changes in the Organization of Industrial Production in the Bengal Presidency in the Early Nineteenth Century', in Ganguli, B. N. (ed.), *Readings in Indian Economic History*, London: Asia Publishing House, 1964, pp. 124–33.

Gieryn, T. F. *Cultural Boundaries of Science. Credibility on the Line,* Chicago and London: The University of Chicago Press, 1999.

Gilchrist, J. B. *The General East India Guide and Vade Mecum for the Public Functionary, Government Officer, Private Agent, Trader or Foreign Sojourner, in British India and the Adjacent Parts of Asia immediately connected with the Honourable the East India Company. Being A Digest of the Work of the Late Capt. Williamson, with many Improvements and Additions; Embracing the Most valuable Parts of Similar Publications on the Statistics, Literature, Official Duties, and Social Economy of Life and Conduct in that Interesting Quarter of the World,* London: Kingsbury, Parbury, and Allen, 1825.

Goodman, J. *Tobacco in History: The Cultures of Dependence,* London and New York: Routledge, 1993.

Grierson, G. A. *Bihar Peasant Life being a Discursive Catalogue of the Surroundings of the People of that Province with many Illustrations from Photographs taken by the Author, prepared under Orders of the Government of Bengal,* Delhi: Cosmo Publications, 1975 (reprint; originally published in 1885).

Guha, R. *The Rule of Property for Bengal. An Essay on the Idea of Permanent Settlement,* Paris: Mouton, 1963.

Habib, I. *The Agrarian System of Mughal India,* Bombay: Asia Publishing House, 1963.

Hamilton, W. *A Geographical, Statistical, and Historical Description of Hindostan, and the Adjacent Countries,* in two volumes, Vol. I, London: John Murray, 1820.

Hay, J. *Memorial of Mr James Hay, Indigo Planter, Poorneah, to the Hon. East India Company, appealing against the Proceedings of Mr William Wollen, Judge of Poorneah,* London: C. H. Reynell, 1826.

Headrick, D. *The Tentacles of Progress: Technology Transfer in the Age of Imperialism, 1850–1940,* Oxford: Oxford University Press, 1988.

Herbert, E. W. *Flora's Empire: British Gardens in India,* Philadelphia: University of Pennsylvania Press, 2011.

Hill, C. V. and Stoll, M. R. (ed.) *South Asia: An Environmental History (Nature and Human Societies),* Santa Barbara and Oxford: ABC-CLIO, 2008.

Hobhouse, H. *Seeds of Wealth. Four Plants that Made Men Rich,* Washington DC: Shoemaker and Hoard, 2004.

Hobsbawm, E. *The Age of Capital 1848–1875,* London: Abacus, 1997.

Hooker, J. D. *Himalayan Journals or Notes of a Naturalist in Bengal, the Sikkim and Nepal Himalayas, the Khaisia Mountains, etc,* Vol. VI, Kew, 1854 (E-book obtained through the Gutenberg Project).

Hough, W. *India as It Ought to be under the New Charter Act.* Improvement suggested, London: Messrs. W. Thacker & Co., 1853.

Houlton, J. *Bihar: The Heart of India,* Mumbai: Orient Longmans, 1949.

Howard, A. 'Agriculture and Science', *Indian Science Congress Association Presidential Addresses,* Vol. 1, 1914–47, Hyderabad: Universities Press (India), 2003, pp. 176–88.

Howard, A. *The Soil and Health. A Study of Organic Agriculture,* with a new introduction by Wendell Berry, Kentucky: University Press of Kentucky, 2006.

Howard, A. and Howard, G. L. C. *The Improvement of Tobacco Cultivation in Bihar, Pusa, Bulletin,* Calcutta: Superintendent Government Printing India, No. 50, 1915.

Howard, G. L. C. and Ram, K. 'Studies in Indian Tobaccos', *Memoirs of the Department of Agriculture in India* (Nos. 4 and 5), Pusa: Agricultural Research Institute.

"Howard, L. E. *Sir Albert Howard in India,* London: Faber and Faber Ltd., 1953.

Huggins, W. *Sketches in India, Treating on Subjects Connected with Government; Civil and Military Establishments; Characters of the European, and Customs of the Native Inhabitants*, London: John Letts, 1824.

Hull, E. C. P. *The European in India or Anglo-Indian's Vade-Mecum*, New Delhi: Asian Education Service, 2004.

Hume, A. O. *Agricultural Reform in India*, London: W.H. Allen & Co., 1879.

Hunter, W. W. *A Statistical Account of Bengal: Monghyr and Purniah*, London: Trübner & Co., 1877.

Hunter, W. W. *A Statistical Account of Bengal: Vol. XIII (Tirhut and Champaran)*, compiled by A. W. Mackie, London: Trübner & Co., 1877.

Hunter, W. W. *The Imperial Gazetteer of India*, Vol. IX, London: Trübner and Co., 1881.

Hunter, W. W. *The Indian Empire: Its People, History and Products*, New Delhi and Madras: Asian Educational Services, 2005 (original London: Trübner & Co., 1886).

Indian Leaf Tobacco Development Co., *Indian Tobacco Leaves. A Story of Co-operation in India*, London: Harrison & Sons, n.d.

Jha, H. (ed.) and Colebrooke, H. T. *Remarks on the Husbandry and Internal Commerce of Bengal*, Darbhanga: MaharajadhirajKameshwar Singh Kalyani Foundation, 2007, Heritage Series 11.

Kiyokawa, Y. and Ohno, A. 'Technology and Labour Absorption in the Indigenous Indian Sugar Industry: An Analysis of Appropriate Technology', in Robb, P., Sugihara, K. and Yanagisawa, H. (eds.), *Local Agrarian Societies in Colonial India. Japanese Perspectives*, Richmond Surrey: Curzon, 1996.

Kling, B. B. *The Blue Mutiny: The Indigo Disturbances in Bengal 1859–1862*, Philadelphia: University of Pennsylvania Press, 1966.

Kozlowski, L. T., Henningfield, J. E., and Brigham, J. *Cigarettes, Nicotine, & Health: a Biobehavioral Approach*, London, Thousand Oaks: Saga Publications, 2001.

Krishna, B. *Commercial Relations between India and England (1601–1757)*, London: George Routledge & Sons, 1924.

Kumar, A. *Community Warriors, State, Peasants and Caste Armies in Bihar*, New Delhi: Anthem Press, 2008.

Kumar, D., Damodaran, V., and D'Souza, R. (eds.) *The British Empire and the Natural World, Environmental Encounters in South Asia*, New Delhi: Oxford University Press, 2011.

Kumar, P. *Indigo Plantations and Science in Colonial India*, Cambridge: Cambridge University Press, 2012.

Laufer, B. *Tobacco and its Use in Asia*, Anthropology Leaflet 18, Chicago: Field Museum of Natural History, 1924.

Lauterbach, F. *Der Kampf des Waidesmitdem Indigo,* Inaugural Dissertation, Universität Leipzig, Leipzig: Veit & Comp., 1905.

Leake, M. H. *The Bases of Agricultural Practice and Economics in the United Provinces*, Cambridge: Heffers & Son, Ltd, 1920.

Lees, S. H. B. *India and the Tariff Problem*, London: Constable & Company Ltd., 1909.

Lethbridge, R. *Swadeshi and British Fiscal Policy*, Delhi: Gian Publishing House, n.d., (reprint in 1988).

Letters from an Artist in India to his Sisters in England. Rural Life in Bengal; Illustrative of Anglo-Indian Suburban Life; The Habits of the Rural Classes, the Varied Produce of the Soil and Seasons, and the Culture and Manufacture of Indigo, London: W. Thacker & Co., 1866.

Long, J. *Strike, But Hear!: Evidence Explanatory of the Indigo System in Lower Bengal,* Calcutta: R.C. Lepage and Co., 1861. (La Vergne, TN US, Nabu Public Domain Reprints, 2010).

Ludden, D. (ed.) *Agricultural Production and Indian History,* Delhi: Oxford University Press, 1994.

Ludden, D. *An Agrarian History of South Asia: The New Cambridge History of India (IV),* Cambridge: Cambridge University Press, 1999.

Lupton, A. *Happy India as It Might be if Guided by Modern Science,* n.p., 1922.

Macaulay, Z. *A Letter to William W. Whitmore, ESQ.MP. Pointing out Some of the Erroneous Statements Contained in a Pamphlet by Joseph Marryat Entitled* 'A Reply to the Arguments contained in Various Publications, Recommending an Equalization of the Duties on East and West India Sugars' by the Author of a Pamphlet entitled East and West India Sugar', London: Lupton Relfe and Hatchard and Son, 1823.

Macdonald, B. *India Sunshine and Shadows,* London: BACSA, 1988.

MacDonnell, A. *Colonial Commerce: Comprising an Inquiry into the Principles upon which Discriminating Duties Should Be Levied on Sugar, the Growth Respectively of the West India British Possessions, of the East Indies, and of Foreign Countries,* London: John Murray, 1828.

MacInnes, C. M. *The Early English Tobacco Trade,* London: Kegan Paul, Trench, Trübner & Co., Ltd., 1926.

Mair, R. S. 'Medical Guide for Anglo-Indians, Being a Compendium of Advice to Europeans in India, etc.', in Hull, E. C. P. (ed.), *The European in India or Anglo-Indian's Vade-Mecum. A Handbook of Useful and Practical Information for Those Proceeding to or Residing in the East Indies, relating to Outfits, Routes, Time for Departure, Indian Climate and Seasons, Housekeeping, Servants, etc., etc.,* (3rd edn) with additions, New Delhi and Chennai: Asian Educational Services, 2004 (first published in 1878 by C. Kegan Paul & Co, London).

Majumdar, R. C. *The Mughul Empire*, Mumbai: Bharatiya Vidya Bhavan, 2007.

Malekandathil, P. *The Mughals, the Portuguese and the Indian Ocean: Changing Imageries of Maritime India*, Delhi: Primus Books, 2013.

Malleson, G. B. *The Indian Mutiny of 1857*, New Delhi: Rupa Publications, 1998.

Mangles, R. D. *Wrongs and Claims of Indian Commerce*, Edinburgh: Ballantyne and Hughes, 1841.

Maori (Inglis, J. A. S.) *Tirhoot Rhymes*, Calcutta: Wyman & Co., 1873.

Maori (Inglis, J. A. S.) *Sport and Work on the Nepaul Frontier or Twelve Years Sporting Reminiscences of an Indigo Planter*, 1878 (Project Gutenberg an e-Book).

Marshall, P. J. *East Indian Fortunes. The British in Bengal in the Eighteenth Century*, Oxford: Clarendon Press, 1976.

Martin, M. *The History, Antiquities, Topography, and Statistics of Eastern India; Comprising the Districts of Behar, Shahabad, Bhagulpoor, Goruckpoor, Dinajepoor, Puraniya, Ronggopoor, and Assam, in the relation to their Geology, Mineralogy, Botany, Agriculture, Commerce, Manufactures, Fine Arts, Population, Religion, Education, Statistics, ETC. Surveyed under the Orders of the Supreme Government, and Collated from the Original Documents at the E.I. House, with the permission of the Honourable Court of Directors*, in three volumes, London: Wm H. Allen and Co., 1838.

Martin, R. M. *Statistics of the Colonies of the British Empire in the West Indies, South America, North America, Asia, Austral-Asia, Africa, and Europe; Comprising the Area, Agriculture, Commerce, Manufacture, Shipping, Custom Duties, Population, Education, Religion, Crime, Government, Finances, Laws, Military defence, Cultivated and Waste Lands, Emigration, Rates of Wages, Prices of Provinces, Banks, Coins, Staple Products, Stock, Moveable and Immoveable Property, Public Companies, &c. of Each Colony; with the Charters and the*

Engraved Seals. From the Officials Records of the Colonial Office, London: Wm. H. Allen and Co., 1839.

Martin, M. *The Progress and Present State of British India. A Manual for General Use, Based on Official Documents, Furnished under the Authority of Her Majesty's Secretary of State for India*, London: Sampson Low, Son, & Co., 1862.

Metcalf, B. D. and Metcalf, T. R. *A Concise History of Modern India*, Cambridge: Cambridge University Press, 2006.

Mishra, S. G. *History of Bihar 1740–1772*, New Delhi: MunshiramManoharlal, 1970.

Misra, B. B. *Mahatma Gandhi's Movement in Champaran*, Patna: Government of Bihar, 1963.

Mitra, M. *Agrarian Social Structure. Continuity and Change in Bihar 1786–1820*, New Delhi: Manohar, 1985.

Mittal, S. K. *Peasant Uprisings & Mahatma Gandhi in North Bihar (A Politico-Economic Study of Indigo Industry 1817–1917 with Special Reference to Champaran)*, Meerut: AnuPrakashan, 1978.

Molla, M. K. U. *The New Province of Eastern Bengal & Assam 1905–1911*, Rajshahi: The Institute of Bangladesh Studies, 1981.

Moreland, W. H. (ed.) *From Akbar to Aurangzeb: A Study in Indian Economic History*, London: MacMillan, 1923.

Moreland, W. H. (ed.) *Relations of Golconda in the Early Seventeenth Century*, London: Hakluyt Society, 1931.

Moreland, W. H. (ed.) *India at the Death of Akbar*, Delhi: Atma Ram, 1962.

Mukerji, N. G. *Handbook of Indian Agriculture*, Calcutta: Thacker, Spink and Co., 1915.

Mukherjee, M. *Colonializing Agriculture: The Myth of Punjab Exceptionalism*, New Delhi: Sage, 2005.

Mukherjee, R. (ed.) *Networking in the First Global Age*, Delhi: Primus, 2011.

Mukherji, S. *Peasants' Politics and the British Government 1930–40: A Study on Eastern Bihar*, Delhi: AnamikaPrakashan, 1993.

Munro, J. F. *Maritime Enterprise and Empire: Sir William Mackinnon and His Business Network 1823–1893*, Woodbridge, Suffolk: Boydelland Brewer, 2003.

Nadri, G. A. 'The Archaeology of Indigo Manufacture', in Mohan, S. K. (ed.), *Reason and Archaeology*, Delhi: Association for the Study of History and Archaeology, pp. 159–63.

Nayak, A. K. J. R. 'FDI in a Developing Country: Case of British American Tobacco', *Multinationals in India*, Case Research Series, Bhubaneshwar, 2008.

Nevile, P. *Sahib's India. Vignettes from the Raj*, New Delhi: Penguin Books, 2010.

O'Malley, L. S. S. *Bihar and Orissa District Gazetteer Patna* (revised edition by J. F. W. James, I.C.S.), New Delhi: Logos Press, 2005 (reprint of 1924).

O'Malley, L. S. S. *Bihar and Orissa District Gazetteers Shahabad* (revised by J. F. W. James), New Delhi: Logos, 2005 (original 1924).

O'Malley, L. S. S. *Bengal District Gazetteers Muzaffarpur*, Calcutta: The Bengal Secretariat Book Depot, 1907.

O'Malley, L. S. S. *Bihar and Orissa District Gazetteers, Monghyr*, revised edition, New Delhi: Logos Press, 2007 (original 1926).

O'Malley, L. S. S. *Bengal District Gazetteers, Champaran*, revised edition, New Delhi: Logos Press, 2013 (original 1907).

O'Malley, L. S. S. *Bengal District Gazetteers, Darbhanga,* revised edition, New Delhi: Logos Press, 2013 (original 1907).

Peggs, J. *India's Cries to British Humanity, Relative to Infanticide, British Connection with Idolatry, Ghaut Murders, Suttee, and Colonization in India; to which are added Humane Hints for the Melioration of the State of Society in British India,* London: Simpkin and Marshall, 1832 (third edition revised and enlarged with a book on colonisation in India).

Petitjean, P. (ed.) *Colonial Sciences: Researchers and Institutions,* Paris: Orstom, 1996.

Petition against the Income Tax of the Zemindars of Bengal, Behar, and Orissa to the Imperial Parliament, Calcutta: Printed at Scott and Co's Press, 1861 (LSE Selected Pamphlets).

Pinto, C. *Trade and Finance in Portuguese India. A Study of the Portuguese Country Trade 1770–1840,* New Delhi: Concept, 1994.

Playne, S. (compiler) *Bengal and Assam, Behar and Orissa. Their History, People, Commerce, and Industrial Resources,* assisted by J. W. Bond, edited by A. Wright, London: The Foreign and Colonial Compiling and Publishing Co., 1917.

Pogson, F. *Manual of Agriculture for India,* Calcutta: Thacker, Spink and Co., 1883.

Pollan, M. *The Botany of Desire: A Plant's-Eye View of the World,* New York: Random House, 2002.

Pouchepadass, J. *Land, Power and Market. A Bihar District under Colonial Rule, 1860–1947,* New Delhi: Sage, 2000.

Prinsep, J. 'Bengal Sugar: An Account of the Method and Expense of Cultivating the Sugar-cane in Bengal: with Calculations of the First Cost to the Manufacturer and Exporter and Suggestions for Attracting that Article of

Eastern Produce Exclusively to Great Britain' in *A letter from a Planter and Distiller in Bengal, to His Friend in London*, London: Debrett, 1794.

Radhakrishna, M. *Dishonoured by History: 'Criminal Tribes' and British Colonial Policy*, Hyderabad: Orient Longman, 2001.

Raha, A. K. and Basu, S. *Evolution of Calcutta Customs: A Study in History*, New Delhi, Rupa & Co., 2000.

Ram, B. *Land and Society in India. Agrarian Relations in Colonial North Bihar*, Chennai: Orient Longman, 1997.

Raychaudhuri, T. 'European Commercial Activity and the Organization of India's Commerce and Industrial Production, 1500–1750', in Ganguli, B. N. (ed.), *Readings in Indian Economic History. Proceedings of the First All-India Seminar on Indian Economic History*, Delhi School of Economics, 1961, London: Asia Publishing House, 1964, pp. 64–77.

Reid, W. M. *The Culture and Manufacture of Indigo: with a Description of a Planter's Life and Resources*, Calcutta: Thacker, Spink and Co., 1887.

Renford, R. K. *The Non-Official British in India to 1920*, Delhi: Oxford University Press, 1987.

Robb, P. *The Evolution of British Policy towards Indian Politics 1880–1920. Essays on Colonial Attitudes, Imperial Strategies, and Bihar*, New Delhi: Manohar, 1992.

Robb, P. (ed.) *Meanings of Agriculture. Essays in South Asian History and Economics*, Delhi: Oxford University Press, 1996.

Robb, P. *Peasants, Political Economy, and Law (Empire, Identity, and India)*, New Delhi: Oxford University Press, 2007.

Robb, P., Sugihara, K., and Yanagisawa, H. (eds.) *Local Agrarian Societies in Colonial India. Japanese Perspectives*, Richmond Surrey: Curzon, 1996.

Robins, N. *The Corporation that Changed the World. How the East India Company Shaped the Modern Multinational*, Hyderabad: Orient Longman, 2006.

Robinson, S. H. *The Bengal Sugar Planter: Being a Treatise on the Cultivation of the Sugar-cane and Date-tree in Bengal, and the Manufacture of Sugar and Rum therefrom*, Calcutta: Bishop College Press, 1849.

Roy, R. N. *Sugar Industry in Darbhanga Division*, Delhi: Capital Publishing House, 1988.

Roy, T. *The Economic History of India 1857–1947*, New Delhi: Oxford University Press, 2011.

Royal Commission on Agriculture in India, *Evidence of Officers Serving under the Government of India*, Vol. 1, Part II, Calcutta: Government of India Central Publication Branch, 1928.

Royle, J. F. *Essays on the Productive Resources of India*, London: H. Allen, 1840.

Russell-Wood, A. J. R. *The Portuguese Empire 1415–1808*, Baltimore: Johns Hopkins University Press, 1998.

Ryot, A. (compiler) *Selections from Papers on Indigo Cultivation in Bengal, with an Introduction and a few Notes, by a Ryot*, Calcutta: I.C. Bose & Co., 1858.

van Schendel, W. *Reviving a Rural Industry: Silk Producers and Officials in India and Bangladesh 1880s to 1980s*, New Delhi: Manohar, 1995.

Schiebinger, L. *Plants and Empire: Colonial Bioprospecting in the Atlantic World*, Cambridge: Harvard University Press, 2004.

Schiebinger, L. and Swan, C. (eds.) *Colonial Botany, Science, Commerce, and Politics in the Early Modern World*, Philadelphia: University of Pennsylvania Press, 2007.

Schrottky, E. C. *The Principles of Rational Agriculture Applied to India and its Staple Products*, Bombay: Times of India Office, 1876.

Scott, J. C. *Seeing Like a State: How Certain Scheme to Improve the Human Condition Have Failed*, New Haven and London: Yale University Press, 1998.

Serajuddin, A. M. *Revenue Administration of the East India Company in Chittagong, 1761–1785*, Chittagong: Chittagong University, 1971.

Seton-Karr, W. S. *Selections from Calcutta Gazettes of the Years 1789,1790,1791,1792,1793,1794, 1795, 1796, and 1997, Showing the Political and Social Condition of the English in India Seventy Years Ago*, Vol. II, Calcutta: O.T. Cutter, Military Orphan Press (under the sanction of the Government of India), 1865.

Sharma, K. K., Singh, P. P., and Kumar, R. (eds.) *Peasant Struggles in Bihar, 1831–1992: Spontaneity to Organisation,* Patna: Centre for Peasant Studies and Janaki Prakashan, 1994.

Shaw, F. J. F. and Ram, K. *Production of Cigarette Tobacco by Flue-Curing'*, Pusa *Bulletin*, No. 187, Pusa: Agriculture Research Institute, 1928.

Shukla, P. K. 'Indigo Cultivation and the Rural Crisis in North Bihar in the Second Half of the Nineteenth Century', *Proceedings of the Indian History Congress*, Forty-Ninth Session 1988, Dharwad: Karnatak University, 1989, pp. 463–69.

Shukla, P. K. *Indigo and the Raj. Peasant Protests in Bihar 1780–1917,* Delhi and Patna: Pragati Publications, 1993.

Singh, N. P. 'Growth of Sugar Culture in Bihar (1793–1913)', *Proceedings of the Indian History Congress*, Forty-fifth session (1984) in Annamalainagar, Delhi: Indian History Congress, 1985, pp. 58894.

Singh, R. S. *Sugar Industry (A Case Study of Champaran),* Delhi: Capital Publishing House, 1988.

Singh, S. B. *European Agency Houses in Bengal (1783–1833)*, Calcutta: K.L. Mukhopadhyay, 1966.

Singh, S. K. *Press, Politics & Public Opinion in Bihar (1912–1947)*, New Delhi: Manak, 2010.

Singh, U. N. *Some Aspects of Rural Life in Bihar (An Economic Study, 1793–1833)*, Patna: Janaki Prakashan, 1980.

Sinha, C. P. N. *From Decline to Destruction. Agriculture in Bihar during the Early British Rule (1765–1813)*, New Delhi: Manak Publications, 1997.

Sinha, R. *Aspects of Society & Economic of Bihar 1765–1856,* New Delhi: Commonwealth Publishers, 1989.

Sinha, S. K. *The Bhumihars: Caste of Eastern India,* New Delhi: Raj Publications, 2005.

Smith, A. C. *The Serampore Mission Enterprise,* Bangalore: Centre for Contemporary Christianity, 2006.

Spry, H. H. (compiler) *Suggestions Received by the Agricultural & Horticultural Society of India for Extending the Cultivation and Introduction of Useful and Ornamental Plants: with a View to the Improvement of the Agricultural and Commercial Resources of India,* Calcutta: Bishop's Press, 1841.

Srinivasachari, C. S. *Tobacco and Areca Nut,* Chennai: Orient Longman, 2001.

Storey, W. K. *Science and Power in Colonial Mauritius*, Rochester: University of Rochester Press, 1997.

Temple, R. C. (ed.) *A Geographical Account of Counties Round the Bay of Bengal,* Nendeln/Liechtenstein: Kraus, 1967.

Tendulkar, D. G. *Gandhi in Champaran*, The Publication Division. Ministry of Information and Broadcasting Government of India, Published under the Auspices of the Bihar Government, October 2, 1957.

Tennant, W. *Indian Recreations; Consisting Chiefly of Strictures on the Domestic and Rural Economy of the Mohammedans & Hindoos*, Vol. II, Edinburgh: C. Stewart, 1803.

Thiselton-Dyer, W. T. *The Botanical Enterprise of the Empire*, London: Her Majesty's Stationery Office, 1880.

Thompson, E. and Garrett, G. T. *History of British Rule in India*, New Delhi: Atlantic Publishers, 1999.

Tilley, H. *Africa as a Living Laboratory, Empire, Development, and the Problem of Scientific Knowledge, 1870–1950*, Chicago: The University of Chicago Press, 2011.

Toppo, R. *Dynamics of Tribal Migration in India*, Ranchi: XISS, 2007.

Tripathi, A. *Trade and Finance in the Bengal Presidency 1793–1833*, Bombay: Orient Longmans, 1956.

Tuck, P. (ed.) *The East India Company: 1600–1858*, Vol. III, London and New York: Routledge, 1998.

Various, *The Indian Problem Solved. Undeveloped Wealth in India and State Reproductive Work. The Ways to Prevent Famines and Advance the Material Progress of India*, London: Virtue, Spalding, and Co., 1874.

Warnford, L. C. G. *Tobacco: Growing, Curing & Manufacturing. A Handbook for Planters in all Parts of the World*, London: E & F.N. Spong, 1886.

Watson, F. *New Zealand Exhibition, 1865. A Classified List of Contributions from British India and its Dependencies*, forwarded by order of the Secretary of State for India, from the Indian Museum, London, London: W. Trounce, 1864.

Watson, F. *Report on the Cultivation and Preparation of Tobacco in India. An Appended Manual of Practical Operations connected with the Cultivation, &C. of Tobacco in Hungary*. Extracted from a *Treatise* by Mr J. Mandis, Financial

Counselor and Inspector for the purchase of tobacco in Austria. With Plates, London: India Museum, India Office, 1871.

Watt, G. *A Dictionary of Economic Products of India*, in six volumes, Calcutta: Superintendent of Government Printing, 1885.

Watt, G. *The Commercial Products of India being an Abridgment of 'the Dictionary of the Economic Products of India'*, London: John Murray, 1908.

Wilkins, W. J. *Daily Life and Work in India*, London: T. Fisher Unwin, 1888, pp. 221–23.

Williamson, T. and Blagdon, F. W. *The European in India: From a Collection of Drawings by Charles Doyleyengraved by J. H. Clark and C. Dubourg with a preface and copious descriptions by* T. Williamson accompanied with *a Brief History of Ancient and Modern India from the Earliest Periods of Antiquity to the Termination of the Late Mahratta War by F. W. Blagdon*, New Delhi and Madras: Asian Educational Services, 1995 (reprint of London: Edward Orme, 1813).

Wilson, M. J. *History of Behar Indigo Factories; Reminiscences of Behar; Tirhoot and its Inhabitants of the Past; History of Behar Light Horse Volunteers (1908)*, Kessinger Legacy Reprints, Original Version: Calcutta: The Calcutta General Printing Company, 1908.

Worboys, M. 'British Colonial Science Policy, 1918–1939', in Petitjean, P. (ed.), *Colonial Sciences: Researchers and Institutions*, Paris: Orstom, 1996, pp. 99–111.

Wyatt, A. *Geographical and Statistical Report of the District of Tirhoot*, Calcutta: Thos. Jones, 'Calcutta Gazette' Office, 1854.

Wylie, M. *The Commerce, Resources, and Prospects of India*, London: W.H. Dalton, 1857.

Yang, A. A. *Bazaar India. Markets, Society, and the Colonial State in Bihar*, Berkeley, Los Angeles, London: University of California Press, 1989.

Yang, A. A. *The Limited Raj. Agrarian Relations in Colonial India, Saran District, 1793–1920,* Berkeley, California: The University of California Press, 1989.

Yang, A. A. *Bazaar India. Markets, Society, and the Colonial State in Gangetic Bihar,* Berkeley, Los Angeles and London: University of California Press, 1998.

Articles

Agnani, S. 'Jacobinism in India, Indianism in English Parliament: Fearing the Enlightenment and Colonial Modernity with Edmund Burke', *Cultural Critique,* Vol. 68, Winter 2008, pp. 131–62.

Alder, G. J. 'The Origins of "The Pusa Experiment": The East India Company and Horse-Breeding in Bengal, 1793–1808', *Bengal Past and Present,* Vol. XCVIII, Part I, Serial No. 186, January–June 1979, pp. 10–32.

Anonymous. 'On the Growth and Peculiar Qualities of Tobacco', *London Magazine or Gentleman's Monthly Intelligencer,* 21 December 1752, p. 605.

Anonymous. 'Remarks on the Husbandry and Internal Commerce of Bengal, Svo. Blacks & Parry, 1806', *The Edinburgh Review,* Art. II, April 1807, pp. 27–40 (book review).

Anonymous. 'The Introduction and Early Use of Tobacco in England', *Asiatic Journal,* Vol. XXII, No. 128, 1826, pp. 137–42.

Anonymous. 'On the Agriculture of Hindostan', *The Quarterly Journal of Agriculture,* Vol. VIII, June 1837–March 1838, pp. 29–63.

Anonymous. 'The Bengal Indigo Planter and His System', *Macmillan's Magazine,* Vol. XLIX, 1884, pp. 221–30.

Anonymous. 'Indigo Plantation', *Journal of the Society of Arts,* 19 October 1900, pp. 847–48.

Anonymous. 'Indian Tobacco Industry', *Journal of the Royal Society of Arts*, Vol. 67, No. 3493, 31 October 1919, p. 777.

Anonymous. 'Progress of Agricultural Research in India', *Current Science*, Vol. 9, No. 3, March 1940, pp. 152–53.

Arents, G. 'The Seed from Which Virginia Grew', *William and Mary College Quarterly Historical Magazine*, 2nd Series, Vol. 19, No. 2, April 1939, pp. 123–29.

Arnold, D. 'White Colonization and Labour in Nineteenth-Century India', *The Journal of Imperial and Commonwealth History*, Vol. 11, No. 2, 1982–1983, pp. 133–58.

Arnold, D. 'Agriculture and "Improvement" in Early Colonial India: A Pre-History of Development', *Journal of Agrarian Change*, Vol. 5, No. 4, October 2005, pp. 505–25.

Arnold, D. 'Plant Capitalism and Company Science: The Indian Career of Nathaniel Wallich', *Modern Asian Studies*, Vol. 42, No. 5, September 2008, pp. 899–928.

Ashworth, W. J. 'Quality and the Roots of Manufacturing "Expertise" in Eighteenth-Century Britain', *Osiris,* Vol. 25, No. 1 (Expertise and the Early Modern State), 2010, pp. 231–54.

Asiaticus. 'The Rise and Fall of the Indigo Industry in India', *The Economic Journal*, Vol. 22, No. 86, June 1912, pp. 237–47.

Baber, Z. 'Colonizing Nature: Scientific Knowledge, Colonial Power and the Incorporation of India into the Modern World-System', *British Journal of Sociology*, Vol. 52, No. 1, March 2001, pp. 37–58.

Bagchi, A. K. 'Colonialism and the Nature of "Capitalist" Enterprise in India', *Economic and Political Weekly,* July 30, 1988, PE-38–50.

Barber, C. A. 'Studies Indian Sugarcanes, No. 5. On Testing the Suitability of Sugarcane Varieties for Different Localities, by a System of Measurements, Periodicity in the Growth of Sugarcane', *Memoirs of the Department of Agriculture in India,* Agricultural Research Institute, Pusa, Botanical Series, Vol. 10, No. 3, August, Calcutta: Thacker, Spink & Co. (for the Imperial Department of Agriculture in India), 1919.

Barendse, R. J. 'Trade and State in the Arabian Seas: A Survey from the Fifteenth to the Eighteenth Century', *Journal of World History,* Vol. 11, No. 2, Fall 2000, pp. 173–225.

Barik, R. 'Tenancy Reforms Act in Bihar during the First Congress Government: 1937–39', *Social Scientist,* Vol. 20, No. 5/6, May–June 1992, pp. 3–20.

Barton, G. 'Sir Albert Howard and the Forestry Roots of the Organic Farming Movement', *Agricultural History,* Vol. 75, No. 2 (Spring), 2001, pp. 168–87.

Bayley, S. C. 'Discussion of Cultivation, Manufacture, and Uses of Indigo', *Journal of the Society of Arts,* Vol. 48, 6 April 1900, pp. 431–32.

Beighton, D. T. 'The Possibilities of the Indian Tobacco Industry', *The Imperial and Asiatic Quarterly Review and Colonial Record,* Vol. 19, No. 37, January 1905, pp. 82–111.

Bellon, R. 'Joseph Dalton Hooker's Ideal for a Professional Man of Science', *Journal of the History of Biology,* Vol. 34, No. 1, Spring 2001, pp. 51–82.

Bhattacharyya, A. 'Random Notes on Bengali Enterprise 1900–1920', *Journal of History,* Jadavpur University Calcutta, Vol. V., 1984, pp. 112–38.

Bhattacharya, S. 'Indigo Planters, Ram Mohan Roy and the 1833 Charter Act', *Social Scientist,* Vol. 4, No. 3, October 1975, pp. 56–65.

Birdwood, G. 'The Quest and Early European Settlement of India', *Journal of the Society of Arts,* 7 February 1879, pp. 192–223.

Bombay Gazette, 'The Indian Tobacco Manufacture', *Tropical Agriculturist*, 1 February 1884, p. 604.

Bradburn, D. 'The Visible Fist: The Chesapeake Tobacco Trade in War and the Purpose of Empire, 1690–1715', *The William and Mary Quarterly*, Vol. 68, No. 3, July 2011, pp. 361–86.

Bradley, A. G. 'Colonial Virginia', *MacMillan's Magazine*, n.s., No. 2, October 1906, pp. 335–43.

Brockway, L. H. 'Science and Colonial Expansion: The Role of the British Royal Gardens', *American Ethnologist*, Vol. 6, No. 3, August 1979, pp. 449–65.

Broughton, H. 'Letters from a Competition Wallah: Letter III', *MacMillan's Magazine*, Vol. 8, May–October 1863, pp. 267–79.

Brown, G. 'Scientific Research in Relation to Economic and Agricultural Development in India', *The Imperial and Asiatic Quarterly Review and Oriental and Colonial Records*, Vol. 15, No. 29, January 1903, pp. 182–84.

Burt, B. C. 'The Indian Sugar Industry', *Journal of the Royal Society of Arts*, Vol. LXXXIII, No. 4317, 16 August 1935, pp. 919–40.

Cain, P. J. 'J.A. Hobson, Cobdenism, and the Radical Theory of Economic Imperialism, 1898–1914', *The Economic History Review*, n.s., Vol. 31, No. 4, November 1978, pp. 565–84.

Card, D. G. 'Review of the Bright Tobacco Industry, 1860–1929 by Nannie May Tilley', *Journal of Farm Economics*, Vol. 30, No. 4, November 1948, pp. 794–96.

Chakravarti, R. 'Early Medieval Bengal and the Trade in Horses: A Note', *Journal of the Economic and Social History of the Orient*, Vol. 42, No. 2, 1999, pp. 194–211.

Chakre, O. J. 'The Wealth of India – a CSIR's Encyclopaedia of Information Resource on Economic Plants, Animals and Minerals', *Current Science*, Vol. 99, No. 7, 10 October 2010, pp. 969–71.

Chaplin, J. 'The Natural History of British Imperialism', *The Journal of British Studies*, Vol. 42, No. 1, January 2003, pp. 127–31.

Chaudhuri, B. 'Growth of Commercial Agriculture in Bengal (1859–1885)', *Indian Economic and Social History Review*, Vol. 7, No. 25, 1970, pp. 25–60.

Chaudhuri, K. N. 'India's Foreign Trade and the Cessation of the East India Company's Trading Activities, 1828–1840', *The Economic History Review*, New Series, Vol. 19, No. 2, 1966, pp 345–63.

Clark, J. F. M. 'Bugs in the System: Insects, Agricultural Science, and Professional Aspirations in Britain, 1890–1920', *Agricultural History*, Vol. 75, No. 1, Winter 2001, pp. 83–114.

Clarke, N. G. 'The Flavour of Tobacco', *Contemporary Review*, Vol. 75, January to June 1899, pp. 880–85.

Cotton, A. 'The Indian Famine: With Special Reference to the Means Which Should Be Adopted for the Alleviation or Prevention of Future Famines', *Journal of the Society of Arts*, 24 April 1874, pp. 501–9.

Council of Agricultural Research. *Agriculture and Animal Husbandry in India 1937–38*, Delhi: The Imperial Council of Agricultural Research, 1940.

Coventry, B. 'Rhea Experiments in India', *Agricultural Journal of India*, Vol. II, Agricultural Institute Pusa, Calcutta: Thacker and Spink, 1907, pp. 1–14.

Cox, H. 'International Business, the State and industrialisation in India: Early Growth in the Indian Cigarette Industry, 1900–1919', *Indian Economic Social History Review*, Vol. 27, No. 3, 1990, pp. 289–312.

Crawford, J. 'On the History and Consumption of Tobacco', *Journal of the Statistical Society of London*, Vol. 16, No. 1, March 1853, pp. 45–52.

Crawfurd, J. 'On the History and Migration of Cultivated Narcotic Plants in Reference to Ethnology', *Transactions of the Ethnological Society of London*, Vol. 7, 1869a, pp. 78–91.

Crawfurd, J. 'On the History and Migration of Textile and Tinctorial Plants in Reference to Ethnology', *Transactions of the Ethnological Society of London*, Vol. 7, 1869b, pp. 1–15.

Damodaran, V. 'Review of Tropics and the Traveling Gaze: India, Landscape and Science, 1800–1856 by David Arnold', *Victorian Studies*, Vol. 49, No. 4, Summer 2007, pp. 710–11.

Datta, K. K. 'India's Trade with Europe and America in the Eighteenth Century', *Journal of the Economic and Social History of the Orient*, Vol. 2, No. 3, December 1959, pp. 313–23.

D'Cruz, J. 'Remarks on Certain Varieties of Sugar-cane in the Nursery Garden of the Agricultural and Horticultural Society, with a Few Hints for Their Cultivation', *Journal of the Agricultural & Horticultural Society of India*, edited by The Committee of Papers, Vol. VI, Part I, January to December 1848, pp. 56–67.

De, A. 'Flourishing Stage of Indigo Plantation', *Journal of History*, Jadavpur University Calcutta, Vol. IV, 1983, pp. 106–19.

Deshpande, A. 'An Historical Overview of Opium Cultivation and Changing State Attitudes towards the Crop in India, 1878–2000 A.D.', *Studies in History*, Vol. 25, No. 1, n.s., 2009, pp. 109–43.

Donnelly, A. 'That Bewitching Vegetable – Tobacco', *Asia: The American Magazine on the Orient*, Vol. XXXI, June 1931, pp. 345–52 and pp. 405–7.

Douie, J. M. 'Review of Indian Offer of Imperial Preference by Roger Lethbridge', *The Economic Journal*, Vol. 23, No. 92, December 1913, pp. 572–76.

D'Souza, R. 'Rigidity and Affliction of Capitalist Property: Colonial Land Revenue and the Recasting of Nature', *Studies in History*, Vol. 20, No. 2, n.s., 2004, pp. 237–72.

Dutta, K. 'Portugal's Experiment with Brazilian Tobacco in India in the Eighteenth Century', *Indica*, Vol. 28, No. 2, 1991, pp. 95–111.

Endersby, J. 'A Garden Enclosed: Botanical Barter in Sydney, 1818–1839', *British Journal for the History of Science,* Vol. 33, No. 3, September 2000, pp. 313–34.

Farooqui, A. 'Opium Enterprise and Colonial Intervention in Malwa and Western India, 1800–1824', *The Indian Economic and Social History Review,* Vol. 32, No. 4, 1995, pp. 447–73.

Farooqui, A. 'Colonialism and Competing Addictions: Morphine Content as Historical Factor', *Social Scientist,* Vol. 32, No. 5/6 (May–June), 2004, pp. 21–31.

Filgalt, T. R. 'Research Work on Natural Indigo', *Nature*, Vol. 78, No. 2031, 1908, p. 540.

Findlay, S. G. 'Report of the Royal Commission on Agriculture in India 1928', *The Economic Journal: the Journal of the Royal Economic Society,* Vol. 38, 1928, pp. 677–79.

Foster, W. 'English Commerce with India', *Journal of the Royal Society of Arts,* Vol. LXVI, No. 3413, 19 April 1918, pp. 361–72.

Fox-Genovese, E. 'Book Review of Jacob Price's "France and the Chesapeake: A History of the French Tobacco Monopoly, 1674–1791, and of its Relationship to the British and American Tobacco Trades"', *The Journal of Modern History,* Vol. 46, No. 4, December 1974, pp. 691–701.

Frey, J. W. 'Prickly Pears and Pagodas: The East India Company's Failure to Establish a Cochineal Industry in Early Colonial India', *The Historian*, Vol. 74, No. 2, Summer 2012, pp. 241–66.

Galloway, J. H. 'Botany in the Service of Empire: The Barbados Cane-Breeding Program and the Revival of the Caribbean Sugar Industry, 1880–1930s', *Annals of the Association of American Geographers,* Vol. 86, No. 4, December 1996, pp. 682–706.

G.D.K. 'Buy Swadeshi (Indian)', *Indian Journal of Economics,* Vol. 13, No. 1, July 1932, pp. 89–91.

Ghildiyal, S. 'Moral Economy and the Indigo Movement', *Economic and Political Weekly,* 20–26 February, Vol. XLV, No. 8, 2010, pp. 67–72.

Gibbon, J. 'Remarks on the State of Agriculture in Behar', *Transactions of the Agricultural and Horticultural Society of India,* Vol. II, 1836, pp. 181–91.

Gokhale, B. G. 'Tobacco in Seventeenth-Century India', *Agricultural History,* Vol. 48, No. 4, October 1974, pp. 484–92.

Goswami, O. 'Sahibs, Babus, and Banias: Changes in Industrial Control in Eastern India, 1918–50', *The Journal of Asian Studies,* Vol. 48, No. 2, May 1989, pp. 289–309.

Gray, S. and Wyckoff, V. J. 'The International Tobacco Trade in the Seventeenth Century', *Southern Economic Journal,* Vol. 7, No. 1, July 1940, pp. 1–26l.

Grove, R. 'Indigenous Knowledge and the Significance of South-West India for Portuguese and Dutch Constructions of Tropical Nature', *Modern Asian Studies,* Vol. 30, No. 1, February 1996, pp. 121–43.

Guha, R. 'Neel-Darpan: The Image of a Peasant Revolt in a Liberal Mirror', *Journal of Peasant Studies,* Vol. 2, No. 1, October 1974, pp. 1–46.

Hahn, B. 'Making Tobacco Bright: Institutions, Information, and Industrialization in the Creation of an Agricultural Commodity, 1617–1937', *Enterprise & Society,* Vol. 8, No. 4, December 2007, pp. 790–98.

Hanson, C. A. 'Monopoly and Contraband in the Portuguese Tobacco Trade 1624–1702', *Luso-Brazilian Review,* Vol. 19, No. 2 (Winter), 1982, pp. 149–68.

Harnetty, P. 'The Cotton Improvement Program in India 1865–1875', *Agricultural History,* Vol. 44, No. 4, October 1970, pp. 379–92.

Hastings, R. B. 'The Relationships between the Indian Botanic Garden, Howrah and the Royal Botanic Gardens, Kew in Economic Botany', *Bulletin of the Botanical Survey of India,* Vol. 28, Nos. 1–4, 1986, pp. 1–12.

Hazareesingh, S. 'Cotton, Climate and Colonialism in Dharwar, Western India, 1840–1880', *Journal of Historical Geography,* Vol. 38, 2012, pp. 1–17.

Headrick, D. R. 'Botany, Chemistry, and Tropical Development', *Journal of World History,* Vol. 7, No. 1, Spring 1996, pp. 1–20.

Hindoo, A. 'Smoking in India', *Frank Leslies Popular Monthly,* Vol. 26, September 1888, pp. 375–76.

Hines, J. W. 'Recent Trends and Developments in the Flue-Cured Tobacco Export Trade', *Southern Economic Journal,* Vol. 18, No. 3, January 1952, pp. 381–90.

Homburg, E. 'The Emergence of Research Laboratories in the Dyestuffs Industry, 1870–1900', *The British Journal for the History of Science,* Vol. 25, No. 1, Organic Chemistry and High Technology, 1850–1950, March 1992, pp. 91–111.

Howard, A. 'The Improvement of Crop Production in India', *Journal of the Royal Society of Arts,* Vol. LXVIII, No. 3530, 16 July 1920, pp. 555–64.

Howard, A. 'An Experiment in the Management of Indian Labour', *International Labour Review,* Vol. 23, No. 1, 1923, pp. 636–43.

Howard, A. 'Agriculture and Science', *The Shaping of Indian Science: Indian Science Congress Association Presidential Addresses,* Vol. 1, 1914–47, Hyderabad: University Press (India) Private Limited, 2003, pp. 176–87.

Howard, A. 'A Criticism of Present-Day Agricultural Research', reproduced in *Asian Agri-History,* Vol. 8, No. 3, 2004, pp. 163–78.

"Howard, A. and Howard, G. L. C. 'Soil Deficiencies in India, with Special Reference to Indigo', *Journal of the Royal Society of Arts*, Vol. 67, No. 3492, 21 October 1919, pp. 762–64.

Jackson, M. G. *Asian Agri-History*, Vol. 9, No. 2, 2005, pp. 157–63.

Jha, H. 'Lower-Caste Peasants and Upper-Caste Zamindars in Bihar (1921–1925): An Analysis of Sanskritization and Contradiction between the Two Groups', *Indian Economic and Social History Review*, Vol. XIV, No. 4, 1977, pp. 549–59.

Johnson, E. H. 'Review of Crop Production in India by Albert Howard', *Economic Geography*, Vol. 1, No. 2 (July), 1925, p.266.

Jones, J. B. 'Particulars Relating to the Agriculture of Jounpoor', *Transactions of the Agricultural and Horticultural Society of India*, Vol. III, 1837, p. 101.

Joseph, E. 'Entwicklung und Vervall der Indigo-Kultur in Britisch-Inden', *Zeitschrift für Sozialwisssemschaft*, Vol. 4, 1913, pp. 117–20.

Kay, J. W. 'The History of the Sepoy War', Vol. I, London: 1864, *The Edinburgh Review or Critical Journal* for July 1866–October 1866, Vol. CXXIV, 1866, pp. 299–340.

Kumar, D. 'Science in Agriculture: A Study in Victorian India', *Asian Agri-History*, Vol. 1, No. 2, 1997, pp. 77–103.

Kumar, P. 'Scientific Experiments in British India: Indigo Planters, Scientists, and the State, 1890–1930', *Indian Economic and Social History Review*, Vol. 38, No. 3, June–September 2001, pp. 249–70.

Kumar, P. 'Plantation Science: Improving Natural Indigo in Colonial India, 1860–1913', *British Journal for the History of Science (BJHS)*, Vol. 40, No. 4, December 2007, pp. 537–65.

Lal, P. 'Bidi – A short History', *Current Science*, Vol. 96, No. 10, 25 May 2009, pp. 1335–37.

Leake, H. M. 'Sir Albert Howard – An Appreciation', *Organic Gardening Magazine* (Sir Albert Howard Memorial Issue), Vol. 13, No. 8, September 1948, available at: http://www.soilandhealth.org/01aglibrary/010142howard.misc/010140memorial.issue.htm (last accessed on 7 September 2014).

Leake, H. M. 'Rationalisation', *Tropical Agriculture*, Vol. VII, No. 9, 1930, pp. 240–42.

Leake, H. M. 'An Historical Memoir of the Indigo Industry of Bihar', *Economic Botany*, Vol. 29, No. 4, October–December 1975, pp. 361–71.

Lethbridge, R. 'The Enhanced Duties on Indian Tea and Tobacco', *The Imperial Asiatic Quarterly Review and Oriental and Colonial Record*, Vol. 18, No. 35, July 1904, pp. 73–82.

Levett-Yeats, G. 'In the Land of the White Poppy', *MacMillan's Magazine*, No. 77, 1897, pp. 188–95.

Llewellyn-Jones, R. 'Claude Martin – A Very Ingenious Man', *Asian Affairs*, Vol. 30, No. 2, June 1999, pp. 164–72.

Lyall, A. 'The Rise of British Dominion in India', *MacMillan's Magazine*, Vol. 63, June 1891, pp. 81–94.

MacKenna, J. 'Scientific Agriculture in India', *Journal of the Royal Society of Arts*, Vol. LXIV, 9 June 1916, pp. 537–46.

MacLeod, R. M. 'Scientific Advice for British India: Imperial Perceptions and Administrative Goals, 1898–1923', *Modern Asian Studies*, Vol. 9, No. 3, 1975, pp. 343–84.

Majumdar, B. 'Agricultural Labour in Bihar in the First Half of the Nineteenth Century', *Indian Journal of Economics*, Vol. 15, No. 4, April 1935, pp. 669–76.

McCook, S. 'Promoting the "Practical": Science and Agricultural Modernization in Puerto Rico and Colombia, 1920–1940', *Agricultural History*, Vol. 75, No. 1, 2001, pp. 52–82.

McCook, S. 'Giving Plants a Civil Status: Scientific Representations of Nature and Nation in Costa Rica and Venezuela, 1885–1935', *The Americas*, Vol. 58, No. 4, April 2002, pp. 513–36.

McKeich, C. 'Botanical Fortunes', *re-Collections, Journal of the National Museum of Australia*, Vol. 3, No. 1, pp. 1–11.

McLane, J. R. 'The Decision to Partition Bengal in 1905', *Indian Economic and Social History Review*, Vol. 2, No. 3, July 1965, pp. 221–37.

Meldola, R. 'Research Work on Natural Indigo', *Nature*, Vol. 78, No. 2031, 1908, pp. 540–41.

Mishra, G. 'Indigo Plantation and the Agrarian Relations in Champaran during the Nineteenth Century', *Indian Economic and Social History Review*, No. 3, 1966, pp. 332–57.

Monckton, J. M. E. 'Free and Open Trade in Bengal', *The English Historical Review*, Vol. 30, No. 117, January 1915, pp. 28–41.

Moubray, J. M. 'The Book of the Quarter: An Agricultural Testament by Sir Albert Howard, C.I.E., M.A.', *Journal of the Royal African Society*, Vol. 39, No. 157, October 1940, pp. 367–75.

Mukherjee, B. B. 'Agricultural Labour in North Bihar', *Indian Journal of Economics*, Vol. 11, No. 3, 1931, pp. 320–28.

Mundargi, T . 'Congress and Zamindars. Collaboration and Consultation in Bihar, 1915–36', *Economic and Political Weekly*, Vol. 25, No. 22, 2 June 1990, pp. 1217–22.

Mylne, J. 'Experiences of a European Zamindar (Landholder) in Behar', *Journal of the Society of Arts*, Vol. 30, May 12, 1882, pp. 688–708.

N.A. 'The Opium Trade with China', *Fraser's Magazine for Town and Country*, Vol. XX, No. CXIX November 1839, pp. 572–88.

N.A. 'Tobacco', *Journal of the Society of Arts*, 3 February 1871, p. 216. Vol.19 (XIX)

N.A. 'Opium in India', *Journal of the Society of Arts*, Vol. 23, 26 March 1875a, p. 408.

N.A. 'Tobacco Cultivation in Jamaica', *Journal of the Society of Arts*, 8 October 1875b, pp. 932–35.(Vol.XXIII) (23)

N.A. 'Tobacco Cultivation in the Madras Presidency', *Journal of the Society of Arts*, Vol. 38, No. 1961, 20 June 1890, pp. 731–32.

N.A. 'Ramie in Tirhut', *Bulletin of Miscellaneous Information (Royal Gardens of Kew)*, No. 1, 1907. Published in London for His Majesty Stationery Office by Darling & Son, No.1 and Artcile III, pp.4-9.

N.A. 'Indian Tobacco', *Journal of the Royal society of Arts*, Vol. 63, No. 3264, 11 June 1915, pp. 696–97.

N.A. 'Tobacco Fertiliser from Indigo Plant', *Journal of the Royal Society of Arts*, Vol. 64, No. 3312, 12 May 1916, pp. 479–80.

N.A. 'Indigo in Behar', *Nature*, Vol. 101, No. 2542, 18 July 1918, pp. 388–89.

N.A. 'Tobacco Growing in the British Empire', *Journal of the Royal Society of Arts*, Vol. 70, No. 3643, 15 September 1922, pp. 752–53.

N.A. 'Empire Tobacco', *Tropical Agriculture*, Vol. VII, No. 9, 1930, p. 240

N.A. 'Tobacco Culture in Mauritius', *United Empire*, Vol. 28, No. 6, 1937, pp. 359–60.

"Nagendrappa, G. 'Chemistry Triggered the First Civil Disobedience Movement in India. Indigo in Indian Independence: Role of a Broken Thermometer', *Resonance*, Vol. 8, No. 3, March 2003, pp. 42–48.

Nayak, A. K. J. R. 'Does Direct Investment in Complementary Business Make Business Sense to Foreign Companies in an Emerging Economy? Case of British American Tobacco in India, 1906–2004', *Global Business Review*, Vol. 8, No. 2, 2007, pp. 189–204.

Oddie, G. A. 'Protestant Missionaries and Social Reform: The Indigo Planting Questions in Bengal 1850–1860', *Journal of Religious History*, Vol. 3, No. 4, pp. 314–26.

Perkin, A. G. 'The Indigo Question', *Nature*, Vol. 78, No. 2033, 1908, pp. 604–5.

Perkins, E. J. 'Review of W.D. and H.O. Wills and the Development of the U.K. Tobacco Industry, 1786–1965 by B. W. E. Alford', *The Journal of Economic History*, Vol. 36, No. 2, June 1976, pp. 450–51.

Perrott, H. R. 'The Family Budget of an Indian Raiyat', *The Economic Journal*, Vol. 22, No. 87, September 1912, pp. 493–98.

Phayre, A. P. 'Memorandum Accompanying a Sample of Tobacco from Sandoway, in the Province of Arracan', *Journal of the Agricultural & Horticultural Society of India*, Vol. III (Part I), January to December 1844, pp. 219–21.

Price, J. M. 'What Did Merchants Do? Reflections on British Overseas Trade, 1660–1790', *The Journal of Economic History*, Vol. XLIX(49), No. 2, June 1989, pp. 267–84.

Prinsep, A. 'On the Traces of Feudalism in India, and the Condition of Lands Now in a Comparative State of Agricultural Infancy', *Journal of the Royal Asiatic Society of Great Britain and Ireland*, Vol. 8, 1846, pp. 390–406.

Quick, R. 'Native Smoking Pipes from Burma', *Man*, Vol. 2, 1902, pp 4–5.

Radhakrishna, M. 'From Tribal Community to Working Class Consciousness. Case of Yerukula Women', *Economic and Political Weekly*, Vol. 24, No. 17, 29 April 1989, pp. WS2–WS5.

Radhakrishna, M. 'The Construction of a "Criminal" Tribe: Yerukulas of Madras Presidency', *Economic and Political Weekly*, Vol. 35, Nos. 28/29, 15–21 July 2000, pp. 2553–63.

Ray, C. S. 'The Hookah – the Indian Waterpipe', *Current Science*, Vol. 96, No. 10, 25 May 2009, pp. 1319–23.

Rawson, C. 'Report on the Cultivation and Manufacture of Indigo in Bengal (for the Indigo Defence Association Limited)', *Journal of the Society of Dyers and Colourists*, Vol. 15, No. 7, July 1899, pp. 166–77.

Rawson, C. 'The Cultivation, Manufacture, and Uses of Indigo', *Journal of the Society of Arts*, Vol. 48, 6 April 1900, pp. 413–34.

Read, D. H. M. 'A Word on Empire-Grown Tobacco', *United Empire: The Royal Colonial Institute Journal*, Vol. 3, No. 5, 1912, pp. 405–10.

Reed, P. 'The British Chemical Industry and Indigo Trade', *The British Journal for the History of Science*, Vol. 25, No. 1, Organic Chemistry and High Technology, 1850–1950, March 1992, pp. 113–25.

Reid, D. N. 'The Disaffection in Behar', *The Fortnightly Review*, Vol. 55, 1894, pp. 808–16.

Reid, D. N. 'A Behar Planter on the Opium Question', *The Imperial and Asiatic Quarterly Review and Oriental and Colonial Record*, Vol. 22, No. 43, 1906, pp. 42–51.

Richards, J. F. 'The Indian Empire and Present Production of Opium in the Nineteenth Century', *Modern Asian Studies*, Vol. 15, No. 1, 1981, pp. 59–82.

Robb, P. 'Hierarchy and Resources: Peasant Stratification in Late Nineteenth Century Bihar', *Modern Asian Studies*, Vol. 13, No. 1, 1979, pp. 97–126.

Robb, P. 'Bihar, the Colonial State and Agricultural Development in India, 1880–1920', *Indian Economic Social History Review*, Vol. 25, 1988, pp. 205–32.

Robb, P. '"Peasants" Choices? Indian Agriculture and the Limits of Commercialization in Nineteenth-Century Bihar', *The Economic History Review*, new series, Vol. 45, No. 1, February 1992, pp. 97–119.

Routledge, J. 'Indian Notes: No. III. Commerce and Manufactures', *Macmillan's Magazine*, Vol. 32, May/October 1875, pp. 457–68.Sah, R. 'Features of British Indigo in India', *Social Scientist*, Vol. 9, Nos. 2/3, September–October 1980, pp. 67–79. Sajjad, M. 'Local Resistance and Colonial Reprisal: Tirhut (Muzaffarpur) Muslims in the Ghadar, 1857–59', *Contemporary Perspectives: History and Sociology of South Asia,* Vol. 2, No. 1, January–June 2008, pp. 25–45.

Sampson, H. C. 'The Royal Botanic Gardens, Kew, and Empire Agriculture', *Journal of the Royal Society of Arts*, Vol. 83, March 1935, pp. 404–19.

Sangwan, S. 'Plant Colonialism (1786–1857)', *Proceedings of the Indian History Congress (PIHC)*, Vol. 43, Indian History Congress, December 1983, pp. 414–24.

Satya, L. 'British Imperial Railways in Nineteenth Century South Asia', *Economic and Political Weekly*, Vol. 43, 22 November 2008, pp. 69–77.

Seshagiri, R. P. 'What Future for Exports of Cigars and Cheroots?' *World Tobacco*, Vol. 87, December 1984, pp. 81–82. Available at: http://tobaccodocuments.org/nysa_ti_sl/TI56322112.pdf (last accessed on 7 September 2014).

Serajuddin, A. M. 'The Salt Monopoly of the East India Company's Government in Bengal', *Journal of the Economic and Social History of the Orient*, Vol. XXI, Part III, 1978, pp. 304–22.

Shah, N. C. 'Hugh Martin Leake: A Historical Memoir', *Indian Journal of History of Science*, Vol. 37, No. 4, 2002, pp. 337–46.

Sharma, K. K. 'Congress, Peasants and the Civil Disobedience Movement in Bihar (1930–1932)', *Social Scientist*, Vol. 16, No. 3, March 1988, pp. 47–61.

Shaw, F. J. F. 'India and the Leaf Tobacco Trade of the British Empire', *The Agricultural Journal of India*, Vol. 23, 1929, pp. 267–70.

Shaw, F. J. F. and Ram, K. 'The Production of Cigarette Tobacco by Fine-Curing', *Experiment Station Record*, Vol. 62, January–June 1930, p. 226.

Sheel, A. 'South Bihar Geography and the Agricultural Cycle', in Sheets-Pyenson, S. *Review of Science and Colonial Expansion: The Role of the British Royal Botanic Gardens by Lucile H. Brockway, Isis*, Vol. 72, No. 3, September 1981, pp. 495–96.

Sikka, S. M. and Swaminathan, M. S. 'Fifty years of Botanical Research at the Indian Agricultural Research Institute', *Euphytica*, Vol. 4, 1955, pp. 173–82.

Smith, S. 'Review of Colebrooke's "Remarks on the Husbandry and Internal Commerce of Bengal", Svo. Blacks & Parry, 1896', *The Edinburgh Review or Critical Journal*, Vol. 10, No. 19, April 1807, pp. 27–40.

Stopford, J. M. 'The Origins of British-Based Multinational Manufacturing Enterprises', *The Business History Review*, Vol. 48, No. 3, Multinational Enterprise, Autumn 1974, pp. 303–35.

Storey, W. K. 'Small-Scale Sugar Cane Farmers and Biotechnology in Mauritius: The "Uba" Riots of 1937', *Agricultural History*, Vol. 69, No. 2, Agribusiness and International Agriculture, Spring 1995, pp. 163–76.

Swaroop, R. 'Some Aspects of the 1857 Rebellion in Bihar', *People's Democracy* (weekly organ of the Communist Party of India (Marxist), Vol. XXXI, No. 18, 6 May 2007, available at: http://archives.peoplesdemocracy. in/2007/0506/05062007_1857.htm (last accesed on 7 September 2014).

Sykes, W. H. 'Contributions to the Statistics of Sugar Produced within the British Dominions in India', *Journal of the Statistical Society of London*, Vol. 13, No. 1, February 1850, pp. 1–24.

Thavaraj, M. J. K. 'Framework of Economic Policies under British Rule', *Social Scientist*, Vol. 7, No. 5, December 1978, pp. 13–44.

The Times, 'Imperial Tobacco', *Tropical Agriculture*, Vol. 3, No. 1, 1926, p. 11.

The Edinburgh Gazetteer or Geographical Dictionary: Containing a Description of the Various Countries, Kingdoms, States, Cities, Towns, Mountains, &C of the World; an Account of the Government, Customs, and Religion, of the Inhabitants; the Boundaries and Natural Productions of Each Country, &c, &c. Forming a Complete Body of Geography, Physical, Political, Statistical, and Commercial, In Six Volumes. Accompanied by an Atlas, Volume Sixth, Edinburgh: Printed for Archibald Constable and Co., 1822 ('Tirhoot', p. 256).

Thomas, A. P. 'The Establishment of Calcutta Botanic Garden: Plant Transfer Science and the East India Company 1786–1806', *Journal of the Royal Asiatic Society*, Vol. 16, 2006, pp. 165–77.

Times. 'On the Resources of India, and the Cultivation of East India Tobacco', *The Mechanics' Magazine, Museum, Register, Journal, and Gazette*, Vol. XXIV, 3 October to 2 April 1836, pp 519–23.

Tomlinson, B. R. 'The Political Economy of the Raj: The Decline of Colonialism', *The Journal of Economic History*, Vol. 42, No. 1, The Tasks of Economic History, March 1982, pp. 133–37.

Tripp, C. 'The Tobacco Industry of India and the Far East', *Journal of the Society of Arts*, Vol. 44, 13 March 1896, pp. 367–79.

T.W.G. 'An Up-Country Fair in Behar, India', *Bentley's Miscellany*, Vol. 60, 1866, pp. 514–21.

Valpy, R. 'On the Recent and Rapid Progress of the British Trade with India', *Journal of the Statistical Society of London*, Vol. 23, No. 1, March 1860, pp. 66–75.

Vella, S. 'Imagining Empire: Company, Crown and Bengal in the Formation of British Imperial Ideology, 1757–84', *Portuguese Studies*, Modern Humanities Research Association, 1 January 2000, pp. 276–297.

Vijayaraghavacharya, T. 'Measures for Improvement of Agriculture', *Annals of the American Academy of Political and social Science*, Vol. 233, India Speaking, May 1944, pp. 92–98.

Wallerstein, I. 'Incorporation of Indian Subcontinent into Capitalist World-Economy', *Economic and Political Weekly*, Vol. XXI, No. 4, Review of Political Economy, 25 January 1986, PE-28–39.

Watson, F. 'The Cultivation and Preparation of Tobacco in India', *Journal of the Society of Arts*, Vol. 19, 14 July 1871, pp. 658–59.

Watson, F. 'Agriculture in India', *Journal of the Society of Arts*, Vol. 26, 7 June 1878, p. 691.

W.H.A.W. 'Reviews', *The Geographical Journal*, Vol. 72, No. 6, December 1928, p. 571.

Whitehead, J. 'John Locke and the Governance of India's Landscape: The Category of Wasteland in Colonial Revenue and Forest Legislation', *Economic and Political Weekly*, Vol. XLV, No. 50, 11–17 December 2010, pp. 83–93.

Wickens, G. E. 'What is Economic Botany?', *Economic Botany*, Vol. 44, No. 1, 1990, pp. 12–28.

Wickens, G. E. 'Two Centuries of Economic Botanists at Kew', Part I: *Curtis's Botanical Magazine*, Vol. 10, No. 2, 1993, pp. 84–94 and Part II: *Curtis's Botanical Magazine*, Vol. 10, No. 3, 1993, pp. 131–37.

Wigglesworth, A. 'The Agricultural Research Institute, Pusa', *United Empire: The Royal Colonial Institute Journal*, Vol. 17, No. 3, 1926, pp. 140–42.

Woodhouse, T. 'Indigo Days in India. A Plantation "Sahib's" Experiment in Friendliness to the Unfriendly', *Asia*, Vol. 26, No. 1, 1926, pp. 32–37 and pp. 76–79.

Wright, H. R. C. 'The Abolition by Cornwallis of the Forced Cultivation of Opium in Bihar', *Economic History Review,* New Series, Vol. 12, No. 1, 1959, pp. 112–19.

Wynne, W. D. 'Fields of Cultural Contradictions: Lessons from the Tobacco Patch', *Agriculture and Human Values,* Vol. 22, No. 4, 2005, pp. 465–77.

Yardumian, R. 'Record of the Kisan Sabha', *Far Eastern Survey,* Vol. 14, No. 11, 6 June 1945, pp. 141–44.

ENDNOTES

Introduction

1   Hyam, R. *Britain's Imperial Century, 1815–1914,* Lanham, MD: Barnes & Nobles, 1993, p. 97.

2   Hyam, R. *Britain's Imperial Century, 1815–1914,* 1993, p. 98 and p. 121.

3   For a similar project in British colonies on the African subcontinent, see Tilley, H. *Africa as a Living Laboratory. Empire, Development, and the Problem of Scientific Knowledge, 1870–1950,* Chicago and London: The University of Chicago Press, 2011.

4   While I do use the term 'British Empire' in this book, I realise that there never was a global imperial system, any all embracing or monolithic empire but 'only a congeries of individual attempts by a large power to impose its will on diverse and unique weaker territories', in Hyam, R. *Britain's Imperial Century,* p. 2.

5   Cf. Mukherjee, M. *Colonializing Agriculture. The Myth of Punjab Exceptionalism,* New Delhi: Sage, 2005.

6   Cf. Baber, Z. 'Colonizing Nature: Scientific Knowledge, Colonial Power and the Incorporation of India into the Modern World System', *British Journal of Sociology,* Vol. 52, No. 1, 1 March 2001, pp. 37–58 and Cf. Osborne, M. A. 'Acclimatizing the World: A History of the Paradigmatic Colonial Science', *Osiris,* 2nd Series, Vol. 15, Nature and Empire: Science and the Colonial Enterprise, 2000, pp. 135–51.

7   Cf. Schiebinger, L. and Swan, C. (eds.) *Colonial Botany: Science, Commerce, and Politics in the Early Modern World,* Philadelphia: University of Pennsylvania Press, 2007, p. 3.

8   For a similar scheme that aimed at the 'revival' of silk production in Bengal, see Schendel, W. . *Reviving a Rural Industry. Silk Producers and*

Officials in India and Bangladesh 1880s to 1980s, New Delhi: Manohar, 1995.

9   *The Edinburgh Review*, April 1807, Art. II, 'Remarks on the Husbandry and Internal Commerce of Bengal, London and Calcutta: Svo. Blacks & Parry, 1806', pp. 27–40.

10   *The Edinburgh Review*, April 1807, pp. 28–29.

11   *The Edinburgh Review*, April 1807, p. 34.

12   *The Edinburgh Review*, April 1807, pp. 36–37.

13   *The Edinburgh Review*, April 1807, pp. 39–40.

14   *The Edinburgh Review*, April 1807, p. 40.

15   Cf. Arnold, D. 'Agriculture and "Improvement" in Early Colonial India: A Pre-History of Development', *Journal of Agrarian Change*, Vol. 5, No. 4, October 2005, pp. 505–25.

16   See also in this regard: 'Oppressive Taxation of British Indian Subjects', in Wilson, H. J. *Anti-Slavery Collection (1840)*, available from the John Rylands University Library, Manchester: University of Manchester.

17   Cf. Agnani, S. 'Jacobinism in India, Indianism in English Parliament: Fearing the Enlightenment and Colonial Modernity with Edmund Burke', *Cultural Critique*, Vol. 68, Winter 2008, pp. 131–62.

18   Arnold, D. 'Plant Capitalism and Company Science: The Indian Career of Nathaniel Wallich', *Modern Asian Studies*, Vol. 42, No. 5, September 2008, pp. 899–928.

19   Studying a different region, Londa Schiebinger also described how 'European trading companies and states claimed exclusive rights to the natural resources of the territories they could hold military'. She named such hunters after (knowledge regarding) natural resources 'bioprospectors'. Shiebinger, L. *Plants and Empire. Colonial Bioprospecting in the Atlantic World*, Cambridge: Harvard University Press, 2004, p. 45.

20   Habib, I. *Essays in Indian History. Towards a Marxist Perception*, New Delhi: Tulika, 2011 (1995), p. 319.

21   I appreciate Jonathan Curry-Machado's remark: 'Put simply, a 'commodity' is the product of human labour combining 'use' and 'exchange value'. Thus, a plant becomes a commodity, 'when it is no longer produced for immediate consumption but is part of an economic relationship whereby it is traded for other commodities or an abstract

monetary representation of its worth'. Curry-Machado, J. (ed.) *Global Histories, Imperial Commodities, Local Interactions*, New York: Palgrave Macmillan, 2013, p. 2.

22 Mukherjee, R. (ed.) *Networks in the First Global Age 1400–1800*, Delhi: Indian Council of Historical Research and Primus, 2011, pp. 318–19.

23 Cf. Habib, *Essays in Indian History*, p. 300.

24 Nigel Dalziel defined 'plant hunting' as the 'quest for botanical knowledge, especially in identifying plants of economic value', and described how in the late eighteenth and nineteenth centuries Britain supported this 'programme of worldwide scientific exploration'. According to Dalziel, this programme 'had an important influence in determining imperial expansion'. Dalziel, N. *The Penguin Historical Atlas of the British Empire*, London: Penguin Books, 2006, p. 100.

25 Cf. Habib, *Essays in Indian History*, p. 319.

26 See Chapter One for an elaboration.

27 For an in-depth analysis of William Bolts's controversial work 'Considerations on India Affairs' published in 1772, see an introduction to this work by Patrick Tuck editor of *The East India Company: 1600–1858*, Vol. III, London and New York: Routledge, 1998, pp. V–XXV. This volume also encompasses another work controversial at the time and authored by Harry Verelst of the EIC: 'A View of the Rise, Progress and Present State of the English Government in Bengal'. The latter was, in fact, a reply to the work by Bolts.

28 Cf. Sharma, J. 'Making Garden, Erasing Jungle: The Tea Enterprise in Colonial Assam', in Kumar, D., Damodaran, V., and D'Souza, R. (eds.) *The British Empire and the Natural World. Environmental Encounters in South Asia*, Oxford: Oxford University Press, p. 120. Jayeeta Sharma also quoted Satpal Sangwan who termed such an 'imperial plan' as 'plant colonialism', and Sharma finds that this was 'a significant part of the East India Company's activities, evident in systematic surveys of the company's territories, where collection of plant and herbal knowledge took a prominent role'. Sharma added that 'such activities were dictated as much by a new improving agenda as by their avowed scientific and material purpose'. Thus, 'nature's bounty was to be discovered and thereafter improved upon by its dissemination through empire'. *Ibid.*, p. 120–21.

29 Vella, S. 'Imagining Empire: Company, Crown and Bengal in the Formation of British Imperial Ideology, 1757–84', *Portuguese Studies*, Modern Humanities Research Association, 1 January 2000. See also: Dirks, N. B. *The Scandal of Empire. India and the Creation of Imperial Britain*, Delhi: Permanent Black, 2007.

30 Quoted by Shiebinger, *Plants and Empire*, p. 46.

31 Cf. Sharma, 'Making Garden, Erasing Jungle', p. 119.

32 David Arnold described this 'tropicalisation' of India in his book: *The Tropics and the Traveling Gaze. India, Landscape, and Science 1800– 1856*, Delhi: Permanent Black, 2005.

33 By the 1880s, this nomenclature had become common. See for instance, Warnford, L. C. G. *Tobacco: Growing, Curing and Manufacturing. A Handbook for Planters in all Parts of the World*, London: E & F.N. Spong, 1886.

34 See for instance, MacLeod, W. *The Commerce, Resources, and Prospects of India*, London: W.H. Dalton, 1857.

35 Cf. Whitehead, J. 'John Locke and the Governance of India's Landscape: The Category of Wasteland in Colonial Revenue and Forest Legislation', *Economic and Political Weekly*, Vol. XLV, No. 50, 11–17 December 2010, pp. 83–93.

36 Cf. Baber, 'Colonizing Nature', pp. 37–58.

37 Cf. Royle, J. F. *Essays on the Productive Resources of India*, London: H. Allen, 1840.

38 Hill, C. V. and Stoll, M. R. *South Asia: An Environmental History*, Santa Barbara, Oxford: ABC and CLIO, 2008, p. xxi.

39 Hill, *South Asia, Ibid.* Compare this with the concluding remarks by Rohan D'Souza in his article on land revenue and the recasting of nature: 'For the British East India Company however, land (nature) was legible only as an economic form, a rent-seeking alienable commodity and a monopolized means of production.' (D'Souza, R. 'Rigidity and Affliction of Capitalist Property: Colonial Land Revenue and the Recasting of Nature', *Studies in History*, Vol. 20, No. 2, n.s., 2004, p. 272.)

40 This implies that 'native' or 'indigenous' knowledge systems of those at the colonial periphery could become integrated into 'colonial science' if such accommodation would serve colonial (commercial) interests of

British. Being in control, the latter would than define such indigenous knowledge as 'useful'. (Cf. Potukuchi, S. 'Controlling Commodity Culture: Indigenous Knowledge and Indian Cotton Textile Industry: Andhra Region, 1790–1900', Unpublished paper present at the 2nd Annual Workshop of the Commodities of Empire Project: Commodities in Evolution: Historical Change in Different Ages of Globalization, 1800–2000, 11–12 September 2008.)

41   Robb, P. (ed.) *Meanings of Agriculture. Essays in South Asian History and Economics*, Delhi: Oxford University Press, 1996, p. 3.

42   Cf. Sangwan, S. 'Plant Colonialism (1786–1857)', *Proceedings of the Indian History Congress (PIHC)*, December 1983, pp. 414–24.

43   Darwin, J. *After Tamerlane: The Rise and Fall of Global Empires, 1400–2000,* London: Penguin Books, 2008, p. 109.

44   Darwin, *After Tamerlane*, p. 111.

45   Darwin, *After Tamerlane,* p. 264.

46   Darwin, *After Tamerlane,* p. 265.

47   Nater, L. 'Colonial Tobacco: Key Commodity of the Spanish Empire, 1500–1800', in Topik, S., Marichal, C., and Frank, Z. (eds.), *From Silver to Cocaine. Latin American Commodity Chains and the Building of the World Economy, 1500–2000,* Durham and London: Duke University Press, 2006, pp. 93–118.

48   Malekandathil, P. *The Mughals, the Portuguese and the Indian Ocean. Changing Imaginaries of Maritime India,* Delhi: Primus Books, 2013, p. 192.

49   Majumdar. *The Mughul Empire,* pp. 718–19.

50   Cf. Habib. *Essays in Indian History,* p. 324.

51   Majumdar, R. C. (General Editor) 'The Mughul Empire', in Series: Bhavan's Book University. *The History and Culture of the Indian People,* Mumbai: Bharatiya Vidya Bhavan, 2007, pp. 719–20.

52   Cf. Markovits, C. 'The Political Economy of Opium Smuggling in Early Nineteenth Century India: Leakage or Resistance', in Eaton, R. M., Faruqui, M. D., Gilmartin, D., and Kumar, S. (eds.), *Expanding Frontiers in South Asian and World History. Essays in Honour of John F. Richards,* Cambridge: Cambridge University Press, 2013, pp. 82–83 (81–103).

53 Roy, T. *The Economic History of India*, New Delhi: Oxford University Press, 2011, p. 50.

54 Thiselton-Dyer, W. T. *The Botanical Enterprise of the Empire*, London: Her Majesty's Stationery Office, 1880 (Foreign and Commonwealth Office Collection), p. 4.

55 Hastings, R. B. 'The Relationships between the Indian Botanic Garden, Howrah and the Royal Botanic Gardens, Kew in Economic Botany', *Bulletin of the Botanical Survey of India*, Vol. 28, Nos. 1–4, 1986, p. 1.

56 Thiselton-Dyer. *The Botanical Enterprise*, p. 23 and p. 3.

57 Sheets-Pyenson, S. 'Review of Science and Colonial Expansion: The Role of the British Royal Botanic Gardens by Lucile H. Brockway', *Isis*, Vol. 72, No. 3, September 1981, pp. 495–96. See also Brockway, L. H. 'Science and Colonial Expansion: The Role of the British Royal Gardens', *American Ethnologist*, Vol. 6, No. 3, August 1979, pp. 449–65.

58 Grove, R. 'Indigenous Knowledge and the Significance of South-West India for Portuguese and Dutch Constructions of Tropical Nature', *Modern Asian Studies*, Vol. 30, No. 1, February 1996, p. 121.

59 Damodaran, V. 'Review of Tropics and the Travelling Gaze: India, Landscape and Science, 1800–1856 by David Arnold', *Victorian Studies*, Vol. 49, No. 4, Summer 2007, pp. 710–11. In similar fashion, Joyce Chaplin argued against 'studies that presented colonisation and science as forms of extractive imperium over nature' and instead indentified 'a reforming and somewhat more positive impulse within modern imperialism: a desire to conserve natural resources'. Richard Grove did not deny, however, that 'this was meant to serve imperial ends by guaranteeing future supplies of key commodities'. Chaplin, J. 'The Natural History of British Imperialism', *The Journal of British Studies*, Vol. 42, No. 1, January 2003, pp. 127–31.

60 Thiselton-Dyer. *The Botanical Enterprise*, p. 23.

61 Hastings, R. B. 'The Relationships between the Indian Botanic Garden, Howrah and the Royal Botanic Gardens, Kew in Economic Botany', *Bulletin of the Botanical Survey of India*, Vol. 28, Nos. 1–4, 1986, p. 3.

62 Cf. Bellon, R. 'Joseph Dalton Hooker's Ideal for a Professional Man of Science', *Journal of the History of Biology*, Vol. 34, No. 1, Spring 2001, pp. 51–82.

63   Hastings. 'The Relationships', *Ibid.* Also: Thomas, A. P. 'The Establishment of Calcutta Botanic Garden: Plant Transfer Science and the East India Company 1786–1806', *Journal of the Royal Asiatic Society,* Vol. 16, 2006, pp. 165–77. See for an analysis of a botanical garden in another English colony (Australia): Endersby, J. 'A Garden enclosed: botanical barter in Sydney, 1818–1839', *British Journal for the History of Science,* Vol. 33, No. 3, September 2000, pp. 313–34. This study takes issue, however, with the notion that British colonial botanic gardens were established as part of a botanical empire, with Kew Gardens at its centre. Endersby argued that casual botanical networks created by gardens like Sydney to serve their own, local needs formed the basis for the more formal networks that Kew would later use for its imperial plant transfers. 'Kew's empire', Endersby concluded, 'was actually founded by colonies, not the centre, and the botanical practices it utilised were partially developed in places like Sydney'. I would agree with this, yet it has to be realised that 'local needs' in the case of Calcutta meant serving the needs of whites in the city and not necessarily of the colonised.

64   Hooker, J. D. *Himalayan Journals, or Notes of a Naturalist in Bengal, the Sikkim and Nepal Himalayas, the Khaisia Mountains, etc.,* Vol. VI, Kew, 1854 (E-book obtained through the Gutenberg Project).

65   Hastings. 'The Relationships', pp. 1–2.

66   Wickens, G. E. 'What is Economic Botany?', *Economic Botany,* Vol. 44, No. 1, 1990, p. 19. Also: Chakrabarti, P. *Western Science in Modern India. Metropolitan Methods, Colonial Practices,* Ranikhet: Permanent Black, 2004 (paperback printing used of 2010), in particular p. 73, p. 82 and 83 and pp. 298–99.

67   Wickens, G. E. 'Two Centuries of Economic Botanists at Kew', Part I: *Curtis's Botanical Magazine,* Vol. 10, No. 2, 1993, pp. 84–94 and Part II: Vol. 10, No. 3, 1993, pp. 131–37.

68   Royle, J. F. *Essay on the Productive Resources of India,* London: Wm. H. Allen and Co., 1840, p. vi.

69   Hough, W. *India as it Ought to Be. Improvements Suggested,* London: Messrs.W. Thacker & Co., 1853.

70   Related to this Roy M. MacLeod commented: it is well known that India was the 'jewel in the imperial diadem', holding, before the World War I, the 'key to Britain's whole payments pattern'. It is less

commonly appreciated that, in her cultivated plantations and her critical natural resources, India's wealth was repeatedly tapped through the use of scientific knowledge and techniques. In fact, applied science and technology became indispensable tools in the creation and consolidation of Britain's economic hegemony. MacLeod, R. M. 'Scientific Advice for British India: Imperial Perceptions and Administrative Goals, 1898–1923', *Modern Asian Studies*, Vol. 9, No. 3, 1975, p. 344 (pp. 343–84). See also: Harnetty, P. 'The Cotton Improvement Program in India 1865–1875', *Agricultural History*, Vol. 44, No. 4, October 1970, pp. 379–92.

71   MacLeod. 'Scientific Advice', p. 346.

72   Accounts and Papers: Thirty-Eight Volumes, *East India. Bengal and Orissa Famine*, Session 5 February–21 August 1867, Vol. 13, 1867.

73   Hume, A. O. *Agricultural Reform in India*, London: W.H. Allen & Co., 1879, pp. 1–6.

74   William Kelleher Storey warned in the case of (colonial) Mauritius: 'Scientists were not impartial bystanders, but participated in colonial political, social, and economic discourses. They produced the knowledge and tools that perpetuated the colonial economy. They also implemented decisions on how to manage natural resources. In Mauritius, colonial politicians and agricultural scientists were partners in a symbiotic relationship.' Storey, W. K. *Science and Power in Colonial Mauritius*, Rochester: University of Rochester Press, 1997, p. 10.

75   MacKenna, J. 'Scientific Agriculture in India', *Journal of the Royal Society of Arts*, Vol. LXIV, 9 June 1916, p. 538. See also: Vijayaraghavacharya, T. 'Measures for Improvement of Agriculture', *Annals of the American Academy of Political and Social Science*, Vol. 233, India Speaking, May 1944, pp. 92–98 and Thavaraj, M. J. K. 'Framework of Economic Policies under British Rule', *Social Scientist*, Vol. 7, No. 5, December 1978, pp. 13–44.

76   Cf. Arnold, D. 'White Colonization and Labour in Nineteenth-Century India', *The Journal of Imperial and Commonwealth History*, Vol. 11, No. 2, 1982–1983, pp. 133–58.

77   Cf. Renford, R. K. *The Non-Official British in India to 1920*, Delhi: Oxford University Press, 1987.

78   In 1903, George Brown, in an article on 'Scientific Research in Relation
      to Economic and Agricultural Development in India', illustrated this
      view as follows: 'India has been said to be "an epitome of the whole
      earth", as it combines in its large extent every variety of clime, from
      mountains clad with perpetual snow to plains with intense hear, sandy
      wastes, broad and fertile districts, and impenetrable forests. It has, then,
      an advantage in the field of research it is developing, and, in widening
      and enlarging those fields, may be looked upon as a pioneer in discoveries
      of value, not only to its own people but to other nations whose resources
      require only such a scheme (scientific research) to unfold their wealth
      and increase the industry of the people.' Brown, G. 'Scientific Research
      in Relation to Economic and Agricultural Development in India', *The
      Imperial and Asiatic Quarterly Review and Oriental and Colonial Records*,
      Vol. 15, No. 29, January 1903, p. 184 (pp. 182–84). Cf. McCook, S.
      'Promoting the "Practical": Science and Agricultural Modernization in
      Puerto Rico and Colombia, 1920–1940', *Agricultural History*, Vol. 75,
      No. 1, 2001, pp. 52–82.

79   See for example Schrottky, E. C. *The Principles of Rational Agriculture
      Applied to India and its Staple Products*, Bombay: Times of India Office,
      1876.

80   Headrick, D. R. 'Botany, Chemistry, and Tropical Development',
      Journal of World History, Vol. 7, No. 1, Spring 1996, p. 3.

81   Headrick. 'Botany', pp. 5–6.

82   Ludden, D. (ed.) *Agricultural Production and Indian History*, Delhi:
      Oxford University Press, 1994, p. 6. See also: Ludden, D. *An Agrarian
      History of South Asia*, The New Cambridge History of India, IV,
      Cambridge: Cambridge University Press, 1999.

83   See for instance, *The Indian Problem Solved. Undeveloped Wealth in
      India and State Reproductive Work. The Ways to Prevent Famines and
      Advance the Material Progress of India*, London: Virtue, Spalding, and
      Co., 1874 (various authors).

84   Thiselton. 'The Botanical Enterprise', p. 3.

85   Sampson, H. C. 'The Royal Botanic Gardens, Kew, and Empire
      Agriculture', *Journal of the Royal Society of Arts*, Vol. 83, March 1935,
      pp. 404–19.

86 Cf. McCook, S. 'Giving Plants a Civil Status: Scientific Representations of Nature and Nation in Costa Rica and Venezuela, 1885–1935', *The Americas*, Vol. 58, No. 4, April 2002, pp. 513–36.

87 Cf. Bhattacharya, K. R. 'Science and Scientists in the Service of Imperialism', *Social Scientist*, Vol. 2, No. 2, September 1973, pp. 52–59.

88 Though this book takes a more anthropocentric approach, I do recognise that plant engineering was not an easy task and more often failed than succeeded. I do, however, pay more attention to human factors than biological reasons for failure. Yet Michael Pollan reminds us of the power of plants which makes it very difficult to engineer plants exactly according to human desires. Polan, M. *The Botany of Desire: A Plant's-Eye View of the World*, New York: Random House, 2002.

89 'On the Agriculture of Hindostan', *The Quarterly Journal of Agriculture*, Vol. VIII, June 1837–March 1838, p. 37.

90 'On the Agriculture of Hindostan', p. 56.

91 Crawfurd, J. 'A view of the present and future prospects of the free trade & colonization of India', second edition enlarged, London: James Ridgway, Piccadilly and Egerton & John Smith, Liverpool, 1829, p. 1., *Knowsley Pamphlet Collection,* Liverpool: University of Liverpool, 1829. http://www.jstor.org/stable/60100332 (Accessed on 14 January 2011).

92 'Indian monopolies, &c. &c.', *Knowsley Pamphlet Collection,* Liverpool: University of Liverpool, 1829. http://www.jstor.org/stable/60100827 (Accessed on 14 January 2011).

93 'Remarks on Crawfurd's letters from British settles in the interior of India', Calcutta: Indian Gazette Press, 1832, in *Hume Tracts*, 1832, UCL Library Services. http://ww.jstor.org/stable/60204197 (Accessed on 14 January 2011), p. 1, p. 23, and p. 24.

94 Mangles, R. D. *Wrongs and Claims of Indian Commerce*, No. 146, Ballantyne and Hughes, 1841, p. 42 (from the *Edinburgh Review* No CXLVI).

95 'Remarks on Crawfurd's letters', p. 37.

96 For Bihar, I refer to: Datta, K. K. (ed.) *Unrest Against British Rule in Bihar, 1831–1859*, Patna: Superintendent Secretariat Press, 1957. Also: Sajjad, M. 'Local Resistance and Colonial Reprisal: Tirhut (Muzaffarpur) Muslims in the Ghadar, 1857–59', *Contemporary Perspectives: History*

and *Sociology of South Asia,* Vol. 2, No. 1, January–June 2008, pp. 25–45.

97 Valpy, R. 'On the Recent and Rapid Progress of the British Trade with India', *Journal of the Statistical Society of London,* Vol. 23, No. 1, March 1860, p. 66.

98 Martin, M. *The Progress and Present State of British India. A Manual for General Use, Based on Official Documents, Furnished under the Authority of Her Majesty's Secretary of State for India,* London: Sampson Low, Son, & Co., 1862, p. viii.

99 Hobsbawm, E. *The Age of Capital 1848–1875,* London: Abacus, 1975, p. 153.

100 Martin, M. *The Progress and Present State of British India,* pp. 284–85.

101 Fuller, B. *The Empire of India,* London: Elibron Classics, 2006, p. 201.

102 Satya, L. 'British Imperial Railways in Nineteenth Century South Asia', *Economic and Political Weekly,* 22 November 2008, pp. 69–77 and Clarke, H. 'Colonization, Defence, and Railways in Our Indian Empire', *Knowsley Pamphlet Collection (1857),* Liverpool: University of Liverpool (online available).

103 For instance, Watson, F. *New Zealand Exhibition, 1865. A Classified List of Contributions from British India and Its Dependencies,* forwarded by order of the Secretary of State for India, from the Indian Museum, London, London: W. Trounce, 1864. Also Watt, G. (assisted by numerous contributors) *A Dictionary of Economic Products of India* in six volumes, Calcutta: Superintendent of Government Printing, 1885. For a discussion of the latter and other works by Watt, see: Chakre, O. J. 'The Wealth of India – a CSIR's Encyclopaedia of Information Resource on Economic Plants, Animals and Minerals', *Current Science,* Vol. 99, No. 7, 10 October 2010, pp. 969–71.

104 McKeich, C. 'Botanical Fortunes', *reCollections: Journal of the National Museum of Australia,* Vol. 3, No. 1, pp. 1–11.

105 Basak, S. *Socio-Cultural Study of a Minority Linguistic Group (Bengalees in Bihar 1858–1912),* Delhi: B.R. Publishing Corporation, 1991, pp. 24–27.

106 Habib. *Essays in Indian History,* p. 280.

107 Cf. Habib. *Essays in Indian History,* pp. 331–35.

108   Wallerstein, I. 'Incorporation of Indian Subcontinent into Capitalist World Economy', *Economic and Political Weekly*, Vol. XXI, No. 4, Review of Political Economy, 25 January 1986, PE-28–39.

109   Cf. Hazareesingh, S. 'Cotton, Climate and Colonialism in Dharwar, Western India, 1840–1880', *Journal of Historical Geography*, Vol. 38, 2012, pp. 1–17.

110   Cf. Frey, J. W. 'Prickly Pears and Pagodas', pp. 241–66.

111   Cain, P. J. 'J.A. Hobson, Cobdenism, and the Radical Theory of Economic Imperialism, 1898–1914', *The Economic History Review*, n.s., Vol. 31, No. 4, November 1978, pp. 565–84.

112   MacLeod. 'Scientific Advice', p. 376 and p. 345.

113   Cf. MacLeod. 'Scientific Advice', p. 379.

114   Cotton, A. 'The Indian Famine: With Special Reference to the Means Which Should Be Adopted for the Alleviation or Prevention of Future Famines', *Journal of the Society of Arts*, 24 April 1874, pp. 501–9.

115   The difference between British/English and European men and women was normally considered irrelevant as long as they were of 'pure white stock'. Quite some of the early settlers in Bengal were, in fact, not born in Britain and were known as 'Europeans'. Such Europeans did even join the EIC. Yet at times, due to political rivalry or wars among the European countries, tensions did develop. See in this regard: Llewellyn-Jones, R. 'Claude Martin – A very Ingenious Man', *Asian Affairs*, Vol. 30, No. 2, 1999, pp. 164–72.

116   MacLeod. 'Scientific Advice', p. 345.

117   Cf. Scott. *Seeing Like a State*, pp. 307–42.

Chapter One:
British Interest in Tobacco Trade and Improvement in Bengal

118   Arents, G. 'The Seed from which Virginia Grew', *William and Mary College Quarterly Historical Magazine*, 2nd Series, Vol. 19, No. 2, April 1939, p. 124.

119   'The Introduction and Early Use of Tobacco in England', *Asiatic Journal*, Vol. XXII, No. 128, 1826, pp. 137–42. Also 'On the Growth, and Peculiar Qualities of Tobacco', *London Magazine or Gentleman's Monthly Intelligencer*, Vol. 21, December 1752, pp. 605–6.

120   Donnelly, A. 'That Bewitching Vegetable – Tobacco', *Asia: the American Magazine on the Orient*, Vol. xxxi, June 1931, p. 346.

121   The quest at the time was to prepare a tobacco plant that could be used for chewing and as snuff in England. Compare this with a later 'Quest for the Golden Leaf' to be used as cigars and cigarettes. Card, D. G. 'Review of "The Bright Tobacco Industry, 1860–1929" by Nannie May Tilley', *Journal of Farm Economics*, Vol. 30, No. 4, November 1948, p. 795 (Book Review).

122   Cf. Hahn, B. 'Making Tobacco Bright: Institutions, Information, and Industrialization in the Creation of an Agricultural Commodity, 1617–1937', *Enterprise & Society*, Vol. 8, No. 4, December 2007, pp. 790–98.

123   Arents. 'The Seed', pp. 125–26. In particular: Hahn, B. *Making Tobacco Bright. Creating an American Commodity, 1617–1937.* Baltimore: The Johns Hopkins University Press, 2011.

124   See for instance: Bradburn, D. 'The Visible Fist: The Chesapeake Tobacco Trade in War and the Purpose of Empire, 1690–1715', *The William and Mary Quarterly*, Vol. 68, No. 3, July 2011, pp. 361–86. For a description of the English 'tobacco *nabob*' in colonial Virginia, see for instance: Bradley, A. G. 'Colonial Virginia', *MacMillan's Magazine*, n.s., Vol. 2, October 1906, pp. 335–43. Compare this 'tobacco *nabob*' with the 'indigo planter' introduced later on in this book.

125   James I was king of Scots as James IV and James VI were kings of England and Ireland as James I from the union of the English and Scottish crowns in 1603 until his death. The kingdoms of England and Scotland were individual sovereign states, with their own parliaments, judiciary, and laws, though both were ruled by James in personal union.

126   Gately, I. *Tobacco. A Cultural History of How an Exotic Plant Seduced Civilization*, New York: Grove Press, 2001, pp. 67–69.

127   Kozlowski, L. T., Henningfield, J. E., and Brigham, J. *Cigarettes, Nicotine, & Health: a Biobehavioral Approach*, London and Thousand Oaks, 2001, pp. 24–25.

128   See for instance, Jacob Price's 'France and the Chesapeake: A History of the French Tobacco Monopoly, 1674–1791, and of its Relationship to the British and American Tobacco Trades', reviewed by Elizabeth Fox-Genovese in *The Journal of Modern History*, Vol. 46, No. 4, December 1974, pp. 691–701.

129 If not mentioned otherwise in this book, 'England' or 'English' does normally also refer to the other parts of Great Britain, that is Scotland and Wales and even to Ireland.

130 Beer, G. L. *The Origins of the British Colonial System 1578–1660*, Gloucester, MA: Peter Smith, 1959 (1908), p. 175.

131 Gray, S. and Wyckoff, V. J. 'The International Tobacco Trade in the Seventeenth Century', *Southern Economic Journal*, Vol. 7, No. 1, July 1940, pp. 1–26l.

132 MacInnes, C. M. *The Early English Tobacco Trade*, London: Kegan Paul, Trench, Trübner & Co., Ltd., 1926, pp. 1–4.

133 In 1908, George Louis Beer wrote a treatise on 'the old British Empire' in order to understand the 'colonial system'. The latter term was defined by him as 'synonymous with that complex system of regulations by means of which, though to a different extent, the economic structures of both metropolis and colony were moulded to confirm to the prevailing ideal of a self-sufficient empire'. Beer also emphasised that 'economic and political systems were inseparably connected', and Beer singled out tobacco as the most important commodity within this old colonial system. Beer, *The Origins of the British Colonial System*, New York: Macmillan Company, pp. v–vi.

134 Crawford, J. 'On the History and Consumption of Tobacco', *Journal of the Statistical Society of London*, Vol. 16, No. 1, March 1853, p. 48.

135 Arents established a 'tobacco library' as 'what could be more natural for me, with a background of tobacco in my family, to specialise on books relating to 'the divine herb'. 'I was seventeen when I started this collection; I am now sixty-three. So for nearly half a century I have been adding books and manuscripts to this library.' Arents, 'The Seed', p. 124.

136 Arents. 'The Seed', p. 129.

137 Price, J. M. 'What Did Merchants Do? Reflections on British Overseas Trade, 1660–1790', *The Journal of Economic History*, Vol. XLIX, No. 2, June 1989, pp. 283–84.

138 Majumdar, R. C. (general editor) *The Mughal Empire*, Mumbai: Bharatiya Vidya Bhavan, 2007, pp. 511–12 and pp. 714–22 and in particular pp. 728–29 (for tobacco).

139   Laufer, B. *Tobacco and Its Use in Asia*, Anthropology Leaflet 18, Chicago: Field Museum of Natural History, 1924, pp. 11–14.

140   Yet Lieutenant Pogson, an officer in the English 'Her Majesty's Bengal Army' but also an honorary member of the Agri-Horticultural Society of India, wrote in 1883 that tobacco, according to him, had been known and used in India, 'when it was inhabited by a remarkably intellectual race of men, whose mother tongue was Sanskrit'. He proposed that in the inner Himalayas, a wild variety of the tobacco plant could be found which very much resembled the Virginian tobacco though it was perennial and not annual like all other known varieties of tobaccos. He, furthermore, thought it quite possible that this wild tobacco had been cultivated in the plains of India and its leaves made into snuff and smoked in different ways. He even argued there were several words in Sanskrit which indicated the various parts of the Indian water pipe, known to Europeans as the 'Hubble-Bubble'. As the latter had a special form of bowl called *chillum* for holding the smoking preparation, this indirectly proved the use of tobacco in it. Pogson added that as the Sanskrit word *nauslena* meant to take snuff, the art of its preparation and the cultivation of the tobacco plant must have been known even before the arrival of the Portuguese in India. Pogson, F. *Manual of Agriculture for India*, Calcutta: Thacker, Spink and Co., 1883, p. 240. However, Crawfurd, in 1869, had argued that 'Tobacco was unquestionably first made known to the nations of Asia and Africa through the people of Europe'. Crawfurd, J. 'On the History and Migration of Cultivated Narcotic Plants in Reference to Ethnology', *Transactions of the Ethnological Society of London*, Vol. 7, 1869, p. 81.

141   Pinto, C. *Trade and Finance in Portuguese India. A Study of the Portuguese Country Trade 1770–1840*, New Delhi: Concept, 1994. Yet Russell-Wood described how 'homeward bound East Indiamen' halted in Rio de Janeiro and Salvador and unloaded substantial quantities of Indian cloth, Chinese silks and porcelain, lacquer objects, and spices in exchange for contraband tobacco, gold, and diamonds, as well as that these engaged in 'legal commerce in sugar, tobacco, hides, and woods'. 'Bahia was', Russell-Wood furthermore explained, 'the source for the top-quality tobacco leaf of the first harvest', (*de primeira folha*) which was exported to Goa and distributed further. Though, Russell-Wood

added that it remained unclear whether this tobacco was transported on 'the vessels of the *carreira da India*' by the outward-bound 'Indiaman put into a Brazilian port' as well as by what routes and precisely when. However, tobacco was grown inland in Bijapur, villages near Surat, and in Golconda, and it had spread to Sambhal and Bihar by the mid-seventeenth century. Russell-Wood concluded that long before the end of Aurangzeb's reign in India in 1707, 'tobacco smoking was commonplace, either in the form of a pipe or *cheroot,* both on India's west coast as well as in northern India. Besides, there were 'grounds for believing that although the sixteenth century was characterised by trading rather than cultivating of the spice by the Portuguese at an early date the Portuguese did conduct experiments into the adaptation of plants of different zones and climates.' Russell-Wood, A. J. R. *The Portuguese Empire 1415–1808*, Baltimore: Johns Hopkins University Press, 1998, p. 140, p. 170, and p. 150. See also in this regard: Dutta, K. 'Portugal's Experiment with Brazilian Tobacco in India in the Eighteenth Century', *Indica*, Vol. 28, No. 2, 1991, pp. 95–111.

142 The *hookah*, a water pipe, became popular for smoking tobacco in India. It acquired other names like *nargile, shisha, goza,* and hubble-bubble. In a small bowl at the top, tobacco, flavoured with molasses, was kept smouldering with burning charcoal. When the smoker puffed on the *hookah*, the smoke passed down through a tube and then through a jar of water before being inhaled. See for instance Ray, C. S. 'The Hookah – the Indian waterpipe', *Current Science*, Vol. 96, No. 10, 25 May 2009, p. 1319.

143 See for instance, Fisher, M. H. (ed.) *Beyond the Three Seas. Travellers' Tales of Mughal India,* New Delhi: Random House, 2007.

144 Though tobacco was not the main research interest of these scholars, at least some mention of it is made by; for instance, W. H. Moreland's (edited) works: *India at the Death of Akbar,* Delhi: Atma Ram, 1962, p. 148; *Relations of Golconda in the Early Seventeenth Century*, London: Hakluyt Society, 1931, p. 36; and *From Akbar to Aurangzeb, A Study in Indian Economic History*, London: MacMillan, 1923, p. 189. See also the works by Temple, R. C. (ed.) *A Geographical Account of Counties Round the Bay of Bengal,* Nendeln/Liechtenstein: Kraus, 1967, p. 20, p. 30, p. 107 and note 1, 289, note 5, by Elliot, H. M. and Dowson, J. (eds.), *The*

History of India as Told by Its Own Historians, Allahabad: Kitab Mahal, 1964, pp. 165–67 and by Beveridge, H. (ed.) and Rogers, A. (tr.), *The Tuzuk-i-Jahangiri or Memoirs of Jahangir*, 2 volumes, Delhi: Munshiram Manoharlal, 1968, Vol. 1, p. 370 and p. 371. See also Donnelly, 'That Bewitching Vegetable', p. 347, p. 348, p. 350, p. 351, and p. 352.

145   Hanson, C. A. 'Monopoly and Contraband in the Portuguese Tobacco Trade 1624–1702', *Luso-Brazilian Review*, Vol. 19, No. 2 (Winter), 1982, pp. 149–68.

146   Gokhale, B. G. 'Tobacco in Seventeenth-Century India', *Agricultural History*, Vol. 48, No. 4, October 1974, pp. 484–92.

147   Gokhale. 'Tobacco', p. 485.

148   Habib, I. *The Agrarian System of Mughal India*, Bombay: Asia Publishing House, 1963, p. 45 and p. 46.

149   Barendse, R. J. 'Trade and State in the Arabian Seas: A Survey from the Fifteenth to the Eighteenth Century', *Journal of World History*, Vol. 11, No. 2, Fall 2000, pp. 220–21.

150   Marshall, P. J. *East Indian Fortunes. The British in Bengal in the Eighteenth Century*, Oxford: Clarendon Press, 1976, p. 109.

151   Pommaret, F. 'Ancient Trade Partners: Bhutan, Cooch Bihar and Assam (17th–19th Centuries)', available at: https://www.repository.cam.ac.uk/bitstream/handle/1810/227005/JBS_02_01_02.pdf?sequence=2 (last accessed on 6 September 2014).

152   For the working of such farms at Chittagong see Serajuddin, A. M. *Revenue Administration of the East India Company in Chittagong, 1761–1785*, Chittagong: University of Chittagong, 1971, pp. 165–68.

153   Marshall. *East Indian Fortunes*, p. 109.

154   Marshall, *East Indian Fortunes*, pp. 111–12. J. Talboys Wheeler, who wrote a history of the English settlements in India on basis of early records, provides a detailed description of this fight for dominance over the internal tobacco trade in Bengal between the EIC and local rulers. Talboys, W. J. *Early Records of British India: A History of the English settlements in India, as told in the Government Records. The Works of Old Travellers and Other Contemporary Documents, from the Earliest Period Down to the Rise of British Power in India*, London: Trübner and Company, 1878, pp. 298–317.

155 Foster, W. 'English Commerce with India', *Journal of the Royal Society of Arts,* Vol. LXVI, No. 3413, 19 April 1918, pp. 361–72.

156 See for an analysis of European trade with India during this period: Raychaudhuri, T. 'European Commercial Activity and the Organization of India's Commerce and Industrial Production, 1500–1750', in Ganguli, B. N. (ed.), *Readings in Indian Economic History. Proceedings of the First All-India Seminar on Indian Economic History,* Delhi School of Economics, 1961, London: Asia Publishing House, 1964, pp. 64–77.

157 Price. 'What Did Merchants Do?', p. 272.

158 The EIC was established in 1600 as a joint-stock association of English merchants trading with the 'Indies', and it was to continue its trading monopoly until 1813 when an Act of Parliament opened the trade with India to all shipping. The seizure of Calcutta by the nawab of Bengal and Robert Clive's subsequent defeat of the nawab at Plassey in 1757 marked the beginning of the company's change in function. Following the Mughal emperor's grant of the *diwani* (authority to collect revenue) of Bengal, Bihar, and Orissa in 1765, the EIC assumed administrative control of these provinces. The administration developed under Warren Hastings, and in 1773, the government of Bengal assumed supervisory powers over the other India presidencies. To administer the ever-increasing number of territories in the subcontinent (including present-day Pakistan and Bangladesh), the presidencies developed complex administrative structures. Besides, although often remaining important centres of trade, the factories (trading posts) gradually became absorbed into the territorial administration as well. Though the trade monopoly of EIC was already abolished in 1813 and the company's trade altogether abolished in 1833, the EIC continued as administrators, drawing their dividends from revenues of India. This 'company rule' lasted until 1858 when, following the events of the 'Indian Rebellion' or so-called Mutiny of 1857 and under the Government of India Act of 1858, the British Crown assumed direct administration of India, known as the British Raj. The company itself was finally dissolved in 1874 as a result of the East India Stock Dividend Redemption Act. See for instance, Chaudhuri, K. N. *The Trading World of Asia and the English East India Company 1660–1760,* Cambridge: Cambridge University Press, 1978 and Robins, N. *The Corporation that Changed the World. How the East*

India Company Shaped the Modern Multinational, Hyderabad: Orient Longman, 2006.

159   In the case of tobacco, this 'new' connection between England and India was to the disadvantage of tobacco growers in England itself. In order to stimulate tobacco in the English colonies such as Virginia, the ruling Stuarts had forbidden the home growth of tobacco within the British Isles. Moreover, the prohibitive duties on home-grown tobacco had become a secure source of revenue. Moreover, in 1817, *The Port Folio* (p. 352) pointed to the 'curious fact' that 'at the close of the American war, when the colonies had become virtually a foreign state', the British parliament had not lifted 'this penalty for the cultivation of tobacco in Great Britain'.

160   Along with the presidencies of Madras and Bombay, Bengal also became part of a 'presidency' with Calcutta as capital. Yet though Calcutta (present-day Kolkata in West Bengal) was declared a presidency town of the EIC in 1699, the beginnings of the Bengal presidency date from the treaties of 1765 between the EIC and the Mughal emperor and nawab of Oudh, which placed East and West Bengal, Assam, Tripura, Meghalaya, Bihar, Jharkhand, and Orissa under the administration of the company. At his height, the presidency encompassed regions that had gradually been annexed such as the so-called princely states of Uttar Pradesh, Uttarakhand, Punjab, Haryana, Himachal Pradesh, portions of Chhattisgarh, Madhya Pradesh, Maharashtra in present-day India as well as the provinces of the northwest frontier and Punjab, both now in Pakistan, and most of Burma (present-day Myanmar).

161   Hamilton, W. *A Geographical, Statistical, and Historical Description of Hindostan, and the Adjacent Countries. In Two Volumes,* Vol. I, London: John Murray, 1820, p. v.

162   Metcalf, B. D. and Metcalf, T. R. *A Concise History of Modern India,* Cambridge: Cambridge University Press, 2006 (second edition), p. 53.

163   Monckton Jones, M. E. 'Free and Open Trade in Bengal', *The English Historical Review,* Vol. 30, No. 117, January 1915, p. 29.

164   Cf. Srinivasachari, C. S. *Tobacco and Areca Nut,* Chennai: Orient Longman, 2001, p. xxix.

165   Thompson, E. and Garrett, G. T. *History of British Rule in India,* New Delhi: Atlantic Publishers, 1999, p. 101.

166 Monckton Jones. 'Free and Open Trade', p. 32.

167 Monckton Jones, p. 40.

168 Chaudhuri, K. N. 'India's Foreign Trade and the Cessation of the East India Company's Trading Activities, 1828–1840', *The Economic History Review*, New Series, Vol. 19, No. 2, 1966, pp 345–46.

169 An abstract of the regulations of government in the Department of Miscellaneous Revenue and Commerce in force within the provinces of Bengal, Behar, and Orissa from the years 1793 to 1826 inclusive with an index and notes of references to any enactments by which the provisions of the regulations in force may have been modified or extended, Vol. IV, Calcutta: Huttmann, G.H. Government Gazette Press, 1828.

170 'Affairs of the East India Company, Minutes of evidence: April 6, 1830', *Journal of the House of Lords*, Vol. 62, 1830, pp. 1040–44.

171 Mangles, *Wrongs and Claims of Indian Commerce*, p. 37.

172 Crawford, J. 'On the History and Consumption of Tobacco', p. 51.

173 Crawfurd, J. *Notes on the Settlement or Colonization of British Subjects in India: with Appendix of Proofs and Illustrations*. London: James Ridgway, 1833, in particular p. 11 and p. 44. See for an in-depth analysis of the salt monopoly of the EIC in Bengal. Serajuddin, A. M., 'The Salt Monopoly of the East India Company's Government in Bengal', *Journal of the Economic and Social History of the Orient*, Vol. XXI, Part III, 1978, pp. 304–22.

174 Stanley, E. G., 'Indian Monopolies', *Knowsley Pamphlet Collection*, 1829, Liverpool: University of Liverpool, pp. 71–72. Available online.

175 Crawfurd, J. *A View of the Present and Future Prospects of the Free Trade & Colonization of India*, second edition, enlarged, London: James Ridgway, 1829, pp. 16–17.

176 Mangles, pp. 38–39.

177 In a footnote, Crawfurd had added: 'Trifling quantities of tobacco are sent to the Paguans and Malays, people less civilized than the Hindoos themselves. Such are the total exports in this great staple, by one hundred and thirty-four millions of people!' Crawfurd, *A View of the Present and Future Prospects*, p. 32.

178 Cf. Ashworth, W. J. 'Quality and the Roots of Manufacturing 'Expertise' in Eighteenth-Century Britain', *Osiris*, Vol. 25, No. 1, Expertise and the Early Modern State, 2010, pp. 231–54.

179   Peter Robb explained that gradually, the British formulated a policy representing 'a conscious development strategy' that was 'concerned with all questions . . . from the field to the factory' and which was 'designed for the organized export sector: best suited not only for one kind of product but for one mode of production'. Robb, P., 'Bihar, the Colonial State and Agricultural Development in India, 1880–1920', *Indian Economic Social History Review*, Vol. 25, 1988, p. 230 and p. 231.

180   Sinha, C. P. N. *From Decline to Destruction. Agriculture in Bihar during the Early British Rule (1765–1813)*, New Delhi: Manak Publications, 1997, p. 150.

181   The Hunter Report of 1877 mentioned, for instance, that tobacco cultivation had already received some official attention in 1789 when experiments with 'foreign seeds' had been made in Purnea and sent to Calcutta for evaluation. Hunter, W. W. *A Statistical Account of Bengal: Monghyr and Purniah*, London: Trübner & Co., 1877, p. 290.

182   Tennant, W. *Indian Recreations; Consisting Chiefly of Strictures on the Domestic and Rural Economy of the Mohammedans & Hindoos*, Vol. II, Edinburgh: C. Stewart, 1803, pp. 301–4.

183   *Transactions of the Agricultural and Horticultural Society of India*, Vol. II, 1836, p. iv.

184   *Transactions of the Agricultural and Horticultural Society of India*, Vol. II, 1836, p. 279. See also in this volume: From Capt. Basil Hall's Travels, 'On the culture of *Tobacco* in Virginia', pp. 50–51; Capt. C. Cowles, 'On *Tobacco* produced at Diamond Harbour, from Virginia, Maryland and Persian Seed', pp. 148–50; adapted by Mr G. F. Hodgkinson, at Garden Reach, 'Particulars of the mode of cultivating and curing *Tobacco*', pp. 150–51 and Dr. Cassanova, 'Remarks on the proper Soil, and best mode of curing *Tobacco*', pp. 151–53. See also: Phayre Captain A.P., 'Memorandum accompanying a sample of Tobacco from Sandoway, in the province of Arracan', *Journal of the Agricultural & Horticultural Society of India*, Vol. III (Part I), January to December 1844, pp. 219–21.

185   *Reports by the Juries on the Subjects in the Thirty Classes into which the Exhibition was divided*, Presentation Copy, London: William Clowes & Sons (printed for the Royal Commission), 1852, p. 60.

186   For instance, in Capper, J. *The Three Presidencies of India. A History of the Rise and Progress of the British Indian Possessions from the Earliest*

Records to the Present Time with an Account of their Government, Religion, Manners, Customs, Education, etc. etc., New Delhi and Madras: Asian Educational Services, 1997 (Reprint, first published in London by Ingram, Cooke, and Co. in 1853), p. 28.

187   Renford. *The Non-Official British in India*, p. 3.

188   This quotation as well as all other evidence before the Commons' and Lords' Committees (the Parliamentary records) and recorded between 1830 and 1832 are taken from Dutt, Romesh, *The Economic History of British India. A Record of Agriculture and Land Settlements, Trade and Manufacturing Industries, Finance and Administration. From the Rise of the British Power in 1757 to the Accession of Queen Victoria in 1837,* London: Kegan Paul, Trench, Trübner & Co, 1902, pp. 271–88. For all the witness reports see *Appendix to the Report from the Select Committee of the House of Commons on the Affairs of the East-India Company, 16th August 1832, and Minutes of Evidence*. II. Finance and Accounts-Trade. Part II. Commercial, London: Printed by Order of the Honourable Court of Directors, by J. L. Cox and Son, 1833.

189   Tripathi, A. *Trade and Finance in the Bengal Presidency 1793–1833,* Bombay: Orient Longmans, 1956, p. 6, p. 7, and p. 30.

190   Renford. *The Non-Official British in India*, p. 14.

191   During the first half of the nineteenth century, it had been debated in England whether sugar could better be produced in 'our Eastern empire' or 'by the West Indian planters'. In this regard, two extreme and opposite opinions were those of 'Mr Trevelyan' and of 'Mr Larpent'. Most felt, however, 'the truth' must lie somewhere in between. The former believed 'the valley of the Ganges could supply the whole world'. The latter felt that no 'English capital and energy' should be applied to the agriculture of British India except in the case of indigo, Mangles. *Wrongs and Claims*, p. 10.

192   Cf. Achaya, K. T. *The Food Industries of British India*, Delhi: Oxford University press, 1994, pp. 24–29.

193   Bagchi, A. K 'Colonialism and the Nature of 'Capitalist' Enterprise in India', *Economic and Political Weekly*, July 30, 1988, PE-38–50.

194   See for the ups and downs of the sugar and indigo export from Bengal to Great Britain around this time. Trueman and Cook, 'The State of the Commerce of Great Britain with reference to colonial and other produce

for the year 1831', *Bristol Selected Pamphlets*, 1831 (Bristol: University of Bristol Library) and 'The State of the Commerce of Great Britain with reference to colonial and other produce for the year 1832', *Hume Tracts*, 1832. Both sources are available online.

195 Royle, *Essay*, p. 250. See also Times, 'On the resources of India, and the cultivation of east India tobacco', *The Mechanics' Magazine, Museum, Register, Journal, and Gazette*, 3 October to 2 April, Vol. XXIV, 1836, pp 519–23.

196 *Reports from the Select Committee of the House of Commons*, London: J.L. Cox, 1830, p. 990 (Appendix VIII: Cotton and Tobacco). See also: Affairs of the East India Company, Appendix A (5) No. 2: Correspondence relating to the Cultivation of Cotton and Tobacco in the East Indies.

197 *Reports from the Select Committee of the House of Commons*, London: J.L. Cox, 1830, p. 990 (Appendix VIII: Cotton and Tobacco).

198 During the later part of the nineteenth and the beginning of the twentieth centuries, Englishmen and Americans often commented on Burma's tobacco tradition as well as its smoking habits. See for instance, Quick, R. 'Native Smoking Pipes from Burma', *Man*, Vol. 2, 1902, pp 4–5.

199 Appendix to the Report from the Select Committee of the House of Commons on the Affairs of the East India Company, 16th August 1832, London: Printed by Order of the Honourable Court of Directors, J.L. Cox and Son, 1833, p. 612. Henry Thomas Colebrooke – as mentioned in the introduction – an Indologist employed by the EIC and for some time assistant collector of Tirhut and Purnea in Bengal had around 1804 already vehemently urged the government to pay more attention to tobacco in Bengal, which he considered a very profitable culture among the peasants in Bengal who eagerly pursued it. Though it required an excellent soil and its culture was laborious, tobacco, Colebrooke had judged, could be 'produced in the greatest abundance to supply the consumption of Europe, and if raised cheaply, it would yield a considerable profit to the exporter upon moderate freight'. Yet Colebrooke agreed that the tobacco of Bengal was not yet of the quality and was not the preparation desired by the European consumer. He was, however, convinced that 'under the immediate direction of

persons sufficiently acquainted with the quality that is preferred in foreign markets, tobacco might be raised that suited their tastes at no greater expense than in the present management'. Colebrooke warned, however, that the profits the cultivators would get had to be very high in order to induce them to grow tobacco for remote foreign instead of local markets. Thomas, H. *Remarks on the Husbandry and Internal Commerce of Bengal,* Darbhanga: Maharajadhiraj Kameshwar Singh Kalyani Foundation, 2007, Heritage Series 11 edited by Hetukar Jha, pp. 90–91 (original version of 1795 was republished in 1804 and 1806 and again published and edited in 1884).

200   Mangles, p. 37.

201   Chowdhury, B. *Growth of Commercial Agriculture in Bengal (1757– 1900),* Vol. I, Calcutta: Indian Studies Past and Present, 1964, p. 49.

202   Chowdhury, B. *Growth of Commercial Agriculture in Bengal, Ibid.*

203   However, exports of sugar were reduced almost to nothing by 1811, whereas the export of indigo had increased. Nevertheless, a revival of sugar export from India to Great Britain could be witnessed after 1813. See for instance, Datta, K. K. 'India's Trade with Europe and America in the Eighteenth Century', *Journal of the Economic and Social History of the Orient,* Vol. 2, No. 3, December 1959, p. 321.

204   *Bengal Hurkaru,* 3, 15, and 16 December 1829.

205   Spry, H. H. (compiler) *Suggestions Received by the Agricultural & Horticultural Society of India for extending the cultivation and introduction of useful and ornamental plants: with a view to the improvement of the agricultural and commercial resources of India,* Calcutta: Bishop's Press, 1841, p. iii.

206   Mangles, p. 38.

Chapter Two:
Away from Bengal Proper: Colonial Gaze Drawn to Bihar

207   Roy, R. N. *Sugar Industry in Darbhanga Division,* Delhi: Capital Publishing House, pp. 24–25.

208   Burt, B. C. 'The Indian Sugar Industry', *Journal of the Royal Society of Arts,* Vol. LXXXIII, No. 4317, 16 August 1935, p. 921.

209 'Crisis of the Sugar Colonies', *The Edinburgh Review or Critical Journal,* Vol. 1, Chapter XXVII, 1803, pp. 216–37.

210 See for the contemporary debate on this all-important issue at the time; for instance: MacDonnell, A. *Colonial Commerce; Comprising an Inquiry into the Principles upon which Discriminating Duties should be levied on Sugar, the Growth Respectively of the West India British Possessions, of the East Indies, and of Foreign Countries,* London: John Murray, 1828, and Macaulay, Zachary. *A Letter to William W. Whitmore, ESQ.MP. Pointing out some of the Erroneous Statements contained in a Pamphlet by Joseph Marryat entitled 'A Reply to the Arguments contained in Various Publications, Recommending an Equalization of the Duties on East and West India Sugars by the Author of a Pamphlet entitled East and West India Sugar',* London: Lupton Relfe and Hatchard and Son, 1823. Also: Macaulay, Z. *East India Sugar, or, an Inquiry Respecting the Means of Improving the Quality and Reducing the Cost of Sugar Raised by Free Labour in the East Indies. With an Appendix Containing Proofs and Illustrations,* London: Richard Taylor (Sold by Hatchard and Sons, Picadilly), 1824. See in particular: Bosma, Ulbe. *The Sugar Plantation in India and Indonesia. Industrial Production 1770–2012,* New York: Cambridge University Press, 2013, pp. 44–87.

211 For the north-western provinces (Uttar Pradesh) see for instance: Sykes, W. H. 'Contributions to the Statistics of Sugar Produced within the British Dominions in India', *Journal of the Statistical Society of London,* Vol. 13, No. 1, February 1850, p. 24.

212 Prinsep, J. 'Bengal sugar: an account of the method and expense of cultivating the sugarcane in Bengal: with calculations of the first cost to the manufacturer and exporter and suggestions for attracting that article of eastern produce exclusively to Great Britain.' *A letter from a Planter and Distiller in Bengal, to His Friend in London,* London: Debrett, 1794. See also: Singh, R. S. *Sugar Industry (A Case Study of Champaran),* Delhi: Capital Publishing House, 1988, p. 9.

213 Singh, N. P. 'Growth of Sugar Culture in Bihar (1793–1913)', *Proceedings of the Indian History Congress,* Forty-fifth Session, Annamalainagar, 1985 (1984), p. 591 and p. 592.

214 Kiyokawa, Y. and Ohno, A. 'Technology and Labour Absorption in the Indigenous Indian Sugar Industry: An Analysis of Appropriate

Technology', in Robb, P., Sugihara, K., and Yanagisawa, H. (eds.), *Local Agrarian Societies in Colonial India. Japanese Perspectives,* Richmond Surrey: Curzon, 1996, p. 320.

215   Cf. Finance and Accounts-Trade, Part II- Commercial, *Appendix to the Report from the Select Committee of the House of Commons on the Affairs 16th August 1832 of the East-India Company, 16th August 1832 Minutes and Evidence,* London: J.L. Cox and Son, 1833, p. 612.

216   *Quarterly Journal of Agriculture,* Vol. VIII, June 1837–March 1838, p. 58.

217   D'Cruz, J. 'Remarks on certain varieties of Sugarcane in the Nursery Garden of the Agricultural and Horticultural Society; with a few hints for their cultivation', *Journal of the Agricultural & Horticultural Society of India edited by The Committee of Papers,* Vol. VI, Part I. January to December 1848, pp. 56–67.

218   Robinson wrote: 'At a time when the attention of our Statesmen and Merchants is directed to the sugar statistics of the world, and with no slight degree of interest to those of India [. . .],' and he indulged: 'The hope that the following pages may prove acceptable, as well by helping to afford a right estimate of the capabilities of Bengal for the production of this valuable staple, as by assisting those who are already engaged in it'. Robinson concluded his introduction hoping 'that the facts, and figures founded on fact, gleaned together in the following pages, will afford sufficient evidence of what can be done in this country for the production of cheap sugar to encourage all those engaged in the trade to persevere in their labours; and sufficient proof that both in its cultivation and manufacture we possess all the elements of ultimate success in competition with the whole world. Let India fairly prepare herself for the struggle, and a fair share of the victory is assuredly hers!' Robinson, S. H. *The Bengal Sugar Planter: Being a Treatise on the Cultivation of the Sugar-cane and Date-tree in Bengal, and the Manufacture of Sugar and Rum therefrom,* Calcutta: Bishop College Press, 1849, p. vi and p. 11.

219   Robinson, *The Bengal Sugar Planter,* p. 1.

220   Robinson, *Ibid,* p. 2.

221   Romesh Dutt, in 1902, processed testimonies that had been submitted before the Lords' Committee of 1830 that provide a very good idea of developments in the field of sugar cultivation and manufacture around

1830: 'Europeans did not engage in the culture and manufacture of sugar in the same manner as they did in the manufacture of indigo. They simply purchased it in the bazaars or from the cultivators to whom advances were made. The machinery used in India was inferior to that of the West Indies, and there were no large sugar plantations in India. The Indian sugar was inferior to the West Indian sugar. In Bengal, the sugar cane was as good as in the West Indies, and some superior sugar had been manufactured after undergoing a special process, but at a cost too high to make it profitable. Bengal sugar was subjected to a duty of 120 per cent on the gross price, which was equivalent to a duty of 200 per cent on the prime cost.' Dutt, R. *The Economic History of British India. A Record of Agriculture and Land Settlements, Trade and Manufacturing Industries, Finance and Administration. From the Rise of the British Power in 1757 to the Accession of Queen Victoria in 1837,* London: Kegan Paul, Trench, Trübner & Co., 1902, p. 281.

222 Bosma, *The Sugar Plantation in India,* p. 75. Bosma added: 'Since industrial sugar was not in demand locally, the newly established factories were squeezed between declining prices on the world market and fierce competition for cane from the Indian khandsari producers', Bosma, p. 75.

223 Quoted from George Watt. *Pamphlet on Indigo,* Calcutta, 1890, p. 17 Mishra, Girish. 'Indigo plantation and the agrarian relations in champaran during the nineteenth century', *Indian Economic and Social History Review,* Vol. 3, 1966, p. 334.

224 Sinha, *From Decline to Destruction,* p. 142.

225 Bosma, *The Sugar Plantation in India,* p. 85.

226 McCoy, A. W. 'Opium History Up To 1858 A.D.'. **http://opioids.com/ opium/history/index.html** (last downloaded on 30 June 2011).

227 Cf. Singh, U. N. *Some Aspects of Rural Life in Bihar (An Economic Study, 1793–1833),* Patna: Janaki Prakashan, 1980, p. 222.

228 This was a risky business as in China the emperor had banned the import of opium. For the workings of this opium monopoly in Bihar from 1765 to 1856, see for instance, Sinha, R. *Aspects of Society & Economy of Bihar 1765–1856,* New Delhi: Commonwealth Publishers, 1989, pp. 89–94.

229   Richards, J. F. 'The Indian Empire and Present Production of Opium in the Nineteenth Century', *Modern Asian Studies*, Vol. 15, No. 1, 1981, p. 72. See also the chapter on opium which provides a detailed account of poppy cultivation and manufacture of opium in the Tirhut District of Bihar in Hunter, W. W. *A Statistical Account of Bengal*, Vol. XIII (Tirhut and Champaran) compiled by A. W. Mackie, London: Trübner & Co., London, 1877, pp. 92–98. Many more scholars commented, like Richards, on the fact that poppy had been cultivated by the *koeries*. See for instance, Mitra, M. *Agrarian Social Structure. Continuity and Change in Bihar 1786–1820*, New Delhi: Manohar, 1985, p. 149. In an article on the state of agriculture in Bihar published in 1833, it was remarked: 'The agriculture of the coery caste is most worthy of notice. Perhaps there is no example to be found where agriculture approaches so nearly to gardening. A portion of the finest land called dhee, that nearest and surrounding country by the village, which is elevated above the surrounding country by the wreck of mud houses, ashes, fragments of pottery, and decayed vegetable and animal matter is chosen for this purpose [. . .] In these, grain crops are sown and watered, but more particularly the poppy.' Gibbon, J. 'Remarks on the state of agriculture in Behar', *Transactions of the Agricultural and Horticultural Society of India*, Vol. II, 1836, p. 187.

230   McCoy, 'Opium History', *Ibid.*

231   The Edinburgh Gazetteer of 1822 had included 'this extensive district of Hindostan' located in the 'province of Bihar' in its geographical dictionary and reported that although 'not hilly, the surface of this district is more elevated, the soil drier, and the climate healthier than Bengal. It is, generally speaking, well cultivated and very productive of grain, sugar, indigo, tobacco, opium, and saltpeter, and of late years the breeding of horse and cattle has received much encouragement from government.' 'Tirhoot', *The Edinburgh Gazetteer, or Geographical Dictionary: Containing a Description of the Various Countries, Kingdoms, States, Cities, Towns, Mountains, &C of the World; an Account of the Government, Customs, and Religion, of the Inhabitants; the Boundaries and Natural Productions of Each Country, &c, &c. Forming a Complete Body of Geography, Physical, Political, Statistical, and Commercial. In Six*

Volumes. Accompanied by an Atlas, Volume Sixth, Edinburgh: Printed for Archibald Constable and Co., 1822, p. 256.

232   The district of Tirhut was also appreciated by the EIC as it provided them with 'large quantities of saltpetre'. Wyatt, A. *Geographical and Statistical Report of the District of Tirhoot,* Calcutta: Thos. Jones, 'Calcutta Gazette' Office, 1854, p. 2 and p. 3.

233   Richards explained that so-called Bengal opium was actually the product of an elongated zone equivalent to the eastern Gangetic valley in present-day eastern Uttar Pradesh and Bihar (i.e., in the nineteenth century the north-western provinces and Oudh to the west and (Bihar) Bengal Province to the east). Richards, J. F. 'The Indian empire and present production of opium in the nineteenth century', *Ibid,* pp. 69–70.

234   Farooqui, A. 'Opium enterprise and colonial intervention in Malwa and western India, 1800–1824', *The Indian Economic and Social History Review,* Vol. 32, No. 4, 1995, p. 450. See also: N.A. 'Opium in India', *Journal of the Society of Arts,* Vol. 23, March 26, 1875, p. 408.

235   'The Opium Trade with China', *Fraser's Magazine for Town and Country,* Vol. XX, No. CXIX (November), 1839, p. 576. (Based on book by Rev. Thelwall, A. S. *The Iniquities of the Opium Trade with China,* London: Allen and Co., 1839). A Bengal retired major objected in 1853, however, that 'as to the morality of the question, it is difficult to levy a tax upon the principles of morality. It may well be that the opium is costly, or it might be a greater evil. Surely, if we drink wine and beer after our meals, the Chinese may take a little stimulant. A warm climate renders a little stimulant requisite.' Hough, W. *India as it ought to be under the New Charter Act. Improvement suggested,* London: Messrs. W. Thacker & Co., 1853, p. 97.

236   See for instance, Fairbank, J. K. *Trade and Diplomacy on the China Coast; the Opening of the Treaty Ports, 1842–1854,* Cambridge, MA: Harvard University Press, 1953.

237   Farooqui, A. 'Colonialism and Competing Addictions: Morphine Content as Historical Factor', *Social Scientist,* Vol. 32, No. 5/6 (May–June), 2004, pp. 21–31.

238   Richards. *'The Indian Empire',* p. 69.

239   For instance, H. Broughton wrote regarding the opium monopoly: 'What a book might be made of "the Confessions of an English Opium

Agent"! It is the most romantic of manufactures. Everywhere the drowsy scent of the poppy prevails, and lulls the pleased visitor into a delightful consciousness of oriental languor and boundless profits, and into a sweet oblivion of the principles of competition and Free Trade.' Broughton, H. 'Letters from a Competition Wallah: Letter III', *MacMillan's Magazine*, Vol. 8, May–October 1863, p. 275.

240 John Crawfurd in one of his many papers read before the Ethnological Society of London in 1868 mentioned about this 'most important and valuable dye of the vegetable kingdom, Indigo' that 'several genera of plants will yield this blue-colouring matter, but the indigo of commerce is supplied by the botanical genus to which it gives name, *Indigofera*, and of the many species of this genus, chiefly by two. For India, its islands, and China, it is furnished by the *Indigofera tinctoria*, and for America by the *Indigofera anyl*'. Crawfurd also explained that 'The Hindus were the first, and indeed, the only, people of the Old World, who had acquired the art of precipitating the fecula containing the colouring matter from the watery infusion of the fresh plant, and drying them into cakes or balls, so as to make them portable'. It was, Crawfurd was convinced, 'but for this discovery, indigo never would have reached distant Greece and Italy'. The Sanskrit name of the plant was *Nila*, Crawfurd further explained, which was corrupted in the vernacular Hindi into *nil*, which also signified 'blue'. One of Crawfurd conclusions of his study into the history and migration of plants was 'the art of extracting a blue dye from the indigo plant was the invention of the Hindus of Upper or Northern India.' Crawfurd, J. 'On the History and Migration of Textile and Tinctorial Plants in Reference to Ethnology', *Transactions of the Ethnological Society of London*, Vol. 7, 1869, p. 12 and p. 13. G. A. Nadri in his article on 'The Archaeology of Indigo Manufacture' also explained that the remains of pre-modern and modern indigo vats at different places in North India 'provide a very interesting archaeological evidence for the history of indigo-processing technology.' Shrimali, K. M. (ed.) *Reason and Archaeology*, Delhi: Association for the Study of History and Archaeology, pp. 159–63.

241 See for a detailed discussion of this act of law which lasted for about hundred and sixty years and took more than twenty years to assume the form in which it was proclaimed in 1793. Guha, R. *The Rule of Property*

for Bengal. An Essay on the Idea of Permanent Settlement, Paris: Mouton, 1963.

242   Krishna, B. *Commercial Relations between Indian and England (1601 to 1757)*, London: George Routledge and Sons, 1924, pp. 94–96 and 155–57.

243   Cited in Bose, S. *Peasant Labour and Colonial Capital: Rural Bengal Since 1770*. The New Cambridge History of India, III: 2, Cambridge: Cambridge University Press, 1993, p. 45.

244   For a fuller treatment of the rise of indigo in Bengal (proper): Darrac, P-P. and van Schendel, W. *Global Blue. Indigo and Espionage in Colonial Bengal*, Dhaka: The University Press Limited, 2006.

245   Indigo and Indigo Planting, *Calcutta Review*, Vol. XXX, January–June 1858, pp. 190–91.

246   Sah, R. 'Features of British Indigo in India', *Social Scientist*, Vol. 9, No. 2/3, September and October 1980, p. 67.

247   Seton-Karr, W. S. *Selections from Calcutta Gazettes of the Years 1789,1790,1791,1792,1793,1794, 1795, 1796, and 1997, Showing the Political and Social Condition of the English in India Seventy Years Ago*, Vol. II, Calcutta: O.T. Cutter, Military Orphan Press (under the sanction of the Government of India), 1865, p. 9.

248   Board of Trade (Commercial) 12 September 1787.

249   Seton-Karr. *Selections from Calcutta Gazettes*, p. 11.

250   Sah. 'Features of British Indigo', p. 67.

251   Bose. *Peasant Labour and Colonial Capital*, p. 45.

252   Board of Trade (Commercial), 'Proceedings on Fertility of Soil for Indigo', No. 85, 12 September 1787.

253   Seton-Karr. p. 551.

254   'Indigo and Indigo Planting', *Calcutta Review*, Vol. XXX, January–June 1858, p. 214.

255   'Indigo and Indigo Planting', *Calcutta Review*, 1858, p. 190.

256   *Calcutta Review*, Vol. VII, January–June 1847, p. 188.

257   *Calcutta Review*, 1858, p. 205.

258   Bose. *Peasant Labour and Colonial Capital*, p. 50.

259   Cf. Ghosal, H. R. 'Changes in the Organization of Industrial Production in the Bengal Presidency in the Early Nineteenth Century', in Ganguli, B. N. (ed.), *Readings in Indian Economic History*, London:

Asia Publishing House, 1964, pp. 124–33. Yet for some time, 'natives' remained competitors to some extent. Robert Montgomery Martin's compilation of 1839, for instance mentions: 'there are from 300 to 400 (indigo) factories in Bengal, chiefly in Jessore, Kishnagur, and Tirhoot. The factories are principally held by Europeans; but many natives have factories of their own, and in several instances produce indigo equal to any manufactured by Europeans.' Martin, R. M. *Statistics of the Colonies of the British Empire in the West Indies, South America, North America, Asia, Austral-Asia, Africa, and Europe; Comprising the Area, Agriculture, Commerce, Manufacture, Shipping, Custom Duties, Population, Education, Religion, Crime, Government, Finances, Laws, Military defence, Cultivated and Waste Lands, Emigration, Rates of Wages, Prices of Provinces, Banks, Coins, Staple Products, Stock, Moveable and Immoveable Property, Public Companies, &c. of Each Colony; with the Charters and the Engraved Seals. From the Officials Records of the Colonial Office*, London: Wm. H. Allen and Co., 1839, p. 363.

260   *Calcutta Review*, 1858, p. 189.

261   *Calcutta Review*, 1858, p. 201.

262   *Calcutta Review*, 1858, p. 202.

263   *Calcutta Review*, 1858, p. 204.

264   Sah. *Ibid*, p. 68.

265   Board of Trade (Commercial) October 28, 1796.

266   Papers Relating to East India Affairs. *Advances by the Bengal Government to Indigo Planters: Financial Letter from Bengal (August 1809) and one from the Court of Directors in answer thereto*, Ordered, by the House of Commons, to be printed, 10 July 1813.

267   In fact, a growing class of Indian merchants with landed interests had supported the British indigo trade and clearly perceived the advantages which would result from free trade and the investment of European capital and skill in Indian agriculture. Some of them such as Dwarkanath Tagore and Prasanna Kumar Tagore and also Rammohan Roy went so far as to openly advocate the cause of (European) indigo planters. Salahuddin, A. A. F. *Social Ideas and Social Change in Bengal 1818–1835*, Leiden: E.J. Brill, 1965, pp. 8–10.

268   Singh, S. B. 'Indigo and the Agency Houses', *European Agency Houses in Bengal (1783–1833)*, Calcutta: K.L. Mukhopadhyay, 1966, pp. 211–43.

269   Bose. *Peasant Labour and Colonial Capital*, p. 49.

270   Bose. p. 50.

271   For an insight in a 'battle' between the supporters of this Union Bank and supporters of a scheme that proposed the establishment of a new bank called the 'Bank of India' in 1836 see: An India Merchant, *Review of a Pamphlet entitled 'Reasons for the Establishment' of a New Bank in India*, Glasgow: R. Malcolm, 1836.

272   Bose. *Peasant Labour and Colonial Capital*, p. 51.

273   'Indian and Colonial Intelligence', *Hume Tracts*, 1820, p. 674.

274   Crawfurd, J. *A View of the Present State and Future Prospects of the Free Trade & Colonization of India*, London: James Ridgway, 1829, pp. 16–17 and p. 23. Related to this see also: Crawfurd, J. *Letters from British Settlers in the Interior of India, Descriptive of Their Own Condition, and That of the Native Inhabitants under the Government of the East India Company. With Notes*, London: James Ridgway, 1831. Also: *Appendix to the Report from the Select Committee of the House of Commons on the Affairs of the East-India Company, 16th August 1832 and Minutes and Evidence*, Finance and Accounts-Trade. Part II: Commercial, London: J.L. Cox and Son, 1833 (printed by order of the Honourable Court of Directors).

275   Peggs, J. *India's Cries to British Humanity, Relative to Infanticide, British Connection with Idolatry, Ghaut Murders, Suttee, and Colonization in India; to which are added Humane Hints for the Melioration of the State of Society in British India*, London: Simpkin and Marshall, 1832 (third edition revised and enlarged with a book on colonisation in India), pp. 418–19 and p. 425. In 1829, some 'merchants and agents of Calcutta' had written a letter to the 'Right Honorable Lord W. C. Bentinck (governor general in Council) in which they asked for attention to be paid to 'the various inconveniences experienced by Indigo planters from their inability to hold lands in their own names' and in which they 'opposed such obstacles to the successful prosecution of their industry as could never have been compensated but by extraordinary fertility of soil and cheapness of labour.' Territorial Revenue Proceedings 6th to 26th February 1829, *Proceedings of the Revenue Department, February 17, 1829, Nos 2–4 (Land Rights of Indigo Planters)*, Vol. 821, No. 2.

276 John Crawfurd, born in Scotland, compiled these letters and added his own 'notes' started off as a surgeon in EIC service followed by being a colonial administrator, diplomat, political candidate, and orientalist scholar. He served the British East India Company in northern India, Penang, Java, Singapore, and as a diplomat to Burma and Siam. He strongly argued against mercantilism and supported 'free trade' as well as the settlement of Englishmen and (indigo) planters in particular in India. In one of his 'notes' to a letter by an English planter, he commented: 'If it were possible for the English Government to learn wisdom by experience, which Governments rarely do, it might here, at least, see with regret, some effects of that illiberal, cowardly, and short-sighted policy, under which it has taken the most solicitous precautions to prevent the settlement of Englishmen in India; trembling, forsooth, lest Englishmen, if allowed to settle in India, should detest and cast off its yoke.' Crawfurd, J. *Letters from British Settlers in the Interior of India, Descriptive of Their Own Condition, and That of the Native Inhabitants under the Government of the East India Company. With Notes*, London: James Ridgway, 1831, p. 18. See also: Crawfurd, J. *Notes on the Settlement or Colonization of British Subjects in India*. London: James Ridgway, 1833. For a discussion of his work see: Knapman, G. 'Race, Empire and Liberalism: Interpreting John Crawfurd's History of the Indian Archipelago', available at: artsonline.monash.edu.au/mai/files/2012/07/garethknapman.pdf (last accessed on 6 September 2014).

277 Crawfurd. *Letters from British Settlers*, p. 20.

278 Crawfurd. *Letters from British Settlers*, p. 24.

279 Crawfurd agreed and quoted from Mills's 'History of British India' who had argued in 1826 that these English gentlemen settled in the country knew more about the 'natives' than the company's servants, a knowledge that would aid in the administration of justice on which 'good administration' was based. The character of their work forced them 'into an intimate intercourse with the natives' from which an 'intimate knowledge' would arise, which provided them with 'local influence of great efficacy', and they would 'be useful, beyond all calculation, in maintaining order in a wide circle around them, among a people is such a state of society as that at present found in Bengal.' *Letters from British Settlers*, p. 26.

280 Bhattacharya, S. 'Indigo Planters, Ram Mohan Roy and the 1833 Charter Act', *Social Scientist*, Vol. 4, No. 3, October 1975, p. 60.

281 *Calcutta Review*, 1858, p. 225.

282 *Calcutta Review*, 1858, p. 207.

283 Cf. *Letters from an Artist in India to his Sisters in England. Rural Life in Bengal; Illustrative of Anglo-Indian Suburban Life; The Habits of the Rural Classes, the Varied Produce of the Soil and Seasons, and the Culture and Manufacture of Indigo*, London: W. Thacker & Co., 1866, p. 72.

284 Crawfurd, *Letters from British Settlers*, pp. 20–21.

285 Crawfurd, *Letters from British Settlers*, p. 29.

286 Ryot A. (Compiler), *Selections From Papers on Indigo Cultivation in Bengal, with an Introduction and a few Notes, by a Ryot*, Calcutta: I.C. Bose & Co., 1858, pp. 71–72.

287 The *Calcutta Review*, Vol. II, January–June 1847, p. 216.

288 Cf. Reports from Committees: Thirteen Volumes. *Fourth Report from the Select Committee on Colonization and Settlement (India); together with the Proceedings of the Committee, Minutes of Evidence, and Appendix.* Ordered by the House of Commons, to be Printed, 23 July 1858, p. 14 and 'Report of the Select Committee appointed to inquire into the Progress and Prospect, and the best means to be adopted for Promotion of European Colonisation and Settlement in India, especially in the Hill Districts and healthier climates of that Country, as well as for the extension of our Commerce with Central Asia. Ordered by the House of Commons to be printed. 9 August 1859', The *Calcutta Review*, No. LXVII, March 1860, pp. 16–34.

289 The *Calcutta Review*, Vol. II, January–June 1847, p. 219.

290 *Calcutta Review*, 1858, p. 197.

291 The *Calcutta Review* felt that the Indigo planters should bestir themselves in this matter. The Planters' Association might offer a premium of 10,000 rupees to any party who should within a certain time invent the best and cheapest plan for precipitating the fecula, with, say, one-fourth of the present manual labour, *Calcutta Review*, 1858, p. 201.

292 The *Calcutta Review* elaborated: 'As short time as possible should elapse between the cutting and stacking of the plant. The vats should be filled before night otherwise everything falls into arrear, all the work being done carelessly and badly. The coolies also are unnecessarily

harassed, and should the weather be bad, they are sure to become sick; the factory thus losing their services at a most important time [. . .] They should (therefore) have good, airy houses, well raised, protected from the weather, and with facilities for cooking. During the manufacturing season a *moodie's* shop should be established in the factory, with proper supplies to be sold at fair rates', *Calcutta Review*, 1858, p. 200.

293 Ryot, A. *Selections From Papers*, p. ii. Also: Freeman, John. *A Reply to the Memorandum of the East India Company: or, An Insight into British India*, London: Robert Hardwicke, 1858. Freeman himself 'Twenty-Five Years a Resident in Bengal; a Landed Proprietor, and Extensive Indigo Planter in Bhaugulpore and various other Districts' asked rhetorically on p. 67 of his book: 'And who are the indigo planters, the silk growers, and others, who distribute upwards of three millions sterling a year in the Lower Provinces of Bengal? Where else, in the possessions of the East-India Company, is there prosperity? Where is the soil made to yield more? In what part is there more material comfort? Where is the heavy revenue from the land paid with such punctuality; and where are the natives more advanced and more civilized than in these Lower Provinces? And why? because here reside a greater number of European independent settlers than in any other part of India-men who have shown sufficient moral courage to live isolated from their fellows, and trust their lives and properties in the interior of the country'.

294 This 'Ryot' added: '[. . .] that his own countrymen and missionaries denounce his doings and dealings, and that the administrators of the country trace in his conduct the evils of Western plantation. The system which he has adopted for success in Indigo is clearly based on fraud and oppression, and his trade, as his own Missionary tells the world, is actually stained with blood', Ryot, A. *Selections From Papers*, p. 2.

295 Ryot, A. *Selections From Papers*, p. 3.

296 This 'Ryot' felt that 'the planter is too cunning and selfish to bear the loss, and the load must necessarily fall on the already over-burdened back of the ryot. It is then the interest of the zemindar to relieve the ryot of this load, and the planter successfully imposes upon the public by pointing to this circumstance as the source of all the evils. He is not slow to aver that the zemindar is the author of all mischief, and that without his interference the ryot would be a mild and pretty manageable creature

[. . .] It is also in the interest of the zemindar, as Mr. Sconce has clearly shown, to promote the ryot's advance in life, and when he neglects to attend to it, he transgresses one of his primary duties and violates his Charter which the Permanent Settlement may not improperly be called. It is then not surprising that perpetual jealously should exist among zemindars and planters, and that this jealousy should lead both of them to social disturbances and infractions of peace', Ryot, A. *Selections From Papers,* p. 3 and p. 4.

297   Ryot, A. *Selections From Papers,* p. 29. See also: Reports from Committees, *Colonization and Settlement, 1857–58,* in particular pp. 53–54. On p. 54 evidence of witnesses is summarised concerning 'the subject of the state of feeling existing in Bengal, more especially in Lower Bengal, between the European indigo planters and the zemindars, and the ryots'. One such witness mentioned: 'the planters in many instances bear the character of violent and oppressive men, though there are doubtless many who are exceedingly benevolent and popular'.

298   Ryot, A. *Selections From Papers,* pp. 2–3.

299   The compiler of this treatise asked: 'If however the lower orders of the Natives are so hard to be dealt with, if they are such thorough – going rogues and so entirely lost to moral sense, as the Planter says [. . .] why not the Silk Grower, the Sugar Planter, and other European Agriculturists in India, who are required to deal with the same class of people, why do they not complain of their dishonesty, trickery and indolence?' Ryot, A. *Selections From Papers,* p. 2.

300   Ryot, A. *Selections From Papers,* p. 31.

301   Despite these problems in the indigo fields of Bengal proper, Amalendu De, however, analysed that, 'The period from 1850 to 1860 was the most flourishing period of the indigo factories in Bengal (proper)', De, A. 'Flourishing Stage of Indigo Plantation', *Journal of History,* Department of History, Jadavpur University Calcutta, Vol. IV, 1983, pp. 106–19. Moreover, according to J. C. H. MacNair who reflected in 1928 on the 'old indigo plantations' of Bengal (mainly those in the Nuddea District), the plantations in Bihar became only more important after 1870, *The Edinburgh Review or Critical Journal,* 1928, Vol. 248, No. 505, p. 164.

302   Ryot, A. *Selections From Papers,* pp. 4–5.

303 Historian Sanjay Ghildiyal explained that 'during 1859–61, a large portion of colonial Bengal became a site of contest between the indigo peasants and English planters, with the Bengali *bhadralok* and British officialdom as important stakeholders'. Ghildiyal commented that 'on the face of it, the Indigo movement was against the oppressive and un-remunerative system of indigo cultivation. It was perceived by the ryot as a threat to his security of subsistence, but there was more than that'. According to Ghildiyal, the indigo system in Lower Bengal was 'an affront to the use of customary rights held by the peasants and was a constriction or denial of choice where earlier there was complete freedom to choose the crop for cultivation'. For an adequate understanding of 'the Indigo movement', Ghildiyal therefore concluded, 'both political and moral economy approaches need to be taken into consideration.' Ghildiyal, S. 'Moral economy and the indigo movement', *Economic and Political Weekly*, Vol. XLV, No. 8, February 20–26, 2010, p. 67. See for contemporary sources for instance: 'Indigo Planters and Missionaries', *The Calcutta Review*, No. LXVII, March 1860, pp. 113–42; 'British Settlers. Report of the Commissioners on Indigo. 1860', *The Calcutta Review*, March 1861, pp. 19–53. A Member of the Calcutta Missionary Conference, 'Missionaries and indigo planting', *Knowsley Pamphlet Collection*, 1861, online; Rev. Long, J. *Strike, But Hear!: Evidence Explanatory of the Indigo System in Lower Bengal*, Calcutta: R.C. Lepage and Co., 1861; Lamb, G. 'The experiences of a landholder and an indigo planter in eastern Bengal', *Knowsley Pamphlet Collection*, 1859, online; *Brahmins and Pariahs. An Appeal by the Indigo Manufacturers of Bengal to the British Government, Parliament, and People, for Protection against the Lieut.-Governor of Bengal; Setting forth the proceedings by which this high officer has interfered with the free course of justice, has destroyed capital and trade of British settlers in India, and has created the present disastrous condition of incendiarism and insurrection now spreading in the rural districts of Bengal*, London: James Ridgway, 1861, online and Dickinson, J. 'Reply to the indigo planters' pamphlet entitled 'Brahmins and Pariahs', *Knowsley Pamphlet Collection*, 1861.

304 Around 1765, Bihar consisted of the Patna Division (Gaya, Shahabad, Muzaffarpur, Darbhanga, Saran, and Champaran), the Bhagalpur Division (Monghyr, Bhagalpur, Purnea, Malda and the Santhal

Parganas), the Chota Nagpur Division (Hazaribagh, Lohardagga, Manbhum and Singhbhum), and Orissa granted in Diwani as far as the Subarnrekha river (i.e., part of Midnapur district), Mishra, S. G. *History of Bihar 1740–1772*, New Delhi: Munshiram Manoharlal, 1970, p. 135. This book mainly concerns the regions of Muzaffarpur, Darbhanga, Monghyr (Munger), and Purnea to some extent.

305 Bose, *Peasant Labour and Colonial Capital*, p. 52.

306 Quotation from the unpublished version of his paper entitled 'Science and the Improvement of Indigo Dye in Colonial India, c. 1860–1913', available online.

307 Cf. Wynne, W. D. 'Fields of Cultural Contradictions: Lessons from the Tobacco Patch', *Agriculture and Human Values*, Vol. 22, No. 4, 2005, pp. 465–77. A British civil servant in 1883 observed: 'Meanwhile the planters in Upper Bengal were in great alarm lest the indigo contagion (in Lower Bengal) might spread to them, and took every precaution in their power to keep matters smooth till the agitation should blow over. Beyond some vague rumours, nothing definite reached the distant country places unpenetrated by the native press, and distance and difference of language saved the planters in Upper Bengal.' N.A. 'The Bengal Indigo Planter and His System', *MacMillan's Magazine*, Vol. XLIX, November 1883 to April 1884, p. 223.

308 Hamilton mentioned in 1820 that Tivabhucti or Tirhut had been a component part of Maithila, which comprised a great proportion of three districts: Tirhut, Purneah, and Sarun. The limits of the whole were the Gunduck and Kosa Rivers and the mountains of Nepal. Tirhut seemed to have continued as an independent Hindu principality until 1237 when Toghan Khan, the Muslim governor of Bengal, took charge. In 1325, it was annexed to the throne of Delhi. Along with the rest of the province, it devolved to the British government of the EIC in 1765 but was only permanently assessed for revenue since 1794. Its principal towns were Hajipur, Singhea, Durbunga, and Mowah. Hamilton had added that 'on account of its natural advantages in soil and climate, this district was originally selected by the British government as an eligible station for improving the breed of horses in their territories'. Hamilton, W. *Geographical, Statistical, and Historical Description of Hindostan, and the Adjacent Countries. In two volumes*, Vol. I, London: John Murray,

1820, p. 270. The erudite scholar Mohammad Sajjad mentioned that 'Tirhut' is said to be a corrupted version of the Sanskrit words *tira* and *bhukti*, which means 'people living on the riverbank'. The area played an important part in the history of Indo-Nepalese relation during the colonial period. Muzaffarpur was made into the district headquarters of Tirhut. When Muzaffarpur and Darbhanga were made into two separate districts in 1875, the word Tirhut disappeared from the terminology of the colonial administrators. Yet in 1907, a 'modern Tirhut' was created, under a separate commissionership comprising of the districts of Muzaffarpur, Darbhanga, Saran, and Champaran. Presently, Tirhut is a division or commissionership with headquarters in Muzaffarpur consisting of six districts, viz., Muzaffarpur, Vaishali (headquarters Hajipur), Sitamarhi, Sheohar, and East and West Champaran. Sajjad. 'Local Resistance and Colonial Reprisal', pp. 25–45.

309 Reid, W. M. *The Culture and Manufacture of Indigo; with a Description of a Planter's Life and Resources,* Calcutta: Thacker, Spink and Co., 1887, p. 103.

310 Shukla, P. K. *Indigo and the Raj. Peasant Protests in Bihar 1780–1917,* Delhi and Patna: Pragati Publications, 1993, p. 13 and p. 19.

311 Sinha, R. *Aspects of Society and Economy of Bihar,* New Delhi: Janaki Prakashan for Commonwealth, 1989, p. 84. For indigo in other districts in Bihar see for instance the chapter on 'Plants used for dying' in Martin, Montogomery. *The History, Antiquities, Topography, and Statistics of Eastern India; comprising the Districts of Behar, Shahabad, Bhagulpoor, Goruckpoor, Dinajepoor, Puraniya, Ronggopoor, and Assam, in the relation to their Geology, Mineralogy, Botany, Agriculture, Commerce, Manufactures, Fine Arts, Population, Religion, Education, Statistics, ETC. Surveyed under the Orders of the Supreme Government, and Collated from the Original Documents at the E.I. House, with the permission of the Honourable Court of Directors,* in three volumes, London: Wm H. Allen and Co., 1838, pp. 248–57. See also Sinha, C. P. N. *From Decline to Destruction. Agriculture in Biharm During the Early British Rule (1765–1813),* New Delhi: Manak, 1997, pp. 112–29.

312 In 1935, Majumdar divided the 'agricultural labourers' in Bihar during the first half of the nineteenth century into two classes: 'slaves and free farm labourers'. The first category was again subdivided into a class of

'debtor bondsmen' and a class of 'born slaves performing agricultural operations'. The second category was subdivided by Majumdar into: (1) those who cultivated for a share of the crop, (2) those who were hired by the month or season, and (3) those who were hired by the day. See: Majumdar, B. 'Agricultural Labour in Bihar in the first half of the nineteenth century', *Indian Journal of Economics*, Vol. 15, No. 4, April 1935, pp. 669–76.

313 Sajjad, M. 'Local resistance and colonial reprisal: tirhut (Muzaffarpur) Muslims in the Ghadar, 1857–59', *Contemporary Perspectives: History and Sociology of South Asia*, Vol. 2, No. 1, January–June 2008, pp. 25–45.

314 Hay, James. *Memorial of Mr. James Hay, Indigo Planter, Poorneah, to the Hon. East India Company, appealing against the proceedings of Mr. William Wollen, Judge of Poorneah*, London: C.H. Reynell, 1826, pp. 2–3.

315 Birdwood, G. 'The Quest and Early European Settlement of India', *Journal of the Society of Arts*, Vol. XXVII, 7 February 1879, p. 223.

316 Mittal, S. K. *Peasant Uprisings & Mahatma Gandhi in North Bihar (A Politico-Economic Study of Indigo Industry 1817–1917 with special reference to Champaran)*, Meerut: Anu Prakashan, 1978, pp. 14–15.

317 See for a somewhat detailed description of these happenings in Bihar and in particular in and around Muzzaffarpur in Tirhut: Shukla, *Indigo and the Raj*, pp. 20–22 and Malleson, G. B. *The Indian Mutiny of 1857*, New Delhi: Rupa, 2005, pp. 142–53. Of late many more publications on the Mutiny in Bihar have appeared. Of particular interest are works by Mohammad Sajjad and several volumes edited by Crispin Bates and Marina Carter: *Mutiny at the Margins: New Perspectives on the Indian Uprising of 1857*, New Delhi: Sage, 2014.

318 'Indigo and Indigo Planters', *Calcutta Review*, p. 224.

319 Delta, 'Indigo and its enemies: or, Facts on both sides', *Knowsley Pamphlet Collection*, 1861, p. 71.

320 The *Calcutta Review* of 1859 (Vol. XXXIII, July–December, p. 343) had stated: '[. . .] every line of railway, every river, canal, road and bridge will have to support the wear and tear of imperial traffic. The fields of lower India will pour forth their cereals, fibres, oilseeds; the mines of upper India, their minerals'.

321 The *Calcutta Review. Indigo and Indigo Planting*, Vol. XXX, March 1858, p. 192. In a paper read in 1833 but published in 1836, James Gibbon had already remarked that the state of agriculture in the province of Behar (at the time comprising the districts of Behar, Shahabad, Tirhoot, and Saran) generally was very good – though there were defects in the system too – and as far as the implements of agriculture were concerned this man, felt that 'there are no implements yet invented that would answer so well. The most esteemed ploughs in England are for the double purpose of stirring the earth and laying it up in lands, in order to draw off the superfluous water. Here the lands, whether alluvial or deluvial drain naturally so well, that this forming into lands is unnecessary, there being no wet land except what is actually inundated. However ineffective the single operation of the plough of this country may appear, yet when we compare the frequent stirrings to prepare the land, to the combined ploughing and harrowing which are required in England, and the vast disproportion of the strength and expense of the team, we shall not find that we have much superiority to boast of.' Gibbon, 'Remarks on the State of Agriculture in Behar', p. 185.

322 Bose explained that 'the different configuration of agrarian social classes in the indigo growing parts of Bengal and Bihar stemmed from important differences in the relationship between land and capital', and he added that 'the immense power of Bihar landlords flowed from their control over land and varied, if crude, instruments of extra-economic coercion.' Bose, *Ibid.*, p. 76 and p. 154.

323 Swaroop, R. 'Some Aspects of the 1857 Rebellion in Bihar', *People's Democracy* (weekly organ of the Communist Party of India (Marxist), Vol. XXXI, No. 18, May 6, 2007. For a similar contention, see Shukla, *Indigo and the Raj*, p. 22.

Chapter Three:
Changing Hierarchy of Tobacco Tastes and Colonial Demands

324 Considering that the water pipe already existed in Mughal India (using opium instead of tobacco however) and the fact that the habit of betel leaf (*pan*) and betel nut chewing were widely spread even before that, it is not so surprising that tobacco was consumed in these ways in Bihar.

325 Bal Krishna, who studied the impact of this 'colonisation', concluded that 'the growing participation of Europeans in the Asiatic commerce' resulted, in the case of the tobacco trade at least, in a 'great loss suffered by the Indian merchants.' Krishna, *Commercial Relations,* p. 293.

326 Grierson, *Bihar Peasant Life,* p. 95 and pp. 96–97.

327 Cf. Ray, C. S. 'The Hookah – the Indian Waterpipe', *Current Science,* Vol. 96, No. 10, 25 May 2009, pp. 1319–23.

328 Williamson, T. and Blagdon, F. W. *The European in India. From a Collection of Drawings by Charles Doyley engraved by J.H. Clark and C. Dubourg with a preface and copious descriptions by* Thomas Williamson accompanied with *a Brief History of Ancient and Modern India from the Earliest Periods of Antiquity to the Termination of the Late Mahratta War by F. W. Blagdon,* New Delhi and Madras: Asian Educational Services, 1995 (reprint of London: Edward Orme, 1813).

329 Wilkins, W. J. *Daily Life and Work in India,* London: T. Fisher Unwin, 1888, pp. 221–23.

330 Crawford, J. 'On the History and Consumption of Tobacco', *Journal of the Statistical Society of London,* Vol. 16, No. 1, March 1853, p. 52.

331 Crooke, W. *Hobson-Jobson. A Glossary of Colloquial Anglo-Indian words and Phrases, and of Kindred Terms, Etymological, Historical, Geographical and Discursive,* new edition edited version of book by Col. Henry Yule and A.C. Burnell, New Delhi: Munshiram Manoharlal, 1984, p. 423 (Originally Published in 1903 by John Murray, London).

332 Bhatia, H. S (ed). *European Women in India. Their Life and Adventures,* New Delhi: Deep and Deep, 1979, p. 173.

333 Bhatia, *European Women in India,* p. 174.

334 Bhatia, *European Women in India,* p. 174.

335 Ghosh, S. C. *The British in Bengal. A Study of the British Society and Life in the Late Eighteen Century,* New Delhi: Munshiram Manoharlal, 1998, pp. 145–46 (originally published in 1970 by E.J. Brill, Leiden).

336 Nevile, P. *Sahib's India. Vignettes from the Raj,* New Delhi: Penguin Books, 2010, p. 1 and pp. 3–4 and pp. 75–81.

337 Gauhgan, J. M. *The 'Incumberances'. British Women in India 1615–1856,* New Delhi: Oxford University Press, 2013, p. 184.

338 Gilchrist, J. B. *The General East India Guide and Vade Mecum for the Public Functionary, Government Officer, Private Agent, Trader, or Foreign*

Sojourner, in British India and the Adjacent Parts of Asia immediately connected with the Honourable the East India Company. Being A Digest of the Work of the Late Capt. Williamson, with many Improvements and Additions; Embracing the Most valuable Parts of Similar Publications on the Statistics, Literature, Official Duties, and Social Economy of Life and Conduct in that Interesting Quarter of the World, London: Kingsbury, Parbury, & Allen, 1825, pp 231–32. This *East India Guide* also provides extensive discussions of the *hooqqu-burdar*, the *Hooqqu* itself and of various types of *cheroots. Ibid*, pp. 117–22 and pp. 230–32

339 Gilchrist, *The General East India Guide*, p. 231.

340 Gilchrist, *The General East India Guide* pp. 117–22.

341 Indeed, the habit of smoking remained throughout the nineteenth century and was in particular popular with the indigo planters in Bihar. One planter even saw smoking (and drinking) as a survival strategy and penned a poem in 1873 that talked about the severe loneliness a European planter in Bihar faced: 'With a pipe and a *peg* you *might* do it, For a week you might live like a lord; But then your beer, who is to brew it? And pipes on 'lone isles' aren't stored.' Maori, *Tirhoot Rhymes*, Calcutta: Wyman & Co., 1873, p. 39. These planters now, however, criticised 'native' tobacco and demanded 'good-quality' cigars or *cheeroots*. A *Medical Guide* for the European in India of 1878, however, warned: 'The excessive use of tobacco, in which many Anglo-Indians indulge, has much greater influence on the health than they imagine'. It was advised: 'But as smokers will smoke [. . .] confine their indulgence within limits [. . .] it may be safely stated that three or four ordinary cigars a day should be the *utmost limit*.' Mair, R. S. 'Medical Guide for Anglo-Indians, Being a Compendium of Advice to Europeans in India, etc.', in Hull, E. C. P. *The European in India or Anglo-Indian's Vade-Mecum. A Handbook of Useful and Practical Information for Those Proceeding to or Residing in the East Indies, relating to Outfits, Routes, Time for Departure, Indian Climate and Seasons, Housekeeping, Servants, etc., etc.*, (3rd edn) with additions, New Delhi and Chennai: Asian Educational Services, 2004, pp. 252–53 (first published in 1878 by C. Kegan Paul & Co, London).

342 Cf. Ghosh, *The British in Bengal*, p. 156.

343 Fairholt, F. W. *Tobacco: Its History and Associations: Including an Account of the Plant and Its Manufacture; with Its Modes of use in All Age and Countries*, London: Chapman and Hall, 1859, p. 213 and pp. 217–20.

344 Billings, E. R. *Tobacco: Its History, Varieties, Culture, Manufacture and Commerce, with an Account of its Various Modes of Use, from its First Discovery until Now, with Illustrations by Popular Artists*, Hartford, Conn.: American Publishing Company, 1875 (EBook version obtained through Project Gutenberg).

345 Though in its infancy and hand-rolled, cigarettes were already on the market in England around 1860 when the paper of which cigarettes were made was of a peculiar structure, 'porous-like India paper', Fairholt had explained, and 'smoldering without smoke'. The best, Fairholt had judged in 1859, were the cigarettes made at Valencia. Fairholt, *Tobacco: Its History and Associations,* p. 217.

346 Billings, *Tobacco,* p. 194.

347 Fairholt, *Tobacco: Its History and Associations,* p. 217.

348 Therefore, at the time, it was already understood that tobacco varieties are not born but made. That they are the outcome of human effort and constructed through technological manipulation (during seed production, cultivation, curing, and manufacturing processes), sociocultural preferences, political change, and different and changing market demands and supplies. Cf. Hahn B. *Making Tobacco Bright,* p. 12.

349 Watt, Sir George, *The Commercial Products of India being an Abridgment of 'the Dictionary of the Economic Products of India',* London: John Murray, 1908, p. 807.

350 Rao, P. S. 'What Future for Exports of Cigars and Cheroots?' *World Tobacco,* December 1984, pp. 31–32. See also: 'Tobacco Cultivation in the Madras Presidency', *Journal of the Society of Arts,* June 20, 1890, pp. 731–32.

351 *Bombay Gazette,* 'The Indian Tobacco Manufacture', *Tropical Agriculturist,* February 1, 1884, p. 604.

352 Hindoo, A. 'Smoking in India', *Frank Leslie's Popular Monthly,* Vol. 26, September 1888, p. 375.

353 Peggs, J. *India's Cries to British Humanity, Relative to Infanticide, British Connection with Idolatry, Ghaut Murders, Suttee, Slavery,*

and Colonization in India; to which are added Humane Hints for the Melioration of the State of Society in British India, London: Simpkin and Marshall, 1832 (3rd edn Revised and Enlarged with a book on colonisation in India), p. 426.

354 Crawford, J. 'On the History and Consumption of Tobacco', p. 46.

355 Royle, J. F. *Essay on the Productive Resources of India*, London: Wm. H. Allen and Co., 1840, pp. 249–57.

356 Martin, M. *The Progress and Present State of India. A Manual for General Use, Based on Official Documents, furnished under the Authority of Her Majesty's Secretary of State for India.* London: Sampson Low, Son and Co., 1862, p. 283.

357 O'Connor, J. E. 'Report on the Tobacco Production in India', *Reports on the Tea and Tobacco Industries in India. Presented to both Houses of Parliament by Command of Her Majesty*, East India (Products), Part I, London: Printed by George Edward Eyre and William Spottiswoode, 1874, p. 139. O'Connor's report was widely quoted by subsequent government officers, and it was the second of the series of monographs on 'the more important products of India' which was compiled by the newly established Department of Revenue, Agriculture, and Commerce. O'Connor was registrar of the department.

358 J. E. O'Connor in this voluminous report on tobacco in India also pointed to the 'stupid practice' of the native tobacco planter who was 'in many points' 'very far behind his American or European brother'. Though, O'Connor agreed with 'some advocates of the *laisser-faire* system in connection with Indian agriculture' that in 'some matters, his inferiority is the result of want of means' (but not of manure which was available but not intelligently applied) but more often than not it was 'the result of ignorance, of apathy, and an inveterate dislike of abandoning the customs of those who went before him.' O' Connor, 'Report on the Tobacco Production of India', p. 218.

359 O'Connor, 'Report on the Tobacco Production of India', pp. 216–19.

360 Watson, F. 'Agriculture in India', *Journal of the Society of Arts*, June 7, 1878, p. 690.

361 Watson, 'Agriculture in India', p. 691.

362 Watson, 'Agriculture in India', p. 689.

363 'Tobacco', *Journal of the Society of Arts*, Vol. 19, 3 February 1871, p. 216.

364   *The Agricultural Gazette of India*, Vol. IV, No. 2, September 1872, p. 37.

365   'Tobacco ultivation in Jamaica', *Journal of the Society of Arts,* October 8, 1875, pp. 932–35.

366   O'Connor explicated that the growth of tobacco in accordance with 'the principles of modern agricultural science' was not enough for the production of tobacco which would be good for consumption in Europe: 'After all the processes of cultivation have been successfully carried out, the planter has still to go through the processes of curing and preparation before he can send his tobacco to market. The best grown tobacco will be fit for nothing but to throw away if it is not properly cured'. In this task', according to O'Connor, 'the natives fail even more egregiously than they do in growing the tobacco.' O'Connor, *Ibid,* pp. 218–19. Mr. Wace reported in a similar way on 'the native method of curing', Hunter, W. W. *A Statistical Account of Bengal* (Vol. XIII: Tirhut and Champaran), London: Trübner & Co., 1877, pp. 90–91.

367   Watson, F. 'The Cultivation and Preparation of Tobacco in India', *Journal of the Society of Arts*, Vol. 19, 14 July 1871, p. 659.

368   'Resolution by the Government of Bengal on Tobacco Cultivation', General Department, Agriculture, September 1873, File No. 12, No. 6.

369   O'Connor, *Ibid,* p. 219.

370   O'Connor, *Ibid,* p. 219.

371   Annual General Report of the Patna Division, No. 85, Bankipore, September 1873.

372   O'Connor, *Ibid,* p. 218.

373   Anonymous. *The Cultivation and Curing of Tobacco in Bengal,* Calcutta: Bengal Secretariat Press, 1874, p. 5.

374   O'Connor, *Ibid,* pp. 171–83 ('Bengal').

375   Watson, F. *Report on the Cultivation and Preparation of Tobacco in India. An Appended Manual of Practical Operations connected with the Cultivation, &C. of Tobacco in Hungary, Extracted from a Treatise by Mr. J. Mandis, Financial Counselor and Inspector for the purchase of Tobacco in Austria. With Plates,* London: India Museum, India Office, 1871, pp. 12–13.

376   For a detailed discussion of the model farm at Barirhat, situated about 5 miles north of Rangpur town (now in Bangladesh), see: Molla, M. K.

U. *The New Province of Eastern Bengal & Assam 1905–1911*, Rajshahi: The Institute of Bangladesh Studies, 1981, pp. 141–48.

377 *The Cultivation and Curing of Tobacco in Bengal*, pp. 5–6.

378 Alder, G. J. 'The origins of 'The Pusa Experiment': the East India company and horse-breeding in Bengal, 1793–1808', *Bengal Past and Present*, Vol. XCVIII, Part I, Serial No. 186, January–June 1979, p. 12.

379 This was one William Malet. See: Alder, 'The Origins', pp. 15–16 and p. 31 note 28.

380 Alder, The Origins' p. 28.

381 Anonymous. 'The Cultivation', p. 159.

382 General Department, Branch II, Agriculture, Collection 2, No. 127–28, September 1875.

383 General Department, Branch II, Agriculture, Collection 2, No. 127–28, September 1875.

384 Watson, *Report on the Cultivation*, p. 12.

Chapter Four:
Taking in the Private Capitalist: European Planters in Tirhut

385 An Ex-Civilian. *Life in the Mofussil or The Civilian in Lower Bengal*, London: C. Kegan Paul & Co., 1878, p. 88.

386 A most important source used in this regard remains Minden J. Wilson, an indigo planter himself who penned down a very detailed history of the indigo factories in this region. It is from this work that I came to know that many of these so-called indigo factories had been started as sugar factories or that sugar and indigo were worked side by side. Wilson, for instance, mentioned that the Doomra indigo concern had started a sugar factory with a vacuum pan which had made 'very good sugar'. This concern had been owned by the Tirhoot Indigo Association of London. The Dholi, Motipore, the Husna outworks of the Munghulgurh factory, all had been sugar factories first. Importantly, Wilson also mentioned that some indigo concerns later on around the end of the century became (again) sugar factories, turned into general 'farms' or worked as a *zemindari* and grew 'crops that paid', like tobacco. Wilson, M. *History of Behar Indigo Factories*, Calcutta: The Calcutta General Printing Company, 1908, p. 9. p. 19, p. 36 and pp. 53–54.

387   William Sharpley had come to India to join his uncle as an assistant. His uncle had been a planter in Bihar and around 1845 had worked at the Ramcollah Factory. When Sharpley arrived, he found out that he was expected to become a 'sugar planter' having to supervise the fabrication of an engine and machinery for crushing cane, yet he wrote in his private diary that this soon had been 'knocked on the head when my Uncle saw the irregular growth of the cane following on a former year's crop and it was as well for the price of sugar was going down.' Sharpley, W. *Autobiographical Sketch of My Life and Times for My Children*, Unpublished. Later on, Sharpley did involve himself at times in sugar making, producing 'Muscovada' sugar. Sharpley explained this was a 'West Indian name', and he added, 'Our sugar was different from that of the natives' who had 'coarse and dark soft sugar [. . .] with which we always sweetened our tea'. Most of the sugar machinery in Champaran in Tirhut had been set up under the superintendence of Mr. Robinson, who had come out to look after H. J. Robinson Engineers. Sharpley also narrated and added, 'There are few factories where someone has not boiled to death by falling in from sitting evaporators or clarifiers, or (crushed) by the mill, rollers, or bu. . .spur [sic] wheels. It is a rare case indeed when no serious accident has occurred through sugar making.' *Ibid.* See also: Royle, J. F., 'Culture of Sugar in India', *Essay on the Productive Resources of India*, pp. 85–94.

388   Other indigo-growing districts in Bihar included Champaran, Saran, Patna, Shahabad, and Munger. After around 1850, in particular Champaran became an important indigo-growing district, yet before that date, English planters in Champaran had been more interested in the development of the sugar industry in that region. Mishra, G. 'Indigo Plantation', p. 333.

389   Huggins, W. *Sketches in India, Treating on Subjects Connected with Government; Civil and Military Establishments; Characters of the European, and Customs of the Native Inhabitants*, London: John Letts, 1824, pp. 138–39.

390   Huggins, *Sketches in India*, p. 140 and p. 141.

391   Huggins, *Sketches in India*, p. 140.

392   Huggins, *Sketches in India*, p. 143.

393   Huggins, *Sketches in India*, p. 144.

394 Huggins, *Sketches in India*, pp. 148–49.

395 General Department *Annual General Reports, Patna Division, 1876–77*, November 1877 (report quoted herein: Calcutta 5th February 1801).

396 General Department, *Annual General Reports, Patna Division, 1876–77*, November 1877 (report quoted herein: Shahpur Oondee, July 7, 1808).

397 General Department. *Annual General Reports, Patna Division, 1876–77* (report quoted herin: No. 11, July 14, 1828).

398 Robins, N. *The Corporation that Changed the World, Ibid.*

399 On May 9, 1793 in the *The Calcutta Gazette*, the EIC had 'great pleasure' in announcing to the public, 'an event which immediately concerns the native land-holders and is certainly an object of the greatest political importance to the welfare of these provinces. The circumstance we mention is a proclamation issued by the Governor-General in Council, declaring that the jumma which has been assessed on the lands of the different descriptions of proprietors in Bengal, Behar, and Orissa, under the regulations for the decennial settlement of the public revenue, is from henceforth fixed for ever'.

400 Seton-Karr, *Ibid*, p. 366 and p. 367.

401 Prinsep, A. 'On the Traces of Feudalism in India, and the Condition of Lands Now in a Comparative State of Agricultural Infancy', *Journal of the Royal Asiatic Society of Great Britain and Ireland*, Vol. 8, 1846, p. 402.

402 *The Calcutta Review*. 'Indigo Planters and Missionaries', Vol. XXXIV, Janaury–June 1860, 113. See also: Rev. Long, J. *Strike, But Hear!: Evidence Explanatory of the Indigo System in Lower Bengal*, Calcutta: R.C. Lepage and Co., 1861.

403 At the same time, such planters did not desire to become EIC servants. William Sharpley, for instance, had been advised by his uncle to apply for the post of deputy magistrate at Bhagalpur. Yet as Sharpley did not know 'the language and the custom and the manner of the people' well enough at the time (around 1845), he had waited for another opportunity. Yet this did not come, but Sharpley had concluded that though this might have set him free from Sunday duties after a few years of service, 'I felt I would rather be free as a planter than bound down as a Government Servant.' *Ibid.*

404 Jones, J. B. 'Particulars relating to the Agriculture of Jounpoor', *Transactions of the Agricultural and Horticultural Society of India*, Vol. III, 1837, 101.

405 *The Calcutta Review*, 'Indigo Planters', p. 124.

406 *The Edinburgh Review*, Vol. CCLIV, October 1866, pp. 313–20.

407 The list of studies that analyse '1857' is endless; I here like to mention just one – adding to the one already mentioned in the previous chapter – which is a collection of essays, reviews, past debates and presents new research into the events constituting 1858. Bhattacharya, Sabyasachi (ed). *Rethinking 1857*, Hyderabad: Orient Blackswan, 2008.

408 The company was, however, officially dissolved in 1874 only, and Nick Robins rightly concluded, 'It continued to shape the economics and societies it had left behind.' Robins, p. 167.

409 *The National Review*. 'Bengal Planters and Ryots', Vol. XIV, January and April 1862, 114.

410 *The Edinburgh Review*, Vol. CCLIV, October 1866, pp. 299–340.

411 *The National Review*. 'Bengal Planters', p. 133.

412 *The National Review*. 'Bengal Planters', p. 133.

413 *The National Review*. 'Bengal Planters', pp. 133–34.

414 'English Life in Bengal', *The Calcutta Review*, Vol. XXXIII, July–December 1859, 345.

415 'Indigo and Indigo Planting', *The Calcutta Review*. Vol. XXX, March 1858, 228.

416 *The National Review, Ibid*, p. 134.

417 *The National Review, Ibid*, p. 130.

418 See for instance, Oddie, G. A., 'Protestant missionaries and social reform: the indigo planting questions in Bengal 1850–1860', *Journal of Religious History*, Vol. 3, No. 4, 314–26. Also: Dutta, A. *Christian Missionaries on the Indigo-Question in Bengal (1855–1861)*, Calcutta: Minerva Associates, 1989. At this juncture, missionaries did definitely not favor indigo planters. However, A. Christopher Smith described how the early Serampore Mission had been involved in an 'awkward indigo venture.' Smith, C. A. *The Serampore Mission Enterprise*, Bangalore: Centre for Contemporary Christianity, 2006, pp. 231–73.

419 Das, P. (editor and compiler). *Report of the Indigo Commission 1860*, Darjeeling: The Registrar, North Bengal University, 1992. See also:

Report of the Bengal Indigo Commission, 1860, with the Minutes of Evidence and Appendix, Calcutta: Printing and Publishing Press Government of India, 1860.

420 Kling, B. B. *The Blue Mutiny: The Indigo Disturbances in Bengal 1859–1862*, Philadelphia: University of Pennsylvania Press, 1966. For some reviews of this work, see for instance, K.N. Chaudhuri in *Bulletin of the School of Oriental and African Studies*, Vol. 31, No. 1, 1968, pp. 170–71 and by Barbara Ramusack. *The Journal of Asian Studies*, Vol. 26, No. 3, May 1967, pp. 511–12.

421 The play was translated into English by Michael Madhusudan Datta at the time. Guha, Ranajit., 'Neel-Darpan: The Image of a Peasant Revolt in a Liberal Mirror', *Journal of Peasant Studies*, Vol. 2, No. 1, October 1974, pp. 1–46. See also: *The National Review*. 'Bengal Planters', p. 119.

422 *The National Review*. 'Bengal Planters', p. 123.

423 Guha called this resistance 'one of the mightiest peasant revolts in the subcontinent.' Guha, 'Neel-Darpan', p. 1.

424 *The National Review*. 'Bengal Planters', p. 115.

425 *The National Review*. 'Bengal Planters', p. 129.

426 Sah, R. 'Features of British Indigo in India', *Social Scientist*, Vol. 9, No. 2/3, September–October 1980, 71. In a *Minute* by Lt. Gov. G.P. Grant of September 17, 1860 on a petition of the Indigo Planters' Association, Grant ruled: 'To calm the minds of the Ryots, and to secure the tranquility of the country, it appears to me essential that such a proclamation shall be immediately issued, as will make the ryots feel secure against coercion.' Judicial Department, *Indigo Protest*, September 1860, Proceedings No: 236.

427 This refers to the region later known as the Samastipur subdivision, the southern subdivision of the new Darbhanga District (of the six subdivisions, the three western had been formed into the new district of Muzaffarpur and the three eastern, viz. Darbhangah, Madhubani, and Tajpur, had been reconstituted into the district of Darbhanga). With the exception of the low lands (for rice cultivation) between the Bhagmati and Burhi Gandak Rivers, the subdivision consisted of a large block of upland (*bhith*) which was considered 'the richest and most fertile part of the district, producing the most valuable *rabi* and *bhadoi* crops, and it is also the centre of the indigo industry'. The government estate of

Pusa was located in this subdivision, *The Imperial Gazetteer of India*, new edition, published under the authority of His Majesty's Secretary of State for India in Council, Oxford: Clarendon Press, 1908–1931 (Vol. 1, 1909), Vol. 22, p. 2 (obtained through Digital South Asia Library).

428 See also Shukla, P. K. 'Indigo Cultivation and the Rural Crisis in North Bihar in the Second Half of the Nineteenth Century', *Proceedings of the Indian History Congress*, Forty-Ninth Session 1988, Karnataka University Dharwad, 1989, p. 463.

429 Sah, 'Features of British Indigo, p. 74.

430 Houlton, *Bihar*, p. 117. Also: Mittel, *Peasant Unprisings*, p. 13 and p. 14. This did not necessarily mean, however, that sugarcane cultivation by peasants reduced, and even indigo planters remained somewhat involved in the trade if not production of *khandsari* to supply the European market with Indian sugar, as pointed out in Chapter Three. Indian traders retained control of the export of this sugar from Bihar, however, as Bosma described, 'Via either Calcutta or the caravan trade over the Hindu Kush to Central Asia.' Bosma, *The Sugar Plantation in India*, p. 79, pp. 85–86.

431 Cf. Pouchepadass, J. *Land, Power and Market. A Bihar District under Colonial Rule, 1860–1947*, New Delhi: Sage, 2000.

432 Most indigo concerns were owned or managed by Europeans, and an (British) administrative servant of the government in 1872 reported, 'The value and quantity of European indigo is out of all proportion compared to the native-made indigo', and it added that, 'In Behar, as in Bengal, the industry is almost entirely managed by Europeans, for the few native zemindars and bankers who have invested their money directly in the business almost all employ European managers.' Bagchi, A. K. and Bandopadhyay, A. (eds.). *Eastern India in the Late Nineteenth Century, Part I: 1860s–1870s*, Documents on Economic History of British Rule in India, 1858–1947, New Delhi: Manohar, 2009, p. 143 and p. 144.

433 Royle, p. 101.

434 Cf. Royle, p. 101.

435 D'Oyly, Sir Hastings. *Tales Retailed of Celebrities & Others*, London: John Lane, The Bodley Head and New York: John Lane Company: 1920, p. 53. On p. 55. D'Oyly ended this story by narrating that, 'On

arrival at Mozufferpore we found the 19th Regiment were still there as the country had not yet quietly settled down after the exciting times of the Indian Mutiny'.

436 Wilson, M. *History of Behar Light Horse Volunteers*, pp. 305–19. See also the cover photograph of this book. A concise history of the Bihar Light Horse mentioned: 'The following three remarks have been overheard about the Bihar Light Horse:

1. *Do you know what BLH stands for?—Britain's last hope!*

2. Ek Hath Per Zin – one hand on the saddle

   Ek Hath Per Ras – one hand on the reins

   Kon Hath Per Kirich! – what hand for the sword!

   Bihar Light Harse—Bihar Light Horse

3. By a staff sergeant to a GOC who came up to inspect the Bihar Light Horse and inquired what sort of men the Bihar Light Horse were. His answer was: 'They salutes no-one! Cleans nothink! Takes no h'orders! But rides like 'ell!' But from the following extracts from three different viceroys, you will find what a very fine volunteer regiment the Bihar Light Horse always were. Lord Curzon, Viceroy and Governor General of India, wrote 1st April 1905:

'Their famous and traditional loyalty has for nearly half-a-century presented to the Government one of the finest Volunteer regiments in India'. Available in library of the Centre of South Asian Studies Cambridge University, Cambridge.

437 Mishra, 'Indigo Plantation and the Agrarian Relations in Champaran', p. 335.

438 'Bengal Planters', p. 130. Compare this with P.K. Shukla who formulated this as follows: 'The experiences of the Mutiny and the motives of imperial interest caused the expediency of creating pockets of European population intended to support the empire in times of emergency.', p. 464.

439 Cf. Bagchi and Bandopadhyay. *Eastern India in the Late Nineteenth Century*, p. 94.

440 See for instance for employment to the 'Dhangads' as the migrant labourers (mainly Oraons) from Chota Nagpur were called, Toppo, Ranjit. *Dynamics of Tribal Migration in India*, Ranchi: XISS, 2007, pp. 151–66; for employment to the 'Nooniah', a class which had formerly

'gained their livelihood by preparing the saltpeter in its crude state and supplying in to the refiners', but of late years, a famine report of 1866 stated, 'Owing to the imposition of a considerable export duty and the successful competition of the substitute for saltpetre which is now manufactured in Europe, the trade has gradually declined, and at the present prices obtainable, the Nooniahs can no longer make a living out of it' (saltpeter), Bagchi and Bandopadhyay, p. 242. See also: Bagchi, A. K. and Bandopadhyay, A. (eds). *Eastern India in the Late Nineteenth Century, Part II: 1880s–1890s*, 2011, p. 368: 'The condition of artisans is treated very shortly, and people who subsist on charity are declared very few. Artisans appear, as in other places, to be better off than the lowest class of cultivators. In Mozuffarpore, about the indigo factories, this is true also of the laborers'.

441 Yet G. Levett-Yeats in a study of poppy cultivation in Bihar that was published at the end of nineteenth century qualified that although the cultivation of the poppy 'is extremely profitable, and hence popular among all castes, it is not followed with equal success by all of them. The brahmin, the thakur, the raj, and the mussulman are considered to be the least able to make the crop pay.' 'In the Land of the White Poppy', *MacMillan's Magazine*, No. 77, 1897, p. 188.

442 'Document 17. Famine Report: Famine in Behar and Sonthal Pergunnahs, 1866. Papers and correspondence, including the report of the Famine Commission and the Minutes of the Lieutenant-Governor of Bengal and the Governor-General', Bagchi and Bandopadhyay, pp. 239–97.

443 D'Oyly remembered that when Lord Mayo had come to inspect the government stud at Pusa in 1869, Captain Farquhar had been in charge and had opened a school for the children of natives employed at the stud/farm. D'Oyly narrated that Lord Mayo 'and the ladies of his party', who had known 'Johnny Farquhar as a smart man about town', had been 'astonished to find him taking an interest in schools for native children! It was too funny for words.' D'Oyly, *Tales Retailed*, p. 83.

444 An Ex-Civilian, *Life in the Mofussil*, p. 101. For instance, W. H. Urquhart, a deputy opium agent at Mozaffarpur had two sons, both planters, D'Oyly, *Tales Retailed*, p. 67.

445 An Ex-Civilian, *Life in the Mofussil,* p. 83. D'Oyly described various members among the more or less white society in rural Bihar during those decades: 'At Beheea in a magnificent house lived three men, Messrs. Burrowes, Mylne, and Thomson, who made large fortunes in the Shahabad district of Bengal. They made themselves very useful in the Mutiny and by their knowledge of the district they gave valuable assistance to Sir Vincent Eyre's forces, as guides, when he fought and pursued the rebel Koer Singh's army up to Sasseram, where he finally and completely defeated them. After the Mutiny was over Messrs. Thomson, Burrowes, and Mylne got from Government as reward for their valuable services a long lease, at a very low rental, of the whole of Koer Singh's extensive estates which had been sequestered. These estates were mostly covered with jungle which the lessees cleared, and many thousands of acres were thus brought under cultivation and let out in regularly defined plots to the ryots. The wilderness was turned into a fruitful land, much to the advantage of both the landlords and ryots. When I was Magistrate [. . .] [T]hey kept open house and nearly always had some guests staying with them. Michael Fox's brother (from the adjoining estate and had become partner), Charles Fox, was Manager of the estates of the Maharajah of Doomraon, who during the Mutiny remained loyal to the Government.' D'Oyly, *Tales Retailed,* p. 89. These three men from Beheea also invented a new type of sugar mill which became famous all over somewhat later (see also Chapter Eight).

446 Denis Hayes Crofton, who was an Indian Civil Servant (ICS) in Bihar during the 1930s and 1940s, had written at the age of eighty-four that 'the competitive examination by which I passed into the I.C.S. was on lines very similar to that recommended by Lord Macaulay's Committee in 1854 for recruiting officers to the service of the East India Company in place of the system of nomination by Directors which had hitherto prevailed'. Such recruits were known as 'competition wallahs', Hayes explained, and this is, 'what I am entitled to call myself.' Crofton, D. H. *Souvenirs of a Competition Wallah. Letters and Sketches from India 1932–1947,* Kent: Volturna Press, 1994, p. xii.

447 Wilson, M. J., *History of Behar Indigo Factories; Reminiscences of Behar; Tirhoot and its Inhabitants of the Past; History of Behar Light*

Horse Volunteers (1908), Kessinger Legacy Reprints, Original Version: Calcutta: The Calcutta General Printing Company, 1908.

448   D'Oyly, *Tales Retailed*, p. 56. Yet, on p. 60, D'Oyly described a scene during the famous Sonepur Fair in Sarun district in Bihar, 'where the Gunduk River separates it from the district of Tirhoot and flows into the Ganges'. During this large fair, 'thousands of Hindoos from almost all parts of India' assembled yet stayed apart from the 'Europeans' who had the western part of the fair reserved for them. Besides, apart from a 'military camp for the officers of the regiments stationed at Dinapore on the opposite side of the Ganges', there had been a separate 'planters' camp', and each of these camps had their own dining tents. The fair would last ten days during which horse races made the Europeans mix. Besides, one day 'is given up to calling at the various camps and to going over the native fair'. Cf. Yang, A. A. *Bazaar India. Markets, Society, and the Colonial State in Bihar*, Berkeley, Los Angeles, London: University of California Press, 1989, pp. 123–28 and pp. 158–59. Horses played an important role in the lives of these two groups of Englishmen at the time, and the government stud at Pusa before becoming a model farm for tobacco experiments had been their central meeting point. See for instance D'Oyly, *Tales Retailed*, pp. 82–83.

449   I will not much more elaborate upon the way indigo planters looked upon government officials in Bihar, yet I have enough material to do so as I have been fortunate enough to come across some autobiographies of indigo planters in Bihar. These 'jewels' convey the 'culture of indigo' in Tirhut at different points in time. One of best, I acquired through Bob Janes and is the unpublished *Autobiographical Sketch of My Life and Times for My Children* by William Sharpley of Yorkshire and Tirhut, transcribed by Bob Janes (RDJ) who is still working on it. Unfortunately, however, the version of the manuscript which I received from Bob Janes personally does not contain any chronology or dates in the text. I, therefore, used for the purpose of this book the version of the manuscript which I already found on the Internet on March 23, 2010 and which contains such chronology. This version had last been modified on September 4, 2005 (starting date 1991). I am greatly indebted to Bob Janes. The second autobiography is a published one entitled *Sport and Work on the Nepaul Frontier or Twelve Years Sporting*

Reminiscences of an Indigo Planter by 'Maori' (James, A. S. Inglis), which is now thanks to Project Gutenberg an e-Book released on January 24, 2004 and downloaded on September 18, 2008. The original book was written in 1878. The third jewel used by me for this chapter is another published one entitled *The Culture and Manufacture of Indigo: With A Description of A Planter's Life and Resources* by W.M. Reid published by Thacker, Spink and Co., Calcutta in 1887. The last autobiography is the more quoted but nevertheless valuable one by Wilson, Minden J., *History of Behar Indigo Factories, Ibid*. There are more 'memoirs' and 'reminiscences' of Tirhut by indigo planters as well as civil servants which have helped me to shape my argument for this chapter and foremost are: Houlton, J. *Bihar: The Heart of India*, Mumbai: Orient Longmans, 1949, Chapter XXI: 'Indigo. The Planters of Tirhut', pp. 115–19 and Beames, John. *Memoirs of a Bengal Civilian. Lively Narrative of a Victorian District Officer*, London: Chatto & Windus and Hippocrene, 1961.

450   Cf. An Ex-Civilian. *Life in the Mofussil*, p. 101.

451   There also were differences between those working in what were known as the 'uncovenanted' and 'covenanted' services of the government (i.e., without or with a formal contract and having passed an examination, the 'competition *wallahs*'). The work of the former (very often carried out by so-called Eur-Asians), D'Oyly argued, 'was hard and the pay comparatively poor.' D'Oyly. *Tales Retailed*, p. 64.

452   An Ex-Civilian. *Life in the Mofussil*, p. 251.

453   Letters from an artist in India to his sisters in England, p. 72.

454   General Department. *Administrative Report of the Bhaugulpore Division for 1872–73*, No. 1266, July 5, 1873.

455   General Department. *Administrative Report of the Bhaugulpore Division for 1872–1873*, No. 1266, July 5, 1873. Rev. G. G. Cuthbert mentioned around 1858: 'I had often heard that a better system prevails in Tirhoot; but, I met, not long ago, a professional gentleman, who had been for some years resident in that district, and knew both the Planters and the people well; and from what he told me I could not but come to the conclusion that the same evils which I was aware of in the system nearer Calcutta, prevail to an equal extent in Tirhoot'. Yet, 'I ought in candour to add, that I have, still more lately, conversed with a friend in the Civil

Service, who was for some time stationed in that district, and it is in his opinion that the Indigo cultivation does not press so heavily there upon the ryots as in some other places, which he ascribes to a larger proportion of *neej* cultivation, (i.e. cultivation on his own account of lands held on lease or otherwise by the Planter himself) that prevails in those parts.' A Ryot. *Selections from Papers on Cultivation in Bengal*, p. 36.

456 D'Oyly, for instance, had admired Mr. George Grant, who 'commenced his career in India as an impecunious adventurer' but later on had turned everything he touched into gold: 'He got employment in an indigo factory near Colgong. Living with his boss, the manager, he had few expenses and so was able to save. He increased his savings by lending small sums to native ryots, at a high rate of interest. Thus after a few years he was able to buy a small share in the factory. Eventually he became the sole owner [. . .] Later he built a small branch factory ('outwork') on a spot where a stream ran out from the hills into the plains. He selected this spot because he had observed that the crops on each side of this steam were particularly fine, owing to the iron and other ingredients in the water. For the indigo manufactured there, he always got the highest prices in the Calcutta market [. . .] I gave him a lease of the forests and mineral products of the Khuruckpore estate, belonging to the Maharajah of Durbhunga, who was a minor, whose estates were under the Court of wards, and I had to manage such of them as were in my district. Gregor Grant was a wonderfully healthy and very strong man [. . .] After thirty years or more in India he became a very rich man, worth a good many lacs of rupee.' D'Oyly, *Tales Retailed*, pp. 107–08.

457 General Department (Misc.). *Annual General Report, Patna Division, 1876–77*, Proceedings No.1–15, November 1877.

458 In an illuminating article, Colin Fisher explained why indigo cultivation had been disliked by peasants even in these *zeerat* lands (i.e., the *neej* cultivation mentioned above): 'The cultivators/labourers blamed the high costs of food on indigo, the rich cultivators resented planter's control over their holdings, and the landowners and controllers objected to the planter's increasing influence in the villages'. Fisher concluded: 'The pre-conditions existed for a widespread popular revolt against

indigo.' Fisher, Colin M. 'Planters and Peasants: The Ecological Context of Agrarian Unrest on the Indigo Plantations in North Bihar', Dewey, Clive and Hopkins, A.G. (eds), *The Imperial Impact: Studies in the Economic History of Africa and India*, London: The Athlone Press, University of London, 1978, p. 127.

459   Bengal Judicial Department Proceedings No.: 49–55 of February 1867 (Indigo Revolt in Tirhut).

460   Judicial Department, No. 232, 1868. See also: Mishra, 'Indigo Plantation', pp. 349–50.

461   Choudharym R.B. 'Lawrence and Indigo Cultivation in Bihar', *Proceedings of the Thirty Third Session of the Indian History Congress*, Muzaffarpur, 1972, p. 546.

462   Judicial Department, October 1868, Part I, Proceedings 209–32. Interestingly, D'Oyly remembered that around this time, Sir William Hudson, known to his friends as Paddy Hudson, had been president of the Bihar Planters' Association. When D'Oyly had been the opium agent at Patna, his brother-in-law, Fred Halliday, had been the commissioner of Revenue and Circuit of the Patna Division. The latter had been called upon by the government to inquire and report 'on some contemplated legislation in connection with the relations between indigo planters and the natives of the districts where indigo was cultivated', and Fred Halliday had sent copies of the correspondence to Paddy Hudson for a report on the views held by indigo planters. After a short time, Hudson, who according to D'Oyly 'was a bit of a wag', had submitted his 'so-called report which consisted of a number of sheets of foolscap headed this: From W.B. Husdon, President, Behar Planters' Association. To the Commissioner of the Patna Division. Dated Mozufferpore the of – Then had followed many '*blank* pages at the end of which were the words: I am, Sir, your obedient servant, *Signed* W.B. Hudson'. Attached to this had been a note from Hudson, in which he had said, 'I submit the annexed report; will you kindly fill up the hiatus?' D'Oyly concluded the story: 'Of course the papers were returned to Paddy to be filled up and eventually Fred Halliday got a very good report on the subject.' D'Oyly, *Tales Retailed*, pp. 80–81.

463   Judicial Department, Judicial Department, October 1868, Part I, Proceedings 209–32.

464 Revenue Department, Proceedings No. 61 and 62, File No. 4–13, February–April 1873.

465 Judicial Department, No. 228, May 17, 1868.

466 Choudhary, 'Lawrence and Indigo Cultivation', p. 547.

467 W.W. Hunter in 1886 noted down that even the *zeerat* system which prevailed in Muzaffarpur and Dharbhanga (Tirhut) – but not in Champaran where the *assamiwar* form of indigo production was dominant—'for a time gave rise to strained relations between the planters, the native landholders, and the tenants', and the system had 'its own complications.' Hunter, W.W. *The Indian Empire. Its People, History and Products*, New Delhi and Madras: Asian Educational Services, 2005 (original London: Trübner & Co., 1886), p. 497.

468 Choudharym, 'Lawrence and Indigo Cultivation', p. 550.

469 Annual General Report of the Patna Division, *From S.C. Bayley, Esq., Offg. Commissioner of the Patna Division to The Secretary to the Government of Bengal, General Department*, No. 85, dated Bankipore, the September 8, 1873.

470 Judicial Department (Police), *Mozufferpore Indigo Riot Case*, Proceedings No.37–44, File No. 278, April–June 1875. See for another case of enforced cultivation of European indigo planters by violent or illegal measures: File 429, Proceedings No. 14–18, August 1876. For the same case in which 'two Europeans and four natives in their employ were charged with having forcibly attempted to sow indigo on certain village lands', Proceedings No. 3, No. 819, June 15, 1876. In this case, one of the 'Europeans' had been employed in the Tirhoot state railway but was now no longer permitted to remain in government service. For the same case see also: Judicial Department (Police) Proceedings 1–2, September 1876 and Proceeding No. 14, December 1876.

471 Judicial Department (Police), *Mozufferpore Indigo Riot Case*, Proceeding No. 44, No. 1147, June 19, 1875.

472 Judicial Department, File 1–146, Proceedings 56–61, *Relation between Indigo Planters and their Ryots*, August 1877. See also Mishra in 'Indigo Plantation', who commented on p. 352: 'As the mood of the Government became favorable to the appointment of an enquiry commission, the planters formed their association in 1877–1878 and gave an undertaking to the government to behave themselves'.

473 Sah, *Social Scientist,* p. 70.

474 In 1875, during the rule of Sir Richard Temple in Bengal, the establishment of a second district in Tirhut in Bihar, with headquarters at Darbhanga, was proposed as the area was considered too great (with a population of 4,350,000 persons) and thus beyond the power of the collector for effective management and supervision. It was considered to be 'double the average size in difficulty and importance of an ordinary district in Bengal'. The result was, administrators judged, food scarcity in Bihar, and therefore, it was decided there would be an 'East Tirhoot' (with 'Mudhoobunnee, Durbhunga, and Tajpore') as new district with headquarters at 'Durbhunga'. The remainder of the old district (Mozufferpore, Hajeepore, and Seetamurhee) would hence be called 'West Tirhoot.' Report on the Administration of Bengal 1873–1874, Calcutta Secretariat Press, 1875, p. 5. See also General Miscellaneous Branch (File 2J-2 B Proceedings 248–250, December 1908), in which it was mentioned that in that year (1908), the Tirhut Division was created comprising the districts of Muzaffarpur, Darbhanga, Saran, and Champaran.

475 Mishra, 'Indigo Plantation', p. 352.

476 Interestingly, Fisher noted that the government had also had a problem with indigo in this particular area as they felt that the planters 'were filching opium land'. These, thus, were, Fisher concluded, 'squabbles between capitalists and capitalists.' Fisher, 'Planters and Peasants', p. 125.

477 Hunter, *The Indian Empire,* p. 498. Compare with Shukhla, *Indigo and the Raj,* p. 101: 'The basic identity of interests of the planters, the zamindars and the government comes out clearly from the evidence available for Bihar in the second half of the nineteenth century. While the planters were interested in the profit, the zamindars in rent and the government in remittance – all of them at the cost of the raiyats and the common masses – collaboration among them was an essence of their relationship'. Indeed, the government had also to 'pacify' the *zamindars* who in 1861 had staged protest, see for instance: Petition Against the Income Tax of the Zemindars of Bengal, Behar, and Orissa to the Imperial Parliament, Calcutta: Printed at Scott and Co's Press, 1861 (LSE Selected Pamphlets). The relation between Indian landholders

and British indigo planters was in particular testing, and both sides had not much commitment in their partnership in the field of 'agrarian improvement'.

478 Cf. Mittal, *Peasants Uprisings*, p. 22. Within Germany, there had been a different competition, see: Lauterbach, Fritz, *Der Kampf des Waides mit dem Indigo,* Inaugural Dissertation, Universität Leipzig, Leipzig: Veit & Comp., 1905.

479 Though European planters had almost abandoned industrial sugar manufacturing, sugarcane *(akh)* was still grown 'on first-class highland' and made into *gur* by Indian cultivators in particular in the Darbhangah Subdivision. *Gur* was largely used for sweetmeats and for mixing with tobacco which was intended for smoking in *hookahs*. Hunter, W.W. *A Statistical Account of Bengal,* Vol. XIII, Tirhut and Champaran, (This volume was compiled by A. W. Mackie), London: Trübner & Co., 1877, p. 87.

480 Huggins, p. 163.

481 The Cultivation and Curing of Tobacco in Bengal, pp. 81–84.

482 Hunter, *A Statistical Account of Bengal,* p. 89.

483 One report added that 'in addition to the staple crops, the Koiris largely cultivate potatoes and country vegetables. In cultivation, however, they are not so niggardly as the Goala; they live on better grain and give the husks to their cattle; they also do not breed cattle or sell milk, butter, etc., nor do they steal. A few of them are merchants in the town-avocation in which their industry usually renders them successful.' O'Malley, L. S. S. S., *Bihar and Orissa District Gazetteer (Patna)* (revised edition by J. F. W. James, I.C.S.), New Delhi: Logos Press, 2005 (reprint of 1924). *The Imperial Gazetteer of India* of 1881 (Vol. IX, Tapti-Zut-Thut and Index) on p. 85 mentioned: 'Koeris (227,046) are the best spade-husbandsmen in the country; they are identical with the Kachis of the North-Western Provinces, and are the chief cultivators of the poppy'. Yang summarised that 'Koeries and Kurmis were widely regarded throughout Bihar as the major, as well as the most efficacious, 'cultivating class.' Fourth in numerical strength among the district's castes, Koeris were represented in almost every village. Among the more important Kurmi caste clusters—the Ayodhiya, Saithwar and Jaiswar – the Ayodhias were particularly singled out as the 'substantial

farmers and . . . the most influential sub-caste.' Yang also argued that rates of rent were more directly related to local power configurations than they were to ecological factors. He quoted W. W. Hunter who had reported that high castes held the best lands in a village at rates varying from 50–75 per cent below what castes such as koeries and kurmis and chamars paid for inferior lands. Yang, p. 47 and p. 166.

484 Pogson, *Ibid*, p. 242.

485 Royle, *Ibid*, p. 102.

486 Quoted in Royle, *Ibid*, p. 97.

487 Wyatt, *Ibid*, p. 10

488 A British planter had cautioned, however, that till then his endeavour to 'improve' tobacco cultivation had 'met with the greatest *passive resistance* [emphasis mine] even by the people who cultivate my own fields.' N.A. *The Cultivation*, p. 168. T.F. Peppe, an opium officer in 1874 already guessed that 'possibly *the native idea might be found to be antagonistic to European ideas* [emphasis mine]; and the tobacco, liked by the natives would not be relished by Europeans.' *Ibid*, p. 177.

489 N.A. *The Cultivation*, pp. 165–66.

490 'Letter from Mr. R. Bathurst, collector of Tirhut to Mr. J. White, subsecretary, reporting that the cultivation of the Virginia tobacco will be taken up on the arrival of the seed.' Home Department. *A Public Consultation*, August 6 1790, No. 28.

491 Apart from indigo planters, a civil surgeon in a lunatic asylum in Dacca was, for instance, asked to do some experimental cultivation with Virginia tobacco seed, and the latter had made 'lunatics' to taste the result and asked them to tell him whether they liked the tobacco or not (the report added that the latter thought the tobacco was 'excellent'). In another instance, seeds were distributed among the gardeners in a jail in Faridpur, and prisoners were now asked their opinion regarding the results (Revenue Dept. Sept. 1872). The army constituted another 'experimental group.' Report on the Administration of Bengal for 1876–1877, Calcutta, 1878, Part: Agriculture and Horticulture, p. 139.

492 See for instance, the *Pall Mall Gazette* which in 1870 stated: 'We owe our supplies of Indian cotton to the American war, and we may have to refer the cultivation of tobacco in our colonies to the present campaign. A good deal of the leaf employed in the manufacture of cut tobacco

comes to us from the Continent, and of course that source is now closed; but the smoker may be consoled by hearing that India, Jamaica and Natal are all engaged in cultivating the plant [. . .] What the Indian government has already done for the cultivation of tea, cinchona, and ipecacuanha, it is now doing for the tobacco plant. Seeds of the best varieties have been distributed in suitable districts, and the time may speedily come when the Bengal cheroot may be a production of the presidency.' 'Indian Tobacco', *Journal of the Society of Arts*, December 30, 1870, p. 117.

493   Hunter, *A Statistical Account,* p. 92.

494   A report on the Ghazipur tobacco farm mentioned that the tenants induced to settle there were mostly of the *kachhi* or *koeri* caste without occupancy rights and on short-term leases and did not attach much importance to *belatee* tobacco, and 'If the choice were left to the tenants, and there was no management to take the crop off their hands, they would certainly not grow Virginia tobacco, since it is too sweet and too mild to sell in the native market'. The report added: 'They probably would not grow tobacco at all, as tobacco-merchants do not come to Gházipur, and the local demand is precarious.' Government of India. Finance and Commerce Department. Accounts and Finance (Provincial Finances), A-Proceedings, July Nos. 776–781. Subject: Proposed surrender of the lease of the Ghazipur Tobacco Farm by Messrs. Begg, Dunlop & Co, p. 3.

495   Tripp, C. 'The tobacco industry of India and the far East', *Journal of the Society of Arts*, Vo. 44, March 13, 1896, p. 369 and p. 370.

496   Report on the Administration of Bengal, 1871–1872, 1873, p. 21

497   Report on the Administration of Bengal, 1870–1871, 1872, pp. 21–22.

498   See for more information on the Pusa Estate: Hunter, W.W., *Statistical Account of Bengal*, Vol. 13: Tirhut and Champaran, London: Trübner & Co, 1877, pp. 64–67.

499   Financial Department, Branch II, Agriculture, Head No. 2. Produce and Cultivation, Tobacco Cultivation, Collection 8: Extracts from the proceedings of the Government of India, in the Department of Revenue, Agriculture and Commerce, 1875.

500   Report from Mr. Paterson, superintendent of the Poosah Model Farm, on the plot of land at Durbhunga, where tobacco is proposed to be

grown, Collection 2, No. 30, February 4, 1875. See also: The Report on the Administration of Bengal 1875–1876, 1877, p. 166.

501 Government of India. Finance and Commerce Department. Accounts and Finance (Provincial Finances), A-Proceedings, July No. 776–781. Subject: Proposed surrender of the lease of the Ghazipur Tobacco Farm by Messrs. Begg, Dunlop & Co.

502 The Report on the Administration of Bengal for 1876–1877, 1878, pp. 138–39.

503 Cambell, G. 'Communication to the Government of India', *Proceedings,* No. 2270, August 12, 1873.

504 Begg, Dunlop & Co. had been in tea, indigo, and coffee and even had possessed coal mines, and Dr. David Begg had been a medical man turned indigo planter and merchant himself, yet for this venture, the company promised the government it would not cultivate indigo in Pusa. Cf. Munro, J. F. *Maritime Enterprise and Empire: Sir William Mackinnon and his Business Network 1823–1893*, Woodbridge, Suffolk: Boydell and Brewer, 2003, p. 39, pp. 96–97, p. 102 and p. 237.

505 Cambell, G. 'Communication to the Government of India', *Proceedings,* No. 2270, August 12, 1873. On the Ghazipur experiments by Messrs Begg, Dunlop & Co. see also: Director of Agriculture and Commerce in the NWP, 'Note on Tobacco Curing', *Collection 8, Proceedings No.: 5/6B,* March 1878.

506 Hume, *Ibid,* p. 102.

507 Report on the internal trade of Bengal for the year 1879–1880, Calcutta: Government of Bengal, 1880, 'Chapter III: Trade of large towns and commercial centres'.

508 Hunter, *The Indian Empire*, p. 500.

509 The Bengal District Gazetteer of Muzaffarpur, 1907, p. 104

Chapter Five:
Colonisation of Plants through British Scientists

510 MacLeod. *Scientific Advice for British India*, p. 344n8.

511 For a detailed discussion on 'the massive predatory and exploitative nature of the imperial railway project under the façade of Britain's benevolence to the people of India', Satya, L. 'British imperial railways

in nineteenth century South Asia, *Economic and Political Weekly*, November 22, 2008, p. 69.

512   Mukerji, N. G. *Handbook of Indian Agriculture*, Calcutta: Thacker, Spink and Co., 1915, p. 1

513   Thavaraj, M. J. K., 'Framework of economic policies under British rule', *Social Scientist*, Vol. 7, No. 5, December 1978, p. 26.

514   Watt. *A Dictionary of the Economic Products of India*, preface.

515   MacLeod. *Scientific Advice for British India*, p. 344. See also: Kumar, D. 'Science in Agriculture: a study in Victorian India', *Asian Agri-History*, Vol. 1, No. 2, 1997, pp. 77–103.

516   Cf. MacLeod, *Scientific Advice for British India*, p. 343–84.

517   Robb. 'Bihar, the Colonial State', p. 215.

518   The director of the Pusa Institute and the agricultural adviser to the Government of India became vested in one and the same incumbent, Royal Commission on Agriculture in India, *Evidence of Officers Serving Under the Government of India*, Vol. 1, Part II, Calcutta: Government of India Central Publication Branch, 1928, p. 125.

519   MacLeod. *Scientific Advice for British India*, p. 352.

520   After a huge earthquake in 1934, the main building of the institute at Pusa was damaged beyond repair. In 1935, the institute was shifted to Delhi, but Pusa survived in independent India as the Indian Agricultural Research Institute and remained under the Government of India till 1966.

521   Wigglesworth, A. 'The Agricultural Research Institute, Pusa', *United Empire: The Royal Colonial Institute Journal*, Vol. 17, No. 3, 1926, pp. 140–42.

522   Sikka, S. M. and Swaminathan, M. S. 'Fifty years of Botanical Research at the Indian Agricultural Research Institute', *Euphytica*, Vol. 4, 1955, p. 173.

523   Chakravarti, R. 'Early Medieval Bengal and the Trade in Horses: A Note', *Journal of the Economic and Social History of the Orient*, Vol. 42, No. 2, 1999, p. 197.

524   *The London Gazette*, August 10, 1888 mentioned on p. 4304 that 'the partnership between merchants Donald Horne Macfarlane, Henry Holmes Sutherland, David Cruickshank, and John Frederick Macnair who carried on business in London, and at Calcutta, under the style or

firm of Begg, Dunlop, and Co., and at Cawnpore, under the style or firm of Begg, Sutherlands, and Co., was dissolved, as far as regards the said Henry Holmes Sutherland, by his retirement from the firms'.

525 Even before Curzon, lieutenant governor of Bengal, Sir R. Temple had already aimed at (and also shown in Chapter Four), 'developing the resources of the country by scientific methods'. 'It had been found necessary', he had written, 'to close the several model farms which had been temporarily established in Bengal because it was found that success could not be attained without scientific means and appliances much beyond any resources which we have at our command'. Instead of all these model farms, Temple had proposed to concentrate on one of them only, the Pusa farm, and convert this into a place not only for tobacco experimentation but possibly also 'for the establishment of an Agricultural College for Bihar'. Moreover, the experiments in Pusa had to be conducted by 'trained scientific officers', that was 'men of high scientific acquirements.' Buckland, C. E. *Bengal under the Lieutenant-Governors; being a Narrative of the Principal Events and Public Measures during their Periods of Office, from 1854 to 1898,* in two volumes, Vol. II., Calcutta: S.K. Lahiri & Co., 1901, p. 616.

526 However, MacKenna had argued it was only 'till the Indian Budget of 1905–06 that Lord Curzon's Government found it possible to place the scientific study of agricultural problems on a thoroughly sound basis', MacKenna, J. 'Scientific agriculture in India', *Journal of the Royal Society of Arts*, Vol. LXIV, June 9, 1916, pp. 540–41.

527 O'Malley L. S. S. *Bengal District Gazetteers.* Darbhanga, New Delhi: Logos Press, 2013 (Reprint of 1907), p. 154.

528 Curzon also introduced closer relations between the Government of India and the commercial world, and a special Department of Commerce and Industry was established in 1905, to which were handed most of the existing government functions with regard to industry and commerce. Anstey, V. *The Economic Development of India.* London: Longmans, Green and Co., 1952, p. 347.

529 Cf. McLane, J. R. 'The decision to partition Bengal in 1905', *Indian Economic and Social History Review,* July 1965, Vol. 2, No. 3, pp 221–37.

530 Rothamsted is known in England as the oldest agricultural research station in the world. It was established in 1843 and was the first

institution to start long-term field experiments. By 1900, the need for statistical methods was felt, however, and presently, Rothamsted is known as the birthplace of modern statistical theory and practice. Cf. MacLeod. *Scientific Advice for India,* p. 364.

531 MacLeod. 'Scientific Advice for British India', p. 364.

532 Buckland, C. E. *Bengal under the Lieutenant-Governors,* p. 616.

533 The textbooks prepared and used by the institute adopted a botanical and an economic classification of crops.

534 Cf. McKeich, C. 'Botanical Fortunes', *re-Collections: Journal of the National Museum of Australia,* Vol. 3, No. 1, p. 2.

535 Cf. Galloway, J. H., 'Botany in the service of empire: the Barbados cane-breeding program and the revival of the Caribbean sugar industry, 1880–1930s', *Annals of the Association of American Geographers,* Vol. 86, No. 4, December 1996, pp. 682–706.

536 The emblem of the Pusa Institute in 1905 read the motto of the British Monarch: 'Dieu et Mon Droit; Honi Soit Qui Mal Y Pense' (God and my Right; Evil to him who Evil thinks).

537 Economic Botany had, thus, finally got 'disciplinary status.' Cf. Clark, J. F. M., 'Bugs in the System: Insects, Agricultural Science, and Professional Aspirations in Britain, 1890–1920', *Agricultural History,* Vol. 75, No. 1, Winter, 2001, p. 97 and p. 98.

538 For instance, Scientific Reports of the Agricultural Research Institute and College, Pusa; Bulletins; Memoirs (with separate Series) of the Department of Agriculture in India; Annual Reports of the Imperial Department of Agriculture in India; Annual Reviews; Proceedings of the Board of Agriculture in India; The Agricultural Journal of India; books and dedicated publications such as the 'Indigo Publications'.

539 Cf. Lupton, A. *Happy India as it Might be if Guided by Modern Science,* NP, 1922. Lupton was a British Liberal Party politician.

540 Worboys, M. 'British Colonial Science Policy, 1918–1939', Patrick Petitjean. (ed) *Colonial Sciences: Researchers and Institutions,* Paris: Orstom, 1996, pp. 108–09.

541 Mukerji, *Handbook,* p. 603.

542 For the connection between the Botanical Garden in Calcutta and the Kew Gardens in London, see also: Chakrabarti, *Western Science in Modern India,* p. 10, p. 73 and pp. 82–83 and p. 94.

543 These were known as 'economic products' that were arranged in geographical order and displayed in the public galleries of the Imperial Institute. The following 'British Colonies and Dependencies' were represented: Canada, Newfoundland; Jamaica, Turks Islands, British Honduras, British Guiana, Bahama Islands, Trinidad and Tobago, Barbados, Windward Islands, Leeward Islands, Bermuda Islands Falkland Islands, New South Wales, Victoria, Queensland, Tasmania, South Australia, Western Australia, New Zealand, Fiji; Cape of Good Hope, Natal, Transvaal, Orange River Colony, Rhodesia, Nyasaland, St. Helena; Gambia, Sierra Leone, Gold Coast, Northern Nigeria, Southern Nigeria, British East Africa, Zanzibar and Pemba; Uganda; Somaliland; the Anglo-Egyptian Soudan; Malta; Cyprus; Ceylon; Hong Kong; Mauritius; Seychelles; Straits Settlements and Federated Malay States; and India, *Bulletin of the Imperial Institute*, Vol. VII, 1909, p. ii.

544 In 1907, in virtue of an arrangement made with the Board of Trade and with the approval of the secretary of state for India, the management of the Imperial Institute was transferred to the Secretary of State for the Colonies, subject to the responsibility of the Board of Trade under the Act of 1902, *Bulletin of the Imperial Institute*, Vol. VII, 1909, p. i.

545 The work of the Scientific and Technical Department was chiefly initiated by the Home and Colonial Governments and the Government of India. Besides, arrangements had been made by the Foreign Office, 'whereby British representatives abroad may transmit to the department for investigation of such natural products of the countries in which they are appointed to reside as are likely to be of interest to British manufacturers and merchants', *Bulletin of the Imperial Institute*, Vol. VII, 1909, p.iii and iv.

546 When Lord Reading, viceroy of India at the time, reviewed the progress of the institute around 1926, he was happy to have observed that 'careful research and experiment by scientists in their laboratory and experimental farms had 'added in the past few years crores of rupees to the wealth of the agriculturists'. Besides, it had not only benefitted India but also 'other possessions of the empire'. Moreover, this research had improved the 'fertility of the land', and plant breeding had evolved 'types of seed capable of giving the best results under certain conditions',

and it was believed that the establishment of such research institutes 'throughout the empire is certain to form one of the bonds which will link the English-speaking people together'. Such a bond of union could not 'be too intimate', the Viceroy felt, and added that more of these institutes should be established 'to show the world the capacity of Great Britain to come into the front rank in regard tropical agriculture', Wigglesworth, The Agricultural Research Institute, p. 140.

547   Galloway, '*Botany in the Service of Empire*', p. 683.

548   Cf. James MacKenna, agricultural adviser to the Government of India and director of the Pusa Institute from 1916 to 1920, described in this article on scientific agriculture in India that it had to be realised that it was only since about the year 1900, that agricultural science and education in England had boomed. In England, 'the development of scientific agriculture was forced by necessity and 'by the clamant voice of youth anxious to get the equipment of scientific knowledge and exploit it, in most cases, far from their native land'. In India, too, MacKenna had continued, 'The appeal was irresistible, and, just as England had its early enthusiasts, so these young exiles, influencing the Government under which they worked, stirred up from the beginning an agricultural policy and directed the attention of Government to improvement of agriculture.' MacKenna, 'Scientific Agriculture in India', p. 538, p. 539.

549   Baber. 'Colonizing nature', p. 37.

550   Prakash Kumar considered indigo, unlike sugarcane, not 'a native crop of Bihar'. My reasoning differs, however, and I argue that around 1760, all the three plants, that is sugarcane, tobacco, and indigo producing plants. could be called 'native plants' (or colonised by different forces than the British), but by 1900, indigo had been fully 'colonised' by British (interests) and thus had become a 'foreign' plant. As I will show in this chapter, further efforts to colonise sugarcane and tobacco in similar way continued after 1900. Cf. Kumar, P. 'Scientific experiments in British India: Indigo Planters, Scientists, and the State, 1890–1930', *Indian Economic and Social History Review*, Vol. 38, No. 3, 2001, p. 264.

551   Nitya Gopal Mukerji, an Indian scientist employed as professor of agriculture in the Civil Engineering College in Sibpur (Bengal), emphasised, however, in 1915 that this 'crisis' was much complicated and caused by various factors: '(1) the quarrel between indigo planters and

raiyats on the one hand and zemindars on the other, (2) the extension of indigo cultivation in the United Provinces, the Punjab [. . .] and in Madras, and the consequent competition which reduced the price to the lowest level, (3) the passing of the industry into Indian hands almost everywhere except in Tirhut, which has resulted in inferiority of produce and (4) the manufacture of the dye by the synthetic process in Germany.' Mukerji, *Handbook, Ibid.*, p. 299. Donald Reid, an indigo planter managing a concern in Bihar's Saran District, elaborated on Mukerji's explanation one and explained: 'I have always felt that the most hopeless and demoralising part of a Behar planter's system of working with the ryots of his farm villages is a knowledge of the fact that he is doing harm to the helpless people and their cattle instead of good. And, even although he may not have business relations with one-tenth of the men in the neighbourhood of his factories, still the terror of his name and his reputation as a land-grabber are sufficient to induce the wretched ryots to submit to the most galling imposition from their landlord in preference to having their villages made over in farm to the planter.' Reid, Donald N. 'The disaffection in Behar', *The Fortnightly Review*, Vol. 55, p. 814.

552   Of course, this was not only to help these 'poor planters' but more an effort to salvage the economic hegemony of the British Empire which was in particular threatened by Germany in matters of colours.

553   Fraser, L. *India Under Curzon & After*, London: William Heinemann, mcmxi (1911), p. 319.

554   There were still problems with the artificial indigo of commerce manufactured by several factories in Germany as it was 'almost pure indigotin, containing no indigo red and no indigo brown, which is a disadvantage, as these substances have some beneficial effects in dyeing'. But these defects could be remedied by 'artificial means'. An Indian agricultural scientist working in British empire service also stated that when woollen fabrics dyed with vegetable indigo, they emitted 'an agreeable odor' while 'the chemical indigo will give out a tarry smell', yet he confessed in 1915 that 'we cannot hope that this advantage will be maintained forever.' Mukerji. *Handbook*, p. 302.

555   Playne, S. (compiler), *Bengal and Assam, Behar and Orissa. Their History, People, Commerce, and Industrial Resources*, assisted by J. W. Bond, edited

by Arnold Wright, London: The Foreign and Colonial Compiling and Publishing Co., 1917, p. 209.

556   In order to compete more successfully with artificial dyes, particularly with synthetic indigo, extensive experiments were carried out by Rawson from 1898 to 1903 on behalf of the Indigo Defence Association, assisted by 'many planters and others'. Rawson's conclusions were that improvement was possible but more research was needed and 'plenty of useful work' could be done by a number of chemists who also should concentrate on making indigo production cheaper (than the artificial dye from Germany). Rawson, C. 'Report on the cultivation and manufacture of indigo in Bengal (for the Indigo Defence Association Limited)', *Journal of the Society of Dyers and Colourists*, Vol. 15, No. 7, July 1899, pp. 166–77. Mr. Hancock, Pusa's agricultural chemist, had also been hired by the indigo planters for some years. Many of such experiments had been carried out in the Dalsinghserai research station which was the center of Tirhut's indigo belt at the time, Bloxam, W. Popplewell and Leake, Martin H. *An Account of the Research Work in indigo carried out at Dalsinghserai Research Station (under subsidy of the Government of Bengal) from 1903 to March 1904*, Calcutta: Bengal Secretariat Book Depot, 1905. Another scientist who carried out research for indigo planters was, for instance, C. J. Berkeley. In one of his papers, W. Popplewell Bloxam had asked, whether it still was 'possible to save the Indian indigo industry'? Bloxam believed, quite predictably, it was but that 'more research' should be carried out. Yet in 1908, even the general secretary of the Bihar Planters' Association in Muzaffarpur, T. R. Filgalt, himself had concluded that 'nothing further can be done in improving the main processes'. See related to this discussion: Filgalt, T. R. 'Research work on natural indigo', *Nature*, Vol. 78, No. 2031, 1908, p. 540 and Perkin, A. G., 'The indigo question', *Nature,* Vol. 78, No. 2033, 1908, pp. 604–05. See also: 'Indigo in Behar', *Nature*, Vol. 101, No. 2542, July 18, 1918, pp. 388–89. Nevertheless, the Agricultural Research Institute in Pusa kept on assigning indigo research work to its scientists till 1920 at least and one main scientist in this field had been W.A. Davis. Others in Pusa who published research papers on indigo were Albert and Gabrielle Howard and Bhailal M. Amin, the first assistant to the Indigo Research Chemist at Pusa. For an in-depth discussion of indigo experiments

by many a scientist: Kumar, P. 'Plantation science: improving natural indigo in colonial India, 1860–1913', *British Journal for the History of Science (BJHS)*, Vol. 40, No. 4, December 2007, pp. 537–65. Also: Kumar, P. *Indigo Plantations and Science in Colonial India*, Cambridge: Cambridge University Press, 2012.

557   Cf. Meldola, R. 'Research work on natural indigo, *Nature*, Vol. 78, No. 2031, 1908, pp. 540–41.

558   Cf. Asiaticus. 'The rise and fall of the indigo industry in India', *The Economic Journal*, Vol. 22, No. 86, June 1912, pp. 237–47. Interestingly, this article was translated in German in 1913 (Germany being the big rival at the time): Joseph, E. 'Entwicklung und Vervall der Indigo-Kultur in Britisch-Inden', *Zeitschrift für Sozialwisssemschaft*, Vol. 4, 1913, pp. 117–20. It should also be realised that during this time in England, too, experimentation with 'artificial' dyes had been going on. See: Reed, P. 'The British Chemical Industry and Indigo Trade', *The British Journal for the History of Science*, Vol. 25, No. 1, Organic Chemistry and High Technology, 1850–1950. March 1992, pp. 113–25 and for an earlier period also: Homburg, E. 'The Emergence of Research Laboratories in the Dyestuffs Industry, 1870–1900', *The British Journal for the History of Science*, Vol. 25, No. 1, Organic Chemistry and High Technology, 1850–1950. March 1992, pp. 91–111.

559   'Java' indigo from plants cultivated in the Dutch-Indies had earlier been Bihar's big rival. Cf. Mukerji. *Handbook*, p. 299.

560   Rawson, who had been hired as a consulting (trade) chemist to the Bihar Indigo Planters' Association, alleged that 'with a view of fostering the industry in India, the English government has wisely decided that all blue cloth supplied to the Royal Army and Navy Clothing Departments shall be dyed with *natural* indigo'. During the discussion that had followed the paper read by Rawson, the chairman of the session, Sir William Brereton Hudson – now a knight commander of the Order of the Star of India (a senior order of chivalry associated with the Empire of India) as well as a member of the Indian Public Service Commission but before had been an indigo planter who commanded the Bihar Light Horse – wanted to call attention 'to another side to what Spencer calls the 'faint aggregate'—in other words, to the feelings of the planters with regard to their position, past and present'. One of

these feelings had been that planters had 'felt that they can legitimately ask government for protection against the effects on them as producers of deceptions practiced on the public by the use of the words 'Indigo-blue dyed' to describe all kinds of inferior substitutes'. The planters 'did not complain of fair competition – but this filching of the name of their product seemed to be just the reverse—and, in fact, contrary to common honesty. And that, in the interests of the public and the Government of India, as well as of the producer, it ought to be stopped.' Rawson, C. 'The Cultivation, Manufacture, and Uses of Indigo' *Journal of the Society of Arts,* Vol. 48, April 6, 1900, p. 429 and p. 430.

561   Bayley, S. C. 'Discussion of Cultivation, Manufacture, and Uses of indigo', *Journal of the Society of Arts,* Vol. 48, April 6, 1900, pp. 431–32.

562   Note the fact that the word 'indigo' was increasingly left out when administrators referred to this community of British planters in Tirhut. What is more, even the 'Indigo Planters' Association' had changed into the 'Bihar Planters' Association'.

563   Interestingly, in 1909, the Imperial Institute in London had noticed that in Bengal only a few industries 'dealing with economic products' had expanded during the last twenty years and that 'the greater part of this advance is due to European capital and enterprise', yet a movement was now in progress 'for the utilisation of Indian capital under native management' (referring to the indigenous sugarcane industry). The Imperial Institute also reported that in Bengal, some of the proposals then put forward had been considered and recommendations made 'with reference to the future development of the arts and industries'. The assistance of the Government of India had been recommended 'in connection with the industries which appear to offer the best prospects' among the few industries enumerated were the manufacture of sugar and tobacco, *Bulletin of the Imperial Institute,* Vol. II, 1909, p. 220.

564   Proceedings No. 1–2, File No. 2–1/3–1, No. 459/43, dated Calcutta, the March 29, 1900.

565   Proceeding No.3, File 2–1–2–3, No.681 T-R, dated Darjeeling the 31st May 1900.

566   Revenue Department, *Proceedings 7–10,* October 1900: 'Proposals for the Appointment of a Committee to enquire into Prospects of making Sugarcane Cultivation in Bihar a Profitable Industry'.

567   In 1912, Bihar and Orissa had been separated from Bengal (and Assam). In 1936, Orissa was separated from Bihar. Chaudhary, Vijay Chandra Prasad. *The Creation of Modern Bihar*, Patna: Yugeshwar Prakashan, 1964.

568   This decline it was argued was also caused by 'the large importation of beet-sugar from Germany and Austria, and foreign cane-sugar from Java and Mauritius.' Playne, *Bengal and Assam, Behar and Orissa*, p. 209.

569   For instance, Barber, C. A. 'Studies Indian Sugarcanes, No. 5. On testing the suitability of sugarcane varieties for different localities, by a system of measurements, periodicity in the growth of sugarcane', *Memoirs of the Department of Agriculture in India*, Agricultural Research Institute Pusa, Botanical Series, Vol. X, No. 3, August, Calcutta: Thacker, Spink & Co. (for the Imperial Department of Agriculture in India), 1919. As sugar is not only made from sugarcane, research was also carried out on date-palm juice, beet, maize-stalks, stalks of sorghum saccharatum, cocoanut, toddy-palm juices, and other plants. The shift away from indigo research to research on other plants in particular sugarcane, but also tobacco can be witnessed when comparing the *Reports of the Agricultural Research Institute and College, Pusa (Including the Report of the Imperial Cotton Specialist)*, Calcutta: Superintendent Government Printing, India, from 1907–1909 to 1920–1921. In 1921, the Indian Sugar Committee that had been established also published its *Report of the Indian Sugar Committee 1920*, Simla: Superintendent Government Central Press, 1921. Earlier, scientists had found that 'indigo and sugarcane form an excellent rotation' as 'the slack season for indigo, *viz.*, December to April, is the busiest season for sugarcane. From May to November, scarcely anything need to be done to sugarcane. Letting out the water from the fields, tying the canes, and one hoeing are all the operations needed during these seven months when indigo is sown, cut, steeped, and manufactured. This space between two lines of sugarcane is sometimes utilised of crowing crops as groundnut, cowpea, green maize, onions, carrots, cucumber, melons, and so on. Mukherji, *Handbook of Indian Agriculture*, p. 280.

570   The problem was 'defenders of sugarcane in Bihar' argued that the many 'fiscal influences such as cartels, bounties, and countervailing duties, and first beet-sugar and then cane products of Java and Mauritius

seriously competed with home-grown sugar in India.' Playne, *Bengal and Assam, Behar and Orissa*, p. 209.

571 Simultaneously, the Chinese boycotted Indian opium. Sir Joseph Bampfylde Fuller, writer, inventor, and first lieutenant governor of the newly created province of Eastern Bengal and Assam, concluded around 1913 that, therefore, 'the importers, who have stocks on their hands to the value of many millions of sterling, find themselves in a very difficult position'. However, should the new authorities in China be 'able to drive out the poppy' from India, Fuller had added, there was no reason for worrying. Yet Fuller decided, 'the trade can clearly no longer be relied upon as an assured source of income. And, indeed, according to modern notions, it is hardly respectable for a government to make money by the manufacture and sale of an intoxicant.' Fuller, B. *The Empire of India*, London: Elibron Classics, 2006 (1913), pp. 343–44.

572 Though nationalists attacked it, indigo planter Donald Norman Reid defended government's opium policy in 1906 and wrote in a letter that first of all opium was not bad for the health of the poor natives in Bihar but to the contrary was used by them as a medicine. Drinking alcohol was much worse, and this would increase Reid warned as soon as opium use would be banned. Second, the cultivation of poppy was very profitable for native cultivators. Moreover, if indigo was cultivated before poppy, the latter crop was greatly improved upon. His letter, therefore, showed 'how the cultivation of indigo and of poppy in Behar should go hand in hand in promoting the welfare of the native cultivators of that province', but yet, Reid concluded, 'these are the two crops which are being threatened with extinction.' Reid, D. N. 'A Behar planter on the opium question', *The Imperial and Asiatic Quarterly Review and Oriental and Colonial Record*, Vol. 22, No. 43, 1906, pp. 42–51.

573 Wiselius, J. A. B. *De Opium in Nederlandsch en in British-India. Oeconomisch, Critisch, Historisch*, 's Gravenhage: Martinus Nijhoff, 1886 in Dutch). This book was written for the Dutch to learn how well such an opium monopoly like that of the British was for a nation's revenues. The Dutch author provides a very detailed and invaluable description of poppy cultivation and opium manufacture in Bihar. He compares opium exploitation with exploitation of the indigo cultivators by planters. He shows that though very profitable for the government

and Bihari *zamindars* (whom he imagines as the *Deus ex machine* of poppy cultivation), the cultivator suffered according to Wiselius, and it would be much more profitable for him if he were allowed to grow sugarcane, corn, or wheat instead of indigo or poppy.

574   This was a process that had started around 1905 and ended by 1913 by which time the Patna opium agency had already been closed down and further cultivation had been sharply curtailed. Richards, 'The Indian Empire and Peasant Production of Opium', p. 69. See also: Deshpande, A. 'An Historical Overview of Opium Cultivation and Changing State Attitudes towards the Crop in India, 1878–2000 A.D.', *Studies in History*, Vol. 25, No. 1, n.s., 2009, p. 123.

575   See also a book by Roper Lethbridge entitled *Indian Offer of Imperial Preference* in which Lethbridge supported the rapid development of mill industries to relieve India's congested agricultural industries 'and to furnish the government with a means of obtaining money to replace the lost opium revenue.' Douie, J. M. 'Review', *The Economic Journal*, Vol. 23, No. 92, December 1913, p. 57.

576   Levett-Yeats, G. 'In the Land of the White Poppy', *MacMillen's Magazine*, No. 77, 1897, p. 188 and p. 192.

577   Lyall, A. 'The Rise of British Dominion in India', *MacMillan's Magazine*, June 1891, p. 94.

578   'Many factories burn the refuse for feeding engines, which is a great mistake. Some fast-growing tree, such as the casuarinas, should be grown for fuel, and the indigo refuse utilised for manure.' Mukerji, *Handbook,* p. 299. See also an article by Donald N. Reid, an indigo planter himself, published in 1894 already in which Reid not only emphasised the need for an increase in 'the nitrogen and organic matter in the *rabi* fields of north Bihar' and therefore the increase of the manure supply through 'fodder and dairy farms in conjunction with the indigo factories of North Bihar' but also stated that indigo refuse (*seet*) was the 'most valuable highly nitrogenous green manure' and 'the water from the indigo vats is just as forcing in its effect on fodder crops as sewage which is let on to the meadows of Craigentinny, near Edinburgh'. He added, however, this 'will never be done by the people themselves, who are as helpless as children in the hands of the capitalists, who are working them for their own selfish ends'. Reid, while a planter

in Saran District, had experienced with 'organic manures' himself and had very good results not only when applied to rice but equally good 'when applied to maize, millet, wheat, potato, and poppy crops', and it had been 'a real pleasure to me to be welcomed by smiling faces when inspecting the fields and to realise the fact that at last I was doing some good to the people.' Reid. 'The Disaffection in Behar', p. 815. See also: 'Tobacco Fertiliser from Indigo Plant', *Journal of the Royal Society of Arts*, Vol. 64, No. 3312, May 12, 1916, pp. 479–80 (also in *The Agricultural News*, Vol. XV, No. 375, 1916, p. 299). It was reported that these indigo experiments had been made recently by the Agricultural Research Institute at Pusa 'with the object of securing better results from the use of seeth. The substance has been used for years by the natives, but little scientific work has been done in India until the last ten years. The experiments so far indicate that tobacco soil in which seeth and bits of broken tile or broken chatties (baked clay water-jars) are mixed produces better crops than soil under no special treatment. The cost is moderate, and the results achieved warrant the extra expense. A plot of tobacco land near Pusa was treated in this way nine years ago and has shown marked superiority over adjoining plots ever since'. Indigo, it was advised should, therefore, be grown as fertiliser for tobacco, and as there had been 'a remarkable boom', since the war began, the amount of seeth available as fertiliser had increased accordingly. See for this issue also: Howard, A. and Howard, G. L. C. *First Report on the Improvement of Indigo in Bihar (with notes on Drainage and on Green-Manuring)*, Agricultural Research Institute, Pusa, Bulletin No. 51, Calcutta: Superintendent Government Printing India, 1915. The Howards were involved in a heated debate on the issue, with another scientist who carried on indigo research at the time namely Henry E. Armstrong. See: Howard, A. and Howard, G. L. C. 'Soil Deficiencies in India, with Special Reference to Indigo', *Journal of the Royal Society of Arts*, Vol. 67, No. 3492, 21 October 1919, pp. 762–64 and Armstrong, H. E. 'The Indigo Situation in India', in *Journal of the Royal Society of Arts*, Vol. LXX, No. 3623, April 28, 1922, pp. 409–25.

579 Bhattacharyya, A. *Swadeshi Enterprise in Bengal 1900–1920*, Calcutta: Sm. Mita Bhattacharyya, 1986.

580   Bhattacharyya, A. 'Randon Notes on Bengali Enterprise 1900–1920', *Journal of History,* Jadavpur University Calcutta, Vol. V., 1984, pp. 112–13 and pp. 134–35.

581   Douie, J. M. 'Review of Indian Offer of Imperial Preference by Roger Lethbridge'. *The Economic Journal,* Vol. 23, No. 92, December 1913, p. 576. In 1910, import duties on liquor, silver, petroleum, and tobacco had been raised. It was remarked by the finance member in that year that substantial duties on wine, beer, spirits, and tobacco were 'the most legitimate ways of taxation in every civilised country'. He also had quipped: 'I hope I shall not be charged with framing a swadeshi budget [. . .] and if the outcome of the changes I have laid before the Council result in some encouragement of Indian industries, I for one shall not regret it; but I would emphasise the fact that the enhanced Customs Duties are attributable solely to the imperative necessity of raising additional revenue'. However, the so-called swadeshi budget had led to resentment in England particularly on behalf of the tobacco trade and the Government of India was compelled in 1911 to reduce the duty on imported tobacco. Nevertheless, during the war between 1914 and 1918, customs revenue witnessed a big surge with the imposition of fresh levels and duties on tobacco manufactures (mainly cigars and in particular cigarettes) were considerably raised. Importantly, in 1921, when the Government of India faced a large deficit the duties on tobacco, other than manufactured ones were raised to 50 per cent, and in 1927–1928, this duty on unmanufactured tobacco was even further increased. Raha, A. K. and Basu, S. *Evolution of Calcutta Customs. A Study in History,* New Delhi, Rupa & Co., 2000, pp. 82–90. See also: Note by the Board of Customs and Excise, *Imperial Preference. History and Results of Existing Preferences in the British Tariff,* Printed for the Cabinet, C.P. 413 (28), Secret, December 1928.

582   Read, D. H. M. 'A Word on Empire-Grown Tobacco', *United Empire: The Royal Colonial Institute Journal,* 1912, Vol. 3, No. 5, p. 405. See also: 'Tobacco Growing in the British Empire', *Journal of the Royal Society of Arts,* Vol. 70, No. 3643, September 15, 1922, pp. 752–53 and Shaw, F. J. F. 'India and the leaf tobacco trade of the British Empire', *The Agricultural Journal of India,* Vol. 23, 1929, pp. 267–70.

583   Cf. Playne, *Bengal and Assam, Behar and Orissa,* p. 211.

584   Beighton, D. T. 'The Possibilities of the Indian Tobacco Industry', *The Imperial and Asiatic Quarterly Review and Colonial Record*, Vol. 19, No. 37 (January), 1905, pp. 82–111. Roper Lethbridge had agreed with Beighton (Lethbridge, Ropert, *Swadeshi and British Fiscal Policy*, Delhi: Gian Publishing House, nd, (reprint in 1988) and one LLP and summed up his arguments which he felt were 'weighty considerations': 'That India can supply what England needs, and England furnish what India requires, in the way of trade, and that the two, united by preference, can make a further advance toward the goal of a self-contained sufficient business unit than the other constituent portions of the Empire, that special encouragement given to exports from India to the United Kingdom would be in itself of great economic advantage to the former country, would facilitate its moral and material welfare, and would simplify the problem of its finance, and that the political benefits to be derived from diverting the movement for native protection into the channel of mutual preference, and from securing a *quid pro quo* from the self-governing Colonies that recognition of Imperial Citizenship for Indian-born subjects, which they now withhold, would be worth obtaining', *Journal of the Royal Statistical Society*, Vol. 70, No. 2, June 1907, pp. 366–68. D. A. Barker, however, believed that though the 'case for preference between England and India' was a good one, it was not a feasible one, and he concluded that 'it is to be feared that the ideal of a combination of Patriotism and Profit is as distant as ever', *The Economic Journal*, Vol. 17, No. 67, September 1907, pp. 390–92.See also: Lethbridge, R. 'The Enhanced Duties on Indian Tea and Tobacco', *The Imperial Asiatic Quarterly Review and Oriental and Colonial Record*, Vol. 18, No. 35, July 1904, pp. 73–82.

585   Lees, S. H. B. *India and the Tariff Problem*, London: Constable & Company Ltd, 1909, p. 48.

586   Cf. N.A. 'Indian Tobacco', *Journal of the Royal society of Arts*, Vol. 63, No. 3264, June 11, 1915, pp. 696–97.

587   Watt, *The Commercial Products of India*, p. 807.

588   Cf. Goodman, J. *Tobacco in History. The Cultures of Dependence*. London and New York: Routledge, 1993, pp. 193–96; Meinking M. *Cash Crop to Cash Cow. The History of Tobacco and Smoking in America*. Broomall, Pennsylvania: Mason Crest, 2009, pp. 61–75; Brennan, W. A. *Tobacco*

Leaves. Being a Book of Facts for Smokers. Menasha, Wisconsin: George Banta Publishing Company, 1915, pp. 29–39. Hobhouse, H. *Seeds of Wealth. Four Plants that made Men Rich*. Washington: Shoemaker & Hoard, 2004, p. 225.

589   Gately, I. *Tobacco. A Cultural History of how an Exotic Plant seduced Civilization*. New York: Grove Press, 2001.

590   The Imperial Gazetteer of India. *The Indian Empire. Vol. III Economic*, Oxford: Clarendon Press, 1908, p. 51.

591   Cf. Hahn, B. *Making Tobacco Bright.*, p. 8.

592   Gieryin, T. F. *Cultural Boundaries of Science. Credibility on the Line.* Chicago: The University of Chicago Press, 1999, p. 236.

593   Howard, G. L. C. and Ram, K. 'Studies in Indian Tobaccos. No. 4. Parthenocarpy and Parthenogenesis in Two Varieties of *Nicotiana tabacum L.* – var. Cuba and var. Mirodato. No. 5. The Inheritance of Characters in *Nicotiana rustica* L.'. *Memoirs of the Department of Agriculture in India. Botanical Series*, Calcutta: Thacker, Spink & Co. Vol. XIII, No. 1, June 1924.

594   Howard, L. E. *Sir Albert Howard in India*. London: Faber and Faber, 1953, pp. 19–41.

595   *Report of the Agricultural Research Institute and College*, Pusa (1910–1911), including report of the Imperial Cotton Specialist, Calcutta: Superintendent Government Printing, 1911, p. 36.

596   Howard, A. Howard, G. L. C. 'Studies in Indian Tobaccos. No.1. The Types of *Nicotiana rustica*, L. Yellow Flowered Tobacco', *Memoirs of the Department of Agriculture in India. Botanitical Series*, Calcutta: Thacker, Spink & Co, Vol. III, No. 1, March 1910. Howard, A. and Howard, G. L. C. 'Studies in Indian Tobaccos. No. 2. The types of *Nicotiana tabacum*, L.', *Memoirs of the Department of Agriculture in India. Botanitical Series*, Calcutta: Thacker, Spink & Co., Vol. III, No. 2, March 1910.

597   Around 1900, the importance of fermentation for tobacco's aroma had been discovered, and as a result, more emphasis was being paid to curing practices. Bacteriologists in North America had boldly asserted that 'the delicate aroma, the subtle shades of flavour which variously please the palate of the smoker, are, one and all attributable to the agency of microbes alone [. . .] and that it is to bacteria, not to any particular

plant growth, that smokers must henceforth tender their gratitude for their enjoyment'. Clarke, N. G. 'The Flavour of Tobacco', *Contemporary Review*, Vol. 75, January to June 1899, pp. 880–85.

598 Howard, L. E. Sir *Albert Howard in India*. London: Faber and Faber, 1953, pp. 118–25.

599 Howard. *Sir Albert Howard in India*, pp. 122–23.

600 Howard. *Sir Albert Howard in India*, p. 124.

601 *Scientific Report of the Agricultural Research Institute*, Pusa (1925–1926). Including the reports of the Imperial Dairy Expert, Physiological Chemist, Government Sugar Expert and Secretary, Sugar Bureau. Calcutta: Government of India, 1926, p. 3.

602 Shaw, F. J. F. and Ram, K. 'The Production of Cigarette Tobacco by Flue-curing'. *Bulletin of the Agrarian Research Institute*, Pusa. 1928, p. 187.

603 *Zamindars* and/or 'cultivators' did not necessarily gain from a harvest of cigarette tobaccos and seemed to have been hesitant to switch over from producing the local tobacco varieties used in *hookahs*, as snuff and for chewing, to the new tobacco variety. Though they eagerly accepted the seeds freely provided to them by the Agricultural Department located at Pusa for trial, they, in fact, often used these 'improved seeds' to produce 'improved' *hookah* and chewing tobacco leaf. Related to this, the *Madras Mail* had, in 1915, cautioned: 'In securing a tobacco of sufficiently high grade for the manufacture of cigarettes, it goes without saying that promising results have been secured in the improvement of other varieties of tobacco, which was a consummation much to be desired, because we are reminded that from an economic point of view there are obvious drawbacks to the production of a high grade cigarette tobacco only, 'Indian Tobacco.'

604 Cf. 'Indian Tobacco', *The Agricultural News*, Vol. XIV, No. 346, July 1915, p. 251.

605 Cf. Beighton. 'The Possibilities of the Indian Tobacco Industry', p. 109.

606 Cf. Douie, 'Review of Indian Offer of Imperial Preference', p. 574.

Chapter Six:
Cigarette Tobacco in Bihar till the Early 1920s

607   In 1875, Darbhanga was separated and was given the status of a district. In 1908, the Tirhut Division consisted of (1) Darbhanga District, (2) Muzaffarpur District, (3) Champaran District, and (4) Saran District. In 1972, the region was divided into (1) Muzaffarpur District, (2) Darbhanga District, and (3) Samastipur District, and the Tajpur region which had been part of Darbhanga became part of Samastipur District. It may be also mentioned here that the Tirhut District comprised the districts Muzaffarpur and Darbhanga and formed part of the Bhagalpur Division and after that the Tirhut District was placed under the Patna Division. Chaudhury, P. C. R. *Bihar District Gazetteers. Muzaffarpur,* Patna: Superintendent Secretariat Press, 1958, p. 2.

608   The rivers and lakes contained alligators, crocodiles, tortoises and porpoises.

609   O'Malley, L. S. S. *Bengal District Gazetteers Muzaffarpur,* Calcutta: The Bengal Secretariat Book Depot, 1907.

610   O' Malley also critically remarked that sugarcane not only exhausted the soil but also occupied the ground for a long period, extending over a year. Moreover, the crop required 'great care' and 'must have 7 or 8 waterings, even if the other crops have to do without water in consequence.' O'Malley. *Bengal District Gazetteers Muzaffarpur,* p. 57.

611   O'Malley. *Bengal District Gazetteers Muzaffarpur,* p. 58.

612   O'Malley. *Bengal District Gazetteers Muzaffarpur,* p. 59.

613   O'Malley. *Bengal District Gazetteers Darbhanga,* p. 57.

614   For instance: Watson, F. *The Cultivation and Curing of Tobacco in Bengal.* Calcutta: The Bengal Secretariat Press, 1874 and *East India (Product). Part I. Reports on the Tea and Tobacco Industries in India. Presented to both Houses of Parliament by Command of Her Majesty.* London: Her Majesty's Stationery Office, 1874. In this: O'Connor J.E. *Tobacco in India. Report on the Production of Tobacco in India,* pp. 139–219.

615   Watson. *The Cultivation and Curing of Tobacco in Bengal,* p. 1.

616   Watson. *The Cultivation and Curing of Tobacco in Bengal,* pp. 73–7.

617   O'Connor. *Tobacco in India,* pp. 139, 172, 176–77.

618   Grierson, G. A. *Bihar Peasant Life. Being a discursive catalogue of the surroundings of the people of that province with many illustrations from photographs taken by the author, prepared under orders of the government of Bengal,* Delhi, Cosmos, 1975 (1885), p. 239.

619   Cf. Amin, S. (ed.). *A Concise Encyclopaedia of Northern Indian Peasant Life. Being a compilation from the writings of William Crooke, J.R. Reid, G.A Grierson,* New Delhi: Manohar, 2005, p. 147.

620   Amin, A. *Concise Encyclopaedia of Northern Indian Peasant Life,* p. 337.

621   Watt, G. *The Commercial Products of India. Being an Abridgment of 'the Dictionary of the Economic Products of India',* London: John Murray, 1908, p. 798.

622   *World Health Organization. IARC Monographs on the Evaluation of Carcinogenic Risks to Humans. Volume 89. Smokeless Tobacco and some Tobacco-specific N-Nitrosamines,* Lyon Cedex: International Agency for Research on Cancer, 2007, pp. 49–55 and pp. 42–3.

623   World Health Organization. *IARC Monographs,* pp. 49–55 and pp. 113–28.

624   Grierson. *Bihar Peasant Life* pp. 240–41.

625   Pimpalapure, N. *Tendu Leaf and Bidis,* Vol. 3, No. 2, April–June 1999, pp. 111–17.

626   Hindoo, A. 'Smoking in India', *Frank Leslies' Popular Monthly,* Vol. 24, September 1888, p. 376.

627   The Cultivation and Curing of Tobacco in Bengal, p. 81.

628   Goodman, J. *Tobacco in History. The Cultures of Dependence,* London and New York: Routledge, 1993, pp. 90–128.

629   Council of Agricultural Research. *Agriculture and Animal Husbandry in India 1937–38,* Delhi: The Imperial Council of Agricultural Research, 1940, p. 62.

630   Hunter, W. W. *The Imperial Gazetteer of India,* Vol. IX, London: Trübner and Co, 1881, p. 87.

631   Presently, the *koeris,* unlike the *babhans* who now call themselves *bhumihar brahmans,* are listed in the other backward castes (OBC) category, a listing that provides all such designated castes with affirmative action benefits such as fixed quotas in government jobs and higher education and relaxed qualifying criteria in open competitive examinations. Many have left cultivation altogether.

632 The Shahabad District Gazetteer mentioned that there were various traditions as to the origin of the *babhans* or *bhuinhar brahmans* but that whatever their origin, they now (1924) stood on much the same level as *Rajputs* in that district. They were usually landowners and cultivators and fairly prosperous with the best irrigated lands and with not much consideration toward the lower castes. The same Gazetteer stated that the *koiris* were also a large caste and 'skilful and industrious cultivators, who are the best tenants to be found in the district'. They were a 'purely agricultural caste and also work as market gardeners and rear such crops as vegetables, chilies, and potatoes'. They also were, 'proud of their position as adroit cultivators and have been known to outcaste a man for adulterating the opium produced by him for government.' O' Malley, L. S. S. *Bihar and Orissa District Gazetteers Shahabad*, revised by J. F. W. James, New Delhi: Logos, 2005 (original 1924), p. 48. Cf. Sinha, S. K. *The Bhumihars. Caste of Eastern India*, New Delhi: Raj Publications, 2005 and Kumar A. *Community Warriors: State, Peasants and Caste Armies in Bihar*. London: Anthem, 2008, p. 28 and p. 34.

633 Cf. Ram, B. *Land and Society in India. Agrarian Relations in Colonial North Bihar*, Chennai: Orient Longman, 1997, pp. 12–13 and p. 69, p. 111 and p. 133. Anand Yang detailed in his valuable research on colonial Bihar that though *bhumihar brahmins* had been the most prominent caste in some villages, *koeris* had been the most prosperous caste in other places, and some *koeris* had been prosperous enough that they served as the village moneylenders. Yang, A. A. *Bazaar India. Markets, Society, and the Colonial State in Gangetic Bihar*, Berkeley, Los Angeles and London: University of California Press, 1998, p. 219. In another in-depth study on the Saran District in Bihar, Yang had argued, however, that high castes held the best lands and paid much below what low castes such as *koeris* and *kurmis* and *chamars* paid for inferior lands. This differential rent structure for *raiyats* with varying degrees of rights in the land was, according to Yang, designed to acknowledge and reinforce village power realities. Yang, A. A. *The Limited Raj. Agrarian Relations in Colonial India, Saran District, 1793–1920*, Berkeley, California: The University of California Press, 1989, p. 166.

634 For an excellent general description of peasant stratification in Bihar at the time, see Robb, P. 'Hierarchy and resources: peasant stratification

in late nineteenth century Bihar', *Modern Asian Studies*, Vol. 13, No. 1, 1979, pp. 97–126.

635   The Cultivation and Curing of Tobacco in Bengal, p. 81.

636   Richards. 'The Indian Empire and Peasant Production of Opium in the Nineteenth Century', p. 70. See also: Chaudhuri, Binay Bhushan. 'Growth of Commercial Agriculture in Bengal (1859–1885)', *Indian Economic and Social History Review*, Vol. 7, No. 25, 1970, pp. 49–56.

637   Jha, H. 'Lower-Caste Peasants and Upper-Caste Zamindars in Bihar (1921–1925): An Analysis of Sanskritization and Contradiction between the Two Groups', *Indian Economic and Social History Review*, Vol. XIV, No. 4, 1977, pp. 549–59.

638   Richards, 'The Indian Empire', p. 70.

639   See also one 'TWG', who wrote in 1866: 'Here, again, are half a dozen koiries, the most industrious agriculturists in India. The work done by those poor fellows might well make us English hesitate before we apply to all Hindustanees the sweeping epithet of 'lazy.' Before daylight they are in the fields, drawing water from the wells they have dug for irrigating the parched and sandy soil; weeding, ploughing, sowing, or reaping, till eight P.M. or so. Then instead of going home comfortably to bed, they sit up the whole night through to prevent the fruit of these labours of the day being carried off by thievish beast, or more thievish men, in the darkness! It is well known that no landholder would let one of them have a patch of ground on such cheap terms as he would a man of a different stock, because he feels convinced that the poor koiri, by his hard work and perseverance, will make the land yield a better crop than one else would, and he is mulcted for his good qualities accordingly.' T.W.G, 'An up-country fair in Behar, India', *Bentley's Miscellany*, Vol. 60, 1866, p. 519.

640   Peter Robb argued that already by the end of the nineteenth century, some of these poppy cultivators had shifted 'from opium to indigo or (near towns and railways) took to tobacco, potatoes, or other vegetables, either independently or at the behest of patrons and local magnates.' Robb. *Peasants, Political Economy, and Law*, p. 134.

641   In the *First Report of the Royal Commission on Opium* of 1893, one witness (Sir. J. Pease, M.P.) stated that the Bihar opium agent had alleged that 'the opium department have difficulty in maintaining their

position'. Similarly, a 'Calcutta Englishman' had stated in 1891: 'The opium cultivator in India is becoming uneasy concerning the future of the industry. An idea that Government contemplates a cessation of opium manufacture appears to have obtained widespread credence in the opium-growing centers of Bengal, and many ryots, especially those near the great towns, are reported to have abandoned the cultivation of poppy in favour of potatoes or tobacco.' Indian Opium Commission. *First Report of the Royal Commission on Opium; with Minutes of Evidence and Appendices, presented to both Houses of Parliament by Command of Her Majesty*, London: Printed for Her Majesty's Stationery Office by Eyre and Spottiswoode, 1894, p. 10.

642   See for an earlier period: Wright, H. R. C. 'The abolition by cornwallis of the forced cultivation of opium in Bihar', *Economic History Review*, New Series, Vol. 12, No. 1, 1959, pp. 112–19.

643   Robb. 'Peasants', p. 134. See for Gandhi and protest against English indigo planters and the cultivation of indigo in Champaran, Datta, K. K., *Writing and Speeches of Mahatma Gandhi Relating to Bihar, 1917–1947*, Patna: Government of Bihar, 1960; Datta, K. K., *Gandhiji in Bihar*, Patna: Government of Bihar, 1969; Misra, B. B. *Mahatma Gandhi's Movement in Champaran*, Patna: Government of Bihar, 1963; and Pouchepadass, J. *Champaran and Gandhi. Planters, Peasants and Gandhian Politics*, Oxford: Oxford University Press, 1999 (translated from the French by James Walker).

644   Robb, P. 'Peasants' Choices? Indian Agriculture and the Limits of Commercialization in Nineteenth-century Bihar', *The Economic History Review*, new Series, Vol. 45, No. 1, February 1992, p. 115.

645   Robb, 'Bihar, the Colonial State', p. 206.

646   Peter Robb explained that the tobacco plant was grown 'in a small way on a large number of holdings within a complex system of indebtedness and dependence to benefit the profits of intermediaries.' Robb, Peter. *Peasants, Political Economy, and Law* (Series: Empire, Identity, and India), New Delhi: Oxford University Press, 2007, p. 135.

647   Wace had given a description of the costs involved in tobacco cultivation, and though most work was done by family members, 'zamindars' dues' had to be added to production costs. Wace also came to know that a *raiyat* at times paid as much as Rs.15 a *beegha* annual rent for good

land, and even where the land cultivated was a part of a holding at fixed rates, or with a right of occupancy, the actual payments for the land were generally in excess of the rents shown in the *jummabundee*. Wace summed up: 'All ryots cultivating tobacco, except for those of the higher caste and more independent character or position, pay an extra cess to the malik or ticcadar'. The last call on the *raiyat* was the percentage of the *dalal*, 'who helps to drive the bargain between the ryot and the trader who goes about the country buying up tobacco for exportation, in *Ibid*.

648   Kumar, P. *Indigo Plantations and Science in Colonial India*, Cambridge: Cambridge University Press, 2012.

649   Playne, *Bengal and Assam, Behar and Orissa*, p. 258.

650   Interestingly, Kumar also detailed that in addition to the Indigo Defence Association in Bihar, another organisation for the same cause was established in Calcutta, and Begg, Dunlop and Company had been given the responsibility by agents, brokers, and bankers dealing in indigo to coordinate efforts for the scientific improvement of blue dye. Clearly, Begg, Dunlop and Company had given up on tobacco in Bihar. Kumar, *Indigo Plantations and Science*, p. 180.

651   Kumar, *Indigo Plantations and Science*, pp. 274–78.

652   Cf. Howard, L. E. *Sir Albert Howard in India*, London: Faber and Faber Ltd., 1953, pp. 169–80.

653   Leake, H. M. 'An historical memoir of the indigo industry of Bihar', *Economic Botany*, Vol. 29, No. 4, October–December 1975, p. 367.

654   According to a retired scientist from Lucknow, N.C. Shah, who corresponded with Leake when the latter was ninety-eight years old and who had received materials from him too, Leake came to India driven by 'a sense of adventure and curiosity.' Shah, N.C., 'Hugh Martin Leake: a historical memoir', *Indian Journal of History of Science*, Vol. 37, No. 4, 2002, pp. 337–46.

655   Leake, 'An Historical Memoir', pp. 370–71.

656   Shah, 'Hugh Martin Leake: A Historical Memoir', p. 337.

657   Interestingly, Leake had observed that the indigo planters in Bihar had become like *zamindars,* and according to him, it had been the *zamindari* system 'in Bihar in particular that led to the establishment of the major indigo industry in that area, thereby an adequate supply of the crop

assured'. In Cawnpore, in fact, Leake proposed a reform of this system, and 'his main object was the zamindars to play an important role in copartnership with the *raiyats*, i.e., a type of cooperative farming'. His scheme failed, however, 'owing to the noncooperation of the Zamindars.' Shah, 'Hugh Martin Leake: A Historical Memoir', p. 344. See also: Leake, M. H. *The Bases of Agricultural Practice and Economics in the United Provinces*, Cambridge: Heffers & Son, Ltd, 1920.

658   A review of Leake's book *The Bases of Agricultural Practice and Economic in the United Provinces, India* confirmed: 'The author belongs to the body of agricultural experts which since 1906 has formed a very useful branch of the administrative machinery of India', 'Review', *The Economic Journal*, Vol. 31, No. 122, June 1921, p. 258.

659   Shah, 'Hugh Martin Leake: A Historical Memoir', p. 341.

660   Leake, 'An Historical Memoir of the Indigo Industry of Bihar', p. 370.

661   Quoted in: Watt, *The Commercial Products of India*, pp. 810–11.

662   These so-called *swadeshi* factories had been set up as a response to the import of 'foreign goods' in the Bengal Presidency and manufactured cigarettes, cigars, *bidis* (tobacco wrapped up in a leaf and in itself a typical *swadeshi* product), snuff, and so on and thereby added to the list of 'traditional' tobacco products, viz., *khaini* (chewable tobacco), *hookah* tobaccos and *zarda* (addendum to betel leaf). The companies which attained, for some time, a fair measure of prosperity included the Rangpur Tobacco Co. (1907), the India Cigarette Mfg. Co. Ltd. of Murshidabad, the Naidu Cigarette Co. of Howrah, AC Dutt & Co. of Nadia, the Globe Cigarette Co., the Bengal Cigarette Co., the National Tobacco Co., and the East India Cigarette Mfg. Co. (1908) of Calcutta (www. banglapedia.org). See also: Bhattacharyya, Amit. *Swadeshi Enterprise in Bengal 1900–1920*, Calcutta: Sm. Mita Bhattacharyya, 1986, pp. 167–86.

663   BAT gradually reduced the number of expatriates employed in its Indian operation. Nayak explained how Indian managers in ITC subsequently lobbied with the Government of India for the cigarette and tobacco business in India. He also narrated that Abdul Rub Sardar Hussain was the first to be inducted as covenanted Indian assistant on the 1st of September 1934. By 1947, there were 121 Indian managers comprising 44 per cent of the management. Yet Indian managers became treated

on equal terms with the expatriates by the middle of the 1960s only. The last Englishman, Tonny Drayton, left India in September 1979. Indian ITC executives interviewed by Nayak had been surprised when they were told how the transition from BAT/Imperial Tobacco to ITC Ltd. had come about. Nayak, A. K. J. R. 'Does direct investment in complementary business make business sense to foreign companies in an emerging economy? Case of British American tobacco in India, 1906–2004', *Global Business Review*, Vol. 8, No. 2, 2007, pp. 189–204.

664   Munger (previously spelled as 'Monghyr') is a town in Bihar, which during colonial days was part of the Bhagalpur Division of Bihar and Orissa (now Odisha). The town is on the right bank of the river Ganges and in 1931 had already a railway station. For a long time, the manufacture of cigarettes carried out by the Peninsular Tobacco Company/ITC was its chief industry, and in 1925, the factory employed nearly 3,000 workers.

665   The company's ownership progressively Indianised, and the name of the company was changed to India Tobacco Company Limited in 1974. Later, and in recognition of the company's multibusiness portfolio, encompassing a wide range of businesses – cigarettes and tobacco, hotels, information, technology, packaging, paperboards and specialty papers, agri-exports, foods, lifestyle retailing and greeting, gifting, and stationery – the full stops in the company's name were removed in 2001, and the company now stands rechristened 'ITC Limited'.

666   It now identifies as 'The One Stop Shop for Quality Indian Tobaccos'. Its website (www.itc-iltd.com) advertises that 'in a spirit that truly embodies the Company's 'commitment beyond the market', ITC has helped the Indian farmer grow quality leaf tobaccos and linked him to global markets'.Actually, Imperial Tobacco and Imperial Tobacco Company of India Limited, now ITC Limited, was the successor of W.D. & H.O. Wills factory at Bristol, which had been founded in 1786 and became defunct in 1988. See: Perkins, Edwin J. 'Review of W.D. and H.O. Wills and the Development of the U.K. Tobacco Industry, 1786–1965 by B. W. E. Alford', *The Journal of Economic History*, Vol. 36, No. 2, June 1976, pp. 450–51.Its seal is still used in Indian cigarette brands such as Wills's Gold Flake a widely sold cigarette brand in India and Pakistan. This brand and its various varieties such as Gold Flake

Kings, Gold Flake Lights, and so on, is owned, manufactured, and marketed by ITC Limited, which still is a British American Tobacco (BAT) affiliate. ITC is the leading cigarette maker in India, the other three being Godfrey Philips India (GPI), a Philip Morris affiliate, Vazir Sultan Tobacco (VST) also a BAT affiliate, and the Golden Tobacco Company (GTC). Another popular cigarette brand owned by ITC is Wills & Scissors.

667   For an excellent refereed summary of how BAT came into being see Goodman, Jordan. *Tobacco in History*, pp. 230–34. See also: Stopford, J. M. 'The origins of British-Based multinational manufacturing enterprises', *The Business History Review*, Vol. 48, No. 3, Multinational Enterprise, Autumn, 1974, p. 318.

668   Howard Cox further remarked that 'the feature which marks out BAT's operations in India from those undertaken in most other regions before the Second World War was the detailed attention given to the process of leaf cultivation and trade.' Cox, H. *The Global Cigarette. Origins and Evolution of British American Tobacco, 1880–1945*, Oxford: Oxford University Press, 2000, p. 202.

669   This was the Imperial Tobacco Company of India Limited registered in Calcutta in 1910 (present-day Indian Tobacco Company). Its object was, 'To carry on the business of cultivators of tobacco, manufacturers of and dealers in tobacco, cigars, cigarettes, snuff and other products composed wholly or in part of tobacco, snuff-grinders and merchants, box merchants and manufacturers of and dealers in boxes, covers, packages, and other articles and things used in the consumption of tobacco, or which are required by, or may be convenient to smokers, or are commonly dealt in by tobacconists'. The Imperial Tobacco Company wanted, 'To enter into any arrangements with any Governments or authorities, supreme, municipal, local or otherwise, that may seem conductive to the Company's objects or any of them and to obtain from any Government (in Britain or in any colonial or foreign country or state) or any authority any rights, privileges and concession which the Company may think it desirable to obtain; and to carry out, exercise, work and comply with any such arrangements, rights, privileges and concessions', 'Memorandum of Association of the Imperial Tobacco Company of India Limited, registered through the Indian Companies

Act, 1882 Company Limited by Shares incorporated August 24, 1910', *The Indian Companies Acts, 1882 to 1913*, Articles adopted by Special Resolution passed on the 11th day of November 1952.

670   The government had commented at the time of establishment of this factory: 'Many years ago endeavours were made by Messrs. Begg, Dunlop & Co. to establish at Pusa in Darbhanga district tobacco growing and manufacture for the European market. The increased local demand for cigarettes has altered the situation. The Peninsular Tobacco Company, financed by an Anglo-American syndicate, who already have a factory at Karachi, have been building a large manufactory in the vicinity of Monghyr to make cigarettes for the million. Since May 1908 it is in working order [. . .] The new factory will increase the importance of Monghyr as a manufacturing and trading centre, there will be a considerable addition to the demand for labour, and the cultivators of the plant will get better prices for their crops and be stimulated to improve its quality. Tobacco is at present grown over 12,000 acres of land, mainly in Beguserai and the area may be expected to increase considerably in the near future', *Review of the Industrial Position and Prospects in Bengal in 1908 with Special Reference to the Industrial Survey of 1890, Part II of Special Report*, Calcutta, The Bengal Secretariat Book Depot, 1908.

671   Even after repeated requests, I did not get permission to access the ITC materials related to its pre-independence history. Basu's book was commissioned to her in 1985 and Basu's (Ranganathan before marriage) brief had been that her work, 'should be an objective study of the history of the Company, with the implication that the firm's failures should be treated as openly and frankly as its successes', and according to Basu, the result was a book as she saw the facts which 'not necessarily' was the view of the ITC. About why the decision fell on, Monghyr Basu wrote: 'Why Monghyr? In today's context, it seems an extraordinary choice and one that is constantly being bemoaned by those posted there. Not directly connected by rail, the town did not even boast of its own power supply. Living conditions were primitive even by the standards of those far-off days. The town fell within the earthquake belt, the malaria belt and the filarial belt. It was subject to seasonal floods and drought. In addition, perhaps due to its turbulent history of conquest

and reconquest, the people had a profound resentment to authority and to change, and preferred instead to earn their living as dacoits.' Basu, C. *Challenge and Change. The ITC Story: 1910–1985*, Hyderabad: Orient Longman, 1988, p. xiii and pp. 23–24. Fortunately, I located some very useful government reports written during the 1920s, 1930s, and 1940s related to the ITC affairs in Bihar that could be balanced somewhat with Basu's writings (see for these next chapter).

672 O'Malley, L. S. S. *Bihar and Orissa District Gazetteers, Monghyr*, revised edition, New Delhi: Logos Press, 2007 (original 1926), pp. 143–45. Interestingly, this *Gazetteer* also mentioned the existence of a place near Sheikhpura in the Monghyr District which was 'noted for the manufacture of tubes (*naicha*) for the hookah or Indian pipes.' *Ibid*, p. 153.

673 Howard Cox, however, qualified: 'Before the first World War imperial interests, both strategic and economic, held ultimate sway over matters of domestic significance to India. Economically, this implied two broad constraints on policy which were of utmost importance; the avoidance of a budget deficit on behalf of the Government of India and the maintenance of a balance of trade surplus for Britain [. . .] as a consequence of these imperial pressures, India entered the twentieth century with a general tariff set at 5 per cent *ad valorem* for the majority of imports; a rate which was designed merely to raise revenue. Higher tariffs were seen in London as a tax on British exports which served to undermine British trade to the benefit of the indigenous, or Swadeshi, producers of India.' Cox, H. 'International business, the state and industrialization in India: early growth in the Indian cigarette industry, 1900–1919', *Indian Economic Social History Review, 1990*, Vol. 27, No. 3, 1990, pp. 290–91.

674 Government of India Board of Inland Revenue, Question of the place of payment of tax or 'salaries' by a firm or Company or employer having branches in different Provinces (case of Imperial Tobacco Company, Calcutta), Proceedings No. 8 for the month of January 1923.

675 This movement was also directed against cigarette box making by US and German firms in India as well against tobacco (products) from American and Egyptian origin. Numerous so-called *swadeshi* enterprises were set up during this time by 'indigenous businessmen' who started

cigarette production, but as the market of such cigarettes was still small in India, these instead prompted sharp increase of *bidi* cigarettes, which could be manufactured on a small scale, and according to Bhattacharyya *bidi* smoking (and I agree as before this period I have not come across any reference to this tobacco item), was 'probably a direct product of the Swadeshi movement in Bengal'. Significantly, these *swadeshi* firms started somewhere between 1905 and 1913 were all established in and around Calcutta or in Bengal proper (and only one *bidi* industry established itself in Bihar also in Monghyr). This might have been an added reason why the ITC started Peninsular Tobacco in Bihar and not for instance in Rangpur where, as mentioned before, also 'good-quality' tobacco had been cultivated according to government reports. Moreover, Bhattacharyya mentioned that Peninsular in Monghyr remained getting tobacco leaf from Rangpur for quite some time. In the end, there was only one such Indian *swadeshi* firm that really could compete with BAT in India at the time, and that was the East India Cigarette Manufacturing Company which was a Turkish-Indian joint. Bhattacharyya, *Swadeshi Enterprise in Bengal,* pp. 167–86. For the history of the *bidi* industry, see also Pranay Lal's article who traced the origin of the *bidi* to south Gujarat in around 1900. He, however, agreed that the industry received a 'further impetus when the educated class started smoking it instead of cigarettes to show their solidarity to the Swadeshi movement.' Lal, P. 'Bidi- A short History', *Current Science,* Vol. 96, No. 10, 25 May 2009, pp. 1335–37. However, Fazal Ahmed traced the *bidi* to the tribals of Madhya Pradesh and stated that in general tribals, also in present-day Jharkhand, used to smoke *bidi* which consists of tobacco wrapped in *tendu* leaf. The *tendu* leaf is indeed found in Jharkhand's forested areas. Ahmad, Fazal, *Labour in Informal Sector,* Delhi: Manak Publications, 1999, p. 20.

676 Political (Judical) Confidential (J) 86J/1905, *Notes on the Extent to which 'Boycott' has at Present affected Wholesale and retail Trade in Calcutta,* report by the assistant collector of Customs, L.F. Morshead. Another report cited numerous instances of 'swadeshi cigarette manufacturing' in Kolkata such as the Globe Cigarette Company, the East India Cigarette Company, and the Bengal Cigarette Manufacturing Company which had 'been importing cigarette making machinery' and

had 'a well-organised system of distribution' and sold ten cigarettes 'of the cheapest quality, for a price'. Significantly, the government had remarked: 'It would have been better if indigenous manufacturing activities had been diverted into a more productive channel', *Review of the Industrial Position and Prospects in Bengal in 1908, Ibid.* Interestingly, these *swadeshi* factories not only imported foreign machinery but initially also imported foreign tobacco leaf. Yet the imposition of the enhanced duties did, however, 'not only greatly affect the process of displacement of imported cigarettes but also put an abrupt check on the use of foreign leaf in the local production of cigarettes'. This report also mentioned: 'It is said that the Peninsular Tobacco Company has spent considerable sums with the object of improving the curing of Indian tobacco and that consumers have become more accustomed to the alteration of the flavour in the cigarettes due to the increased proportion of Indian leaf used in their manufacture'. Nevertheless, though the factory in Monghyr had a large outturn and still not enough to meet the local demand, it had been 'largely curtailed, and it is estimated that at least half of it has been replaced by the biri'. The government also commented: 'It is, however, probable that the indigenous industry would in any case have captured the cigarette business and that it is now in too strong a position to be displaced.' *Report on the Maritime Trade of Bengal for the year 1908–1909*, Finance Department, File C. 1 R3–1, Proceedings No. 29–30, June 1909 and *Report on the Maritime Trade of Bengal, 1910–1911*, Government of Bengal Financial Department, Customs, File C. 1-R, Proceeding No. 4–8, June 1911.

677   Nayak, 'Does Direct Investment in Complementary Business Make Business Sense?' p. 191. Also: Nayak, A. K. J. R. 'FDI in a Developing Country: Case of British American Tobacco', *Multinationals in India*, Case Research Series, Bhubaneshwar, 2008.

678   However, tobacco was 'of some importance' in the Teghra thana which incidentally also had an indigo factory around 1901–1902. In south Monghyr, it was grown 'here and there close to the village sites but not on any large scale.' O'Malley, *Gazetteer Monghyr*, 1926.

679   Pichai, H. and Lakshminarainan, R. 'A Study of Corporate Diversification in the Indian Context: Does theory explain success stories?', (Unpublished) *Final Report* in partial fulfillment of the

requirements for the Contemporary Concerns Study Course in the Post Graduate Programme in Mangament, Submitted on November 21, 2006 (guided by J. Ramachandran and Sourav Mukerjee), pp. 7–9. Also: Basu, *Challenge and Change,* pp. 45–46. Interestingly, W. S. Seton-Karr had already in 1896 commented during a discussion organised by the Royal Society of Arts on the possibilities of a tobacco industry in India: 'Englishmen who have proceeded to India impressed with the notion that the cultivator is ignorant of the rudiments of his own business, have very soon found out that they have a good deal to learn from him [. . .] It is quite true that tobacco cannot be grown in Bengal in large continuous tracts or in extensive gardens as [. . .] it can be grown to the height of the Sumatra plant. But it does attain to the respectable height of a couple of feet, and I do not think that much fault can be found with the method of cultivation, or that higher results could be produced by what is called 'skilled processes.' But, in the drying of the leaf and the manufacture of the article there is, no doubt, a good deal of room for improvement; and if any capitalist should think of spending money on any such enterprise, it is in this particular direction that he might look for remuneration and success', *Journal of the Society of Arts,* Vol. 44, 13 March 1896, p. 387.

680   Indian Leaf Tobacco Development Co., *Indian Tobacco Leaves. A Story of Co-operation in India,* London: Harrison & Sons, nd, p. 2.

681   *Report on the Administration of the Territories now included in the Province of Bihar and Orissa,* 1911–1912, Patna: Printed at the Bihar and Orissa Government Press, 1913, p. 13.

682   The *Agricultural News* reported in 1915: 'In 1910 or thereabouts, several of the tobacco factories came into existence, and cigarettes made from Indian tobacco began to find their way into the market. The best known of these is the Peninsular Tobacco Co., with factories at Monghyr, Bangalore, and other places. Having the huge and wealthy trust, the Imperial Tobacco Co., behind it, the Peninsular Tobacco Co., has been able not only to undertake the manufacture of cigarettes on a gigantic scale but to experiment on its own account and to cooperate with the Department of Agriculture in trying to secure a tobacco of fixed and uniform grade suitable for the making of cigarettes, Vol. 13, No. 346, July 1915, p. 251.

683 Scientific Reports of the Agricultural Research Institute, Pusa (including the Report of the Imperial Cotton Specialist; note that the latter was replaced in 1919 by the Report of the Secretary of the Sugar Bureau).

684 *Report of the Agricultural Research Institute and College*, Pusa (1907–1909), 1909, p. 7.

685 *Report of the Agricultural Research Institute and College*, Pusa (1907–1909), 1909, p. 36.

686 *Report of the Agricultural Research Institute and College*, Pusa (1909–1910), 1910, p. 20.

687 *Report of the Agricultural Research Institute and College*, Pusa (1910–1911), 1911, p. 37.

688 *Report of the Agricultural Research Institute and College*, Pusa (1911–1912), 1912; p. 7.

689 Howard, G. L. C. 'Studies in Indian Tobaccos, No.3. The inheritance of characters in *Nicotiana tabacum, L.*', *Memoirs Department of Agriculture in India* (Botanical Series), Vol. VI, No. 3, 1912.

690 *Report of the Agricultural Research Institute and College*, Pusa (1911–1912), 1912, pp. 44–5.

691 Mukkerjee also tested 'the effects of manurial and other operations on tobacco', Mukerji, *Ibid.*

692 Howard. *Sir Albert Howard in India*, p. 123.

693 O'Malley. Bengal, Bihar and Orissa, Sikkim, p. 243.

694 Basu. Challenge and Change, p. 47.

Chapter Seven:
End of Cigarette Tobacco Cultivation in Bihar

695 'Full-blood Anglo-Indians' residing in India made a difference between themselves and 'mixed-blood' people of mixed British and Indian descent who were referred to as 'Eurasians'.

696 I remain using this geographical appellation though I realise it was not appropriate anymore as I now refer to the newly established regions of Darbhanga and Samastipur.

697 Cf. Goodman, *Tobacco in History. Ibid.*

698 'Note on Indian Tobacco', p. 15

699   Cf. Pouchepadass, J. 'Peasant Protest in a Global Setting: The Champaran Movement Reconsidered', Unpublished paper presented during an international conference on *Bihar in the World and the World in Bihar. An Interdisciplinary Workshop on and in Bihar,* organised by the Asian Development Research Institute (ADRI), Patna and the European Science Foundation (ESF), Paris, 16–19 December 1997.

700   Cox, 'International Business, the State and Industrialisation in India', p. 312.

701   Cf. Daniel Headrick who argued that for the period up to 1940, Europeans restricted the distribution of technological knowledge as a means of fostering colonial dependency, Headrick, Daniel. *The Tentacles of Progress: Technology Transfer in the Age of Imperialism, 1850–1940,* Oxford, Oxford University Press, 1988. Quoted in: Storey, William Kelleher, 'Small-scale sugar cane farmers and biotechnology in Mauritius: the 'Uba' Riots of 1937', *Agricultural History,* Vol. 69, No. 2, Agribusiness and International Agriculture, Spring 1995, p. 176.

702   Cf. Axelby, R., Nair, S. P., and Cook, A. (ed). *Science and the Changing Environment in India, 1780–1920: A Guide to Sources in the India Office Records,* London: The British Library, 2010, p. 11.

703   Arnold, D. *Science, Technology and Medicine in Colonial India,* The New Cambridge History of India, Cambridge: Press Syndicate of the University of Cambridge, 2000, p. 15.

704   Watt, *The Commercial Products,* p. 808.

705   After 1935, when the Imperial part of Pusa shifted to Delhi, the new capital of British India, the equally new government of Bihar got the charge of the Agricultural Research Institute at Pusa. See Chapter Eight.

706   The work carried out by Albert's wife is grossly neglected by scholars, but unfortunately, I could not trace much of textual material on or produced by her apart from her scientific publications authored single-handedly as well in coauthorship with her husband or assistants as well as a few comments on her by her sister Louise, who became Albert's wife after Gabrielle's death in 1930 and an obituary (most likely written by family friend H. M. Leake). However, Gabrielle's contribution in the field of tobacco 'improvement' was definitely most significant, possibly more than that of her husband. Gabrielle was herself a professionally trained, competent, and recognised botanist during her time. German

but born in London and daughter of a merchant father and a musician mother, she died in 1930 in Geneva, when the couple were on a visit to the International Labour Office there. Gabrielle married Albert in 1905 and became his 'personal assistant' in 1910 and in 1913, Second Imperial Botanist to the Government of India, the First Imperial Botanist being her husband. In that same year, she also received the Kaisar-i-Hind Gold Medal, a medal awarded by the British King to civilians of any nationality who rendered distinguished service in the advancement of the interests of the British Raj. See in particular: Anonymous. 'Mrs Albert Howard', *Nature,* September 20, 1930, pp. 445–46.

707 Barton, G. 'Sir Albert Howard and the Forestry Roots of the Organic Farming Movement', *Agricultural History*, Vol. 75, No. 2 (Spring), 2001, pp. 168–87.

708 Cf. Howard, A. *An Agricultural Testament*, New York and London: Oxford University Press, 1943 (first published in England 1940) (Dedicated 'to Gabrielle who is no more'). Indeed, Howard had his 'enemies', too, during and even now after his death. In 2002, Dr. Dave Wood, an ecologist from the UK who lived in India for a few years, called Howard's ideas 'a testament to pseudo-religious belief rather than farming fact' and felt that Howard had (badly) plagiarised the insights of the agricultural chemist Voelcker whose work appeared much earlier than that of Albert Howard, around 1894 in fact. Dave Wood called Albert 'the imperialist male Howard', 'whose cranky ideas could still damage Indian agriculture'. Interestingly, Wood praised Gabrielle, Howard's first wife, however: 'Mrs Howard was an accomplished professional wheat breeder, working with excellent Indian scientists on the early high-yielding and rust-resistant 'Pusa' varieties'. Wood concluded: 'Gabrielle died in 1930 in the service of Indian agriculture. Her work has proved to be of far more lasting importance to Indian food supply than her husband's dogmas (and the understandable promotion of Albert Howard, rather than Gabrielle, by Howard's second wife, Louise in her book on her husband).' Wood, Dave. 'One Hand Clapping: Organic Farming in India', *Agriculture Information (Online Agriculture Business/Community*, December 12, 2002 (posted by Dr. Seetharam Annadana, Creator & Moderator of Organic Farming Forum on: http://

www.agricultureinformation.com (in May 2006). Last downloaded on 13/04/2009).

709   Her obituary mentioned: 'But Mrs Howard's association with Pusa introduced a definite economic trend, absent from her earlier work but becoming more and more marked with time. In 1905 the agricultural Department in India was but recently reorganised and the impetus given by the rediscovery of Mendel's work was still fresh. The earlier papers are tinged by these facts and many plant breeding problems in this new field were brought to solution by these new methods. But even at this period the economic aspect was not neglected [. . .] It is not possible to estimate the material benefit of her work to India – undoubtedly it has been great; but the greater loss is that which arises from the balanced judgment, on both scientific and practical problems, which she was ever ready to place at disposal of all who sought it.' Anonymous. 'Mrs Albert Howard', *Nature,* September 20, 1930, pp. 445–46.

710   Cf. Goodman, J. *Tobacco in History. The cultures of dependence,* London and New York: Routledge, 1993 and Cox, H. *The Global Cigarette. Origins and Evolution of British American Tobacco, 1880–1945,* Oxford, Oxford University Press, 2000.

711   Cf. Hobhouse, H. *Seeds of Wealth. Four Plants that Made Men Rich,* Washington DC: Shoemaker and Hoard, 2004, pp. 211–17.

712   Benedict, C. *Golden-Silk Smoke. A History of Tobacco in China, 1550–2010,* Berkeley, Los Angeles: University of California Press, 2011, p. 10.

713   For a review of Albert Howard's work, see the biography written by Louise, Albert's second wife and sister of his first wife, Gabrielle: Howard, Louise, E. *Sir Albert Howard in India,* London: Faber and Faber Ltd., 1953.

714   Howard, A. *The Soil and Health. A Study of Organic Agriculture,* with a new introduction by Wendell Berry, Kentucky: University Press of Kentucky, 2006, p. 2

715   Johnson, E. H. 'Review of Crop Production in India by Albert Howard', *Economic Geography,* Vol. 1, No. 2 (July), 1925, p. 266.

716   Quoted from Gieryn, Thomas F. *Cultural Boundaries of Science. Credibility on the Line,* Chicago and London: University of Chicago Press, 1999, p. 236.

717   Howard, *The Soil and Health,* p. 3.

718   Gieryn, *Cultural Boundaries of Science*, p. 255.

719   After the famous 'counterblast' of James I of England against tobacco use in 1604, three centuries later, the Manchester Physical Health Culture Society had prepared a second counterblast which at the time got little support, however. See: 'A Counterblast against tobacco', *The Guardian*, 19 February 1903. The term antismoking movement refers to an organisation that is opposed to cigarettes and smoking and has an agenda to regulate tobacco products due to their addictive nature and because of the heath consequences of smoking on smokers and nonsmokers caused by second-hand smoke. The first evidence based on antismoking movement began in 1929 after Fritz Lickint of Germany published a paper linking tobacco use with lung cancer. Yet this report and the antismoking movement in Germany went largely unnoticed. It was not until the 1950s that the antismoking movement gained force world-wide.

720   Howard, *The Soil and Health*, p. 4.

721   Howard. *Sir Albert Howard in India*, pp. 19–41. In fact, Mr Howard did more 'applied research' and was interested in the introduction of new cultivation methods (such as topping and spiking) and curing practices. Yet the couple soon recognised that they were 'dealing with soils and systems several centuries old' and that research should concern itself more with the existing 'country methods' of curing and improvements on these. Yet since Mr. Howard was also interested in marketing issues and believed that in order to be able to compete with 'the highly organised and heavily capitalised American export market', 'local cultivation practices' had to be changed if having this export market in mind. In this sense only, Albert Howard decided that the existing curing and cultivation practices of the growers had been 'about the worst possible.' Howard. *Sir Albert Howard in India*, pp. 122–23.

722   Cf. Howard, A. 'Agriculture and Science', *Indian Science Congress Association Presidential Addresses*, Vol. I: 1914–1947, Hyderabad: Universities Press (India), 2003, pp. 176–88.

723   Howard, A. 'Witness No.67, Oral Evidence, Muzaffarpur November 24, 1916', Indian Industrial Commission, *Minutes of Evidence 1916–1918*, Vol. VI, Confidential Evidence, Calcutta: Superintendent Government Printing, India, 1918, pp. 23–32.

724   Actually while at Pusa, Albert had complained about the absence of freedom of interaction with 'boys of the cultivating classes'. Albert had also proposed it should be they and not other ordinary students from the Agricultural Colleges (mainly the sons of *zamindars*) that should be educated at Pusa. Howard. *Sir Albert Howard in India*, p. 238.

725   Jackson, M. G. 'The Significance of Albert Howard', *Asian Agri-History*, Vol. 9, No. 2, 2005, p. 157.

726   When in 1931 Albert Howard had become the director of Plant Industry at Indore as well as agricultural adviser to states in Central India and Rajputana, he wrote a very interesting article on his experiment in the management of Indian labourers who were mainly involved in the production of raw cotton. In this article, Howard stated that 'it soon became apparent that if the Institute was to succeed the Director would have to pay attention to the labour problem and devise means by which an efficient and contended body of men, women and children could be attracted and retained for reasonable periods'. Albert had come 'to the conclusion that it could be solved by providing for regular and effective payment of wages, for good housing, for reasonable hours of work with regular and sufficient periods of rest, and for suitable medical attention', Howard, A. 'An experiment in the management of Indian labour', *International Labour Review*, Vol. 23, No. 1, 1923, p. 638. Compare this with what a reviewer of Albert's and Gabrielle's book on *The Development of Indian Agriculture* had to say in 1927 about Howard's novel ideas regarding 'labour': some success, 'taking the line of least resistance', had been arrived at by getting the Indian cultivators to improve his tobacco crops, 'by using seed of better yielding varieties so as to increase production without extra expense'. Yet the reviewer regretted that 'the progress is slow. The chief obstacles to rural uplift are the indifference and illiteracy of the cultivator, his chronic indebtedness, and a mentality enslaved by superstition. Nowhere have the people come forward themselves or through their representatives in the Councils to urge practical steps for agricultural improvement'. This reviewer judged that 'education' was the only solution to these 'labour' problems, and 'excellent suggestions' had been made by the Howards in this regard. WHAW. *Reviews, the Geographical Journal*, Vol. 72, No. 6, December 1928, p. 571. In 1940, a reviewer of Howard's *An Agricultural Testament*

had learnt from Albert Howard that 'the approach to the problems of farming must be made from the field, not from the laboratory. The discovery of the things that matter is three-quarters of the battle. In this the observant farmer and the labourer, who have spent their lives in close contact with Nature can be of the greatest help to the investigator. The views of the peasantry in all countries are worthy of respect; there is always good reason for their practice [. . .] the illusion that the agricultural community will not adopt improvements will disappear once the improver can write his message on the land itself, instead of in the translations of learned societies.' Moubray, J. M., 'The book of the quarter: an agricultural testament by Sir Albert Howard, C.I.E., M.A.', *Journal of the Royal African Society*, Vol. 39, No. 157, October 1940, p. 375. See also in this regard: '[Review of] The Improvement in Crop Production in India', *The Agricultural News*, Vol. 19, No.486, December 1920, p. 398 and Howard, A. 'The Improvement of Crop Production in India', *Journal of the Royal Society of Arts*, Vol. LXVIII, No. 3530, July 16, 1920, pp. 555–64.

727   Peter Robb summarised his very detailed description of the contemporary 'atmosphere' in Bihar by stating: 'Here, economic controls were intermixed with political ones and it is hardly surprising that the social order was correspondingly complex.' Robb, *Peasants, Political Economy, and Law*, p. 33.

728   Leake ended his obituary of Albert Howard stating that 'during the forty years that have intervened, agricultural science had become ever more specialised and the idea of a unity permeating the whole subject has been lost. Soil becomes a simple physio-chemical complex to be studied in the laboratory; nutrition a matter of calories and so on. If 'man has that within him, which no science weighs', so have other organisms; the problems of life are not solved by such crude methods. It is in man's nature to err and it is equally in his nature to resent the exposure of his error. To the complacency with which agriculture since had become impregnated, Howard administered a rude shock'. Yet Leake had observed in 1948, 'slowly but surely, if painfully, recognition is gaining ground that, in agriculture, empiricism has still an important role to play and that, for some time to come, science must fill the humbler role of explaining the teachings of empiricism.' Leake, H. M.

'Sir Albert Howard—An Appreciation', *Organic Gardening Magazine* (Sir Albert Howard Memorial Issue), Vol. 13, No. 8, September 1948.

729 David Arnold agreed that the term 'colonial science' is flawed, but he nevertheless decided that the term is worth retaining, and he used it 'to describe the various technologies of power operating within and through science in a colonial setting.' Arnold. *Science, Technology and Medicine in Colonial India*, p. 15.

730 Howard. *Sir Albert Howard in India*, p. 232.

731 Howard's dissatisfaction with the scientific environment at Pusa as well as that of government administrators with him is very evident from the question–answer session between the Indian Industrial Commission and Howard while still employed at Pusa. Basically, the commission seemed to have had problems with Howard's interdisciplinary approach towards 'agriculture' or the fact that Howard thought that a good investigator needed to know 'the industry well' and thus all members of the Agricultural Department, chemist, botanists or whatever should have knowledge about 'agriculture as a whole', including all aspects, even socioeconomic aspects. For instance, Howard thought that all scientists at Pusa should also pay attention to the marketability of the plant that was at hand. In the case of tobacco, for instance, a scientist should see to it that the standard of tobacco to be exported was always of the same good quality otherwise 'India cannot take a proper place among the producers of raw material'. Generally, his 'independent behaviour' was criticised as well as that to implement his suggestions would be time-consuming and more expensive and such methods of improvement were considered too difficult and impractical. Howard's answer to the question 'whether the Imperial Institute or any similar institution was necessary' had been: 'It is not at all necessary. If the Imperial Institute or any other similar institution were to close tomorrow, it would make no difference at all to agricultural work in India'. His frequent visits to Quetta, where he did research in fruit-growing areas as well as his effort to find a man in England who could help him to market Pusa crops, were also disliked by the commission. Howard had also felt all the research had to be done 'for India', and Indians themselves should be more involved in research matters, in particular 'the cultivators' who were 'practical farmers' different from the 'the zamindars'. Interestingly,

his answers to this commission also show a slight distain towards indigo planters, Indian Industrial Commission, *Minutes of Evidence 1916–1918*, Vol. VI, Confidential Evidence, Calcutta: Superintendent Government Printing, India, 1918, pp. 23–32.

732 Howard, A. 'A Criticism of Present-day Agricultural Research', reproduced in *Asian Agri-History*, Vol. 8, No. 3, 2004, pp. 172. Not all at Pusa had disliked Albert Howard's work at Pusa, however. E. Fairlie Watson, one-time superintendent of the governor's estates, Bengal had felt 'uneasy' over the developments at Pusa, which had created bureaucratic anarchy (my words) in the Imperial Institute. Fairlie Watson had stated: 'It was a great disappointment to me when his work as Economic Botanist to the Government of India came to an end through his insistence on having a free hand to treat agriculture as a whole'. 'But', Fairlie Watson had added in his obituary, 'the loss to Pusa became a gain to the world at large as his inspiring book—*An Agricultural Testament* – shows. It is sad that he is gone just as everyone is accepting his view that health is so much more than freedom from disease. But the sound foundations he had laid are there ready for others to build on', *Organic Gardening Magazine*, *Ibid*. See also: 'Studies in Indian Tobaccos', *The Agricultural News*, Vol. XII, No. 302, 1913, p. 377.

733 Leake, H. M. 'Rationalisation', *Tropical Agriculture*, Vol. VII, No. 9, 1930, pp. 240–42.

734 The Cultivation and Curing of Tobacco in Bengal, p. 84.

735 Cf. Mishra, D. K. 'Structural Inequalities and Interlinked Transactions in Agrarian Markets: Results of a Field Survery', Bhaumik, S. K. (ed.). *Reforming Indian Agriculture. Towards Employment Generation and Poverty Reduction. Essays in Honour of G.K Chadha*, New Delhi: Sage, 2008, p. 235.

736 Kumar, D. 'Science in Agriculture: A Study in Victorian India', *Asian Agri-History*, Vol. 1, No. 2, 1997, p. 83. See for a detailed discussion on the position of various kinds of 'cultivators' in Bihar during the nineteenth century, Robb, P. 'Peasants' Choices? Indian Agriculture and the Limits of Commercialization in Nineteenth-Century Bihar', *The Economic History Review, New Series*, Vol. 45, No. 1, February 1992, pp. 97–119.

737   Cf. Ram, B. *Land and Society in India. Agrarian Relations in Colonial North Bihar,* Chennai: Orient Longman, 1997, p. 12.

738   Playne, S. (compiler). *Bengal and Assam, Behar and Orissa. Their History, People, Commerce, and Industrial Resources,* assisted by J.W. Bond, edited by Arnold Wright, London: The Foreign and Colonial Compiling and Publishing Co., 1917, pp. 350–51.

739   O'Malley, *Bihar and Orissa District Gazetteers Monghyr, Revised Edition,* 1926, p. 146.

740   Collins, B. A. *Bihar and Orissa in 1925–26,* Patna: Superintendent, Government Printing, Bihar and Orissa, 1927, p. 125.

741   Champaka Basu alleged that managers had been plagued 'by the irregular attendance of workers' and 'absenteeism amongst factory workers who were generally also part-time farmers' had not been 'unusual'. Besides, another 'problem' had been that, 'of a woman giving birth to a baby on the factory floor', during which, 'all work came to a stop.' Basu, *Challenge and Change,* p. 35.

742   Howard. *Sir Albert Howard in India,* pp. 124–25.

743   Basu. *Challenge and Change,* p. 37 and p. 41

744   Basu. *Challenge and Change,* p. 44.

745   Cox, H. The *Global Cigarette. Origins and evolution of British American Tobacco, 1880–1945.* Oxford: Oxford University Press, 2000, p. 230.

746   Chaturvdei, R. *Bihar Through Ages.* New Delhi: Sarup and Sons (Vol. 4), 2007, p. 117.

747   Tomlinson, B. R. 'The political economy of the Raj: the decline of colonialism', *The Journal of Economic History,* Vol. 42, No. 1, The Tasks of Economic History, March 1982, p. 133.

748   For a more contemporary account of the *Kisan Sabha,* see: Yardumian, Rose, 'Record of the Kisan Sabha', *Far Eastern Survey,* Vol. 14, No. 11, 6 June 1945, pp. 141–44.

749   Cf. Barik, R. 'Tenancy Reforms Act in Bihar during the First Congress Government: 1937–39', *Social Scientist,* Vol. 20, No. 5/6 May–June 1992, pp. 3–20.

750   Mukherji, S. *Peasants' Politics and the British Government 1930–40. A Study on Eastern Bihar,* Delhi: Anamika Prakashan, 1993, p. 45.

751   Mukherji. *Peasants' Politics and the British Government 1930–40,* p. 53. Shiri Ram Bakshi agreed: 'The Civil Disobedience Movement

swayed the imagination of the people. Boycott of foreign goods gained momentum. Remarkable success was achieved in respect of boycott of cigarettes. They were replaced by the Indian cheroots and bidis. The Imperial Tobacco Company was hard hit.' Bakshi, Shiri Ram. *Advanced History of Modern India*, Delhi: Anmol Publications, 1995, p. 162.

752 Mukherji, *Peasants' Politics and the British Government 1930–40*, p. 71.

753 Bakshi, *Advanced History*, p. 175.

754 Cox. The Global Cigarette, p. 232.

755 Agenda for the meeting of the Advisatory Board of the Imperial Council of Agricultural Research held at Delhi from 25th to 29th January 1932; p. 176.

756 Peninsular Tobacco Company Monghyr. Government of Bihar and Orissa. Special Section. Confidential.File No. 307, 1930.

757 GDK. 'Buy Swadeshi (Indian)', *Indian Journal of Economics*, Vol. 13, No. 1, July 1932, pp. 89–91. Omkar Goswami found that *swadeshi* firms in Bengal proper during the 1930 economic depression faced severe problems, but in particular after 'the emergence of multinational corporations (MNCs), many of which opted for precisely the products that were the lifeblood of *swadeshi* firms', and 'by the mid-1940s, most *swadeshi* firms were in serious trouble in the product market'. He, in particular, mentioned that the Imperial Tobacco Company and such firms had been prompted to move to India as and, 'in sharp contrast to the older colonial firms, all these MNCs catered exclusively to the domestic market'. He also stated that 'the emergence of high tariffs coupled with changes in the government's railways' stores and purchase policy were the critical factors' (for MNCs entrance in India). Yet Omkar Goswami added that 'their entry occurred according to different imperatives. Moreover, jumping tariff walls can only be a necessary, not a sufficient, reason for entry. In the final analysis, entry is contingent on demand. If there is to be a unifying explanation, it must come from the demand side'. He added, 'A rapidly expanding population in cities and towns now demanded new products [. . .] cigarettes instead of *bidis* (which he defined as 'the poor man's smoke—something like cheap, tiny-sized cigarillos—and far cheaper and more humble'). Goswami, Omkar. 'Sahibs, Babus, and Banias: changes in industrial control in

eastern India, 1918–50', *The Journal of Asian Studies,* Vol. 48, No. 2, May 1989, pp. 304–307.

758   Mukherji, *Peasants' Politics and the British Government 1930–40,* p. 83.

759   For the history of the *biri* industry, see Pranay Lal's article who agreed that the industry received a 'further impetus when the educated class started smoking it instead of cigarettes to show their solidarity to the Swadeshi movement.' Lal, Pranay. 'Bidi- A short History', pp. 1335–37.

760   'Information on the spread of hostile feeling in rural areas during the non-cooperation propaganda', Government of Bihar and Orissa Political Department Special Section Confidential, File No. 375 of 1920.

761   Ghosh, P. *The Civil Disobedience Movement in Bihar (1930–1934),* New Delhi: Manak, 2008, pp. 78–79 (published after Papiya Ghosh was brutally murdered in her residence in Patna in 2006).

762   Mansfield, P. T. *Bihar and Orissa in 1930–31,* Superintendent, Government Printing, Bihar and Orissa, Patna, 1932, p. 107.

763   'Monghyr Tobacco Factory', Government of Bihar and Orissa Special Section Confidential, File 207/34, 1934.

764   'Socialist activities in Jamalpur and in the Tobacco Factory in Monghyr. Jamalpur Rly. Labour Union', Political Department Special Section, File No. 11 of 1935. Part II

765   ILTDC. *Indian Tobacco Leaves. A Story of Co-operation in India,* London: Harrison & Sons, 1943.

766   For some general discussions of the peasant movement(s) in Bihar, see for instance: Sengupta, N. 'Regional Characteristics of Peasant Movement in Bihar, 1910–1950', Gopal, S. 'Changing Bases of Peasant Movements in Bihar', Singh, B. P. and Roy, P. K. 'Peasant Protest and Congress Leadership in Bihar, 1930–1934', and Kumar, R. 'Kisan Sabha and the Congress-Socialists in Bihar: Cooperation and Confrontation, 1934–1944', all in: Sharma, K. K., Singh, P. P., and Kumar, R. (eds.), *Peasant Struggles in Bihar, 1831–1992: Spontaneity to Organisation,* Patna: Centre for Peasant Studies and Janaki Prakashan, 1994, pp. 65–83, 84–97, 109–28, 129–45, and 146–58 resp. See also: Mundargi, T. 'Congress and zamindars. Collaboration and consultation in Bihar, 1915–36', *Economic and Political Weekly,* 2 June 1990, pp. 1217–22.

767   B. B. Mukherjee, a contemporary scholar of G.B.B. College in Muzaffarpur in the early 1930s, had analysed the relations between the

labourer and his employer in Bihar and concluded that the labour supply was derived from landless villagers or cultivators having uneconomic holdings. He also found that 'agricultural labour is skilled labour, and the main object of the labourer is to acquire land for himself'. Mukherjee discussed the 'nature of the shortage of agricultural labour' and suggested 'remedies'. In general, he found that 'agricultural wages are not progressive and with the gradual replacement of wages in kind by cash wages, the lot of the agricultural labourer has become miserable'. Importantly, Mukherjee remarked that 'variations in the wages rate depend to a large extent on the costs of living of the labourers, e.g. the Sonthali labourer with his few wants is available at a lower rate than the labourer from Saran, and the Dusadhs and Musahars (described by him as 'semi-serfs' or *kamiyas)* are paid less for the same work than people of higher castes, e.g. the Malahas and Kurmis'. Work that required hard labour, for example, transplanting or digging was 'always paid at a higher rate than lighter work for example, weeding, which in many districts is done by women'. Even more significantly, Mukherjee mentioned that 'in reaping, the wages also vary according to the kind the crop, e.g. the rate for reaping Marua, which requires less labour is considerably lower than the rate for other crops.' Mukherjee, B. B. *Indian Journal of Economics*, Vol. 11, No. 3, 1931, pp. 320–28.

768   Basu, *Challenge and Change*, p. 82.

769   Mukherji also specified that Purnea in Bihar had been known to have suffered more due to this depression, 'because of a fall in the prices of the district's staple products like jute and tobacco'. Yet he added, 'Their cultivation was mainly in the hands of the more prosperous farmers who being more resourceful were in a better position to absorb the shocks of depression.' Mukherji, *Peasants' Politics,* p. 92 and p. 113.

770   'The Trauma of the Thirties', Basu, *Challenge and Change,* pp. 85–88. In 1934, the superintendent of police, Monghyr had received papers signed 'either by H. C. Verna or by Karu Lal, who purport to be organisers of the Tobacco Factory Worker's Trade Union'. These 'concerned grievances of men who have been dismissed or are out of employment' after the earthquake. The superintendent explained that 'prior the earthquake the factory employed 3,300 workers but because the factory being re-modelled and the work curtailed, the number of workers employed was

reduced to 1600', Government of Bihar and Orissa Political (Special), Special Section, Memo No. 10844 S.B., Confidential, 1934.

771   Political (Special), File No. 453 (II), Special Section, 'Report of the Board of conciliation relation to the trade dispute between the Peninsular Tobacco Company Monghyr and the Workmen of the said Company', 1939. See also: *The Bihar Gazette Extraordinary*, Labor Department, Patna, Wednesday January 4, 1950.

772   Basu, *Challenge and Change*, p. 47.

Chapter Eight:
New Ventures in Sugarcane and Tobacco Improvement in Bihar

773   In my afterword I will return to this issue.

774   Robb, P. *The Evolution of British Policy Towards Indian Politics 1880– 1920. Essays on Colonial Attitudes, Imperial Strategies, and Bihar,* New Delhi: Manohar, 1992, p. 7.

775   Arnold, D. *The New Cambridge History of India. Science, Technology and Medicine in Colonial India.* Cambridge: Cambridge University Press, 2000, p. 186.

776   Shirras, G. F. 'Report of the Royal Commission on Agriculture in India 1928', *The Economic Journal: the Journal of the Royal Economic Society,* Vol. 38, 1928, pp. 677–79.

777   Royal Commission on Agriculture in India, *Evidence of the Officers serving under the Government of India,* Vol, I, Part II, Calcutta: Government of India Central Publication Branch, 1928, p. 125.

778   Royal Commission on Agriculture in India, *Evidence,* p. 126.

779   *Proceedings of the Board of Agriculture in India.* Held at Pusa on the December 9, 1929 and following days, with appendices, Calcutta: Government of India Central Publication Branch, 1931, p. 10.

780   Cf. Misra, B. B. *District Administration and Rural Development in India. Policy Objectives and Administrative Change in Historical perspective.* Delhi: Oxford University Press, 1983, pp. 176–77.

781   Mukerji, N. G. *Handbook of Indian Agriculture.* Sibpur: Civil Engineering College, 1901, p. 310.

782 Agenda for the meeting of the Advisory Board of the Imperial Council of Agricultural Research Held at Delhi from 25th to 29th January 1932, p. 176.

783 The *Journal of the Faculty of Agriculture*, Imperial College of Tropical Agriculture in the West Indies, had reported that the recent earthquake severely affected the Pusa Institute, the headquarters of the Imperial Department of Agriculture in India. The building had been damaged beyond repair, and the Imperial Institute in the West Indies tendered its sympathy to the Pusa staff, 'who at one stroke have lost their College, their land, and the fruits of their labours.' *Tropical Agriculture*, Vol. XI, No. 9, 1934, p. 235.

784 Misra, *District Administration and Rural Development in India*, p. 181.

785 Schemes for research on cigarette tobacco and production of Virginian tobacco were initiated by the Imperial Agricultural Research Institute in Delhi, and under the Tobacco Research Scheme, a substation was established in Guntur in August 1936, Department of Education, Health and Lands (Agriculture), Simla, *Imperial Agricultural Research Institute, Schemes (i) Research on Cigarette tobacco – Extension and (ii) Production of Virginian tobacco seed in India*, File 56–13/40-A, 1940.

786 Annual Report of the Imperial Council of Agricultural Research 1940–1941. New Delhi: Manager of Publications Government of India Press, 1941, p. 15.

787 Agriculture and Animal Husbandry in India 1937–1938. Issued under the authority of the Imperial Council of Agricultural Research. Delhi: Manager of Publications, 1940, pp. 60–61, p. 316.

788 Bosma, *The Sugar Plantation in India and Indonesia*, p. 86, pp. 140–42 and pp. 145–46.

789 Bosma, *The Sugar Plantation in India and Indonesia*, pp. 145–46.

790 Cf. Bosma, *The Sugar Plantation in India and Indonesia*, p. 146.

791 Wilson, *History of Behar Indigo Factories*, pp. 61–63.

792 'Miscellaneous. Indigo Plantation', *Journal of Society of Arts*, October 19, 1900, pp. 847–48.

793 Miscellaneous. Indigo Plantation', *Journal of Society of Arts*, Vol. 49, 19 October 1900, p. 848.

794 Coventry, B. 'Rhea Experiments in India', *Agricultural Journal of India*, Vol. II, Agricultural Institute Pusa, Calcutta: Thacker and Spink, 1907,

p. 4. Also: N.A. 'Ramie in Tirhut', *Bulletin of Miscellaneous Information (Royal Gardens of Kew)*, No. 1, 1907. The *Bihar District Gazetteers Muzaffarpur* of 1958 also mentioned that 'the indigo plantations had been substituted by sugarcane and oat plantations. Oat plantations, however, died out when the Pusa horse farm closed', Roy Chaudhury, P.C., p. 53.

795   Mittal, *Peasant Uprisings & Mahatma Gandhi in North Bihar*, p. 58.

796   Another way in which government assisted planters was 'in the provision of railway communication by sidings or portable lines between factories and the main line of the railway system'. The Government of India added that this recommendation was 'also in accordance with one made by the West India Royal Commission', Government of India, Department of Revenue and Agriculture, *Report on the Cultivation of Sugar by Indigo Planters in Bihar*, A Proceedings No.4–7, 1901, pp. 316–19.

797   O'Malley, *Bengal District Gazetteers Muzaffarpur*, p. 81.

798   O'Malley, *Bengal District Gazetteers*, pp. 58–59.

799   Government of Bihar and Orissa, Political (Special), 'Representation of the Planters in Tirhut Division on the Bihar & Orissa Legislative Council', 1912.

800   Bihar and Orissa in 1923, 1924, p. 28.

801   Cf. Royal Commission on the Agriculture in India, pp. 79–80.

802   Murray, C. R. B. *Bihar and Orissa in 1928–1929*, 1930, p. 94.

803   Bihar and Orissa in 1931–1932, 1937, pp. 99–100.

804   Sharma, K. K. 'Congress, Peasants and the Civil Disobedience Movement in Bihar (1930–1932)', *Social Scientist*, Vol. 16, No. 3, March 1988, p. 47.

805   Bosma, *The Sugar Plantation in India and Indonesia*, p. 212.

806   Ulbe Bosma argued that 'actually, the tariff wall that had protected the Indian sugar industry since 1932 was the result of a coalition between the Indian Congress and sugar interests'. He added that since India produced industrial sugar for its home market, this 'created the political conditions to strike a balance between the interests of the factories and the cultivators'. That this was not 'an easy task' as explained in detail by Bosma in his in-depth comparison of *The Sugar Plantation in India and Indonesia*, p. 232.

807 *Report of the Committee on the Agrarian Condition in Champaran*, Vol. I, Patna: Superintendent, Government Printing, Bihar and Orissa, 1917 and Tendulkar, D.G. *Gandhi in Champaran*, The Publication Division. Ministry of Information and Broadcasting Government of India, Published under the auspices of the Bihar Government, October 2, 1957. For Press reports on the so-called anti-indigo movement in Champaran between 1918 and 1919 see: Singh, S. K. *Press, Politics & Public Opinion in Bihar (1912–1947)*, New Delhi: Manak, 2010, pp. 71–76. See also: Shukla, P. K. 'Indigo Peasant Protest in North Bihar, 1867–1916' and Ghosh, Papiya. 'Peasants, Planters and Gandhi: Champaran in 1917', all in Sharma, K. K., Singh, P. P., and Kumar, R. (eds). *Peasant Struggle in Bihar, 1831–1992. Spontaneity to Organisation*, Patna: Centre for Peasant Studies in association with Janaki Prakashan, 1994, pp. 48–64 and pp. 98–108 resp.

808 Government of India, Home Department, Proceedings, June, No.129–137, 'Occurrence of an agitation directed against the indigo and sugar factories in the Bettiah sub-division of Champaran district', Simla Records, 1910.

809 Cf. Mylne, J. 'Experiences of a European Zamindar (Landholder) in Behar', *Journal of the Society of Arts*, Vol. 30, 12 May 1882, pp. 688–708.

810 Mittal, *Peasant Uprisings & Mahatma Gandhi in North Bihar*, p. 58.

811 Government of Bihar, Political Department, Special Section, 'Report by the Superintendent of Police, Purnea of unrest in the Indigo concern of Messer A.G. & C.G. Shillingford', File No. 184 of 1921. Cf. Nagendrappa, G. 'Chemistry Triggered the First Civil Disobedience Movement in India. Indigo in Indian Independence-Role of a Broken Thermometer', *Resonance*, Vol. 8, No. 3, March 2003, pp. 42–48.

812 Playne, *Bengal and Assam, Behar and Orissa*, p. 290.

813 Wilson, *History of Behar Indigo Factories*, p. 15.

814 Yet though many things had changed, the new 'competition *wallah*' of the 1930s and early 1940s discovered similarities to the past too: 'I have been re-reading an old book Professor Troop gave me called *Life in the Mofossil* by a Bengal Civilian, who was posted as an Assistant Magistrate in Muzaffarpur 72 years before I was. The similarity between his experiences and mine is very interesting, e.g. the trial of hotly contested petty cases of assault, with the lawyers egging the parties on and the

inexperienced magistrate becoming very exasperated! You can imagine the scene. The courthouse, which I knew was just about to be built, when he was there, and collapsed in the earthquake about two months after I left.' Crofton, D. H. *Souvenirs of a Competition Wallah. Letters and Sketches from India 1932–1947,* Hythe Kent: Volturna Press, 1994, p. 184.

815   Crofton, *Souvenirs,* p. 33.

816   Crofton, *Souvenirs,* p. 34.

817   Woodhouse, T. 'Indigo Days in India. A Plantation 'Sahib's' Experiment in Friendliness to the Unfriendly', *Asia,* Vol. 26, No. 1, 1926, p. 32.

818   Describing the travel to Samastipur Junction where Joan and her father were to go to attend the funeral of the colonel of the Bihar Light Horse, Joan mentioned: 'Our journey continued and we reached Darbhanga station where a car, with my father's uniform well pressed, and his boots and Boer War medals shining with polish, awaited him. As I shall repeat frequently, Indian servants are wonderful. The car took us to the bungalow of the Manager of the Maharaja of Darbhanga, my godfather Gerald Danby, where everyone was to meet for the funeral.' Allen, J. *'Missy Baba' to 'Burra Mem'. The Life of a Planter's Daughter in northern India, 1913–1970,* Putney, London: BASCA, 1998, pp. 1–12.

819   MacDonald, B. *India. Sunshine and Shadows.* Putney, London: BACSA, 1988, pp. 49–50.

820   Remarks added by E. C. Danby on January 11, 1980. Typed and available in the library of the Centre of South Asian Studies, Cambridge under the title: *A Farmer in Bihar 1919–1944.* Also available here is a letter addressed to Danby and written in 1964 of C. Thakur, principal and regional director of the Tirhut College of Agriculture and Agricultural Research Institute Dholi (Mozaffarpur) (housed in the old Dholi indigo concern and its outworks).

821   Available in the library of the Centre of South Asian Studies, Cambridge.

822   These all are excerpts of a diary P. T. Mansfiled (also commissioner of Tirhut) kept and edited in 1970 and introduced in 1971 in Essex. See also, Mansfield, P. T. *The Story of a Village in Bihar,* Muzaffarpur: S.P.Bhandary, n.d. Also: *A History of Services of Gazetted and other Officers serving under the Government of Bihar,* compiled by the office of the accountant general, Bihar, corrected to July 1, 1939, Patna, 1939,

Vol. 2 All these and *A Concise History of the Bihar Light Horse*, taken from Disney's Filgate's and Kemp's histories, are available in the library of the Centre of South Asian Studies, Cambridge University.

823   Indian Leaf Tobacco Development Co., *Indian Tobacco Leaves*, pp., 2–5.

824   Basu, *Challenge and Change* p. 83.

825   Basu, *Challenge and Change*, p. 48. Interestingly, however, the *Journal of the Society of Arts* of 1919 included an article on the 'Indian Tobacco Industry' (which was also very much located in Bihar at the time) that mentioned the *Indian Trade Journal* calling 'attention to the encouraging prospects of the above industry as a result of the one-sixth preference accorded by the United Kingdom'. The bulk of the tobacco grown in India was consumed locally, but it was mentioned 'there is a large and increasing export trade'. The chief prewar destinations of the leaf were (1) Aden and Dependencies; (2) Hong Kong; (3) France; (4) Straits Settlements; (5) Holland, and (6) Germany. For cigars, the Straits Settlements were India's principal customers. The effect of war was to divert a portion of the exports to the Persian Gulf. The article also stated that in 'recent years', there had been 'a conspicuous increase in the number of cigarette factories in the country'. Repeated efforts had been made to improve the quality of the produce, and it had been concluded that 'these efforts have met with some success, and the equality has improved'. I, therefore, argue that the 'socioeconomic' and 'political' reasons that Basu mentions for shifting away from Bihar to Guntur were much more important than 'quality' as such. The quality of cigarette tobacco in Bihar was as good (or bad) as in southern India, but in Bihar, cigarette (tobacco) had to compete with *deshi* tobacco for chewing and for use in *hookah* and with the wide-spread use of *biri* smoking. Besides other 'pull-related' reasons from Guntur that are exposed next.

826   Basu, *Challenge and Change*, p. 49.

827   Basu, *Challenge and Change*, pp. 49–50.

828   Basu, *Challenge and Change*, pp. 52–53. She further detailed on these pages that: 'Starting in a small way in Kanteru with eight acres, farmers were encouraged to grow Virginia tobacco. All help was given by the Company to them. The Company bought land for nurseries near the Chirala factory, and here seedlings were grown and distributed free of charge to the farmers. They in return bonded their tobacco

crop to the Company who classified the fields into four groups and paid the farmers according to class of tobacco and acreage. The bond obviously worked both ways. When, in 1930, there was boycott of British goods, including those made by British companies in India, and sales of cigarettes were almost nil, the demand for tobacco disappeared. Nevertheless, the Company bought all the tobacco covered by its agreements, though naturally not from those farmers who were not bonded. The arrangement, however, did not include the curing of the tobacco by the farmers and this was done by ILTD'.

829   Radhakrishna, M. 'From Tribal Community to Working Class Consciousness. Case of Yerukula Women', *Economic and Political Weekly*, Vol. 24, No. 17, April 29, 1989, pp.WS2–WS5. See also: Radhakrishna, M. 'The Construction of a 'Criminal' Tribe: Yerukulas of Madras Presidency', *Economic and Political Weekly*, Vol. 35, No. 28/29, July 15– 21, 2000, pp. 2553–2563 and Radhakrishna, Meena. *Dishonoured by History: 'Criminal Tribes' and British Colonial Policy*, Orient Longman: Hyderabad, 2001.

830   Basu, *Challenge and Change*, p. 53.

831   Bihar and Orissa in 1924–1925, 1926, p. 33.

832   Lacey, G. W. *Bihar and Orissa in 1926–27*, 1928, p. 82.

833   Milligan, S. *Review of Agricultural Operations in India, 1920–21*, Calcutta: Superintendent Government Printing, India, 1921, pp. 9–10 and pp. 20–22. See also: *Scientific Reports of the Agricultural Research Institute*, Pusa (Including the Reports of the Imperial Dairy Expert and the Secretary, Sugar Bureau), 1920–1921, Calcutta: Superintendent Government Printing, India, 1921, pp. 14–15.

834   N.A. 'Tobacco Growing in the British Empire', *The Journal of the Royal Society of Arts*, Vol. 70, No. 3643, 15 September 1922, pp. 752–53.

835   The Times, 'Imperial Tobacco', *Tropical Agriculture*, Vol. 3, No. 1, 1926, p. 11. See also: N.A. 'Empire Tobacco', *Tropical Agriculture*, Vol. VII, No. 9, 1930, p. 240 and N.A. 'Tobacco Culture in Mauritius', *United Empire*, Vol. 28, No. 6, 1937, pp. 359–60.

836   *Scientific Reports of the Agricultural Research Institute Pusa* (Including the Reports of the Imperial Dairy Expert, Physiological Chemist, Government Sugarcane Expert, and Secretary, Sugar Bureau), 1927–28,

Calcutta: Government of India, Central Publication Branch, 1928, p. 20.

837   Cunningham, J. C. *Products of the Empire*, Oxford: Clarendon Press, 1927, pp. 153–54.

838   Hines, J. W. 'Recent Trends and Developments in the Flue-Cured Tobacco Export Trade', *Southern Economic Journal*, Vol. 18, No. 3, January 1952, p. 386.

839   Herbert, E. W. *Flora's Empire, British Gardens in India*, Philadelphia: University of Pennsylvania Press, 2011, p. 180.

840   As mentioned above, the Cambridge South Asian Archive (Centre of South Asian Studies) possess the 'Danby Papers' which also contains a photograph of the bungalow built by E. W. Danby 1933–1934 at Dholi and a TS article by E. C. Danby entitled 'Life on an Indigo Estate in North Bihar', 1971 and further autobiographical details of E. C. Danby and correspondence. It also possesses the Gladstone Papers donated to the library by John McAdam. John Gladstone was an indigo planter in Pupri in Tirhut. Fortunately, I could access these documents during a visit to Cambridge during the spring of 2012.

841   All information from Playne, Somerset. *Bengal and Assam, Behar and Orissa*, pp. 290–99.

842   Chaudhury, P. C. R. *Bihar District Gazetteer, Monghyr*, p. 120.

843   L. P. Singh added: 'It seems to be necessary to mention here that some of the chewing types of tobacco can also be used for Hookah purposes or vice-versa depending on the method of curing'. He further detailed that 'Muzaffarpur, Vaishali, Samastipur, Darbhanga and Purnea districts in Bihar produce substantial quantities of chewing and Hookah tobacco', *Economics of Tobacco Cultivation, Production and Exchange*, New Delhi: Deep and Deep, 1992, p. 16 and p. 17.

844   Indian Central Tobacco Committee. Annual report of the hookah & chewing tobacco research station. Pusa; 1960–1961. What is more: traditional appellation returned to Bihar, and now 'desi' is just one of the many varieties of tobaccos in Bihar along with, for instance, 'vilayati', 'motihari', and 'jati' types of tobacco, Singh, *Economics of Tobacco*, p. 16.

845   At the same time, cigarette tobacco was not 'foreign'. The so-called Pusa Type 28 seed that had been engineered by the Howards and was

a 'light-coloured fine product' with the right texture and 'favourably reported upon as suitable for cigarettes' was actually derived from 'indigenous varieties' as the 'American varieties' had been found unsuitable, Sayer, Wynne. 'The Agricultural Research and College, Pusa', Playne, Somerset (compiler) and Wright, Arnold (ed.), assisted by Bond, J.W. *Bengal and Assam, Behar and Orissa*, p. 700. What is more: this Pusa Type 28 was also used by cultivators to manufacture improved *biris* and *hookah* and chewing tobacco preparations. Besides, 'non-improved' tobacco (i.e., nonflue-cured 'Virginia') was also used in cheap types of cigarettes. Cf. Hookah tobacco – ear making of, with starch to prevent its being used in the bidi manufacture report regarding. *Central Board of Revenue, Central Excise,* File No. 41(6) – C. Exc. (T)/45, 1945; Tobacco – Biri and chewing – Sec. 10, T. (E.D.) Act, 1943 and Rule 44, T. (E.D.) Rules. 1943 – Intention: meaning of – Proposal to amend the Rules – (Reflected) – Decision that duty be charged at manufacturers – Ms. Mulla & Mulla, Bombay – R. Dis. No. 14(8) – C. Exc.(T)/43. *Central Board of Revenue, Central Excise*, File No. C. 14(8) C. Exc. (T)/43, 1943; Virginia tobacco for manufacture into hookah tobacco etc. – Exemption from duty in excess of respective rates for country tobacco instructions regarding, *Central Board of Revenue, Central Excise,* File No. 7(2)-C Exc. (T)/43, 1943.

846   Brockway, L. H. *Science and Colonial Expansion, the role of the British Royal Botanic Gardens,* New Haven and London: Yale University Press, 2002, p. 75.

INDEX